The
Necessary
Nature
of
Future
Firms

George P. Huber

University of Texas at Austin

The Necessary Nature of Future Firms

Attributes of Survivors in a Changing World

SAGE Publications
International Educational and Professional Publisher
Thousand Oaks ▪ London ▪ New Delhi

For information:

Sage Publications, Inc.
2455 Teller Road
Thousand Oaks, California 91320
E-mail: order@sagepub.com

Sage Publications Ltd.
6 Bonhill Street
London EC2A 4PU
United Kingdom

Sage Publications India Pvt. Ltd.
B-42, Panchsheel Enclave
Post Box 4109
New Delhi 110 017 India

Printed in the United States of America

Library of Congress Cataloging-in-Publication Data

Huber, George P.
The necessary nature of future firms: Attributes of survivors in a changing world / George P. Huber.
 p. cm.
Includes bibliographical references and index.
ISBN 978-0-7619-3035-8 (cloth :alk. paper)—ISBN 978-0-7619-3036-5 (pbk.: alk. paper)
  1. Organizational change. 2. Organizational learning. 3. Technological innovations—Economic aspects. 4. Organizational effectiveness. I. Title.
HD58.8.H813 2004
658.4′062—c21   2003013102

This book is printed on acid-free paper.

08 09 10 11 12   8 7 6 5 4 3 2

Acquisitions Editor:	Al Bruckner
Editorial Assistant:	MaryAnn Vail
Copy Editor:	Robert Holm
Production Editor:	Diane S. Foster
Typesetter:	C&M Digitals (P) Ltd.
Proofreader:	Scott Oney
Indexer:	Jeanne R. Busemeyer
Cover Designer:	Edgar Abarca

Contents

List of Figures

Preface

Tomorrow's business environment will be different from today's. Chapter 2 of this book makes clear what the differences will be and why these differences are inevitable. Because the environment will be different, and because the firms that survive will be those best suited to this changed environment, it follows that future firms must be, and will be, different from today's. My intent in this book is to describe the necessary nature of these survivors, these future firms.

That said, the usefulness of the book does not lie in the future. Its usefulness is in the here and now, for it is today's management actions and inactions that both enhance and constrain a firm's future survival.

Managers, particularly upper level managers, are held responsible for their firm's future performance and survival. They will be most able to fulfill this responsibility if they understand what attributes firms must possess to survive in the future. In my view, and in the view of many of the thoughtful managers I've taught in my executive MBA classes and the many others whom I've interviewed in my studies of organizational change, the business press doesn't provide reliable guidance about this important matter. It was in response to this problem that I decided to write this book.

That wasn't the only reason I wrote the book. In the three quarters of a century since the Hawthorne experiments at Westinghouse, organizational scientists—and other social scientists and strategic management researchers as well—have conducted thousands of studies of organizational change and have learned a great deal about the determinants of business performance and survival. I believe that this well-grounded knowledge can be explicitly brought to bear on managers' needs to prepare their firms for the future. It was to exploit this resource, and to show how it could be used by upper level managers seeking to position their firms for survival, that I wrote this book.

Of course we'll never know all that we'd like to know. But not to use what we do know is a waste of resources and an insult to the businesses and other societal entities that have supported our research. Managers make commitments in the face of uncertainty and ambiguity all of the time. Waiting until all possible information is logged in, until certainty is achieved, is exactly what managers don't do, and certainly won't be able to do in tomorrow's faster moving business environment. Withholding what we now know because there is more to learn seems foolish. Of course some rigorous sorting is in order. Some areas are in a state of flux. Where I've drawn on work in these areas I've indicated what we do know and what we don't.

I wrote this book principally to inform managers about changes they might want to make to prepare their firm for its future. Of course it could be argued that the future is so unknowable that, rather than project and plan for it, managers should simply maximize their firm's flexibility, thus being prepared for all eventualities. Certainly flexibility is important in a changing world. But organizational survival depends on making commitments. Armies that do not commit troops to action and firms that do not put products into the marketplace don't gain territory—ultimately they lose it. Organizational designs (broadly defined to include strategies, structures, core technologies, other systems, procedures and practices, organizational cultures, human resources, and physical facilities) are laden with weighty commitments. Wise commitments, even those made to ensure the flexibility needed for dealing with unforeseeable events, require assumptions about the organizational characteristics appropriate to the environment the firm will encounter. The need to have some sense of the organization design features and management practices well matched to future business environments cannot be avoided. Prediction is necessary in a non-benign world.

Some managers, fully absorbed in the present, are not thinking about future business environments and the implications of these changed conditions for their firm. Perhaps they do not recognize that the future will be considerably different from the present. Other managers believe that there is nothing they should do now to help their firm be better positioned for the future, that they should "wait and see" what the future brings, and only then should they act. Perhaps they believe in this approach because, in their experience in the slower moving and less competitive world of yesterday and today, this strategy worked. At least it worked for them. It didn't work for the many other firms—no longer to be seen—that waited to act until the future was upon them, and then failed to survive because either their actions or the benefits of their actions arrived too late to avoid disaster.

While I wrote this book principally to inform managers, and also graduate students planning to enter the practice of management, I also intended to share with my organizational science colleagues the idea that we might consider codifying our field's considerable knowledge not only as theories, but as guidelines (or at least as predictions concerning the organizational attributes and management practices that are likely to influence which firms will do well in the future and which will not). The body of systematically obtained, tested, sifted, and winnowed knowledge we've created is potentially a valuable resource for making these predictions, more valuable—I believe—than any other source of knowledge (an idea I develop at length in the appendix to Chapter 1). If we don't codify this knowledge in the form of predictions or guidelines (guidelines implicitly assume a predicted future), it will either be ignored or will be codified less well by others less qualified.

The contents of this book follow from three sources. The first is what I've learned from my own research. I started systematically studying determinants of organizational performance in 1969 while on a 14-month, full-time consulting appointment with the U.S. Employment Service (ES). The assignment of our Washington, D.C.–based, 12-person team was to help ES offices around the country learn to use computer technology for finding jobs for people and employees for firms. Subsequently one of the team members and I obtained a research contract from the U.S. Department of Labor to determine how use of the technology changed the structures and decision processes in the offices and what effects these changes (which varied from office to office) had on the office performance. From this came a book and three articles on the use of performance data to determine optimum designs for like organizations.

During the 1970s and early 1980s I continued to study organizational decision making, with particular emphasis on the effects of the organization's environment and on the use of information technology by the organization's decision makers. In the very early 1980s I became convinced that the combination of a more dynamic business environment and progress in the usefulness of information technology for business decision making would have a great impact on the nature of firms. In 1982, while on a 14-month appointment as a full-time consultant for a startup software firm in Austin, I had a 6-week hiatus between tasks and asked the firm's president if I could work on this idea of the nature of future firms. The president quickly gave his approval. The result was an article, "The Nature and Design of Post-industrial Organizations," published in *Management Science* in 1984.

That the article was awarded first prize in an international competition sponsored by the Institute of Management Sciences and began to be frequently referenced encouraged me to continue work in this area. Dr. Edgar Johnson, Director of the Army Research Institute, found my ideas interesting enough to provide back-to-back research grants. The second of these spanned from 1985 through 1990 and allowed me, along with co-investigators from the Universities of California–Berkeley, Michigan, Oregon, Texas, and Texas A&M University, to interview top managers in over a hundred organizations every 6 months over a period of 2 or 3 years each about changes in their organizations and the causes of these changes. This work resulted in many research products, including *Organizational Change and Redesign*, coedited with my Texas colleague Bill Glick and published by Oxford University Press in 1993, and also—but less directly—*Longitudinal Research Methods: Studying Processes of Organizational Change,* coedited with Andrew Van de Ven of the University of Minnesota and published by Sage Publications in 1995.

The second and most important source of content for the book is the huge body of knowledge discovered and written about by organizational scientists and other researchers, by consultants, and by managers themselves about organizational change, performance, and survival. I began examining this material while a doctoral student and haven't stopped. In the late 1990s, when I decided on the content of this book, I began to read selectively and intensely works most closely allied with its subject matter.

The insights I've obtained from the over 700 executive MBA students who took my course in Organizational Change and Redesign during the past decade represent a third form of information that influenced the book's contents. Each of these managers wrote a 20-page analysis of his or her firm's past, present, and probable future, and provided explanations of the drivers of change in his or her organization's strategy, core processes, structure, culture, personnel, and in the decision, control, and people-management practices. Many of the firms employing these managers were failing. Many had failed—some of the managers wrote retrospectively. Other firms were succeeding wildly. All had changed, were changing, or would be changing in some ways, generally as a result of changes in their environments but sometimes due simply to changes in their life cycle phase or their top managers. These analyses influenced my thinking about change within firms. They especially informed me about the conditions affecting the propensity of upper level managers to create or resist changes in the features of their firm, either in response to changes in the firm's circumstances or in anticipation of such changes.

I've had considerable help and support in making this book a reality. Dr. Jerry Wagner, president of Execucom Systems Corporation, made available the 6 weeks it took to get my early ideas into a publishable form. Dr. Edgar Johnson, director of the Army Research Institute, provided the support needed to conduct the large interview study of the forces provoking organizational change that I described above. My colleague Bill Glick was co-principal investigator on that study; and Ken Bettenhausen, Kim Cameron, Dick Daft, Alan Meyer, and Charles O'Reilly were co-investigators. Arie Lewin, Peter Monge, John Slocum, Andy Van de Ven, and Karl Weick were consultants and advisers. All influenced what we learned from each other, and certainly what I learned. Three former upper level managers, Fred Alexander from TRW, Ted Mueller from Safety-Kleen, and Jim Teegarden from Fisher Controls, and my colleague Reuben McDaniel here at the University of Texas, read the entire manuscript and gave me new ideas and welcome criticisms. People who know a lot about some of the topics treated in specific chapters read those chapters and gave me guidance and critiques. Specifically the book and I benefited from the help given by Ed Anderson, Alison Davis-Blake, Andy Henderson, John Huber, Pamsy Hui, Vish Krishnan, Kyle Lewis, Ithai Stern, and Kathie Sutcliffe.

Proceeds from three endowed appointments provided time and other resources that contributed to the evolution of the book—the Eddy Clark Scurlock Professorship in Management, the Fondren Foundation Centennial Chair in Business, and the Charles and Elizabeth Prothro Regents Chair in Business Administration. I am indebted to these respective benefactors. Most of all, Libby and Sandy provided the support and encouragement that were absolutely critical to writing the book.

To my parents, who gave me the love of learning, and to Libby and Sandy, without whose support and encouragement this book could not have been written.

1

Dangerous Deficiencies

With few exceptions, top managers feel responsible to create organizations well prepared to thrive in the future. This has become an especially relevant goal, as the future more rapidly becomes the present. As a consequence, more so than ever before, managers are actively seeking ideas and insights for creating firms that will succeed in the business environments that lie ahead.

Due to its ready availability and apparent validity, the popular business press is the source where many managers go for guidance. This is unfortunate, as *the material in the business press that purports to be useful to managers attempting to prepare their firms for the future is, on the whole, deficient in three important respects.*

1. Its recommendations concerning organizational attributes and management practices necessary for success in the future rely excessively on projecting the attributes and practices of currently—but often temporarily—high performing firms.

2. It is nearly void of systematic assessments of whether the attributes and practices recommended for mimicry are really the key determinants of exemplar firms' high performance, or are merely correlates of that success.

3. It tends to lack thoughtful analyses of the deep root causes of change in business environments, and, as a result—relying on less substantial bases—it is often misleading.

For these reasons, while it stimulates action, the popular business press tends not to guide action in fruitful directions. It leads to excitement but not to enlightened execution.

The purpose of this book is to remedy each of these deficiencies, systematically and explicitly. I hope and intend that the book will enable managers and their firms to deal more effectively than they otherwise would with the dangers, dilemmas, and opportunities that will characterize future business environments.

Observing the fast-changing environments of their firms, astute managers recognize that past experience is less useful than ever before. With this in mind,

1

they seek reliable guidance from the business press and current "best sellers" about "leading edge" corporate practices. Given their strongly felt need for guidance, many managers are motivated to act on the urgings and recommendations contained in these sources. As a consequence, the three deficiencies just enumerated are more than merely aggravating; they are dangerous.[1]

What Is Happening? What Is Not?[2]

First, let us acknowledge outright that, while it is still fashionable, it has become *tiresomely* fashionable for the business press and the management literature to report on the dynamic and turbulent business environment. We are deluged with stories and statistics informing us of unanticipated events and fast-changing trends. We are inundated with advice, admonitions, and hype about what organizations and managers are doing and what they should be doing to survive these changes.

Second, let's be mindful of what we're *not* receiving. Two items of value are seldom found in the flood. *One* is a truly thoughtful analysis of the fundamental issues and questions. What are the root causes of the increasingly rapid rate of change in today's business environments? Are these change drivers likely to endure? What will be their specific effects on the future environments of business organizations? These are the questions of forward-thinking managers. These are questions I attempt to answer in this book.

The *second* missing element is a broad-ranging and well-grounded description of what future firms must be like. If firms face a future of accelerating change, which organizational attributes and management practices will differ from today's? What will be the nature of the new attributes and practices? These, too, are important questions. Using what I believe is tight reasoning, and drawing on research findings that satisfy the criteria of being relevant, up-to-date, and well grounded, I intend to provide those who manage and study organizations with answers to these questions.[a]

An award-winning article titled "The Nature and Design of Post-industrial Organizations" asserted in 1984 that the fast-changing and turbulent environment then being experienced was not a transition to the future—it was the future.[3]

---

[a]Throughout this book I use *alphabetical* superscripts to indicate footnotes, which are generally short and of general interest. I use *numerical* superscripts to indicate endnotes, which are generally longer and of interest primarily to readers who wish to pursue an issue in more depth. With this first footnote, I call attention to the appendix of this chapter, the only appendix in the book. This appendix explains more fully the dangers associated with the three deficiencies just noted, deficiencies commonly found in magazine articles and trade books attempting to predict the nature of future firms or recommending adoption of particular organizational features or management practices. The appendix also outlines the approach used in this book to identify the necessary nature of future firms, an approach much more likely to result in valid predictions.

That message created a bit of a stir, because *at the time*—strange as it now seems—many people viewed those dynamic conditions as a temporary disequilibrium. As an easily recalled example, the U.S. automobile industry was seeking "temporary" protection from Japanese imports—apparently not recognizing that Japanese car manufacturers would continue to innovate and be competitive,[b] and certainly not anticipating the globalization of the auto industry that has since occurred. Today the message is *not* that the observed high levels of environmental dynamism represent the future. They do not. Rather the message is that, *in the future, environmental dynamism will be greater, and it will be increasing.*

This changed environment will change the nature of the organizations that are able to survive. It cannot be otherwise. People and organizations are "living systems," as are ant colonies and nations.[4] Especially by moving from one environment to another, or manipulating their environment, or adapting to their environment, *higher-order* living systems (those governed by human cognition) attempt to attain and maintain *congruence* with their environments. If they fail, they are "selected out," as were—for example—the manufacturers of mechanical calculators. For managers and other organizational stakeholders, an important outcome of this pervasive ecological dynamic is that when its environment shifts more rapidly than an organization can adjust, the organization will not survive.[5] (Or at least it will not survive beyond the point at which its "reserves"—whatever these may be—are depleted.)

It is important not to misunderstand the broad meaning of *congruence*, sometimes called "fit" or "alignment." Achieving or maintaining congruence often means adapting to a changing environment (for example, continuously reducing the prices the firm asks for its products as the market becomes more densely populated with products comparable to the firm's products). Especially when the firm's environment is moving in a particular direction, as when technological advances are enabling nearly continuous improvement in the performance of competitors' products, congruence must be dynamic rather than static—the firm must frequently initiate the changes necessary to maintain or exceed the performance of its competitors' products. Perfect congruence is rarely achieved—most firms lag their environments most of the time. When perfect or near-perfect congruence is achieved, it is almost always the result of an existing firm successfully shaping its environment or a new firm being designed to fit the environment in place at its birth.

---

[b] For entertaining and informed elaborations of this example, see Lee Iacocca's *Iacocca* (1984) and *Talking Straight* (1988).

The need for firms to be as quick-changing as their environments must be of critical concern to top managers. Attaining and retaining congruence between the firm and its environments is primarily top management's responsibility.[c] Middle- and lower-level managers must focus on delivering goods and services. In contrast, top managers must focus on determining what the nature of their firm must be if it is to survive in the future[6] and then causing the firm to take on the required characteristics. Because future environments will be significantly different from today's and are approaching with increasing velocity, determining the necessary nature of future firms in general, and their firm in particular, is perhaps the most significant issue that faces top managers.

It could be argued that the future is so unknowable that, rather than project and plan for it, firms and their managers should simply maximize the organization's flexibility, thereby being prepared for all eventualities. Certainly flexibility is important in a changing world—Chapters 3 through 8 of this book describe specific approaches to designing agile, responsive organizations. But organizations must make commitments. Armies that do not commit troops to action and firms that do not put products into the marketplace don't gain territory—ultimately they lose it. Organizational designs (broadly defined to include strategies, structures, core technologies, other systems, procedures and practices, organizational cultures, human resources, and physical facilities) are laden with weighty commitments. Wise commitments, *even those made to ensure the flexibility needed for dealing with unforeseeable events,* require assumptions about the organizational characteristics appropriate to the environment the firm will encounter. The need to have some sense of future business environments, and the organization design features and management practices well matched to these environments, cannot be avoided. Prediction is necessary in a non-benign world.

Environments change, select out some of their inhabitants, and retain others. Sometimes firms seem to be selected out, or are at least forced to undergo radical change or extreme hardship, because their leaders—so caught up in current problems—do not look ahead. Consider as an example the near demise and radical transformation of *Encyclopedia Britannica,* as described in the September-October 1997 issue of the *Harvard Business Review.* The encyclopedia had one of the strongest and best known brand names in the world, but

---

[c]For convenience and in accord with convention, I will often write as if firms took actions. In reality, of course, "a firm's actions" arise as a consequence of the interactions between top management's intended actions and the dynamics of the firm's internal and external environments.

since 1990, sales of Britannica's multi-volume sets . . . plummeted by more than 50%. CD-ROMs came from nowhere and devastated the printed encyclopedia business as we traditionally understand it. How was that possible? The *Encyclopedia Britannica* sells for somewhere in the region of $1,500 to $2,200. An encyclopedia on CD-ROM, such as Microsoft *Encarta*, sells for around $50. . . . The cost of producing a set of encyclopedias—printing, binding, and physical distribution—is about $200 to $300. The cost of producing a CD-ROM is about $1.50. . . . Judging from their initial inaction, Britannica's executives failed to understand what their customers were really buying. Parents had been buying *Britannica* less for its intellectual content than out of a desire to do the right thing for their children. Today when parents want to "do the right thing," they buy their kids a computer. The computer, then, is Britannica's real competitor. . . . When the threat became obvious, Britannica did create a CD-ROM version—but to avoid undercutting the sales force, the company included it free with the printed version and charged $1,000 to anyone buying the CD-ROM by itself. Revenues continue to decline. The best salespeople left. And Britannica's owner, a trust controlled by the University of Chicago, finally sold out. Under new management, the company is now trying to rebuild the business around the Internet.[d] (Evans & Wurster, 1997: 71-72)

In retrospect, it seems that Britannica's top managers were not attending to the changing nature of the firm's environment. But was the near demise of Britannica the fault of its top management, or was this hugely painful and costly event inevitable given the inertial nature of organizations, especially large and successful organizations? Would different managers have done differently? Would it have made any difference?

A few years ago, an academic asserted at a national meeting of his professional association that "managers are like light bulbs"—that for all the difference they make they are completely interchangeable. The implication was that managers have no more control than do the occupants of inner tubes attempting to round Cape Horn. In contrast, and equally as ridiculous, I was told a few years ago by a member of an extremely successful top management team that "we can do *anything*" (emphasis is the speaker's). It was clear in the context that he meant exactly what he said. Whoa! What is going on here? Let's try to make some sense of these contradictory points of view.

---

[d]The new management's blueprint for Britannica's survival was described in the October 20, 1997, issue of *BusinessWeek*. There we also get a sharper picture of the pain suffered by the stakeholders—"book sales . . . down 83% since 1990" and the "entire 500 person book sales force . . . sacked." More pain was yet to come. "Any profits from a turnaround (are) several years away at best." We will return to the saga of the Britannica in Chapter 3.

The Role of Top Management

Important as environmental selection is, it is an incomplete representation of ecological dynamics—living systems are not selected out if they change as quickly as their environments change (and if their changes are appropriate to the changed environment). Everyday observation makes clear that some firms adapt swiftly and survive even rapid shifts in their environments.

Indeed, rapid environmental changes sometimes cause top managers to gain new visions of what their firms might be, and prompt them to make radical, performance-enhancing changes. I recently encountered a rather dramatic example while teaching in an executive program in Leon, Mexico. For many decades, the principal industry in this city, situated near the middle of Mexico's ranching country, had been the manufacturing of leather products, primarily shoes. With the huge and relatively rapid market shift to athletic and casual shoes made of nylon and rubber, a large proportion of Leon's leather-goods firms were selected out. Others, quicker afoot, didn't lose a step. They shifted to serving the growing market of leather automobile seat covers. The employment levels, revenues, and profits of these firms went up.

Each of Leon's leather-industry firms was confronted with essentially the same environmental shift. But survivorship varied. The deciding factor between the firms that failed and those that survived and thrived was the vision, entrepreneurship, and change-management effectiveness of their top managers.

Top managers can make an appreciable difference in the nature, performance, and survival of their firms. Asserting, as I did earlier, that environmental changes often lead to organizational demise, is not to deny top managers their role in determining the fate of their firms—as the example of the leather-goods manufacturers shows. Top managers carry out this role (i.e., carry out the tasks of creating and maintaining the alignment between their firm and its environment) in various ways.

1. They sometimes foresee the possibility of critical changes in the market for their product and cause their firms to act preemptively by hedging, as when Toyota began selling hybrid vehicles (in anticipation of a greater demand for eco-friendly cars) while maintaining a position in the SUV market.

2. They sometimes shift the firm to a new environment, as when U.S. baby food and tobacco companies—encountering, respectively, declining U.S. birth rates and increasing regulatory hostility—looked for market growth in other nations.

3. They sometimes manipulate or create their business's environment—as when, for example, they shape their firm's environment with innovative products, or create cooperative arrangements with suppliers, customers, or other firms in the industry, or lobby legislative bodies concerning competition or regulation.

Identifying and choosing among such options is a task of top managers. Some choose more wisely than do others. And, of course, in all cases, top managers choose the timing and manner of implementing their actions. Here, too, some choose more wisely than do others.

> Making choices is one thing. Implementing them is another. Not even top level executives are omnipotent. Evolved organizational designs are often not what top management intended. Intended designs are sometimes modified by other managers with different intentions or understandings. Indeed, due to changes in the marketplace, in internal power distributions, in workforce demands, or in any of a myriad of other forces, intended designs are frequently modified during implementation by the originators themselves.
>
> Then, too, there are the less controllable organizational features. Organizational culture, for example, is notoriously hard to change, being influenced greatly by the organization's history and the values its employees bring to their jobs. And unwanted turnover is to a great extent a consequence of the availability of employment opportunities outside the firm. These examples show that, while top managers have considerable influence, the *nature* of their firm often contains features that do not conform to top management's desires.[7]

In the future, top managers will be able to carry out change actions effectively and before disaster overcomes them only if they have created firms well suited to the increased dynamism, complexity, and competitiveness of future business environments. What will be the necessary nature of such firms? What attributes must they possess? Which management practices must be in place? For those top managers who learn the correct answers to these questions, and effectively implement the necessary changes, it will *generally* be true that they will win the race against the destructive changes in their firms' environments. Their firms will tend to survive to become future firms.[8] In contrast, it will *certainly* be true that those top managers who do not discover the correct answers, or who do not successfully create the congruencies required, will lose the race.[c] Their legacies will be the deaths of their firms.

---

[c]While it is top management's responsibility to ensure that the firm possesses the capabilities needed to attain and maintain congruence with the firm's environment, to achieve this congruence requires managers *at all levels* to choose and implement organizational design features and management practices well matched to the firm's environment.

This book is about *what* the nature of future firms must be. As skeptical and jaded as all readers should be, given the plethora of have-faith-in-the-author predictions that pervade the business and management literature, I required of myself that the book also explain *why* future firms must be what they will be. Thus, more precisely, this book is about the *necessary* nature of future firms. However, the book's usefulness does not lie in the future. Its usefulness is in the here and now, for *it is today's management actions and inactions that both enhance and constrain the firm's performance in the future.*

About This Book

This chapter set forth two ideas: (1) firms must be congruent with their environments and (2) future firms will be different from today's firms because their environments will be different. The next chapter describes the characteristics of these future environments, the factors and forces that—along with actions by top management—will determine the nature and survivability of future firms.

One of the conclusions of Chapter 2 is that the rate of environmental change will itself be changing; it will be increasing. This idea, of *accelerating change,* seems to have taken hold in some quarters, but few seem to understand why this will occur or what its implications are. Without knowing *why* something is occurring, *what* its causes are, and *to what* it will lead, managers are greatly limited in their ability to make sound judgments, and are consequently more likely to misdirect organizational actions. In an attempt to minimize these adverse outcomes, I describe in Chapter 2 the future environments of business organizations, and I explain there why these environments will be what they will be. Because organizations must be congruent with their environments, it is absolutely necessary that managers preparing their firms for the future understand the nature of future environments.

Some managers, fully absorbed in the present, are not preparing their firms for the future. Perhaps they do not recognize that the future will be considerably different from the present. Other managers believe that there is nothing they should do now to help their firms be better positioned for the future, that they should "wait and see" what the future brings, and only then should they act. Perhaps they believe in this approach because, in their experience in the slower moving and less competitive world of yesterday and today, this strategy worked. At least it worked for them. It didn't work for the many other firms—no longer to be seen—that waited to act until the future was upon them, and then failed to survive because either their actions or the benefits of their actions arrived too late to avoid disaster.

Having established in Chapter 2 the nature of future business environments, and knowing that future firms must possess characteristics congruent with these environments, the next seven chapters of this book describe the organizational attributes and management practices that will differentiate future firms from today's firms. While possessing these characteristics does not guarantee survival, not possessing them virtually guarantees that the firm will lose out to its competitors, that it will not survive to be a future firm.

Our task then, in the remaining chapters, is to determine the necessary nature of future firms given the nature of future business environments, with an almost exclusive focus on those features of future firms that will be *different in kind or degree from those predominant in firms today*. This will require us to draw carefully on the soundest knowledge available about the causal relationships between organizational attributes and management practices on the one hand, and organizational performance and survival on the other, *and to do this in the specific context of the environments that will confront firms in the future*. Let us turn, then, to ascertaining the future environments of business organizations.

Endnotes

1. Works based on systematic and truly in-depth studies of multiple firms tend to avoid one, two, or even all of these three deficiencies. Examples are works by Eisenhardt and her colleagues, 1989, 1995; Leifer and his colleagues, 2000; and Van de Ven and his colleagues, 1989, 1999. Such works are scarce and seldom encountered by practicing managers.

2. Early parts of this section draw on and extend parts of Chapter 1 of *Organizational Change and Redesign: Ideas and Insights for Improving Performance*, 1993 (G. Huber and W. Glick, Eds.).

3. G. P. Huber, "The Nature and Design of Post-industrial Organizations," 1984. This article was awarded First Prize in the Institute of Management Sciences' second annual prize competition for Most Original New Contribution to the Field of Organizational Analysis and Design.

4. See J. G. Miller's early monumental work, *Living Systems*, 1978, for a full development of the living systems concept. Also see Sir G. Vickers's *Human Systems Are Different*, 1983, for a broad-ranging examination of the development and ecological position of human systems. In a related vein, the usefulness of a biological metaphor for understanding certain aspects of organizations is convincingly set forth by A. de Geus, longtime strategist at Royal Dutch/Shell Group, in *The Living Company*, 1997; and by J. Moore, management consultant and business writer, in *The Death of Competition*, 1997. Moore's book is an interesting complement to R. A. D'Aveni and R. Gunther, *Hypercompetition*, 1994.

5. Organizational scientists and strategic management researchers will recognize that I have chosen not to call attention here to various organizational science theories (e.g., contingency theory, configuration theory, resource dependence theory, institutional theory, and population ecology) associated with the ideas in this paragraph. Doing so would slow the flow and be of little service to managers, who—for better or worse—care very little about scientific abstractions of what they observe. Nor would

calling attention to the theories, and citing the well-known works, be of real service to academics, who are already familiar with these matters. For anyone wishing to examine elaborations of the ideas set forth in the paragraph, let me suggest examining H. Aldrich, *Organizations Evolving*, 1999; L. Donaldson, *The Contingency Theory of Organizations*, 2001; M. T. Hannan and G. R. Carroll, *Dynamics of Organizational Populations*, 1992; and W. R. Scott, *Organizations: Rational, Natural, and Open Systems* (5th ed.), 2003.

6. International management consultant Elliott Jacques is widely recognized for having developed and elaborated the idea that a manager's "time span of discretion" or "maximum-target-completion-time for tasks" is closely related to the manager's level in the organization. For an articulate elaboration of this idea, see Chapter 2 of his book, *Requisite Organization*, 1989, or for a lighter dose, see Jacques, "In Praise of Hierarchy," 1990.

7. For a comprehensive analysis of managerial influence on organizational actions and outcomes, see D. Hambrick and S. Finkelstein's (1987) Comprehensive analysis, "Managerial Discretion: A Bridge Between Polar Views of Organizational Outcomes"; John Child's (1973) classic article, "Organization Structure, Environment, and Performance: The Role of Strategic Choice"; and W. Dill's (1958) early piece, "Environment as an Influence on Managerial Autonomy." Each takes a different cut at addressing the issue of the relative influence of environment versus managerial preference in determining the nature of organizations, particularly business organizations. Each exemplifies the best thinking of the era in which it was written. For further insight into the "debate" about the relative influence of environment and management, see A. Y. Lewin, C. B. Weigelt, and J. D. Emery, "Adaptation and Selection in Strategy and Change: Perspectives on Strategic Change in Organization," 2004.

8. Continued survival is a goal for most firms during most of their lives. Thus it is that top management's responsibility is generally to ensure that the firm is sufficiently congruent with its environment that it can survive in the short run and that it possesses the capabilities to attain and maintain congruence in the long run. An elaboration and a caveat seem worthwhile. The *elaboration* is to note that most firms must compete for loans and/or for shareholders. Thus, to be "congruent" with one of their key resource-controlling environments, the capital markets, firms must be successful—they must generate returns equal to or greater than the other options available to at least some investors. The *caveat* is to note that, because the infrastructures supporting the markets in which firms and their assets are bought and sold have grown in effectiveness, these markets have come to be a more important component of the business environment. Because these markets will grow further in their effectiveness (as a consequence of increasing globalization and of the increasing effectiveness of the facilitating information technology), they will become an even more important component in the future. We might expect, therefore, that top managers will, in the future, more frequently position the firm and its assets to be attractive in these markets. If so, "attaining and retaining congruence with their environment" will, in the future, more often mean that top managers will intentionally take actions that will not lead to their firm's continuing survival. Instead they will position their firms to be attractive in the mergers and acquisitions market and in markets for their firm's specific assets.

Appendix

Prediction

Explanation Versus Correlation

U nfortunately for managers seeking guidance to prepare their firms for the future, most descriptions of what firms must do, or become, or be like, are based on questionable inferences drawn from correlations in quite small samples.

Everyday observation shows that higher-order living systems, such as humans and organizations, attempt to improve their lot by engaging in exploratory behavior, pushing and testing the current limits of their capabilities and environments. Salespeople try new prospects. Firms try new products. Nations try new conquests. Many such initiatives fail. In today's fast-changing environments, firms are exploring many alternative strategies, structures, technologies, and business practices. Which particular alternatives (which particular management fads or fashions, for example) will survive is difficult to say. Authorities on the nature of social change emphasize that the ratio of tested alternatives to adopted alternatives is large; most innovations fail.[1] This is the case in firms as well: "Quite simply, the vast majority of attempts at innovation fail" (Rosenberg, 1996: 334). For this reason, predicting the nature of future firms on the basis of the newly high-fashion features of high-performing firms is certain to result in a large number of erroneous predictions.

Another reason that using the relative performance of a given company as evidence that some particular one of its features is worthy of replication elsewhere is that the relative performance rankings of (business) organizations change across time.[2] Each of these two facts sharply calls into question the usefulness of extrapolating the newest features of today's high-performing firms as the best approach for ascertaining the necessary nature of future firms.

The usefulness of this *correlational* approach is particularly questionable when the features claimed to enhance performance are not identified using a rigorous screening process. Seldom does it appear that the espoused feature, sometimes portrayed as "the key to success in the future," was the survivor of a systematic sifting and winnowing directed at determining whether the feature is *the* source of the exemplar firm's recent performance (or even whether it is *a* source). This can result in some serious misdirection. For example, it might be that an investigation would show that underperforming firms also manifest the organizational attribute or management practice being lauded as characteristic of high performers, but such an investigation is seldom if ever reported and is very likely not undertaken.

> Unfortunately, it is a hazardous process to search for good examples and then extract lessons from them alone. The sample of successes is biased, the reasons for success are often obscure, and the key buttresses of systematic inquiry are absent. (Miller, Greenwood, & Hinings, 1997)

In place of the correlational approach to identifying the nature of future firms, this book builds on an *explanatory* approach that is more robust and more scientifically grounded. As a consequence, the approach provides a more accurate prediction of what features firms must possess to prosper in the future. It derives from the ecological theory set forth earlier, that organizations must possess—or quickly achieve—features congruent with the requirements of their environment.

Two steps makeup the explanatory approach. The first is to identify the characteristics of future business environments. The second step is to determine the organizational attributes and management practices that will be necessary for firms to be congruent with the predicted environments. Partly due to its systematic nature and partly because it capitalizes on a large body of knowledge about the determinants of business performance, knowledge gained from thousands of field studies, the explanatory approach is more likely than is the more popular correlational approach to provide accurate predictions. Three specific reasons stand out.

The *first* is that it does not suffer from the important shortcomings of the extrapolation approach. As elaborated above, these are three. (1) Most new management practices turn out to be short-lived. Thus the assumption that what is new is an indication of what will be is likely to be incorrect. (2) Selecting exemplar organizations in which to find performance-enhancing features is very risky. Relative performance rankings are unstable across time. (3) Rigorously determining whether a particular feature is actually responsible for the performance of some currently high-performing organizations is a task not often undertaken.

The *second* reason the explanatory approach is more likely to give trustworthy results is that, in its first step—identifying the characteristics of future organizational environments—only environmental characteristics with durable patterns of movement are included. For example, the data sets used in Chapter 2 to examine environmental change generally span decades and, for particularly important issues, span scores of years. This contrasts with the short or nonexistent histories commonly used in the correlational approach.[a] Longer histories protect us from drawing incorrect inferences that might follow from viewing short-term "runs" or other aberrations.

Third and finally, in the explanatory approach used in this book, the causal pathways from these environmental characteristics to the necessary features of future firms are derived from a huge number of rigorous studies of firms of many types in many circumstances. This contrasts with the generally loose reasoning used in the correlational approach to hypothesize connections between the features of some currently high-performing firms and the performance in the future of other firms that adopt these same features.

> Although the explanatory approach is likely to generate predictions that are more accurate, it is worth noting that the gain in predictive power over the alternative correlational approach need not be great for significant performance gains to follow. Drawing on a convenient analogy to compound interest suggests that if better insights about the future lead a firm to employ an organizational attribute just 10% more effective than the next best, then—all else equal—in 7 years the firm will have accumulated twice the resources acquired by a firm using the next best attribute.

Endnotes

1. See, for example, Chapter 11 of Talcott Parsons, *The Evolution of Societies* (1977), and Chapter 13 of Kenneth Boulding's *Ecodynamics: A New Theory of Societal Evolution* (1978).

2. Not long after publication of T. Peters and R. Waterman's highly acclaimed *In Search of Excellence* (1982), *BusinessWeek* (1984) reported that approximately one third

[a]A large proportion of business press articles ignore time entirely, relying entirely on "one-time time-slice" data.

of the "excellent" companies had a poor performance year. This is not to say that the companies were not correctly identified as excellent, but rather to give an example of the difficulty in projecting relative performance. When relative performance is stable, it may have nothing to do with the attribute under discussion but may be the consequence of inertial factors such as reputation, resources, alliances, and so forth. For a follow-up to the *BusinessWeek* article and an excellent statistical analysis of the issue, see T. W. Ruefli and R. L. Jones, "Excellent Companies: An Ordinal Time Series Analysis," in T. W. Ruefli (Ed.) *Ordinal Time Series Analysis* (Quorum Books: New York, 1990).

2

The Future Environments of Business Organizations[1]

S ome managers might still assume that the highly dynamic environments faced by today's business organizations represent a period of transition to a more stable era. They would be wrong.

Other managers might believe that these dynamic environments *are* the new era, that they represent the future. These managers, too, would be wrong.

The fact is that the future environments of business organizations will differ in important respects from the environments in effect near the beginning of the twenty-first century. In particular, they will be characterized by

1. more and increasing *scientific knowledge,*

2. increasingly effective information, transportation, and manufacturing *technologies,*

3. more and increasing *complexity,*

4. more and increasing *dynamism,* and

5. more and increasing inter-firm *competitiveness.*

These five characteristics, in combination, will constitute business environments significantly more challenging than were those of either the growth years of the mid- to late 1990s or the decline years of the early 2000s. They will require today's firms and tomorrow's startups to take on attributes different from those common today. They will be key drivers of organizational change and redesign in the future.

Top managers will, of course, influence the processes through which their firms are changed, and they will influence the specific new features of their changed organizations. We will see, however—as the book progresses—that *the general nature of the differences between tomorrow's firms and today's will be the same in all surviving firms.*[a]

The rapid changes in organizational environments, both today's and tomorrow's, are largely a consequence of the increasing effectiveness of information technologies, transportation technologies, and manufacturing technologies. As an example, manufacturing employment in the United States has decreased and will continue to decrease as a direct consequence of cross-border management (read "information technology"), cross-border importation of manufactured goods (read "transportation technology"), and automation (read "manufacturing technology"). More generally, globalization could not be increasing at the rate it is, and will be, if information, products, and people could not be moved as easily as these technologies now permit.

Scientific Knowledge and Improved Technology

SCIENTIFIC KNOWLEDGE

When predicting future organizational environments, we must not allow ourselves to take the easy path and simply extrapolate from recent events, or even recent trends. History shows that short-term trends are often misleading as indicators of longer term change. To avoid being misled by false indicators, we must

1. select only trends whose existence can be explained with causal reasoning,

2. select only trends for which there is a substantial history and about which we have information relevant to determining the trend's future course, and

3. select only trends that are *logically* antecedent and causally linked to the changes we wish to anticipate and understand.

As will become apparent through the course of this chapter, the growth in scientific knowledge is a trend that satisfies each of these requirements.

Before examining why and how the growth in scientific knowledge will so strongly influence the nature of future business environments, and thus future firms, let us consider the trend itself. It possesses two properties that are

---

[a]When considering the differences between tomorrow's firms and today's and yesterday's firms, we must control for context. That is, while for the sake of readability I will speak generally, in actuality I will be comparing future firms to *their* predecessors, to *their* antecedent counterparts. That is, I will be examining differences between future firms and firms that today or in the past were in the same industry or, more generally, were serving the same societal or economic need in the same country or culture.

highly desirable—it is long-term and it is consistent in its accelerating form. As an indicator of these properties, consider the long-term and accelerating increase in the number of scientific journals. As reported by the historian Derek de Solla Price, after the first scientific journal appeared in the 1660s, it took just under 100 years (until 1750) for the number to grow to approximately 10. Thereafter the growth increased exponentially: 100 journals by 1800, 1,000 by 1850, perhaps 10,000 by 1900. "According to the *World List of Scientific Periodicals* (last published in 1975) . . . we are now well on our way to the next milestone of a hundred thousand journals."[2] By this measure and by others, scientific knowledge has been increasing at an increasing rate for hundreds of years.

The Dutch economist Huppes provides an interesting snapshot of more recent scientific productivity, reporting that on a worldwide basis the number of scientific articles published per day rose from 3,000 to 8,000 in the period 1965 to 1980, a 160% increase in 15 years.[3] Another such snapshot is provided by Tenopir and King, who report that between 1975 and 1995 the average number of scientific journal pages published *per U.S. scientist* increased almost 70% (this in spite of the fact that the number of U.S. scientists more than doubled during the period.)[4] Many other indicators also demonstrate this pattern of accelerating growth in scientific knowledge.

Forecasting the intermediate or longer term future by extrapolating the present or recent past is, of course, very risky and likely to result in major forecast errors. Extrapolations of even long-term trends, although much superior, are not satisfactory bases for predicting future events, at least not by themselves. Thus even when so accomplished an authority as Charles Van Doren writes that

> the rate at which the totality of human knowledge increases varies from age to age; sometimes the rate is very fast (as, for example, it is today or it was during the fifth century BC), while at other times it is very slow (as, for example, it was during the Dark Ages). Nevertheless, this progress essentially never ceases and, most probably, never can cease. (Van Doren, 1991: xvi)

we must ask, Why so? Why is it that the growth in knowledge "never ceases . . . never can cease"? Should we rely solely on data showing that it hasn't ceased yet? *No.* While we are tempted to do so, we should not.

More reliable, and much more important than suggestive data when attempting to predict the future, is a sound argument or set of arguments that explains why the future will be what it will be. There are two reasons why scientific knowledge will continue to grow at an accelerating rate. The *first* is straightforward—knowledge leads to more knowledge. One discovery leads to another. Knowledge is its own generative raw material—the more you have, the more you get; and the more you get, the more you have. And on and on.

The *second* reason new knowledge will continue to be created at an accelerating rate is that increases in the capability and application of communication technologies greatly increase the *availability* of whatever knowledge exists. The invention and use of the printing press is the most noteworthy example. Without it, scientific journals could not have made the huge contribution to the growth of scientific knowledge that they have.[5] Subsequently the Internet also increased the rate at which knowledge leads to more knowledge, as many scientific publications and facts moved to this distribution medium.[b]

Reflecting on some advances in communication technology made during the last 200 years (e.g., the Pony Express, telegraph, radio, telephone, television, and the Internet), each viewed by many at the time of its origin as the apex in communication technology, leads to the conclusion that communication technologies much more effective than those now with us will appear. (Even if they do not, more widespread adoption of current "advanced" technologies is inevitable, and alone will greatly increase the availability of knowledge for knowledge creation.) *Forthcoming adoptions of knowledge-distribution technologies, superimposed on the rapidly growing knowledge base, will create an environment where new knowledge is in much greater supply.*

If this last were so, given the availability in the last decade or two of fax, then e-mail, then the Internet, we would already expect to see an increase in collaboratively developed scientific works, as these information technologies increasingly enable widely separated scientists to collaboratively generate new knowledge. We do. The National Science Foundation's *Science and Engineering Indicators* reports trends showing, for example, that the number of authors per scientific paper has been increasing and that, in particular, inter-institutional and international coauthorships have been increasing.[6] In addition, the facilitating role of knowledge-distribution technology on scientific advancement has much room yet to play out. For example, analyses by Dr. Francis Narin, an international authority on scientific and technological progress, show that "each country's inventors are preferentially building upon their own domestic

(Continued)

---

[b]Even though an ever larger proportion of new scientific knowledge comes from "big science," an article in the April 29, 2000, issue of *The Economist* (77-78) notes the interesting fact that the Internet has made it easier for amateurs to be part of the mainstream scientific community, that is, to collect data, make discoveries, and distribute results.

(Continued)

science" and that "all of these citing phenomena show that there are still very strong national ties between scientists within a country and inventors within a country" (Narin, Hamilton, & Olivastro, 1997:6).

Note to reader: The data referenced here, and that referenced or reported in other of these "windows," are not offered as proof of the conclusion that precedes them. Rather, they are examples of what we should already expect to see if the causal reasoning supporting the conclusion were valid.

These forthcoming changes—these increases in the quantity of knowledge, the availability of knowledge, and the number of nations actively involved in generating knowledge[7]—lead to the conclusion that scientific knowledge will continue to grow at an increasing rate. We are observing a long-term trend that reason maintains will continue. *In the future, the amount of available scientific knowledge will be significantly greater, and its growth will be accelerating.*

Given the new scientific findings we learn about daily, it is hard to imagine that we would think about an end to scientific progress in any broad area. But if we do,

it is prudent to recall that at the end of the nineteenth century the general opinion amongst physicists was that nothing of any great importance remained to be done in physics. And then came radioactivity, X-rays, the discovery of the electron and the nucleus, . . . quantum mechanics and relativity, . . . black holes, chaos, the Big Bang, and so on. (Silver, 1998: xiv)

The rate of knowledge growth in any narrowly defined research area eventually declines, of course, as the area matures and as the scientific establishment shifts its attention to newer areas—where career-rewarding breakthroughs are more likely. On balance, however, and as we noted earlier, new areas are opened up at a rate such that the net growth in scientific knowledge accelerates. At the beginning of the 2000s, the areas of science underlying biotechnology and nanotechnology were among those receiving increasing attention.

IMPROVED TECHNOLOGIES

Increases in scientific knowledge have the important practical effect of enabling improvements in technologies. As examples of this, consider developments in information technology (both communication technologies and decision-aiding technologies, e.g., high-speed computers, cellular phones, the Internet, teleconferencing, massive and easily used databases, and computer simulations) and developments in manufacturing technology (e.g., manufacturing resource planning, computer-aided manufacturing, computer-aided engineering, and use of computer simulations and virtual reality).[8] Developments in both technologies depended on microprocessors, which depend on microchips, which exist and are decreasing in cost in large part due to advances in materials science (an applied area within the *science* of physical chemistry).

Relatively speaking, the contribution of scientific advances to technological advances is a new phenomenon. In earlier eras, technological advances were more likely to result from insights and atheoretic experimentation rather than from advances in scientific knowledge. This is now much less often the case. Certainly the influence of scientific knowledge on technological advances increased greatly during the twentieth century. For example, the economic historian Heilbroner points out that "although scientists played virtually no direct role in the development of the steam, coal, and textile technologies of the opening decades of the century, their work was at the very heart of the ever-more-important electrical technology of its last decades" (Heilbroner, 1995: 46).

Because advances in science lead to increases in the effectiveness of technologies, and because forthcoming increases in the availability and capability of communication devices will make new scientific knowledge more accessible to engineers and other developers of technology, it seems reasonable to conclude that, *in the future, the contributions of science to technology will increase.*[9]

If it were true that the influence of scientific knowledge on technology is increasing, the number of scientific articles cited per new patent would be increasing at an increasing rate. It is, for the United States, the United Kingdom, France, Japan, Germany, and other countries.[10]

Because advances in science lead to improvements in technologies, and because—as we saw earlier—these scientific advances will be forthcoming at an increasing rate, it also seems reasonable to believe that *in the future, the effectiveness of information, transportation, and manufacturing technologies will be greater, and will be increasing.*

Another line of reasoning also supports this conclusion—technological advances often facilitate subsequent technological advances. This can be brought into sharp focus by considering an interesting historical instance where the absence of communication technology interfered with the emergence of an advance in manufacturing technology. In 1041, a movable-type printing system appeared in China. It used clay characters. In 1329, book printing appeared in Korea, using metal plates. So, why not print books with a movable-type printing system using metal characters? In the later decades of the twentieth century (a period characterized by high-speed communication devices, extensive media coverage, and well-hyped product announcements), people in the printing industry would have recognized the possible integration of these two technologies as soon as the second one appeared. Gutenberg's printing press, movable metal type and all, would very likely have become operational in a matter of months. But Gutenberg didn't develop his movable type with metal characters until the 1450s, 120 years after the second of the above two marriageable technologies appeared. Why didn't someone, somewhere, quickly combine these technologies to create a printing press? At least some of the delay, if not all of it, can be attributed to the lack of communication infrastructure.

In contrast to the above, consider how even the mid-twentieth-century communication infrastructure must have facilitated the marriage of the technologies incorporated into industrial robots. Industrial robots became commercially available in the 1960s. Their functioning draws on three technologies: servo-mechanics, developed in the 1940s, and semiconductor electronics and digital computer data processing, both developed in the 1950s. Thus commercialization of industrial robot technology occurred only a decade after the component technologies were developed.

Due to the availability of more effective communication and transportation infrastructures, *in the future, technological advances will more rapidly contribute to other technological advances.*

Advances in technologies not only contribute to advances in other technologies, but they also facilitate advances in scientific knowledge, and in this way further accelerate scientific progress. For example, improvements in measurement technologies and in computing technologies have enabled many advances in science that would have been impossible without these improvements. As a specific example, computing technology was a prerequisite to the development of our understanding of DNA, a scientific breakthrough (a scientific breakthrough that in turn led to new health-enhancing technologies). Such multiplier effects within the scientific knowledge-generating community, within the technology-enhancing community, and between the two communities, lead us to conclude that, *in the future, advances in scientific and technical knowledge will arrive at an accelerating rate.*

If the reasoning of these last few pages were valid, we would expect to see it reflected already as an acceleration in the number of patents granted by the U.S. Patent Office. This has occurred. During the first half of the twentieth century, the number of patents granted increased by 50%. During the second half, the number quadrupled (Technology Assessment and Forecast Seventh Report, March 1977, and U.S. Patent Statistics Report, February 2000, U.S. Patent and Trademark Office). During the 1990s, the number increased by 70% (*BusinessWeek,* August 28, 2000: 78).

MENTAL BLOCKS TO IMAGINING A
DIFFERENT WORLD ON THE SAME PLANET

Given the speed of technological advances that occurred in the last two decades of the twentieth century, it is difficult to imagine that in the future the rate of technological progress will be greater still. What we must do, however, is to rely on reason rather than allow ourselves to be anchored to our observations of the past and present. Reliance on prior experience and current observation has failed even accomplished authorities, as these oft-cited and perhaps all-too-familiar examples of authoritative—but mistaken—perceptions suggest:

Everything that can be invented has been invented.

U.S. Patent Office director, urging
President McKinley to abolish the office (1899)

That is the biggest fool thing we have ever done. . . . The bomb will never go off, and I speak as an expert in explosives.

U.S. Admiral William D. Leahy to
President Truman, on atomic weaponry.

I think there is a world market for about five computers.

Thomas J. Watson, President of IBM (1958)[11]

Computers in the future may weigh no more than 1.5 tons.

Popular Mechanics (March 1949: 259)

Such examples are included here and elsewhere as clarifications rather than as evidence. More relevant than examples is the systematic research indicating that *most people most of the time imagine the future to be much like the present.*[12]

It seems worthwhile to consider how skeptical the everyday person in times past would have been with respect to the likelihood of modern technologies. We needn't restrict ourselves to electronically enhanced technologies. Take, for example, the human-machine technology we call a factory. It had an amazing impact on manufacturing effectiveness:

> Invented in the 1700s to make cotton textiles, the factory model was adapted by entrepreneurs to mass produce guns, tools and other foundations of modern life. Britain considered the textile factory so critical to its economic advancement that it tried to hoard the technology, unsuccessfully, by blocking the emigration of artisans and the export of machine tools. (*Wall Street Journal,* January 17, 1999: R14)

Would the seamstresses, blacksmiths, and wheelwrights of the early eighteenth century have believed that what came to pass would come to pass? Probably not. Could they have imagined the enormous increase in output per person per day? Hardly. It seems unlikely that even the most optimistic entrepreneurs of the period could have foreseen the magnitude of the changes that ultimately occurred.

Because of the pervasive disinclination to imagine unfamiliar futures, we should anticipate skepticism about future factories, factories that accept customized orders and fill them without involving humans; factories where component materials are ordered, received, and integrated into products without human involvement; factories that receive, manufacture, package, and ship orders in a matter of minutes or hours without human involvement; that is, factories that are lifeless.

Even such a visionary as former Microsoft CEO Bill Gates provided in his 1996 book, *The Road Ahead,* only a faint hint of what was to come:

> Soon, shirt-making machines will obey a different set of instructions for every shirt. When you order, you'll indicate your measurements as well as your choices for fabric, fit, collar, and every other variable. The information will be communicated to a manufacturing plant that will produce the shirt for prompt delivery. (Gates, 1996: 189)

Only a few years after Gates made this observation, we saw the retail store fitting to the customer and the subsequent normal production-line manufacture of Levi Strauss' "Personal Pair" jeans, and automobile buyers communicating their preferences for options directly to the manufacturer through the Internet and expecting their custom-assembled automobile to be available in a matter of days.

Advances in overland transportation technology would undoubtedly have encountered skepticism as well. "In 1800, a man could *comfortably* travel overland about twenty-four miles *in a day*" (Van Doren, 1995: 403), whether by foot or by horse, presumably carrying a *small package.* "But only sixty years later, when Abraham Lincoln took the Oath of Office as the sixteenth president of the United States, Americans could move *bulky items* in great quantity farther in an hour than Americans of 1801 could do in a day, whether by land (twenty-five miles *per hour* on railroads) or water (ten miles *an hour* upstream on a steamboat)" (Ambrose, 1996: 54). Would the turn-of-the century horse rider have imagined this? Not, at least, in terms of the volume and size of the items transported.

Given this history, we should expect few people today to envision the everyday transport of trainload-sized orders of goods—over water or through mountains—at speeds approaching the speed of sound, even when an admittedly crude forerunner of such technology seems apparent in the form of the London-to-Paris Eurostar. *Most people most of the time imagine the future to be much like the present.*

It will not be. In the future, advances in science and improvements in technology will arrive at an accelerating rate.

[Perhaps] nothing better illustrates this amazing acceleration in technological change than the realization in the twentieth century of humankind's ancient desire to fly. The first successful motor-driven flight took place in 1903, but the fragile aircraft of Wilbur and Orville Wright traveled only a few hundred feet. Just 66 years later, an astronaut was standing on the moon, talking to another astronaut on earth, and hundreds of millions of people around the world overheard and watched that conversation.

Robert W. Folgel, President of the American Economic
Association in his Presidential Address, January 4, 1999, New York

Who would have imagined these events, or this rate of progress? Not some noted authorities:

Heavier than air flying machines are impossible.

Lord Kelvin, engineer, physicist, and
president of the British Royal Society (1890-1895)

Space travel is utter bilge.

Dr. Richard van der Riet Wooley, upon assuming the post of
British Astronomer Royal (1956).[13] (Sputnik was launched in 1958.)

Most people most of the time do not imagine the future to be much different from the present.[c] Hear James Martin, Pulitzer Prize nominee and world-renowned authority on the impact of computing technology on business and society, address the matter:

> We are all, in differing degrees, prisoners of familiarity. This fact is often true of the technologist viewing his own discipline and the industrialist viewing his own product. The technologist and industrialist understand in such fine detail how things are done today that they cannot imagine the sweeping changes that will come tomorrow; the detail of these is not yet known. They focus on the limitations set by the current state of the art. (Martin, 1977: 10-11)

As example instances of Martin's generalization that people "cannot imagine" the occurrence of really large changes, hear two of the somewhat familiar and (now) humorous responses to Alexander Graham Bell's invention of the telephone: (1) by Western Union's review committee—"In conclusion, the committee feels that it must advise against any investment whatever in Bell's scheme," and (2) by a London newspaper of the day—"The telephone may be appropriate for our American cousins, but not here because we have messenger boys" (Martin, 1977: 12).

INTERIM SUMMARY AND TRANSITION

Before proceeding to the remaining two sections of this chapter, where we will identify and examine other characteristics of future business environments, let us review where we have been and see where we are. We began this section by reviewing some data indicating that scientific knowledge has been growing at an accelerating rate for at least some hundreds of years. Next we examined two reasons why scientific knowledge must continue to grow at an accelerating rate in the future. We moved then to considering the idea that advances in scientific knowledge would lead to improvements in technology, noting some recent examples where this had occurred and some documentary evidence suggesting that it was now occurring on a large scale. Finally, we examined arguments leading to the conclusion that, in the future, the effectiveness of technologies will improve greatly. The next section of the chapter draws on this conclusion—that the future will bring considerable improvement in the effectiveness of technologies.

---

[c] Endnote 12 presents a probable explanation for this bias—people "anchor" on present conditions and, when making predictions about the future, "adjust" from present conditions too little. This suggests that while people may be willing to agree that, in general, the future will be different from the present, with respect to specific phenomena people expect the future to be very much like the present (as the examples noted here suggest).

Our ultimate interest is, of course, determining the nature of future business organizations. Given from Chapter 1 that the nature of future firms will be shaped to a great extent by the nature of future environments, the question arises—what other characteristics of business environments, besides increases in scientific knowledge and improvements in the technologies discussed above, are likely to force changes in the nature of future firms? There are three such characteristics—*environmental complexity, environmental dynamism, and environmental competitiveness.* Let us turn first to examining forthcoming changes in environmental complexity, as these have unassailable implications for changes in organizational structures and because they are important contributors to forthcoming changes in environmental dynamism and competitiveness.

The Complexity of Future Environments

In Chapter 1 we noted the need for living systems to be aligned with their environment. Increases in environmental complexity require organizations either to become more complex themselves or to find or create a less complex environment (perhaps a smaller niche in the overall environment). So, for example, when the U.S. government required firms doing business with it to take "affirmative action" in the employment of minorities and women, many firms found that they needed to add a function, an affirmative action office or officer and a set of procedures, and they became more complex. Similarly, when a new technology critically relevant to a firm's survival appears, the firm must add to its existing capabilities the capability to cope with or exploit the new technology—it must become more complex.[14] Given the relevance of environmental complexity to the design of organizations, it seems important to understand the nature of environmental complexity in the future. Let us turn to this issue.

Environmental complexity is established through three attributes—the *variety,* the *density,* and the *interdependence* of the environment's entities. (Examples of key entities in the environments of business organizations are products, markets, and competitors.) To see why future business environments will be more complex, let us examine why each of the three attributes will be greater. We begin with increases in environmental variety, as it leads to the increases in environmental density and interdependence.

ENVIRONMENTAL VARIETY

Increases in the variety of entities in the business environment, such as products, markets, and firms, follow largely from advances in technology.

Consider, for example, what *did not* occur when confluences of technological advances resulted in videocassettes and video digital disks. Although millions of people became consumers of these new entertainment media, movie theaters did not disappear, as many predicted. And the Hollywood movie-making industry did not decline, as many predicted. What *did* occur? Moviemakers came to have a *greater variety of markets* for their films—to movie theaters were added video rental retailers. Movie viewers came to have a *greater variety of products* from which to choose—rentable movie cassettes and disks as well as rentable seats in theaters. And a *greater variety of business enterprises* came to be—to movie theaters were added movie cassette and disk rental stores.

As another example of how advances in technology increase environmental variety, consider the arrival of fiber-optic cable as a telecommunications medium. It amounted to an *increase in the variety of products* available for use by firms in the telephone, television, and local-area network industries. Because connecting fiber-optic cables was more difficult than connecting copper wires, and because connecting fiber-optic cable to copper wire required specialized devices, there occurred an increase in the *variety of markets* available to manufacturers of telecommunications media connectors. This increase in the variety of products in the market created an increase in the *variety of threats* faced by producers of other telecommunications media (such as copper wire) and an increase in the *variety of opportunities* for consumers of the media (such as telephone companies and other producers of communication services). Finally, because copper-wire manufacturers did not disappear, there occurred a net increase in the *variety of firms.*[d]

We saw earlier that the future environments of business organizations will be characterized by accelerating increases in scientific knowledge and by improvements in technology. Because scientific knowledge and technology effectiveness will increase at increasing rates, and because they are causes of variety in the environment, we can expect that, *in the future, the variety of products, markets, and firms in the environments of business organizations will be greater, and will be increasing at increasing rates.*

---

[d]As another example of how technological advances increase environmental variety, consider the Internet. The Internet created additional markets (e.g., consumers accessed through this new advertising and distribution channel) without reducing the number of existing markets. While large volumes of books and some foodstuffs were sold through the Internet, many people viewed going to book stores and grocery stores as positive experiences, as outings where they could encounter people or enjoy their senses of smell and touch as they browsed. Others wanted instant access and ownership. These walk-in consumers remained as markets to be served. Thus, for books, foodstuffs, and many other products, the effect of the Internet was to increase the *variety* of markets available to producers.

If this prediction were valid, because scientific knowledge has been increasing at an increasing rate, we would expect that the variety of business organizations would already be increasing at a considerable rate. It is. As an indication, consider that the U.S. Bureau of the Census—recognizing in 1997 that the 1987 Standard Industry Classification System (SIC) was no longer representative of the U.S. economy—began using the North American Industry Classification System (NAICS) as a replacement. The total number of industry classifications increased from 1,004 in the SIC to 1,170 in the 1997 NAICS. This NAICS included 351 new industries that were not previously recognized separately under the SIC and 338 industries that had their scopes revised; 475 industries were substantially unchanged.[15] Revision to the NAICS published in 2002 includes 1,179 industry classifications—9 more than the 1997 version. Altogether, then, the 2002 NAICS contains 360 new classifications not previously identified in the SIC, a 36% increase over the number contained in the SIC just 15 years earlier.

ENVIRONMENTAL DENSITY AND INTERDEPENDENCE

The second attribute of environmental complexity is the density of the environment. Let us consider environmental density to refer to the number of entities in the environment, entities such as competitors, customers, and suppliers. Will the number of entities be greater in the future, or smaller? Certainly many firms are disappearing—we read every week about mergers of already gigantic firms. *The vividness of these events misleads us, however.* Research findings are unambiguous on this point—the vividness of events distorts our perception of the likelihood of their occurrence; highly vivid events are perceived to be much more frequent than they really are. In actuality, the number of mergers and acquisitions per year is very small relative to the number of new firms that appear each year (as either entrepreneurial ventures or spin-offs from established firms), and the net effect is an ongoing growth in the number of firms.[16]

So much for the past and present. What about the future? There are two reasons to believe that the number of entities in future business environments will be increasing. *One* is that increases in the variety of firms lead to increases in the number of firms (and we've already established that the variety will be increasing). As an example of this dynamic in action, consider technologies for conveying information over long distances (e.g., radio waves, copper cable, fiber-optic cable, and lasers). We would expect that multiple firms would be engaged in the production and marketing of each technology. The aggregate number of firms providing the several technologies would very likely be greater than the number of firms providing the previous technologies at the time the subsequent technologies appeared (holding other factors constant).

The *second* reason to believe that the entities in the environment of a given firm will become more numerous is that impending improvements in communication and transportation technologies will enable more customers and suppliers to access the firm. *In effect,* there will be more customers and suppliers because a larger proportion of potential customers and suppliers can be engaged. Thus we see again how improvements in technology increase the number of environmental entities with which a firm interacts.[17]

For both of the above reasons, each related to the accelerating advances in science and technology, it seems safe to conclude that, *in the future, the numbers of products, markets, and firms in the environments of business organizations will be greater, and will be increasing at increasing rates.*[e]

An important practical implication of this increase in the variety and number of environmental entities is that future firms, in order to identify the greater variety of threats and opportunities in their environments, will be forced to include within their makeup a greater variety and/or number of sensors. Either that, or they will have to move to simpler environments. We will return to this matter in Chapter 3.

Having examined the accelerating *variety* and *number* of entities in future business environments, let us wrap up by quickly examining the third attribute of environmental complexity, *interdependence.* The increased competition that follows from improvements in communication and transportation technologies forces firms to specialize and focus on core capabilities. As a consequence, they give up certain capabilities (or do not achieve commensurate growth in certain capabilities). This causes them to become dependent on other organizations for the resources they can no longer provide for themselves. Outsourcing and the development of interorganizational relationships are examples of interdependence in action. Because the specialization leading to interdependence has its origins in the growth of knowledge, because knowledge will be growing at an increasing rate, and because increases in the number of entities lead to much larger increases in the number of ways the entities can combine, we can conclude that, *in the future, the interdependence among firms will be greater, and will be increasing at an increasing rate.*

---

[e]The ongoing growth in the number of U.S. firms conforms to this pattern and is documented in the references cited in Endnote 16. Such authoritative data for products is harder to find, but top officers of Cap Gemini Ernst & Young's Center for Business Innovation report that "in 2001, companies introduced 35,000 new consumer products, up from 15,000 ten years ago" (Meyer & Ruggles, 2002: 15).

We observed in the preceding subsections that the variety, number, and interdependence of entities in the future environments of business organizations will be greater and will be increasing at increasing rates. Because an environment's complexity is determined by the aggregate of these three attributes, it follows that, *in the future, environmental complexity will be significantly greater, and will be increasing at an increasing rate.*

So what? What does this increased complexity mean for the nature of business organizations? The answer follows from what was noted earlier— increases in environmental complexity require firms to become more complex, or to reposition themselves into a less complex environment. For example, if a firm producing laptop computers chose to address the arrival of palm-sized computing devices (an increase in environmental complexity) by moving into this technology and market, we would expect to see the firm elaborate its market research efforts, technology monitoring efforts, R&D efforts, engineering efforts, manufacturing units, and distribution efforts or, as an option, extend its capabilities in these areas by engaging in new interfirm relationships. More generally, if a firm chooses to operate in a more complex environment, we can expect that it will exhibit a larger number of specialized functions within itself or in association with other organizations, and more coordinating mechanisms to deal with interdependencies both within the firm and without.

If, instead of becoming more complex, a firm chooses to specialize in a smaller niche where it can be relatively noncomplex, we can expect it to avoid attaining, or to divest itself of, functions not closely related to operations within this niche. For necessary functions not related to its core competence, we can expect the firm to create linkages with other organizations that provide these functions. We can also expect it to join in alliances and networks in order to exploit its special competence.

Recalling the necessity for firms to be congruent with their environments, we see that one consequence of the forthcoming increases in environmental complexity will be that future firms will be characterized by greater complexity than are today's firms. Some will incorporate this increased complexity within themselves. Some will achieve it by engaging in complex webs of relationships with other firms, or with individuals working as independent contractors. Others will use a combination of these approaches to dealing with the increased complexity of their environments. (But we are ahead of ourselves. These are issues to be covered in Chapter 7.) Operationally, forthcoming increases in environmental complexity will require firms and their managers to give more attention to environmental sensing, organizational decision making, organizational learning, and knowledge integration. We will elaborate on these ideas in subsequent chapters.

INTERIM SUMMARY AND TRANSITION

We established earlier that accelerating increases in scientific knowledge will lead to accelerating increases in the effectiveness of technologies. In these last few pages we saw that these two phenomena will lead to accelerating increases in the variety, density, and interdependence of entities in the environments of business organizations. As a result of examining the increases in these three environmental attributes in detail, we concluded that, in the future, environmental complexity will be significantly greater, and will be increasing at an increasing rate.[18] Figure 2.1 summarizes the ideas of this section.

Let us now turn to examining how these forthcoming increases in environmental complexity, and in scientific and technological knowledge, will together lead to increases in the dynamism and competitiveness of future business environments.

Environmental Dynamism and Competitiveness

VELOCITY, TURBULENCE, AND INSTABILITY

The future environments of business organizations will be changing significantly faster than are today's environments. This is unavoidable. It follows from two facts. *First,* as we saw earlier, in future environments, the number of competitors, regulators, suppliers, customers, and other entities will be greater—there will be more sources of threats and opportunities. *Second,* the increased effectiveness of information, manufacturing, and transportation technologies discussed earlier will enable each of these sources to generate more events per unit of time (and each has reason to do so). Given more sources of threat and opportunity events, and given that each source will be generating such events more frequently, we must conclude that in the environments of future firms there will be more events per unit of time and less time between events. The *velocity* of the environment will be greater, and it will be increasing due to the accelerating advances in science and technology.

But the flow of these environmental events as they come at the firm will not be smooth. Individual events will often arrive abruptly—there will also be more *turbulence.*

Actually, while turbulence will be ubiquitous, for firms in some industries the wrenching alternating sequence of *technological discontinuity* and *dominant design* will cause "turbulence" to understate what these firms will experience. To give meaning to these two concepts, let us draw on Tushman and Murmann's (1998) discussion of aircraft propulsion systems as dominant designs and changes in these systems as technological discontinuities.[19]

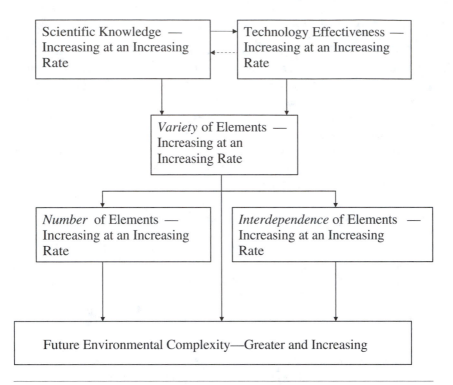

Figure 2.1   Causal Pathway to Increased Environmental Complexity

The propulsion system of the Wright brothers' airplane consisted of an internal combustion engine and two wooden propellers. Metal replaced wood as the dominant material for propeller blades by the 1930s. Trying to scale up propulsive power, engineers examined the effect of mounting up to eight engines on the airplane. Around 1926-1927, the three-engine approach as embodied in the Ford Tri-Motor became the dominant design for commercial airplanes until the emergence of the DC-3 in 1936 ushered in the subsequent period of two-motor designs. The two-motor, internal combustion propulsion period was broken, in turn, by jet engines in 1959 by DeHavilland and Boeing. (Tushman & Murmann, 1998: 233-234)

A new dominant design, such as one of the propulsion systems just noted, separates adjacent *eras of dynamism* or ferment (during which the new design emerges and battles to dominate the current dominant design) from *eras of incremental change* (during which dominant designs are perfected). An era of incremental change ends when a technological discontinuity occurs, that is, when an alternative to the current dominant design emerges and begins to compete.

The dominant design concept helps clarify why, even though *proportional* improvements within any one dominant design (such as multiengine, internal-combustion propulsion) tend to decline across time and to become even incremental, the overall rate at which a given technology (such as aircraft propulsion) advances can nevertheless accelerate due to the arrival of new dominant designs (such as the jet engine). As an example, the overall performance of wire-connected telephones improved incrementally for decades, but a qualitative improvement occurred when a new dominant design, the cellular phone, arrived to dominate its predecessor. Similarly, non-voice data-transmission technologies such as the telegraph and television improved, but more significant technological improvements in non-voice data transmission came through new dominant designs—such as e-mail and the Internet.

In *Only the Paranoid Survive* (1996), Intel's then-CEO Andy Grove gives broad-ranging examples of technological discontinuities, which fit into his category of "very large" or "10X" changes: "When the technology for sound in movies became popular, every silent actor and actress personally experienced the '10X' factor of technological change. When container shipping revolutionized sea transportation, a '10X' factor reordered the major ports around the world" (Grove: 55). These examples highlight *one* effect of the forthcoming acceleration in the rate at which technological advances will arrive—an acceleration in the rate at which technological discontinuities or "breakthrough" products appear, creating highly unstable environments for the firms directly affected and for their buyers and suppliers.

A *second* effect of accelerating technological change we've already noted: improvements in communication and transportation technology allow competitors to penetrate a firm's markets more rapidly, often by enabling whole new ways of doing business, as when encyclopedias became available on CDs and then on the Internet. Given the technological advances that took place during the last two decades of the twentieth century, it is not surprising that in his book, *Hypercompetiton* (1994), Dartmouth Professor Richard D'Aveni concluded that, even in the 1990s, "instead of stable periods punctuated by disruptions, the environment is one of disruptions punctuated by rare stable periods" (D'Aveni: 215).

The technological discontinuities (and other cataclysmic events, such as when a Wal-Mart moves into a small town) surpass what most people think of as turbulence. Rather they exemplify what can be described more appropriately as abrupt changes in environmental *stability*. Because increases in the knowledge and tools of scientists and engineers will cause the intervals between technological breakthroughs to become shorter and shorter, the level of environmental instability faced by future firms will necessarily rise. In combination, these ideas about inevitable changes in environmental velocity, turbulence, and stability lead to the conclusion that, *in the future, environmental dynamism will be significantly greater, and will be increasing at an increasing rate.*

Because the opportunities and (inadequately met) threats associated with environmental dynamism contribute to the arrival of new firms and the departure of existing firms, if the above conclusion were sound, we would expect to see ongoing growth in the rates at which firms have been appearing and disappearing. Data from the U.S. Census Bureau show this to be the case (see the references of Endnote 16). For example, consider that "one third of the giants in America's Fortune 500 in 1980 had lost their independence by 1990 and another 40% were gone five years later" (*The Economist,* January 29, 2000: 22).

Some executives, even now caught up in a world more dynamic than they have ever experienced, might find it difficult to believe that the dynamism of their business environment will be significantly greater and will be increasing at an increasing rate. That would be unfortunate for them and their firms, but it would not be surprising. Not only do most people most of the time imagine the future to be much like the present but, with respect to *specific* phenomena, it seems that people have a particularly difficult time imagining a future different from the present.

We needn't always look to the distant past for examples of where experts are unable to see a future different from the present. An executive of a major consulting firm recently described to one of our University of Texas MBA classes the strategic and organizational changes his company's clients would necessarily be making to adapt to forthcoming changes in their environments. At the conclusion of his formal remarks, the executive was asked by one of the students how *his* company would be changing. *He wasn't able to think of a single change that was likely to occur.* Unless they focus their attention on the matter, it seems that most people most of the time do not imagine a future different from the present. Of course, anecdotes are instructive, but rigorous field studies are more convincing. (For examples of such studies, see Endnote 12.)

ENVIRONMENTAL COMPETITIVENESS

Three factors will, in the future, cause business environments to be even more competitive. *One,* the Internet, exploded onto the consciousness of firms in the industrialized world in the late 1990s. Because the Net allowed customers to identify new suppliers and to make interproduct comparisons conveniently, the proportion of "customer loyalty" that a firm enjoyed due to customer ignorance and inertia declined as a greater number and variety of competitor products appeared on the Internet and as a greater proportion of buyers used the Internet. As the Internet and its communication-technology successors become more effective and their use becomes more pervasive, we can expect their effect on environmental competitiveness to increase.[f]

A *second* factor that will lead to more environmental competitiveness was discussed earlier—improved transportation technologies will further eliminate the distance barriers that many firms have relied on to buffer themselves from competitors. A decade and a half before Japanese automobile manufacturers began building cars in the United States, growth in both the speed and capacity of oceangoing transports helped Japanese manufacturers compete successfully on price with U.S. manufacturers in the U.S. auto market. As with improvements in communication technology, future improvements in transportation technology will enable competitors to steal markets and individual customers more rapidly. The buffering effect of distance for manufacturers of large products or for the providers of face-to-face services will continue to decline.

The *third* factor leading to a more competitive environment for future firms is the progress in science and technology that results in new products that compete with existing products. The variety, and hence the number, of competitors will increase because substitutable products will be invented at an increasing rate.

Because the effectiveness of communication and transportation technologies will be increasing, and because these increases contribute so greatly to competitiveness, we can conclude that, *in the future, environmental competitiveness will be significantly greater, and will be increasing.*

In industries where economies of scale are critical and barriers to entry are high, instances will arise where a relatively few large firms will prevail and form stable oligopolies. Increasing environmental dynamism, combined with governmental intervention where these industrial structures do not well serve society, will, however, limit the number of industries where this level of consolidation can be maintained.

(Continued)

---

[f]Of particular interest are thin markets, markets where—because there are few buyers or sellers—at any one moment a buyer or seller may have little competition, as might be the market for certain used machine tools. With its relatively wideband communication capabilities, the Internet and it successors will enable buyers and suppliers to be well informed about many of the options in such a market, thus removing ignorance as a buffer to competition.

(Continued)

The number of industries dominated by oligopolies is a small proportion of all industries. The number of large firms is a small proportion of all firms. The number of people employed in large firms is a small proportion of people employed in all firms. As we will see in subsequent chapters, the environmental changes described in these pages will enhance these conditions in many contexts. In by far the larger proportion of the world's economy, the increasingly rapid arrival of new products and new competitors, enabled by advances in information and transportation technologies, will lead to increases in environmental turbulence, instability, and competitiveness for firms in most lines of business.

Of the several changes in business environments identified in this chapter, none is more important than the forthcoming increase in environmental competitiveness. This is because competition pressures firms to make changes more quickly and more radically than they otherwise would. Specifically, inertia in organizations, and especially in the minds of management, nearly always causes change to be slower and more incremental than the situation requires. Competition is the driving force that counters these inertial forces.

Chapter Summary and Transition

Building on the idea that advances in science and technology are destined to occur at rates greater than those we now see, and very likely at accelerating rates, we reasoned that these advances will cause most or all entities of the environment (e.g., products, markets, and competitors) to be characterized by greater variety, number, and interdependence. Building on this idea of greater environmental complexity, we then reasoned that future business environments would necessarily become even more dynamic and competitive than they are. In several instances, we noted that, if the explanations were sound, we would already expect to see increases in these several environmental characteristics. In each of these instances, we encountered data showing that, indeed, the environmental characteristics that were asserted to be decidedly different from today's have already begun to exhibit the predicted differences. These ideas are summarized in Figure 2.2.

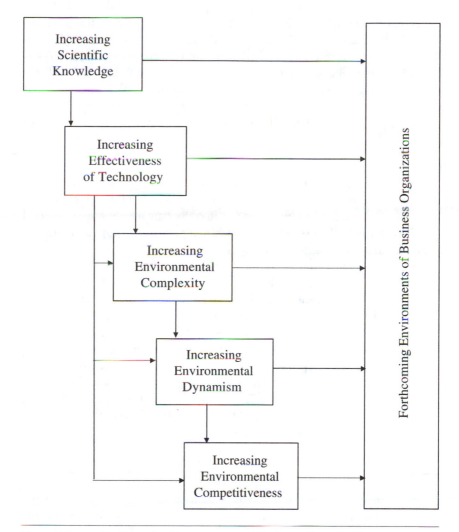

Figure 2.2   Forthcoming Environments of Business Organizations

Some managers may feel or hope that the current environment of business organizations is a period of transition toward a more stable era. Others might believe that the current dynamic environment is here to stay. But the reality is that, in the near, intermediate, and longer term futures, the rate of change in the environments of business organizations will be increasing. *In the future, environmental complexity, dynamism, and competitiveness will each be greater, and each will be increasing.*[g] The result will be threats and opportunities generated at rates considerably greater than those experienced today. The action implication for top managers is to understand what attributes their firms must possess to survive and do well under these conditions, and then to emplace in their firms these attributes *before* the future is upon them and *before* the associated missed opportunities and hostile forces shrink their firm's resources for responding to the point where they are inadequate for survival.

Firms in the future will choose, as do firms today, specific combinations of products and markets for their products. These combinations result in firms having *micro environments* idiosyncratic to themselves—or idiosyncratic to themselves and to the small groups of competitors that have chosen the same combinations. It follows from this chapter's conclusions—about the effects of technological advances on the variety of products and markets—that the business environment of the future will contain more product-market combinations than does today's. That is, *micro environments, in aggregate, will be more varied in the future than they are today.* But at the same time it also follows from this chapter that, while firms will have micro environments peculiar to themselves or to themselves and small groups of like firms, *all firms will be confronted in the future with a macro environment that is more complex, more dynamic, and more competitive than is today's macro environment.* Firms will not be entirely secure in their micro environment. Indeed, one effect of the more complex, dynamic, and competitive macro environment is that, *in the future, individual micro environments will be shorter lived.*

We noted earlier that the nature of firms must be congruent with the nature of their environments. Given this, and because environmental complexity, dynamism, and competitiveness in the future will each be different from what they have been, and are, we must conclude that future firms will also

---

[g]As we have seen in the chapter, this sentence may well understate the facts. Strong arguments were set forth earlier supporting the conclusions that complexity and dynamism will be increasing at *increasing rates.* In the remainder of the book, I do not build on this very defensible point of view. Instead, I build only on a more conservative position; that is, I assume that environmental complexity and dynamism will simply be increasing—at an implied linear rate—rather than increasing at an increasing rate. Some readers may find this assumption more acceptable. I would not retreat from the original conclusion if doing so would cause subsequent conclusions to be invalid, but this is not the case. As it turns out, the necessary nature of future firms is qualitatively the same under either assumption.

be different from what they have been, and are. How will they be different? In the remainder of the book I attempt to answer this question.[h]

An extremely influential component of the environment of any firm is the culture of the nation or society in which the firm resides. To secure legitimacy and other resources, a firm's attributes and management practices must conform to a great extent to values, norms, beliefs, and expectations of the national culture.

For the purposes of this book, perhaps the most important characteristic of national or societal cultures is their inertia; they are very slow to change. As a consequence, national cultures are much more frequently constraints on organizational change than they are drivers of change. This is not to deny their considerable importance when considering the nature of firms but rather is to highlight their role when considering changes in the nature of firms.[20]

The arguments of this chapter are not limited to the United States or the currently industrialized world. Increases in the effectiveness of technologies, a major enabling factor in globalization, will cause the complexity, dynamism, and competitiveness of business environments to increase in all countries. Although the *magnitude of the slope* of change will vary across countries, due to differences in national culture and resources, there seems to be no reason to believe that the *direction* or the *general shape of the graph* of change will vary.

A fact we must keep in mind, as we continue our investigation into the necessary nature of future firms, has been mentioned more than once in this chapter. But it is so important and yet so seldom recognized that I call attention to it once more. *Most people, most of the time, do not imagine a future different from the present.* This is dangerous in a fast-changing environment, especially when the environment is, in many respects, accelerating. I have attempted to capture some of these thoughts with Figure 2.3.

In the environment of the future, with its heightened levels of dynamism, complexity, and competition, firms must be more able to rapidly and correctly sense survival-threatening environmental changes. In addition, much more so than in the past, firms must be more able to rapidly and appropriately interpret

---

[h]To limit its size and to create focus, this book examines not all aspects of future firms but rather focuses on those structures, processes, attributes, and practices that will be *different* in degree or kind from those predominant in firms today.

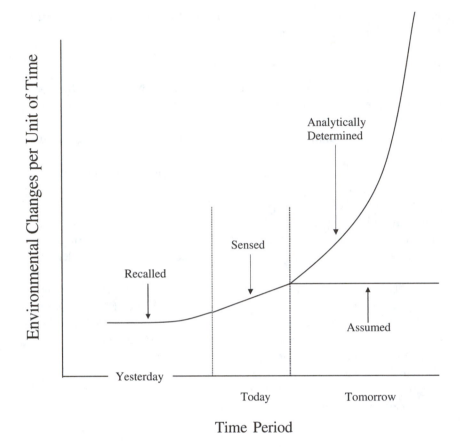

Figure 2.3   Rates of Environmental Change: Recalled, Sensed, Assumed, Determined

these changes, and then to decide quickly and correctly what action to take. Chapters 3 and 4 deal with environmental *sensing* and *interpretation* and with *organizational decision making.*

Endnotes

1. Parts of this chapter draw on and greatly extend my earlier writings on this subject. See Chapter 1 of D. Druckman, J. E. Singer, and H. Van Cott (Eds.), *Enhancing Organizational Performance*, 1997; Chapter 1 of G. P. Huber and W. H. Glick,

Organizational Change and Redesign: Ideas and Insights for Improving Organizational Performance, 1993; and G. P. Huber, "The Nature and Design of Post-industrial Organizations," 1984.

2. Different estimates of the number of scientific journals—see D. Price, *Science Since Babylon,* 1975, 164; D. Bell, *The Coming of Post-industrial Society: A Venture in Social Forecasting,* 1976, 178ff; and D. Goodstein, "Peer Review After the Big Crunch," 1995, for examples—reflect differences in methodology as well as differences in the time period included.

3. See T. Huppes, *The Western Edge,* 1987, 6.

4. C. Tenopir and D. King, "Designing Electronic Journals With 30 Years of Lessons From Print," 1998.

5. In *The Road Ahead* (1996: 8), Bill Gates, whose company is a leader in the development and diffusion of communication technology, makes this point strongly— "The single shift (in technology) that has had the greatest effect on the history of communication took place about 1450, when Johann Gutenberg, a goldsmith from Mainz, Germany, invented movable type and introduced the first printing press to Europe. . . . Before Gutenberg there were only about 30,000 books on the entire continent of Europe, nearly all of them Bibles or biblical commentary. By 1500 there were more than 9 million books, on all sorts of topics."

6. As indications, the percentage of articles published in U.S. scientific and technical outlets that were multiauthored increased 12% from 1988 to 1999 and the percentage where the authorships indicated international collaboration increased by 14% from 1986 to 1999 (National Science Board, *Science and Engineering Indicators— 2002.* Arlington, VA: National Science Foundation, 2002 (NSB-02-1).

7. Besides the facts that knowledge is its own generative material, and that forthcoming increases in the effectiveness of communication technology will make knowledge much more available for scientific use, there is a third line of argument leading to the conclusion that scientific knowledge will grow at an accelerating rate. This argument considers *the economic development cycle,* such as that which began in the newly industrialized economies (of Hong Kong, Singapore, South Korea, and Taiwan) in the 1980s and which was already under way at that time in the emerging Asian economies (of China, India, Indonesia, and Malaysia). The cycle begins with economic growth (often based on cheap labor), then proceeds to further economic growth through implementation of new-to-the-nation technologies, and then to the use of the increasing national wealth to support science (generally heavily oriented toward the development of economy-enhancing technologies). Data supporting this description of the economic maturation of these countries appear in the National Science Foundation, *Human Resources for Science and Technology: The Asian Region* (Washington, DC, 1993), the National Science Foundation, *Asia's New High-Tech Competitors* (Washington, DC, 1995), and the National Science Foundation, *Science & Engineering Indicators* (Washington, DC, 2002). As some or all of the newly industrialized economies and the emerging Asian economies enter actively into the science-supporting phase of the economic development cycle, during the next few decades and beyond, the world will see the knowledge products of a new set of knowledge-generating nations. Also suggestive of this is the fact that other developing countries (e.g., Hungary, Ireland, Israel, the

Philippines) have, as a result of their investments in education and R&D, made significant technological gains and seem, therefore, to be positioned to become exporters of technology and then science (National Science Foundation, *Science & Engineering Indicators,* Washington, DC, 2002).

8.   For an informative article on the increasing use of simulation and virtual engineering in the creation of new products and processes, see *The Economist,* "The Immaterial World," June 1997, pp. 86-87.

9.   For more on the historical influence of science on technology, see Heilbroner, *Visions of the Future: The Distant Past, Yesterday, Today, Tomorrow,* 1995; and J. Mokyr, *The Lever of Riches: Technological Creativity and Economic Progress,* 1990, and *The Gifts of Athena: Historical Origins of the Knowledge Economy,* 2002.

10.   See F. Narin and D. Olivastro, "Linkage Between Patents and Papers: An Interim EPO/US Comparison," 1998, pp. 51-59, but also M. Meyer, "Does Science Push Technology? Patents Citing Scientific Literature," March 2000, pp. 409-434.

11.   These quotations are from C. Cerf and V. Navasky, *The Experts Speak,* 1998.

12.   While people are not so reluctant to believe *in the abstract* that the future will be different from the present, it appears that it is especially *with respect to specific phenomena* that they imagine the future to be much like the present. Hundreds of scientific studies, conducted in a wide variety of contexts, have demonstrated that when making specific estimates, such as projections, people anchor on something conspicuous—such as current conditions—and adjust from this conspicuous something to arrive at their estimate (for elaboration, see A. Tversky and D. Kahneman, "Judgment Under Uncertainty: Heuristics and Biases," 1974; and G. B. Chapman and E. J. Johnson, "Anchoring, Activation, and the Adjustment of Values," 1999). What is so notable is that the adjustments made are almost invariably much smaller than what the unfolded facts show should have been the case. Adjustments are almost always insufficient. The fact that most people most of the time imagine the future to be much like the present is a special case of this pervasively used heuristic; people anchor on current conditions and adjust very little.

For an example of field research demonstrating that people imagine their feelings about the future to be much like those they have at present, see G. Loewenstein and D. A. Schkade, "Wouldn't It Be Nice? Predicting Future Feelings," 1999. See also D. T. Gilbert, E. C. Pinel, T. D. Wilson, S. J. Blumberg, and T. P. Wheatley, "Immune Neglect: A Source of Durability Bias in Affective Forecasting," 1998.

13.   These quotations are from C. Cerf and V. Navasky, *The Experts Speak,* 1998, p. 277.

14.   The need for organizations and other living systems to be as complex as their environment seems obvious, but it is interesting to note the existence of a general proof called "Ashby's Law of Requisite Variety." See W. R. Ashby, *An Introduction to Cybernetics,* 1956; *Design for a Brain: The Origin of Adaptive Behavior* (2nd ed.), 1960.

15.   P. T. Zeisset and M. E. Wallace, "How NAICS Will Affect Data Users," February 23, 1998. Available at http://www.census.gov/epcd/www/naicsusr.html. As an aside, if it were true that the number of environmental entities of relevance to business organizations were increasing, we would also expect to see today's businesses having to deal with more regulations. We do—the budgets for the EPA, EEOC, and OSHA have grown (in real dollar terms, i.e., corrected for CPI) 112%, 47%, and 14% respectively during the

last two decades. (Compiled from data in the *Budget of the United States Government—Appendix for the years 1977, 1982, 1987, and 1997*, and the *Budget of the United States Government for 1992*.).

16. Table No. 876—New Business Incorporations and Business Failures—Number and Liabilities: 1970 to 1988, *U.S. Census Bureau Statistical Abstract of the United States: 1990*; Table No. 877—Business Starts (and Failures) and Employment: 1985 to 1997; and Table No. 884—Mergers and Acquisitions—Summary: 1985 to 1996, *U.S. Census Bureau Statistical Abstract of the United States: 1998*. With regard to the summary conclusion, see Table No. 870—Private Employer Firms, Establishments, Employment, Annual Payroll and Estimated Receipts by Firm Size: 1990 to 1995. *U.S. Census Bureau Statistical Abstract of the United States: 1998*. Data from the U.S. Internal Revenue Service www.irs.treas.gov/prod/tax_stats (October 8, 2002) lead to the same summary conclusion. Using as a proxy for the number of firms, the number of income tax returns, the data indicate that during the last quarter of the twentieth century, the net number of corporations nearly doubled and the number of partnerships grew by more than 50%. These findings tended to be robust across firms in all size categories.

17. It is important to recognize that on occasion *negative feedback forces* arise and curtail or even reverse the growth in variety or number of particular entities (such as specific products or specific types of businesses). For example, markets have shakeouts and consolidations that reduce the number of competitors and suppliers, and in specific markets and trade organizations, standards committees, and supply chain managers sometimes step in to limit the variety of product options. Such negative feedback forces will attenuate some of the rates of change described here, as they do now and have in the past. But—*overall and on balance*—these forces will not negate the indicated acceleration in the total variety and number of entities operating in future business environments, for the same reasons that *negative feedback forces have not negated acceleration in the total variety and number of entities in the past*. These reasons are three in number: (1) no currently imaginable institutions are able to curtail the *positive feedback forces* described here (such as knowledge feeding on itself and science and technology contributing to each other's advances); (2) negative feedback forces are reactive and tend to arise only when economic or social tolerances have been exceeded (thus, for each entity there will tend to be a substantial interval when its growth is accelerating); and (3) the variety and number of entities will be increasing (thus there will be more entities during which these acceleration intervals will be in effect).

18. The speed with which changes in technology create changes in environmental complexity depends in part on how rapidly firms and customers react to the availability of the technology. For a variety of reasons, commercialization and consumer acceptance of new technology seem to have been increasing at an increasing rate. For example, radio and TV were available for 38 years and 13 years, respectively, before 50 million people tuned in, while the Internet (actually, the World Wide Web) hit that benchmark within 4 years ("Internet Commerce Could Pass $300 Billion a Year by 2002, the U.S. Says," *Wall Street Journal*, April 16, 1998). Even accounting for the change in population, this is a remarkable difference.

19. M. L. Tushman and J. P. Murmann, "Dominant Designs, Technology Cycles, and Organizational Outcomes," 1998.

20. A. Y. Lewin and J. Kim, "The Nation-state and Culture as Influences on Organizational Change and Innovation," 2004, is a hugely comprehensive review of the effect that national institutions and culture have on organizations.

Besides changes in national cultures and advances in science and technology, I also considered three other trends (e.g., globalization, increases in the world's population, and rising standards of living). I found, however, these trends to be (1) less strongly linked to changes in the nature of firms than were the increases in environmental complexity, dynamism, and competitiveness, (2) redundant with these increases, or (3) quite slow moving relative to the rapid advances in science and technology. Globalization, for example, I determined to be a consequence of advances in the effectiveness of information, manufacturing, and transportation technologies and of certain consequences of these advances (e.g., larger markets, more competitors, more widespread use of English). Globalization is associated with increases in the variety, number, and interdependence of entities in the environment (recall that we discussed these three attributes as components of environmental complexity) and with increases in the velocity, turbulence, and instability of the environment (recall that we discussed these attributes as components of environmental dynamism), and with reduced buffers to international markets and from international competitors. For me, these several concepts were more easily tied to characteristics of future firms than were the higher level (and often ambiguous or value laden) concepts associated with "globalization." Changes in population and standards of living are, like changes in national culture, slow moving, and to me their effects on the nature of future firms were unclear.

3

Sensing and Interpreting the Environment

Given the forthcoming increases in environmental dynamism, complexity, and competitiveness, it seems clear that environmental sensing and interpreting will be more critical to a firm's survival in the future than in the past. But top management's sensing and interpreting of the firm's environment has always been critical. In this regard, it can be instructive to examine the sudden death of Facit AB, the established and highly successful firm described by New York University's Professor William Starbuck.

Facit AB

Founded in the 1920s, the Swedish multinational firm Facit AB, maker and seller of business machines and office furnishings, grew large and profitable during the 1960s.

Although Facit made many products, the top managers believed the key product line to be mechanical calculators; they saw [other of Facit's business office] products such as typewriters, desks, and computers as peripheral. . . . Facit concentrated on improving the quality and lowering the costs of mechanical cal-culators. . . . In the mid-1960s, Facit borrowed large sums and built new plants that enabled it to make better mechanical calculators at lower costs than any other company in the world. Between 1962 and 1970, employment rose 70% and sales and profits more than doubled. By 1970, Facit employed 14,000 people in factories in 20 cities in 5 countries and in sales offices in 15 countries. . . .

The engineers within Facit concentrated on technologies having clear relevance for mechanical calculators, and Facit understood these technologies well. Top, middle, and lower managers agreed about how a mechanical-calculator factory should look and operate, what mechanical-calculator customers wanted, what was key to success, and what was unimportant or silly. . . . [Operations] were pared to essentials; bottlenecks were excised; no resources were wasted gathering irrelevant information or analyzing tangential issues. . . . Costs were low, service fast, glitches rare, understanding high, and expertise great.

But [understanding was high] only within the programmed domain. . . . Although some of Facit's lower-level managers and engineers were acutely aware of the electronic revolution in the world at large, this awareness did not penetrate upward, and the advent of electronic computers took Facit's top managers by surprise. Relying on the company's information gathering programs, the top managers surmised that Facit's mechanical-calculator customers would switch to electronics very slowly because they liked mechanical calculators. Of course, Facit had no programs for gathering information from people who were buying electronic calculators.[1]

Actual demand for mechanical calculators dropped precipitously, and Facit went through two years of loss, turmoil, and contraction. . . . With bankruptcy looming, the board of directors sold Facit to a larger firm. [It is interesting to observe that Facit's contraction strategy followed from top management's worldview and] aimed perversely at preserving the mechanical-calculator factories by closing typewriter and office furnishings factories. . . . [In contrast,] [T]he new top managers discovered that demand for typewriters was at least three times and demand for office furnishings at least twice the production capacities: sales personnel had been turning down orders because the company could not fill them. (Starbuck, 1983: 92-93)

The top managers emplaced by the new parent firm successfully redirected Facit's resources from mechanical calculators to these markets. Facit, in terms of its top management, its business strategy, and its image-defining product line, was dead.

Importance of Environmental Sensing and Interpretation[2]

The Facit story reminds us that effectively sensing and interpreting the environment have long been important. But the Facit debacle occurred over a third of a century ago. Aren't modern firms managed in ways that enable them to avoid Facit's failings? Certainly many are not, even those thought to be exemplary firms.

Consider, for example, Intel's highly publicized and costly failure to rapidly sense and correctly interpret a shift in the market for computer chips. In the mid-1990s, a huge market began to develop for chips to serve in low-cost consumer products. Intel was late in responding to this market shift. Perhaps its market analysts and other environmental sensors missed the signals. After all, Intel's attention was on the highly profitable high-performance chip market. Or perhaps Intel's management did not correctly interpret what its sensors saw—"For a long time Intel was in denial about the low end" (Intel's Executive Vice President Paul Otellini quoted in the *Wall Street Journal,* February 12, 1998). Intel's strengths ultimately enabled it to become a player in this low-end market, but only after other chip makers had positioned themselves and made enormous profits. If a firm smaller or weaker than Intel had missed—or misinterpreted—the signals, it may well not have survived.[a]

Sensing and interpretation can also, of course, identify opportunities. An instance occurred when Howard Schultz, founder and CEO of Starbucks, went to a conference in Italy, saw the Italian-style coffee bars, and understood that what Starbucks should sell is not coffee as a commodity but rather coffee consumption as an experience. While the coffee bar was a common concept in Italy, it was new to Americans then. The key was Schultz's interpretation of what he saw, an interpretation that many others never arrived at.[3]

As another example of firms identifying opportunities, early in 2000 both Ford and General Motors announced plans for using the Internet to enable customers to order cars custom assembled to the customer's specifications. By actively sensing and interpreting the merchandizing and distribution practices of firms in other industries (Dell Computer in the personal computer industry, for example), Ford and GM came to see that by adopting this practice they might be able to gain market share in their own highly competitive and over-capacitated industry. In this case, an environmental situation was sensed and then reasonably interpreted as an opportunity. Tardy sensing or incorrect interpretations can also, of course, cause a potential opportunity to become a threat.[4]

Let us remind ourselves of three facts frequently observed in organizations: (1) The particular decision process used (including choosing the decision makers) affects the decision made. (2) The decision made influences which actions, if any, are taken. (3) Organizational actions affect organizational performance. From these facts it follows that decision processes affect organizational performance. Clearly the choice of a decision process can have important consequences.

Now let us extend this idea by adding another, one less frequently stated but just as true; namely, in organizations, interpretation of events is often a social process involving a significant portion of the organization's upper echelon. As

---

[a]The correctness, reasonableness, or appropriateness of an interpretation can often be known only in hindsight. Further, it depends in part on the nature of the firm—an environmental change that might be a threat to a small firm might be an opportunity for a large firm. Certainly it also depends on the predispositions of top management. In parts of this chapter, we will describe interpretations as correct or reasonable or appropriate, while at the same time keeping in mind the limitations of these terms in this context.

part of their interpretation, events are categorized. The particular categorization of an event brings into effect corresponding organizational routines, including particular decision processes.

This is an important fact—the interpretation of an event determines whether the response to the event will be a decision process, or a monitoring or probing process, or whether the event will be ignored altogether unless it recurs. Interpretations and categorizations determine whether, or which, decision processes will be initiated. For example, whether a loss in market share is categorized as a marketing problem, as a cost problem, or as a product-design problem will greatly influence (1) who will participate in making the decision about what to do, (2) which criteria and constraints will be considered, and (3) which information and information sources will be accessed. Or, as another example using a quite different categorization, whether an event is labeled as a threat or as an opportunity will also greatly influence these same three phenomena— participation, considerations, and information gathering.[5] An important outcome of interpretations is that *interpretations greatly affect decision processes.*

A second important consequence of the interpretation phenomenon is that *their interpretations of events lead managers to revise the mental models they use to interpret subsequent events.*[b] This occurs in three ways. In one, the event is so unambiguously at odds with the current schema that it severely weakens the schema and, consequently, both changes the schema and opens the way for further change. In another, the scope or richness of an event or its interpretation forces extension and elaboration of the schema and in this way also changes it. Finally, especially because individuals are subconsciously biased to protect their existing views, events are often interpreted as confirming the current schema. But even confirmation changes the schema somewhat— strengthening its intensity although not changing its form. In these ways, then, by causing revisions in interpretive schema, each interpretation affects all future interpretations. Further, by changing interpretive schema, interpretations may also create other important changes, such as changes in thinking about who should make decisions in certain types of situations, and in this way they also affect future organizational decisions. Clearly, *interpretations are important influences on current and future organizational decisions and on decision-shaping schema, and thus on future organizational actions and performance.*

Sensings and interpretations are clearly important, but will environmental sensing and interpreting be any more important in the future? To answer, let us be explicit about conditions that might cause sensing and interpreting to be more important and consider whether these conditions will be more common in the future. At least four conditions would cause sensing and interpretation

---

[b]To add some variety to what our minds and eyes encounter, I will sometimes use "schema" in place of "mental model."

to take on greater importance and would cause firms to be more aggressive in creating sensing and interpretation structures and processes:

1. when knowledge for improving the firm's products or processes becomes much more abundant or faster arriving and must be sifted more swiftly to catch important but brief windows of opportunity,

2. when competition becomes more acute and the basis of competition is knowledge exploitation (forcing firms to scan the environment for knowledge to exploit),

3. when threats and opportunities begin thrusting themselves upon the firm at an accelerated rate, and thus must be responded to more rapidly yet appropriately, and

4. when firms recognize that the nature or sources of threats and opportunities have changed, such that their past surveillance practices are inadequate, and that they must therefore engage in more active sensing (for example, when specific trade barriers are lowered and the firm must identify and monitor new, nondomestic competitors).

As we saw in Chapter 2, each of these four conditions will characterize future environments more than past or current environments. Because forthcoming business environments will be enormously more knowledge-laden, more competitive, and more productive of threats and opportunities—including some threats and opportunities from new sources—future firms must sense and interpret their environments more rapidly and with greater accuracy. Further, the faster paced, more competitive environments of the future will be less forgiving of sensing and interpretations made too late or incorrectly. Altogether, these facts leave no doubt that *sensing and interpreting its environments will be much more important for a firm's performance and survival in the future than in the past.*

Because survival-relevant information will be generated at an increasing rate, firms will necessarily become increasingly vigilant. Increased vigilance can cause firms to experience information overload, but at the same time the increasing numbers of unfamiliar threats and opportunities will cause firms to need information they don't have. One consequence of these facts is that *future firms will more closely manage their sensing and interpretation processes.*[c] What does this mean? What will be the nature of the structures and processes that will

---

[c]This and other of the conclusions in the book imply a comparison between some feature or action of a future firm and the same feature or action of the future firm's *counterpart* firm. By a counterpart firm I mean a firm that played essentially the same role in society, that served the same general market need, that was part of the same industry in the same country, and so on, as will the corresponding future firm. Thus, for example, I intend for future consulting firms in the United States to be compared with today's consulting firms in the United States, rather than with today's hospitals in Japan.

enable future firms to cope with the heightened need to sense and interpret their environment? The remainder of this chapter is directed at answering these questions.

Environmental Sensing in Future Firms

One form of environmental sensing, *intelligence gathering,* occurs when firms scan and probe their environments for major threats and opportunities (e.g., when firms notice and investigate major changes in markets, technologies, regulations, or competitors' strategies). Firms use intelligence gathering to alert themselves to important changes in environmental conditions while there is still time to preempt threats (or to lessen the consequences of threats) or to emplace the resources needed to exploit opportunities quickly. Intelligence gathering is a key early step as firms attempt to determine whether current practices or future plans need changing.

A second form of environmental sensing occurs when firms engage in more focused scanning and probing to acquire knowledge specific to improving their products or operations. Examples of this are employing consultants with specialized knowledge, engaging in technology-exchanging alliances, and sending their personnel to competence-enhancing educational events or programs. We will examine this form of environmental sensing, this *knowledge acquisition* process, in Chapter 5. Intelligence gathering and knowledge acquisition are not mutually exclusive in either definition or practice, but—as will become clear—they tend to differ in importance with respect to the intentions behind them and the use to which their outcomes are put.[d] Below we examine the nature of intelligence gathering in future firms and the poorly understood but highly important role of executive interpretations. Later we will consider how the construction of interpretations will be different in future firms.

INTELLIGENCE GATHERING

In Chapter 2 we saw that the level and growth rate of environmental complexity, dynamism, and competitiveness will be significantly greater in the future than in the past. The aggregate effect of these forthcoming conditions is that the arrival rate of threats and opportunities will be significantly greater. Given the heightened level of competitiveness and increased arrival rate of threats and opportunities, the need for future firms to sense environmental changes more swiftly and more accurately is clear.

---

[d]Let us use "knowledge" broadly, to include information, know-how, and understanding.

This need for greater vigilance is already apparent among the leaders of firms having environments evolving toward those of future firms. It is not surprising that Andy Grove, when he was CEO of Intel, would use the title of his book, *Only the Paranoid Survive,* to highlight his belief that successful companies must be increasingly watchful for powerful impending changes. Or that Bill Gates, when he was CEO of Microsoft, would exclaim—in the context of a discussion of environmental change—"I know very well that in the next ten years, if Microsoft is still a leader, we will have had to weather at least three crises" (*Fortune,* July 20, 1998: 56).

Is this talk about the need for vigilance simply high-fashion, image-managing rhetoric, or is there systematically obtained and evaluated evidence that vigilance, scanning, and probing positively affect firm performance? The fact is that many studies support the ideas of Grove, Gates, and like-minded executives that active sensing contributes to superior performance. For example, "Chief executives in high-performing companies scan more frequently and more broadly in response to strategic uncertainty than did their counterparts in low-performing companies" (Daft, Sormunen, & Parks, 1988: 123), and "Alignment of executives' external ties with the informational requirements of the firm's strategy enhances organizational performance" (Geletkanycz & Hambrick, 1997: 654).

It seems certain, then, that *future firms will more actively engage in intelligence gathering.* Not to do so would be foolish. Foolish firms will not survive. Firms that do not create effective intelligence-gathering systems will not be able to compete with those that do. In placid, benign environments, active engagement in intelligence gathering is not critical. In the future, such environments will not exist. The greater dynamism and competitiveness of future business environments will force future firms to be more actively engaged in intelligence gathering than were their counterparts in the past.[6] Exactly how they do this will necessarily vary with their circumstances and with their management's preferences. Because resources will always be scarce, especially for activities that do not directly create or distribute products, development of the intelligence-gathering function will not be allowed to proceed willy-nilly. It will be managed and, given its heightened criticality, it will be actively managed.

What would it mean for a firm to more actively manage its intelligence gathering? To make this idea more tangible, I will shortly describe some examples of practices that we can expect future firms to employ. First, however, let us examine the possibility that intelligence gathering might become either a widespread staff function or an outsourced function.

INTELLIGENCE GATHERING AS A STAFF FUNCTION? AS AN OUTSOURCED FUNCTION?

Will firms in the future maintain staff units whose function is to gather, interpret, or centrally coordinate the business intelligence function? The answer depends on several factors, such as the firm's industry and strategy. Among the most important factors—for this particular approach to institutionalizing intelligence gathering—are the firm's size and affluence. Certainly large or affluent firms are more able to support such specialized units. Consequently, because the need for reliable intelligence gathering will be greater in the future, we might expect that large and affluent firms—which can more readily afford such units—would have them. The benefits of an intelligence unit can be considerable. The following actual example "alert" from a corporate staff is dated, pertaining to the Iraqi war with Iran, but is worth noting because it so clearly demonstrates both sensing and interpretation.

> If Iraq is ordering such large quantities of army uniform materials, suddenly, fresh army recruitments on a large scale can be anticipated. This may mean that an escalation of the war is imminent. That, in turn, implies that Iraq may face further strain on its resources, particularly with regard to the availability of foreign exchange for payment of non-defense material. They may, therefore, defer payment on such supplies, even if LCs (lines of credit) are opened. We are heavily involved in supplying them with building materials, chemicals, and fertilizers. Caution must be exercised on all future supplies and the payment situation must be monitored very closely. (Ghoshal & Kim, 1986: 52)

On the one hand, tomorrow's business environments will favor the use of business intelligence units. However, on the other hand, the survival of highly specialized staff units is often tenuous. It is hard to imagine units more likely to be deleted when a firm is in a cost reduction frame of mind. On balance, it seems likely that the presence of business intelligence units in large firms in the future will not be greatly different from what it was in large firms in the recent past. And the need for leanness will cause the use of such units not to diffuse to medium or small firms where the cost of maintaining such a unit would be proportionately higher. Less costly approaches to more rapidly and reliably sensing environmental threats or opportunities will necessarily be developed and used in future firms of all sizes. *Except in large firms, intelligence gathering in the future will not be carried out by specialized staff units.*

How, then, will small- and medium-size firms "more actively engage in intelligence gathering," an endeavor much more critical when threats and opportunities appear at an accelerated rate? Some forms of intelligence can be most effectively obtained by people specifically trained or well networked. Examples are information about radical increases in the cost of critical resources or in regulatory legislation. Small- and medium-size firms are especially vulnerable to such threats. What we can expect in the future is for such firms to outsource some of their intelligence gathering to companies that specialize in providing customized intelligence. This practice began to evolve in the United States during the 1990s. As the need for intelligence increases, as intelligence gathering becomes an increasingly specialized competence, and as intelligence providers and their clients become more adept at working together in the acquisition and transfer of intelligence, partial outsourcing of the intelligence-gathering function will become commonplace. *A larger proportion of future firms will purchase intelligence-gathering services from vendors.*

In what other ways can we expect future intelligence-gathering practices to differ from practices of the past? The specific practices that different firms will take when managing their intelligence gathering will vary, but two examples of practices that we can expect to see—rather independent of firm size— are the adoption of specialized accountability and the adoption of eclectic responsibility.[7]

INTELLIGENCE GATHERING AS SPECIALIZED ACCOUNTABILITY

Because forthcoming increases in scientific and technical knowledge cannot help but result in more highly specialized products, markets, and competitors, some greater level of expertise will be necessary for effective environmental sensing. Firms will be forced to use specialists to scan, probe, and interpret these and other components of their environments. This idea we've seen before—a living system's complexity (including the elaborateness of its sensing systems) must be congruent with the complexity of its environment. To ensure that their surveillance systems are sufficiently complex and capable, future firms will arrange for intelligence gathering in specialized environmental sectors to be the formal responsibility of personnel with the relevant expertise. In addition, because delayed or incomplete information acquisition or inaccurate interpretation of information about environmental changes will be more damaging in the future than in yesterday's slower moving environments, intelligence-gathering structures that ensure reliability and timeliness will be more necessary.

Together, the need for specialized sensors and the need for reliable and timely intelligence gathering will require that, in the future, for each significant environmental component, some organizational members with the relevant expertise will be accountable for monitoring and reporting on that component.

In the great majority of cases, the personnel made accountable will be organizational members who already have operational responsibility related to the environmental component, rather than personnel having intelligence gathering as their primary responsibility. Companies will use this approach—of formally allocating intelligence-gathering accountability to personnel with operational responsibility in the area—for three reasons: (1) in general, personnel working in a specialized area are more sensitive to the nature of information relevant to the area, (2) the approach minimizes delays and distortions between those who encounter information and those who interpret or use it, and (3) the approach minimizes personnel costs.

As we examine approaches for more effectively identifying threats and opportunities, we must keep in mind that, more frequently in the future, these events and situations will have their origins in faraway places. This follows from the fact that improvements in information and transportation technologies enable distant events and actions to deeply affect local markets. For example,

> Motorola was caught flat-footed when Nokia emerged from the backwaters of Finland as its main rival. And European retailers were taken by surprise when a Spanish chain, Zara, figured out how to change the fashions in its stores practically every week. (*BusinessWeek*, August 28, 2000: 114)

While the *specialized accountability* just discussed will be necessary in the future, it will not be sufficient to ensure adequate coverage. Not only will the nature of threats and opportunities in tomorrow's fast-changing and erratic environments be less predictable than in the past, the sources of such events will also be less familiar. There will be surprises (as was the attractiveness of electronic calculators to Facit and as was consumer acceptance of e-commerce to many firms in the 1990s). Any specialized accountability structure will be constrained by the firm's current understanding of its environment—and current understandings will be increasingly obsolete. For this reason, reliance solely on preassigned scanning responsibilities would result in many events going unnoticed (until it is too late) because no one had been assigned to monitor the new, unforeseeable event-generating source. One way that many future firms will avoid the "it fell between the cracks" or "it was outside our zone" consequences of specialized sensors will be to create *eclectic responsibility*.

INTELLIGENCE GATHERING AS ECLECTIC RESPONSIBILITY

What approaches might be put in place to ensure that members feel eclectic responsibility for gathering intelligence? *One* approach that we can expect to see frequently is the development of what some firms might choose to call an "Everyone a Sensor" *culture*, a culture where all employees view themselves as potential environmental *sensors* for the organization and see themselves as responsible for fulfilling this role.[c] An engineer who at a trade show learns something useful to a project team other than her own, and who communicates this something to that team because "it's the way we do things here," would be manifesting the "Everyone a Sensor" culture.[8] Symbolic actions and credible pronouncements by top managers and other influential organizational members can help create and maintain such a culture. For example, immediately upon returning from a long business trip, do upper level managers routinely and promptly communicate what they've learned to those who could benefit from this information? Do managers at all levels frequently ask their technical subordinates about new developments that are surfacing in the field and that might become important in the future? Such symbolic acts set examples and send messages about valued behaviors.

Once in place, organizational cultures can be reinforced by recognitions and awards for exemplary actions congruent with the espoused culture. Take as an example the instance of a salesperson quickly investigating customer complaints about a recently encountered product defect and then fighting through a number of organizational obstacles to report the matter to the director of manufacturing. If this person received the firm's Employee of the Month Award, it would send a strong signal about what kinds of actions were valued by the firm, that is, were congruent with the espoused culture.

A *second* approach we can expect firms to use to encourage their members to be alert for firm-relevant information unrelated to their specific job responsibilities, and to communicate it to relevant parties in the organization, will be to establish what some firms might call "Everyone a Sensor" *practices*. Even now, of course, many firms allow and encourage their members to attend trade shows or meetings of professional societies. One of the firm's goals is for its members to learn *on behalf of the organization*. But how many firms strongly encourage recent attendees of professional conferences or trade shows to leverage the firm's investment by reporting what they learned to others who could benefit?

---

[c]A firm's expectations will, of course, vary with the nature of its environment and its personnel. In some cases the firm will expect proactive sensing efforts from all personnel. In other cases the firm will call only for vigilance.

Post-travel and post-meeting reporting are more likely if appropriate information-sharing media and forums are readily available. (Examples of such devices are topic-specific e-mail rosters of need-to-know or want-to-know recipients, user-friendly Web sites, and, if the event warrants, informal but prescheduled meetings or formal presentations.) The heightened importance of disseminating information to all those with a need to know will, in the future, lead many firms to make such forums and media more available. An example would be a "Possible Threats or Opportunities" heading at the end of the *Sales Call Report* form on the company's intranet. Another example would be a "Review of Possible Threats or Opportunities" heading on the board of directors meeting agenda. Such headings can prompt explication of matters that otherwise would be not be surfaced because a convenient forum or medium wasn't available.

When post-travel information dissemination occurs on a regular basis, not only does the breadth of organizational learning significantly increase, but the need to report motivates traveler-sensors to consciously seek useful information to report. Knowing they are accountable for communicating new useful information can cause travelers to greatly increase their ratio of *active search* for information to *passive receipt* of information. The marginal cost of disseminating information is, of course, low compared with the disseminator's already expended travel costs and already invested time.

Eclectic responsibility as an organizational norm is not, of course, limited to sensors who have recently traveled or participated in important meetings. A culture and set of practices that encourage all organizational members to act as sensors and report their observations can be made to fit the whole variety and range of the firm's employees, from globe-traveling CEOs to Internet browsers to delivery personnel.[f]

---

[f]Some speculate that business travel will be less frequent in the future. Certainly advanced communication technologies will eliminate the need for some travel. On the other hand, the need to build trust in the many new relationships associated with the increased complexity and dynamism of the firm's environment, and the need to quickly comprehend the subtleties of new markets, clients, and alliances, will both increase in the future. These needs can best be satisfied with on-site conversation and observation. So it may be that physical travel will be, for many, no less frequent in the future than in the past. In any case, it seems worthwhile to note that the idea of post-travel or post-meeting information dissemination applies as well to cyberspace travel as to physical travel.

In tomorrow's business environment, where sources of change will be less anticipatable than in the past, eclectic responsibility will be needed to complement the practice of assigning specialized personnel to monitor and report on particular environmental components. Without eclectic responsibility, many unanticipated threats and opportunities would go unnoticed because no specialized sensor had been assigned to the source. Given the negative consequences of this, we can expect that, *in future firms, all personnel will be explicitly encouraged to be watchful for threats and opportunities and to report those seen to all other members with a need to know.*

Specialized accountability and eclectic responsibility are mechanisms for motivating people to adopt the sensor role. But assigned accountability for fulfillment of a responsibility, especially in the case of eclectic responsibility, is a motivation mechanism that is never more than partially successful. It invariably must compete with other forces directing members' attention and effort toward other personal and organizational goals. We must emphasize again the importance of establishing an organizational culture that encourages lightly managed people working in unstructured job situations to serve alertly and reliably as sensors. Organizations where recognition for so serving is acknowledged and celebrated will achieve more vigilant intelligence gathering and an increased likelihood of surviving and prospering.

SUPPORTING SENSORS

Motivation does not, of course, guarantee effective action. The likelihood and effectiveness of sensor actions will also depend on affirmative answers to four questions: (1) Does the sensor know what information might be useful? (2) Does he or she know which of the firm's members or units need the information? (3) Are user-friendly devices and facilities for communicating the information in place? (4) Does the sensor know of them?

The trade show–attending engineer attempting to learn about new technologies relevant to her unit's product line might learn instead about a competitor's forthcoming "blockbuster" product designed to compete in another of her firm's markets. Does she know who in the organization needs this information? Will she bother conveying it? Motivation aside, this traveled engineer is not likely to share the information about marketing strategy unless (1) she recognizes the importance of the information to the firm, (2) she can easily find out who needs the information, and (3) she can easily communicate to this person or unit.

To be effective, an organization's intelligence-gathering system must ensure that these conditions are met. How will this be accomplished? We can expect to see implementation of two approaches. *One* will be intensified and formalized efforts to ensure that all of the firm's sensors are attuned to the nature of information important to the organization. Thus we can expect that, more so than in the past, *future firms will more actively educate their members about the organization's current and anticipated objectives, projects, and assignments of responsibility.*[g]

Although these educational efforts will have as their goal ensuring that sensors are able to recognize useful, nonroutine information and to communicate it appropriately, they seem likely to contribute also to two other desirable outcomes—employee motivation and identification with the firm. Especially given (1) an increasingly mobile workforce and (2) the high cost of losing and replacing knowledge workers, creating employee identification with the company will be much more critical than it has been in the past. We will return to this matter in Chapter 8.

As a *second* approach to increasing the likelihood that people with new and useful information actually communicate this to those who need it, we can also expect firms to make available guidelines and devices that facilitate the sensor's making appropriate message-routing decisions. Information technologies will be used much more widely to support sensor-initiated communications. We can expect to see, for example, (1) user-friendly electronic directories that enable a sensor to readily identify those who need to know what the sensor has learned, (2) a greater variety of user-friendly media for sending any message, and (3) aids for determining the best communication medium to use, considering criteria such as the message's criticality and age and the intended recipient's travel and work schedule. Adoption of these communication aids is likely to be initiated less by advances in technology—the technologies are already at hand—than it is by the demands of those who need the sensors' information, or by the expressed frustrations of sensors struggling to rid themselves of the unsatisfied obligation to pass on the specific information they've acquired. To ease the reporting task of their sensors, *future firms will emplace, and inform their members about, efficient and easy-to-use devices that facilitate the routing and distribution of messages.*

Organizations obtain both anticipated information and unanticipated information. Highly structured and formalized mechanistic organizations are superior for dealing with relatively high volumes of anticipated or routine information. (Ineffectual though some say it is, imagine the consequences if the U.S. Internal Revenue Service eliminated specialization

(Continued)

---

[g]Subject, of course, to the constraint that especially sensitive or proprietary information would not be distributed on other than a need-to-know basis.

(Continued)

in its units and personnel and began processing returns in an informal manner.) Less structured and less formalized organic organizations are superior for dealing with unanticipated or nonroutine information. (Imagine the ineffectiveness of negotiating teams, consulting teams, or top management teams if the only permitted communication medium was a set of preformatted forms submitted through preestablished routing networks.) Nowhere do we find guidelines specifically directed at the problem of designing intelligence-gathering and reporting systems that can deal well with high volumes of both anticipated and unanticipated information. The problem seems not to have been explicitly addressed in private-sector organizations—heuristic, make-do solutions seem to have sufficed. Because future environments will impose both routine and nonroutine information in much greater volume, future firms will be forced to address this organization design problem.

As useful as these information dissemination aids will be, their effective use depends on the ability and inclination of the human sensors to recognize and report events significant to the firm. The educational and motivational measures noted above are critical.

PROBING THE ENVIRONMENT

Intelligence gathering includes a wide array of scanning and probing actions, ranging from casual monitoring of the business media to actively investigating competitor intentions. Here is an example of a probe having considerable consequences:

McDonnell Douglas executives were trying to decide whether to launch a new generation of airliners driven by a rear turbo-fan. Although Boeing had stated that it was considering going ahead with a similar plane, McDonnell Douglas needed to know for sure. It assembled a team that over several months studied Boeing's annual reports, 10-Ks, R&D spending, and factory capacity. Conclusion: Boeing could not produce the aircraft as quickly or as cheaply as McDonnell Douglas. . . . The company's intelligence team then recommended to management that the company proceed with the MD 91. Top executives agreed . . . soon afterward Boeing announced it was delaying development of a prop-fan. (*Fortune,* November 7, 1988: 68)

A firm's managers or other sensors often identify events and conditions that require further investigation, that require probes such as McDonnell Douglas's. Events that threaten existing assumptions are especially likely to be probed. While the use of probes is nothing new to the business world, the greatly increased number of threats and opportunities needing further investigation makes it virtually certain that *future firms will more frequently undertake environmental probes.*

Probes vary widely. One form leads to *competitive intelligence,* the product of identifying and interpreting the actions of competitors or of other organizations that affect a firm's competitive environment. The McDonnell Douglas probe just described is an example. Whatever its current level—and by its inherent, sometimes clandestine nature this will forever be hard to know—the development and use of competitive intelligence will be greater in the future than in the past.[9] This must be so—in the future there will be more competitors generating more threats more rapidly. Because knowing the specific nature of competitive threats before they are active can often enable a firm to lessen the damage it might otherwise incur, it seems reasonable to conclude that *in the future, firms will more actively seek and develop competitive intelligence.*[h]

In the 1990s, the growing interest in environmental intelligence and competitive intelligence, combined with advances in information technology, led to a great deal of intelligence information becoming available on the Internet. Some firms, both new and existing firms, developed expertise in tapping into data sources via the Internet and began selling their services as expert generators of client-specific environmental or competitive intelligence.[i] These phenomena—the emergence of intelligence information on the Internet and the increased availability of intelligence gathering services—driven as they are by the demands of the environment, will undoubtedly continue, will make intelligence gathering more effective and less costly, and consequently will strengthen the conclusion that competitive intelligence gathering will be more actively pursued by future firms.

---

[h]Probes of another form are anything but secretive. These probes are actions the firm imposes on its environment and from which it plans to receive diagnostic feedback to use in decision making. Examples are experiments in product offerings, packaging, pricing, and advertising. We will examine action probes in more detail when, later in this chapter, we discuss top managers as sensors and when, in Chapter 5, we examine organizational learning through experience.

[i]In this regard, it is interesting to note that the famous British security agency, MI5, has indicated to Britain's largest companies a willingness to provide them with competitor intelligence (*The Independent,* September 7, 2001: 1, 3).

Tracor was a very successful high-tech defense-industry firm before being acquired in 1987 by Westmark Systems, a holding company. While visiting Tracor on one occasion, I asked a group of mid-level managers about Tracor's environmental scanning. One replied, "We don't do any scanning." I was quite taken aback. To me, any high-tech defense contractor *had* to be actively engaged in intelligence gathering. When I expressed my surprise and asked for an explanation, the manager said: "We don't need to scan because we already know what's happening." Now I was skeptical. Either this guy didn't know what he was talking about, or he was giving me a bad time for the benefit of his audience!

I was wrong on both counts, and the manager was correct in both of his assertions. Further discussion made it clear that Tracor had such a broad range of interactions with the Department of Defense (and with Tracor's own subcontractors) that the firm was always well informed concerning DOD programs, developing technologies, and competitor actions. There were no gaps in Tracor's environmental sensing. There was no need to scan when everywhere was continuously probed. It seems that, in rare cases, extensive probing of an environmental sector can eliminate the need to scan that sector.

SENSING EARLY RESPONSES TO THE FIRM'S ACTIONS AND PRODUCTS

A firm's financial performance is determined by its actions and products and the responses of the firm's environment to these activities and outputs. While other measures of performance are available (e.g., consumer reports of satisfaction with the company's products, ratings by writers of articles in business magazines, and investment analysts' ratings), financial measures tend to capture management's attention.

> Because financial performance measures are highly institutionalized, they become taken-for-granted as "objective" and organizational executives pay greater attention to them as indicators of poor (or good) performance. . . . They are embedded in the organization's systems of information and control and structure the attention of organizational decision makers. (Ocasio, 1995: 322)

The heightened level of future competition will ensure that financial performance will be closely monitored by future firms. But is there a danger that reliance on financial measures such as gross sales, earnings, and profits will preempt the use of other measures that might be more useful as early warning indicators? Many managers monitor financial measures, hoping to identify performance problems before the problems become acute. But is this the best approach for *managing*? Don't financial performance measures sometimes significantly *lag* key events? Of course they do. Precisely speaking, financial performance measures are measures of environmental responses to earlier occurring determinants of firm performance, determinants such as product quality, timely delivery and service, and unwanted personnel turnover.

Professor William Ocasio of Northwestern University's Kellogg Graduate School of Management reminds us that nonfinancial data may be more useful for *early* identification of problems associated with changes in the environment or with the environment's response to changes initiated by the firm. "Nonfinancial measures (e.g., market share, product quality, customer satisfaction, employee morale, safety, and innovativeness) often provide *leading* indicators of economic results. . . . [They have] superior ability to predict future trends" (Ocasio, 1995: 322).

The heightened level of environmental change in the future will require firms to attend more actively to such early warning indicators of downturns in financial performance. In addition, in tomorrow's faster moving environments, such upstream indicators will be especially valuable as diagnostic aids when changes in the levels of financial performance measures signal a problem, or perhaps an opportunity, that needs investigation. As a consequence, in order to respond rapidly to problems and opportunities, whether these be within the firm or in the environment, *firms in the future will direct more attention to nonfinancial measures as leading indicators of environmental change and of firm performance.*

It is necessary, of course, to identify and validate timely and reliable measures of leading indicators, and to verify that they relate to the firm's performance. Naturally the most appropriate indicators will vary across industries and types of firms. For example, using *publicly available* patent-related measures to reflect science-and-technology-based potential and growth, researchers have found that

> patent measures reflecting the volume of companies' research activity, the impact of companies' research on subsequent innovations, and the closeness of research and development to science are reliably associated with the future performance of R&D-intensive companies in capital markets. (Deng, Lev, & Narin, 1999: 20)

For R&D-intensive firms these measures constitute leading indicators of financial performance. More generally, "Research has shown that corporate R&D is strongly associated with subsequent gains in companies' productivity, earnings, and stock prices" (Deng, Lev, & Narin, 1999: 20).

No analysis of a firm's sensing system would be complete without attention to the unique role of the firm's chief sensor, its CEO. We turn now to considering the role and performance of the CEO and other top level managers as firms seek to fulfill their need for vigilant environmental sensing. As an introduction to the topic, we might first recall the earlier example of Starbucks' CEO, Howard Schultz. Schultz's observation of Italian-style coffee bars led him to implement a whole new business model for Starbucks. Here we add the example of Toyota Motor Corporation's CEO, Eiji Toyoda. Partly as a result of observing Ford's immense River Rouge plant at Dearborn, Toyoda was

> impressed with the scale of U.S. automobile production . . . [and] realized that if he could combine the best of U.S. and Japanese production methods, his company could be a world-beater. But Toyoda also found inspiration in other, less obvious, places. At a supermarket, he observed an innovative system of cards used to control the flow of stock from the warehouse to the shelves. What he saw influenced the just-in-time inventory system that would form one of the cornerstones of Toyota's success. (Crainer & Dearlove, 2002: 25)

TOP MANAGERS AS ENVIRONMENTAL SENSORS

In a study informatively titled "Stale in the Saddle: CEO Tenure and the Match Between Organization and Environment," Professor Danny Miller, now at the École des Hautes Études Commerciales (Montreal) and the University of Alberta, reports his finding of a strong *negative* relationship between long CEO tenure and the financial performance of the CEO's firm.[10] The cause of this negative relationship is important as it informs us about a key feature of future firms.

To understand this negative relationship between CEO tenure and firm performance, we must remind ourselves *first* that *CEOs are the most important of the firm's sensors.* One reason is that they have unique access to certain information sources (e.g., other CEOs and top level governmental officials). Their access to these sources enables CEOs to learn early on about key forthcoming events, such as the plans of competitors, suppliers, and regulators. Another reason CEOs are the most important of a firm's sensors is that their interpretations of what they sense have considerable influence on the interpretations of other of the firm's managers.[j]

Second, we must also remind ourselves of the commonsensical and oft-documented fact that firm performance is negatively affected by a mismatch between the firm's environment and its strategy or structure. Knowing this,

---

[j]Later in the chapter we will examine the critical role of interpretations made by CEOs and other top managers.

Miller investigated two relationships: (1) the relationship between long CEO tenure and the firm's environment-strategy fit, and (2) the relationship between long CEO tenure and environment-structure fit. He found both relationships to be negative. That is, Miller found that the environment-strategy fit was poorer in firms headed by long-tenured CEOs, and so was the environment-structure fit. Evidently long-tenured CEOs lost touch with their firm's environment, or didn't appropriately respond to changes in the environment. Because mismatches were greater when long-tenured CEOs were at the helm, and because such mismatches are negatively associated with firm financial performance, it is not surprising that long CEO tenure was associated with poor firm performance.

In a subsequent study of those studio heads who ran all the major Hollywood film studios from 1936 to 1965, Miller and an associate found an inverse U-shaped relationship between top-executive tenure and a firm's financial performance. Using the product-line experimentation undertaken by individual executives as a measure of the executives' attempts to understand the firm's environment, these researchers obtained findings

> consistent with a three-stage "executive life cycle." During the early years of their tenures, top managers experiment intensively with their product lines to learn about their business; later on their accumulated knowledge allows them to reduce experimentation and increase performance; finally, in their last years, executives reduce experimentation still further, and performance declines. (Miller & Shamsie, 2001: 725-745)

What are the implications of this for the nature of future firms? Drawing on their own research and that of others, Professors Sidney Finkelstein and Donald Hambrick, now at Dartmouth College and Pennsylvania State University respectively, concluded, "Executives start their positions with a high degree of task interest, which starts to decline after several years" (Finkelstein & Hambrick, 1996: 84). The resultant decline in top management's attentive sensing of the firm's environment will be more harmful to the firm's performance in the faster-changing environments of the future. Future firms will necessarily guard against this inattentiveness. If they do not, they will not effectively compete with firms that do. *In the future, firms will more actively ensure that their top managers are sufficiently attentive to the firm's environment.*

The increased activism of shareholders and boards of directors initiated in the 1990s will undoubtedly be one mechanism through which this outcome will occur. We can expect that in the future, other approaches, more facilitative of active sensing than preventive of inattention, will be created in response to the increased need for top managers to be attentive to their firm's environment. The specifics of these approaches will often be designed and put into place at the direction of CEOs, as they attempt to effectively fulfill their sensor role as well as their executive role.

That a CEO or other top manager is unaware of a key environmental event or situation is not necessarily a consequence of inattentiveness. It may well be a matter of the time available for scanning. The job of top managers has many facets, many responsibilities. Each needs tending. Important developments are consequently often sensed first by middle- and lower-level managers. Hear Andy Grove speaking while still CEO of Intel:

> [A strategic inflection point] can be a major change due to the introduction of new technologies, a different regulatory environment, a change in customers' values, or a change in what customers prefer. Almost always it hits the corporation in such a way that *those of us in senior management are among the last ones to notice*. (Puffer, 1999: 15-16)

As a result, it will be more important for future firms, facing, as they will, more frequent and more rapidly occurring environmental changes, to ensure that upward communication channels are easily traversed.

The adverse consequences of a CEO's declining attention to the environment are especially serious in that long-tenured CEOs tend to have more within-firm power and influence and to be more committed to the status quo that they've created. It may be that in stable environments, long-term tenure would be found to be related positively to firm performance, as over time CEOs could build up a richly detailed understanding of the firm's environment. In the future, however, environmental stability will be rare, and the benefits of attention and fresh interpretations will more often than in the past outweigh the benefits of those long-accumulated observations and interpretations that lead to elaborate and detailed understanding.

INTERIM SUMMARY AND TRANSITION

The future environments of business organizations will generate threats and opportunities at rates significantly greater than do today's environments. To detect these threats and opportunities early enough to act effectively, future firms will more purposefully design and actively manage environmental sensing systems. For example, increasing specialization in their environments will cause many future firms to create specialized sensors; people and units will be accountable for monitoring and reporting on segments of the environment where they have special expertise.

Specialization of sensors, however, will allow new sources of threats and opportunities to go unnoticed—unless some corrective system design feature is put in place. To minimize the problem, future firms will create a culture and practice of eclectic responsibility for all members of the firm to sense relevant environmental events and conditions and report these to members and units with a need for this information.

The effectiveness of a firm's intelligence-gathering system will depend on (1) the firm's success in motivating and educating its sensors and (2) its success in enabling its sensors to communicate with those who need to know what the sensor has found. Some sensing practices seen in the past will be continued but will be carried out more intensely, in a more coordinated manner, and will more frequently be supported by information technologies. The combination of these and related changes will cause the sensing systems of future organizations to be much more visible, and more recognizable for what they are.

While some firms have had sophisticated systems for monitoring certain aspects of their environment, most firms have had only informal, rudimentary intelligence-gathering systems. Developing and actively managing an effective environmental intelligence–gathering system will be, for most firms, a new endeavor. In most cases, it will require a fresh look at what needs to be done to survive and prosper in an environment the firm has never experienced. We can expect, in particular, that more emphasis will be given to developing competitive intelligence, that more use will be made of nonfinancial performance measures as leading indicators of problems and opportunities, and that more attention will be given to the information-gathering role of the CEO and other upper level managers.

Environmental sensing is a critical organizational function. It helps a firm know when decision making and action taking might be needed. But a firm's sensing of its environment is seldom fully informative. Conditions and events almost always require interpretation. Sense must be made of what has been sensed.

Interpreting What Is Sensed

"Organizations must make interpretations. Managers literally must wade into the ocean of events that surround the organization and actively try to make sense of them. . . . *Organizational interpretation* is . . . the process of translating events and developing shared understanding and conceptual schemes among members of upper management" (Daft & Weick, 1984: 286). This shared understanding and these conceptual schemes, in turn, influence organizational decisions and, in this way, influence organizational actions and performance.

In organizations, interpretation of major environmental events is largely an interactive process. While individual managers often make immediate interpretations of events, drawing on what might be called their "mental model" of the world, their ultimate interpretations tend to be considerably influenced by the views of their associates. Further, the collective interpretation that precedes the majority of a firm's strategic actions is almost invariably the outcome of an interactive process, a process that tends to reduce variation and build consensus among the views of the participants.

Interpreting events and circumstances is something managers do all of the time, although they may not recognize this. Very often arriving at an interpretation of an event is a necessary precursor to making a decision about what to do, or whether to do anything; interpretations shape decisions. Interpretations serve two other roles as well. Developing and communicating their interpretations is frequently necessary as managers carry out the tasks of reducing uncertainty and ambiguity for their subordinates, superiors, or other stakeholders. And interpreting an event or circumstance is frequently the process through which managers update or enrich their mental model of how things were, or are, or should be. Each of these three interpretation outcomes is of great practical importance.[11]

This portion of the chapter, on interpretation, has three remaining sections. The first discusses possible future declines in the quality and timeliness of interpretations. The second describes a management practice that will characterize future firms and that has unintended but positive effects on the firm's interpretations. The third addresses the issue of faulty interpretations.

We noted earlier that the "quality" of an interpretation—its correctness, reasonableness, or appropriateness—can often be determined only in hindsight and, in addition, often depends on the nature of the firm and the predispositions of top management. An example of how interpretations of the same event can vary from firm to firm and yet all be appropriate is provided by Alan Meyer in his classic article, "Adapting to Environmental Jolts," *Administrative Science Quarterly*, 1982. Meyer studied three hospitals, all facing the same strike by San Francisco Bay area physicians. The three hospitals differed in their strategies, structures, and other features. The top managements of the hospitals adopted idiosyncratic-to-the-hospital interpretations of the strike situation, interpretations that allowed them to exploit their hospital's particular strengths and, therefore, evolve from the situation better prepared to compete than before the strike. In retrospect, each of the three different interpretations could readily be described as appropriate, reasonable, correct, and effective.

DECLINES IN QUALITY AND TIMELINESS
OF ORGANIZATIONAL INTERPRETATIONS

In slow-changing environments, events are generally easily and correctly interpreted as they are similar to the events that formed the current interpretive schema itself. In contrast, in fast-changing environments, events tend to be novel. Interpretive schema tend to be ill-suited for interpreting novel events—evolving as they did from interpretations of events that were different from the current, novel events. From these ideas, and the fact that future environments will be faster changing and therefore will be generating more novel events than ever before, it seems reasonable to conclude that, *in the future, unless corrective action is taken, the quality of managers' interpretations of environmental events and conditions will tend to be lower than in the past.*

Managers' mental models *diverge* from one another over time—if the managers encounter different perception-shaping experiences. On the other hand, managers' mental models also tend to *converge* over time—if the managers compare and share interpretations of their experiences. What changes can we expect in the net effect of these two processes as the business environment of the future evolves? On balance—unless an intervention takes place—we can expect divergence to prevail. The reason is that, in many firms, the increased complexity and dynamism of future environments will cause individual managers to have more dissimilar experiences per unit of time. When this divergence of experience is not matched by an increase in the frequency of richly interactive communication sessions (and such sessions seem likely to be less frequent as executive travel stays constant or increases and as global-firm executives are increasingly not collocated), the mental models of the firm's managers will diverge. We can expect that, *in the future, unless corrective action is taken, the degree of overlap among the mental models of the firm's managers will be less than in the past.*

Differences in mental models contribute to difficulties in communication, to misunderstandings, and to conflict. These in turn slow the development of collective interpretations and thus delay the firm's responses to threats and opportunities. Assuming that the commonality of mangers' mental models declines, it follows that, *in the future, unless corrective action is taken, the timeliness of top management's interpretations of environmental events and conditions will be less than in the past, and so will be the firm's responses to these events.*

Whatever corrective actions are used to blunt the adverse effects of tomorrow's rapidly changing environments on the quality and timeliness of interpretations, there is no certainty that the actions will be successful. What is more certain is that firms that do take actions to enhance the quality and timeliness of their interpretations will tend to outperform firms that do not. These will be the firms that survive to be future firms.

ENHANCING INTERPRETATIONS IN FUTURE FIRMS

Managers' minds contain mental models. These models guide the processing of information about events and situations; they shape the development of interpretations. Research shows that a significant degree of *similarity* exists among the mental models of a given firm's top managers about the firm's environment, its objectives, and the most effective means for attaining these objectives.[12] Nonetheless, an important degree of *variation* also exists among the mental models of the firm's top managers. As is well known, this variation has its advantages and disadvantages—while the multiplicity of perspectives among managers can help to identify errors in reasoning, it can also lead to confusion, delay, unresolved conflict, and lack of commitment to the evolved decision process. How will future firms exploit the diversity of their members' perspectives and yet arrive expeditiously at a collective interpretation?

The answer hinges on the fact that groups can reach a working level of agreement more rapidly, and yet still benefit from the diversity of perspectives, when their members understand—without necessarily adopting—the mental models of the other group members. Before examining, shortly, how this state of affairs might be achieved—how managers might be enabled to understand the mental models of their associates—we should consider what might be gained if it could be achieved. It seems that at least two benefits would follow:

1. Information exchange during managers' attempts to arrive at a collective interpretation would be more efficient, as the managers could word their communications so as to be more understandable and acceptable to their listeners. As a result, interpretation processes would be faster and more effective, and the consequent decision process would be more fully informed.[13]

2. Managers' greater cross-understanding of each other's mental models, including the knowledge, assumptions, and values incorporated within the models, would result in more appropriate decision implementation assignments. This, in turn, would generally cause decision implementations to progress more smoothly and expeditiously.

These outcomes seem eminently desirable. They would position a firm to make and implement decisions as rapidly as other conditions permit. The issue is, of course, how to achieve cross-understanding of mental models, especially among the members of the top management team.

On the one hand, it seems unlikely that firms will consciously attempt to increase the interpretive capability of their top management team any more frequently in the future than they have in the past—which is to say hardly ever. Development of an interpretation is largely an implicit process and is generally considered to be so subtle, complex, and individualistic that not much can be done to improve it.[k] As a consequence, most managers and management teams will be intolerant of structured efforts aimed directly at improving someone's understanding of someone else's interpretation-driving mental model.

On the other hand, the upper level managers of future firms will necessarily engage more frequently in a practice that focuses directly on improving operating performance (a practice that has the generally unintended but still desirable side effect of enhancing upper level managers' understanding of their associates' mental models). The occurrence and nature of this practice was brought to the attention of managers and management researchers by Professor Kathleen Eisenhardt of Stanford University in her studies of decision making by top management teams. To identify practices that enabled firms to make swift but still appropriate interpretations, she studied the strategic decision processes of firms in "high velocity environments" (i.e., Silicon Valley firms), firms in environments approaching in their nature the business environments discussed in this book. Based on these studies, Eisenhardt drew three important conclusions.[14] The *first* was that firms where the top managers met more frequently to engage in intensive reviews of the firm's operations, performance, and environment were the higher-performing firms.

A *second* conclusion was that the frequent and intensive reviews that characterized the higher-performing firms enabled the managers involved to learn how their associates think, that is, enabled the team members to develop an understanding of their associates' mental models.

> With intense interaction, managers naturally organize antipodal team-member roles, such as short-term versus long-term or status quo versus change. At Mercury [the pseudonym of a high-performing firm], for example, the vice president of marketing was seen as "constantly thinking about the future" whereas the vice president of engineering was considered to be the keeper of the status quo. Describing the interplay of their relationship, the engineering vice president said, "I depend on her to watch out for tomorrow—I look out for today." (Eisenhardt, 1999: 67)

This conclusion suggests that, if a firm's top management team engaged in frequent and intense reviews such as those Eisenhardt observed, its members would achieve a greater understanding of how their associates think—thus reducing one obstacle to arriving at collective interpretations that are both appropriate and timely.[15]

---

[k]I am making a distinction here between the interpretation-development process and its product, an interpretation. The generally implicit process is very often difficult to understand or communicate, and therefore difficult to argue about. In contrast, the product, the interpretation, is much easier to communicate, and managers (and all people) are prone to try to "improve" the interpretations of others with whom they don't agree about a situation.

Eisenhardt's *third* conclusion was that frequent and intense review of current operating data and of environmental conditions seemed to contribute to the development of rich and accurate mental models, and that, as a result, top management teams that engaged in this review practice were able to interpret new situations quickly and correctly.

So, two outcomes favorable to developing organizational interpretations follow from the use of this particular management practice. Will the top managers of future firms engage in this practice, of intense interaction, more frequently than in the past? The answer is "Yes," for two reasons, neither involving *intentional* development of cross-understanding of mental models. One is that future environments will be more dynamic and demanding. This will force top management to review operations and performance more frequently. The second reason is that firms whose top management teams do not meet more frequently and intensively will be less successful, especially in future environments. These firms will tend not to survive. For both these reasons, we can conclude that *the top management teams of future firms will meet more frequently and intensively to review operations, performance, and environmental events.*

We earlier concluded that, "in the future, unless corrective action is taken, the *quality* of managers' interpretations of events and conditions will be lower than in the past." We also concluded that, "unless corrective action is taken," the *timeliness* of the interpretations would be less. Studies by Eisenhardt and other researchers support the idea that frequent and intensive reviews of operations, performance, and events lead managers to richer and more accurate mental models and to better understanding of their associates' mental models.[16] It seems reasonable, then, to expect that those firms whose top management teams engage in such reviews will be those most likely to survive, and to be future firms.

FAULTY INTERPRETATIONS

Our minds trick us. Our minds cause us to discount information that is not in keeping with what we believe, that is not congruent with our mental models. This pervasive bias often causes us to misinterpret changes as insignificant or unimportant. This is most often the case when the changes are not to our liking.

Consider again the *Encyclopedia Britannica* example noted in Chapter 1. Recall that from 1990 through 1997, CD-ROMs devastated the printed encyclopedia business. Sales of Britannica's multivolume encyclopedia declined more than 50%. According to the October 1997 issue of *BusinessWeek,* "Management was slow to move into electronic media. . . . Britannica continued to market its book to consumers at $1500 a set" while computer manufactures were giving away encyclopedia CDs with every computer sold. How could Britannica not have acted more quickly at a time when the business press and popular media were predicting every day the demise of paper-copy documents and books?

Surely Britannica's top management knew CD-ROMs were being used to convey large volumes of information at very low cost.

As shown below, to the business writers covering the situation, top management's error seemed not to be a matter of not sensing the environment, but rather a matter of misinterpreting it, a matter of holding on to an outdated mental model.

> Imagine what the people at Britannica thought was happening. *The editors probably viewed CD-ROMs as nothing more than electronic versions of inferior products.* Encarta's content is licensed from the *Funk & Wagnall's* encyclopedia, which was historically sold in supermarkets. Microsoft merely spruced up that content with public-domain illustrations and movie clips. *The way Britannica's editors must have seen it, Encarta was not an encyclopedia at all.* It was a toy.
>
> Judging from their initial inaction, *Britannica's executives failed to understand what their customers were really buying.* Parents had been buying *Britannica* less for its intellectual content than out of a desire to do the right thing for their children. Today when parents want to "do the right thing," they buy their kids a computer.
>
> The computer, then, is Britannica's real competitor. And along with the computer come a dozen CD-ROMs, one of which happens to be—as far as the customer is concerned—a more-or-less perfect substitute for the *Britannica.*
>
> *When the threat became obvious,* Britannica did create a CD-ROM version. . . .[1] [Italics are mine.] (Evans & Wurster, *Harvard Business Review*, 1997: 72)

We concluded earlier that "in the future, firms will more actively ensure that their top managers are sufficiently attentive to the firm's environment." We now see the need to extend this idea—*in the future, firms will more actively ensure that their top managers are sufficiently attentive to the firm's environment and that they understand its changing nature.*

While the increased activism of shareholders and boards of directors will undoubtedly contribute to achieving this outcome, we can also expect this outcome to result from top managers responding to increased complexity, dynamism, and competitiveness by adopting the practice of meeting frequently to engage in intense reviews of the firm's operations, performance, and environment.

Chapter Summary and Transition

In the future, the speed and appropriateness of a firm's actions, and hence its performance and survival, will depend more than in the past on the firm's ability to rapidly and effectively sense and interpret environmental changes.

---

[1]Britannica's tardiness in arriving at a correct interpretation of its changing environment created huge losses of jobs and profits. During and subsequent to the late 1990s, Britannica continued to transform the ways in which it marketed and distributed its product, codified knowledge.

Recognizing their need for increased vigilance, some large firms will create staff units to monitor and probe environmental events. The great majority of firms will seek less expensive approaches to obtain environmental intelligence— such as purchasing intelligence-gathering services. Two environmental sensing practices that all future firms will employ in some form will be specialized accountability and eclectic responsibility. In addition, future firms will be more active in supporting and encouraging their members in their sensor roles. The most important of the firm's sensors is, of course, its CEO, and future firms will more actively ensure that their CEOs and other top managers are attentive to the firm's environment and understand its changing nature.

The members of top management teams of future firms will more frequently meet to intensively review operations, performance, and environmental events— for the explicit purpose of improving their performance. While recognizing the primacy of this purpose, we can nevertheless expect some additional beneficial outcomes: (1) team members will tend to develop rich and overlapping under-standings of their firms' context, (2) they will tend to develop cross-understand-ings of each other's mental models, and—as a result—(3) will tend to be more effective communicators, and thus (4) they will tend to be more able to interpret new situations quickly and appropriately.

An important consequence of an organizational interpretation is that it determines if and how a firm will respond to the interpreted situation. In particular, interpretation leads to a situation being categorized, and the particu-lar categorization chosen determines which, if any, decision process is initiated. This determination, in turn, influences organizational actions and, eventually, performance.

A second important consequence of event interpretation is that the process changes the mental models that the firm's top managers use to interpret future events. In these ways, interpretations are important influences on both current and future organizational decisions and performance.

With these ideas in mind, especially that a firm's interpretations strongly influence its decision processes, let us move on to examining the necessary nature of organizational decision making in future firms.

Endnotes

1. For further development of this idea, see F. F. Reichheld, "Learning From Customer Defections," 1996.

2. Parts of this section draw on and extend G. P. Huber, "The Nature and Improvement of Organizational Interpretations," 2000.

3. See H. Schultz and D. J. Yang, "Pour Your Heart Into It," 1997.

4. See J. L. Bower and C. M. Christensen, "Disruptive Technologies: Catching the Wave," 1995; and G. S. Day and P. J. H. Schoemaker, "Avoiding the Pitfalls of Emerging Technologies," 2000.

5. J. E. Dutton and S. E. Jackson, "Categorizing Strategic Issues: Links to Organizational Action," 1987, is the classic work highlighting the ideas that interpretations lead to events being classified as threats or opportunities, and that the classification of an event leads to its being addressed through different people and processes. Numerous authorities and research groups have considered, investigated, and elaborated this *organizational interpretation paradigm* and the closely related *categorization theory*. See, for example, P. Chattopadhyay, W. H. Glick, and G. P. Huber, "Organizational Actions in Response to Threats and Opportunities," 2001; R. Daft and K. E. Weick, "Toward a Model of Organizations as Interpretation Systems," 1984; S. E. Jackson and J. E. Dutton, "Discerning Threats and Opportunities," 1988; R. Klimoski and S. Mohammed, "Team Mental Model: Construct or Metaphor?" 1994; W. H. Starbuck and F. J. Milliken, "Executives' Perceptual Filters: What They Notice and How They Make Sense," 1988; K. Sutcliffe, "Organizational Environments and Organizational Information Processing," 2001; J. B. Thomas, S. M. Clark, and D. A. Gioia, "Strategic Sensemaking and Organizational Performance: Linkages Among Scanning, Interpretation, Actions and Outcomes," 1993; J. B. Thomas and R. R. McDaniel, "Interpreting Strategic Issues: Effects of Strategy and the Information Processing Structure of Top Management Teams," 1990; and Weick, *Sensemaking in Organizations*, 1995.

6. In studies where information gathering and interpretation was an integral part of the firm's sensing and decision-making practices, researchers have found that active engagement in such practices was more positively related to firm performance in more dynamic environments. See, for example, R. B. Duncan, "Multiple Decision Making Structures in Adapting to Environmental Uncertainty: The Impact on Organizational Effectiveness," 1973; and H. Mendelson, "Organizational Architecture and Success in the Information Technology Industry," 2000. This finding and the results from V. K. Garg, B. A. Walters, and R. L. Priem, "Chief Executive Scanning Emphasis, Environmental Dynamism, and Manufacturing Firm Performance," 2003, support the idea that, in the much more dynamic environment of the future, a firm's survival will depend on its active employment of such practices.

7. The next three sections draw on and extend G. P. Huber, "Organizational Learning: A Guide for Executives in Technology-Critical Organizations," 1996, and "Synergies Between Organizational Learning and Creativity & Innovation," 1998.

8. An organization's culture comprises the dominant norms, beliefs, expectations, and values held by members of the organization. It is an organization's most effective behavior-controlling mechanism under conditions (1) where people are faced with situations not neatly matched to their formal job responsibilities and (2) where their actions cannot be closely monitored by their associates or managers. These conditions apply to a large proportion of the instances where personnel encounter firm-relevant information not linked to their regular job responsibilities.

9. Twice toward the end of the twentieth century, business intelligence became a hot topic for the business press. For example, in the late 1990s we saw: "They Snoop to

Conquer," *BusinessWeek,* October 28, 1996; "In the Service Sector, They Snoop to Conquer," *Canadian Business,* January 1997; "Spying for Pills, Not Projectiles," *The Economist,* July 12, 1997; "A Crackdown on Corporate Spies," *BusinessWeek,* July 14, 1997; "Secrets and Lies: The Dual Career of a Corporate Spy," *Wall Street Journal,* October 23, 1997; and "The Spying Game Moves Into the U.S. Workplace," *Fortune,* March 30, 1998.

This was a sequel to what we encountered in the late 1980s: "Business Intelligence— The Quiet Revolution," *Sloan Management Review,* Summer 1986; "Building Effective Intelligence Systems for Competitive Advantage," *Sloan Management Review,* Fall 1986; "Corporate Spies Snoop to Conquer," *Fortune,* November 7, 1988; "The Largest Survey of 'Leading Edge' Competitor Intelligence Managers," *Planning Review,* May/June 1989. For a review of the state of the practice at the time, see T. Lawton, J. Rennie, and T. Eisenschitz, "Business Information From Industrial Espionage—A State-of-the-Art Review," 1988; and H. Sutton, *Competitive Intelligence (Research Report 913)* (New York: The Conference Board, 1988). For a broadened perspective, see J. Fialka, *War by Other Means: Economic Espionage in America,* 1997, especially his extensive bibliography.

10. Knowing as he did from earlier work (see D. Miller and C. Droge, "Psychological and Traditional Determinants of Structure," 1986) that smaller firms provide the best opportunity to study the effects of CEO impact, Miller studied 95 small- and medium-sized, undiversified, autonomous companies (see D. Miller, "Stale in the Saddle: CEO Tenure and the Match Between Organization and Environment," 1991). To help ensure the validity of his results, Miller controlled for the firms' age, size, and technology. Because the median tenure of the CEOs was 10 years, this was the tenure used to distinguish long-tenured CEOs from short-tenured CEOs.

11. For elaboration of the relationships between sensing and interpreting, see the classic work by H. L. Wilensky, *Organizational Intelligence,* 1967. Other insightful works are W. H. Starbuck and F. J. Milliken, "Executives' Perceptual Filters: What They Notice and How They Make Sense," 1988; K. E. Weick, *Sensemaking in Organizations,* 1995; and K. M. Sutcliffe, "Organizational Environments and Organizational Information Processing," 2001.

12. See J. R. Meindl, C. Stubbart, and J. F. Porac, *Cognition Within and Between Organizations,* 1996, for readings regarding the cognitive schemas of individuals, groups, and organizations. The studies of P. Chattopadhyay, W. H. Glick, C. C. Miller, and G. P. Huber, "Determinants of Executive Beliefs: Comparing Functional Conditioning and Social Influence," 1999; K. Daniels, G. Johnson, and L. De Chernatony, "Task and Institutional Influences on Managers' Mental Models of Competition," 2002; and K. M. Sutcliffe and G. P. Huber, "Firm and Industry as Determinants of Executive Perceptions of the Environment," 1998, demonstrate the similarity among the mental models of a firm's top managers.

13. We might speculate that information sharing would be more frequent as well, as managers might be more confident that their communications would be understood. The validity of this speculation is suggested by the work of J. S. Bunderson and K. M. Sutcliffe, "Comparing Alternative Conceptualizations of Functional Diversity in Management Teams: Process and Performance Effects," 2002. These researchers set forth reasoning in accord with this speculation and found that business-unit management

teams composed of managers who individually had broader ranges of functional experience shared more information and achieved higher profits.

14. See K. M. Eisenhardt, "Making Fast Strategic Decisions in High-Velocity Environments," 1989; "Speed and Strategic Choice: How Managers Accelerate Decision Making," 1990; and "Strategy as Strategic Decision Making," 1999.

15. The perhaps intuitively obvious idea that frequent and intense interactions result in understandings of how other group members think is strongly supported by field research, particularly the research drawing on the *transactive memory* paradigm. See, for example, J. R. Austin, "Transactive Memory in Organizational Groups: The Effects of Content, Consensus, Specialization and Accuracy on Group Performance," 2003; K. Lewis, "Measuring Transactive Memory Systems in the Field: Scale Development and Validation," 2003; L. M. Moynihan and R. Batt, "Antecedents and Consequences of Transactive Memory in Shared Services Teams: Theory and Scale Development," 2000; D. Rau, "The Effect of Transactive Memory on the Relationship Between Diversity of Expertise and Performance of Top Management Teams," 2000; D. L. Rulke, S. Zaheer, and M. H. Anderson, "Bringing the Individual Back In: Managers' Transactive Knowledge and Organizational Performance," 2000. T. Simons, L. H. Pelled, and K. A. Smith, "Making Use of Difference: Diversity, Debate, and Decision Comprehensiveness in Top Management Teams," 1999, found that the interaction of top management team diversity and debate within the team resulted in improved firm performance. For reviews of research addressing the interaction between diversity and cognition in strategic management, see G. P. Hodgkinson, "The Psychology of Strategic Management: Diversity and Cognition Revisited," 2001; and K. Y. Williams and C. A. O'Reilly III, "Demography and Diversity in Organizations: A Review of 40 Years of Research," 1998.

It seems to me that certain of the performance problems observed in dispersed teams may be consequences of the participants' difficulty in developing cross-understandings of each other's mental models. Relevant to this question are the pieces by C. Cramton, "The Mutual Knowledge Problem and Its Consequences for Dispersed Collaboration," 2001; T. L. Griffith and M. A. Neale, "Information Processing in Traditional, Hybrid, and Virtual Teams: From Nascent Knowledge to Transactive Memory," 2001; and G. M. Olson and J. S. Olson, "Distance Matters," 2000.

16. Many studies address the development and role of mental models in organizational interpretations and actions. See, for example, P. Barr, J. Stimpert, and A. Huff, "Cognitive Change, Strategic Action, and Organizational Renewal," 1992; W. Bogner and P. Barr, "Making Sense in Hypercompetitive Environments: A Cognitive Explanation for the Persistence of High Velocity Competition," 2000; P. Chattopadhyay, W. H. Glick, and G. P. Huber, "Organizational Actions in Response to Threats and Opportunities," 2001; P. Chattopadhyay, W. H. Glick, C. C. Miller, and G. P. Huber, "Determinants of Executive Beliefs: Comparing Functional Conditioning and Social Influence," 1999; D. Day and R. Lord, "Expertise and Problem Categorization: The Role of Expert Processing in Organizational Sense-Making," 1992; C. M. Fiol, "Consensus, Diversity, and Learning in Organizations," 1994; and M. Kilduff, R. Angelma, and A. Mehra, "Top Management Team Diversity and Firm Performance: Examining the Role of Cognitions," 2000.

4

Organizational Decision Making

Ｗe concluded in Chapter 2 that future firms will be faced with decision situations arriving at unprecedented rates. This condition is hard to imagine, but reason tells us it must be so. That these situations will be arriving with frequencies and speeds significantly greater than those previously encountered suggests that decision making in future firms will differ from decision making in the past or present. Is this true? If so, how will it be different? I attempt to answer these and related questions in this chapter.

> Organizational decision making in the organizations of the post-industrial world shows every sign of becoming a great deal more complex than the decision making of the past. As a consequence of this fact, the decision-making process, rather than the processes contributing immediately and directly to the production of the organization's final output, will bulk larger and larger as *the central activity* in which the organization is engaged. In the post-industrial society, the central problem is . . . how to organize to make decisions. [Italics are mine.]

This is a very powerful statement. When it was made, in 1973, it was an audacious statement. Who would say such a thing?

The author of this audacious assertion is Herbert Simon (1973: 269-270), 5 years later named as the Nobel laureate in economics and especially recognized at that time for his research in organizational decision making. Is there any evidence that he was seeing clearly what was yet to come?

Yes, it seems that there is. It seems that Simon's vision of how firms would be different from what they were in 1973 has been validated by subsequent events.

Consider the major changes to the structure of business organizations that occurred in the last quarter of the twentieth century. One was the widespread replacement or supplement of functional "silo" organizational structures with cross-functional matrix or project team structures. Why did firms make this change? They made it because increased competition and heightened customer expectations forced firms to push for faster completion of projects, and these new structures were able to get decisions concerning multifunctional actions made faster than could the functional structure. So this huge shift in the thinking of U.S. managers, about the best way to design organizations in environments characterized by time-based competition, is an event entirely congruent with Simon's thinking about decision making becoming a central consideration in organizational design.

Another major change that took place in the structure of U.S. firms during this time was hierarchical delayering—the elimination of levels of management. Why did firms delayer? One reason was to save on managerial salaries. An equally important reason was to speed and improve the quality of decisions—by removing levels of management as sources of delay and distortion in the upward and downward flow of decision-related information. This change, too, can be interpreted as an example of designing organizations as if decision making were a centrally important function.[a]

Thus two of the major transformations in the way U.S. firms are designed are in keeping with the idea that organizations should be designed as if a central activity were to make decisions. Was this the sole intent in all instances? Probably not. But it seems very likely, given the extensive business coverage of the decision-related benefits of project-team structures and delayered organizations, that it was an important consideration in a large proportion of the instances where these structural forms were adopted.

If, during the early 1980s, we had suggested to a firm's managers that the firm's functional structure would be displaced or greatly altered within the next (say) 6 to 10 years, the managers would likely have laughed at the apparent absurdity of the idea. Probably viewed as even more absurd would have been the suggestion that, within the same time period, a third or more of the existing managerial levels would be eliminated. Yet such changes occurred in many firms. Most people, most of the time, do not imagine a future much different from the present.

If, even today, we asked managers whether their firms would in the foreseeable future be adopting a specific unfamiliar decision process or structure, they too would very likely be amused. Most people, most of the time, do not imagine a future much different from the present.

---

[a]The third major change was the shift toward eliminating activities not part of the firm's core competence and the associated outsourcing of many activities. The fourth was the widespread use of inter-firm alliances, either to absorb new competencies from alliance partners or to undertake jointly with alliance partners endeavors requiring competencies not possessed, in total, by any one firm (thus creating *virtual organizations*).

The remainder of this chapter has three sections. The first focuses on the nature of decisions in future firms and on the resources that firms will bring to bear on their decision-making function. The second describes how the decision processes used by future firms will differ from those used in today's firms, and examines the apparent trade-off between speed and scope in organizational decision making. The future use of three decision processes that have been commonplace, but that will be used less frequently in future firms, is examined in the third section.

Decisions and Decision-Making Resources in Future Firms

Decision making in future firms will be different. This is a direct consequence of the findings of Chapter 2, that the future environments of business firms will be more *dynamic,* more *complex,* and more *competitive.* Each of these three changed environmental characteristics will cause the nature of decision making and decision-making resources in future firms to be different from those of the past and present.[b] We will first consider the decision-related consequences of forthcoming increases in environmental dynamism and then proceed to those of complexity and competitiveness.

INCREASING ENVIRONMENTAL DYNAMISM AND ITS CONSEQUENCES

From Chapter 2 we have that, "in the future, environmental dynamism will be significantly greater, and will be increasing at an increasing rate." A logical implication of this fact is that, *in the future, firms will encounter problems and opportunities at an increasingly rapid rate.*

Given their more frequent encounters with confrontational events, it follows that—to avoid putting themselves at risk—future firms will have to decide more frequently what action to take, or whether to take any action at all. *In the future, firms will make decisions more frequently.* Their faster moving

---

[b]Here we begin encountering the concept of an organizational decision. By an *organizational decision,* I mean a decision made on behalf of the organization. Organizational decisions can be made by any of a variety of *decision units,* for example, a project-approval committee, an individual manager, or even "the organization" (if the "decision" is an evolved consequence of discussions among members of the firm's upper echelon). In place of the term "decision unit," I will frequently use "decision maker," as it is a more familiar term.

environments will force this condition upon them. As a corollary, it follows that *future firms will make decisions more rapidly.*[c]

If the firm's decision-making performance is not to decline, the firm has as options:

1. increasing the number of decision units to match the increased decision load (e.g., adding loan officers when the number of loan applications jumps), and

2. increasing the efficiency of the decision-making processes (e.g., using triage or other sorting techniques to reduce the number of loan applications that require extensive analysis).

Thus, to make decisions more rapidly without loss of decision quality, either the level or the efficiency of a firm's decision-related resources must be increased. Given that future firms must make decisions more frequently and more rapidly, it follows that *the decision units of future firms will be more numerous or faster acting, or both.*

INCREASING ENVIRONMENTAL COMPLEXITY AND ITS CONSEQUENCES

Also from Chapter 2, we have that, "in the future, environmental complexity will be significantly, and will be increasing at an increasing rate." This fact, that the variety, number, and interdependence of the elements in a firm's environment will be greater and increasing, means that decisions will involve more constraints, more factors, more criteria, and more interactions. Greater numbers of competitors, watchdog groups, customers, suppliers, and alliance partners will see to it that a broader array of considerations will apply to most decision situations. *In the future, the scope of a firm's decision situations will be greater.* Or, put another way and especially in view of the greater interdependencies among these entities, *in the future, a firm's problems and opportunities—its decision situations—will be more complicated.*

Firms not capable of coping with these more complicated decision situations will be less able to compete, will not survive, and will not be around to be counted among future firms. How will firms increase the ability of their decision units to identify and choose actions that effectively respond to the broader scope, more multifaceted decision situations of the future? Pressures to survive will cause firms to adopt two approaches.

One is for firms to instill in their individual decision makers a broader range of knowledge. Business practices designed to do this, such as moving

---

[c]In his book, *The Road to 2015: Profiles of the Future,* futurist and national security consultant John Petersen (1994) expressed this same thought in an interesting way: "Organizations will have to make decisions faster and faster as the metabolism of the larger system increases" (p. 250).

managers through different functional units or across different product lines, or gradually increasing the proportion of the firm's managers having formal business management education (such as a BBA or MBA degree), became commonplace during the last half of the twentieth century.

> Across the last half of the twentieth century, the growing popularity of cross-functional managerial assignments, MBA education, executive and management seminars, and other broadening experiences seems to have caused succeeding cohorts of managers to possess more broadly based mental models, models reflecting views less parochial to the manager's primary functional background. Research near the middle of the twentieth century, for example, seemed to indicate that managers—when faced with a general management situation—focused to a great extent on those aspects of the situation that were related to their particular organizational function. Put differently, managers seemed to possess strong perceptual biases linked to their current functional responsibilities (and presumably to their functional backgrounds). In contrast, research near the end of the century found hardly any evidence of such a bias among members of top management teams and found that CEOs demonstrated essentially no bias related to their primary functional background.[1]

A *second* way for firms to enhance the ability of their decision units to deal with broader scope decision situations is to increase the variety of external knowledge that the decision units can access. So, for example, a top management team might seek legal counsel when faced with an intellectual property issue unlike any previously encountered. Or a marketing manager might hire a consultant when a newly developed product seems applicable to an unfamiliar market as well as the familiar market in which the firm and manager are well versed. These simple examples help make clear that, as situations increase in their complexity, the variety—and thus the number—of people participating tends to increase.

In the past, increasing the number of participants generally meant adding members to the review committee, project team, crisis management team, or other decision unit. It was often the case that—until the point in the decision process was reached when their knowledge, preferences, or opinions were needed—these members had little to contribute to the decision unit's deliberations. During the 1980s and 1990s, decision units began to get around this inefficient use of talent by using communication technologies (such as videoconferenceing, audioconferencing, and speakerphones) to access, *during* decision-making meetings, remotely stationed personnel who possessed the necessary knowledge and who, *during* decision-making meetings, had kept abreast of the discussions by also using the technologies. Use of these and more advanced communication technologies will undoubtedly be more common in the future as the technologies will be more effective, more affordable, and more user-friendly.

I encountered an example of this when sitting in a top management team's two-day strategic planning session. Several of this chemical manufacturer's personnel from around the United States—experts in different product lines or functional areas—were "on call" via a speakerphone hookup, some at appointed times, some continuously. It was clear from the proceedings that the more complicated issues, the ones possessing more facets, were the ones that generated more calls to the off-site personnel, and thereby drew on more participants without enlarging the formal decision unit, the top management team. (The speakerphone hookup seemed adequate and efficient. Today, or especially tomorrow, we might expect firms to use videoconferencing or other more advanced communication technologies for including people not physically present.)

The need for decision units to possess or access knowledge as multifaceted as the decision situations they face, combined with the fact that future decision situations will be more multifaceted, strongly suggests that *future firms will ensure that their decision units possess a broader range of knowledge, or are readily able to access a broader range of knowledge, or both.*

If this prediction were correct, we would already expect to see upward trends in management education focused on acquiring or providing a broad range of business knowledge, and also an upward trend in the use of external consultants. We do. As indications of this: (1) the number of regular MBA program degrees awarded per year in the United States grew from 177,000 in 1967-68 to 430,000 in 1997-98, (2) the number of executive MBA programs grew from 2 in 1963 to 180 in 2002, (3) during the 1980s and 1990s, the compound growth rate of worldwide management consulting revenues averaged 20%, and (4) during the 1990s the amount spent in the United States on management, scientific, and technical consulting grew by over 200%.[2] Individual estimates of the growth in management education offered through distance learning programs, through within-firm programs or corporate universities, or through blends of these channels vary considerably, but in aggregate indicate high rates of growth.

We saw earlier that forthcoming increases in environmental dynamism will require decisions to be made more quickly, and we saw just above that forthcoming increases in environmental complexity will require decisions to account for a broader scope of critical factors. Let us turn now to considering the effects on organizational decision making of forthcoming increases in environmental competitiveness.

INCREASING COMPETITIVENESS AND ITS CONSEQUENCES

Our last conclusion in Chapter 2 was that, "in the future, environmental competitiveness will be significantly greater than it is, and will be increasing." Increases in the level of competition have two important consequences for a firm's decisions.

The *first* is that mistakes are more likely to be disastrous. In the future, competitors will be more numerous. Further, more effective communication and transportation technologies will enable competitors to exploit more quickly whatever vulnerability results from a firm's poor decision. The increased number and nimbleness of competitors means that, *in the future, organizational decisions that arrive late, or that inadequately account for the multiple factors relevant to the situation, will be even more likely to enable competitors to gain advantage and put the firm at risk.*

The *second* important consequence of increasing environmental competitiveness is related to the first, but is more subtle. It has to do with the cumulative effect of numerous small or moderate gains or losses in performance relative to the performance of competitors. If competition is not intense (if the current draw on a market is below what the market can support, for example), it can take some time for changes in relative firm performance to result in lower-performing firms being forced out. But if a market is saturated with competitors, a series of small losses or gains in relative performance will result in the firm—or one or more of its competitors—being forced out of the market very quickly.

Decisions superior to those of the competition tend to result in performance superior to that of the competition. In the more highly competitive environment of the future, a cluster or series of even marginally superior decisions will enable a firm to increase the likelihood of its survival and to decrease this likelihood for its competitors. Thus, *in the future, organizational decisions that are more timely, or that more adequately account for the multiple factors relevant to the situation, will be even more likely to enable the firm to gain advantage and put its competitors at risk.*

In these last few pages we identified nine decision-related consequences of the fact that future business environments will be significantly more dynamic, complex, and competitive. Together these consequences make clear the firm's need for decision makers who can grasp the increasing number of relevant factors, interactions, criteria, and constraints, and convert this information into choices as *effectively* as the situation demands and, at the same time, as *rapidly* as the situation demands. Fulfilling this survival-relevant need will require future firms to devote much more attention to enhancing the capabilities of their decision makers. Let us turn to this issue.

DECISION MAKER CAPABILITIES: PAST, PRESENT, FUTURE

Are today's *athletes* better than the athletes of earlier eras? Of course they are. Track and field athletes, for example, run faster, jump higher, and throw farther than ever before. Records are broken every year. Why? Among the reasons, three are relevant to our discussion of decision maker capabilities.

The *first* reason today's athletes are superior is that the selection processes are more sophisticated than they were in the past. Candidates with athletic promise tend to be identified, selected, encouraged, and slotted by ever more sophisticated institutional machinery. The *second* reason is that today's athletes are the products of countless studies on diet, training methods, conditioning programs, technique, and coaching methods. The *third* reason today's athletes are superior to those who preceded them is that they have far superior equipment (e.g., flexible poles for pole vaulters).

Even though they are superior to their predecessors, today's athletes are no more likely to place first in their event than were the athletes of yesteryear. Each is having "to run faster just to keep up with the competition" which, of course, is composed of athletes who are also superior to their predecessors.

Are today's *managers* better—as decision makers—than were managers in earlier eras? If they are, why would this be?

Three observations support the idea that today's managers are superior—as decision makers—to managers of the past. *One* is that the selection processes are more sophisticated. Candidates with promise tend to be identified, selected, encouraged, and slotted (then rotated) by ever more sophisticated educational and corporate machinery. The *second* is that today's managerial decision makers are shaped by countless studies, courses, seminars, books, and business press articles on how to make better decisions. The *third* observation is that they have far superior decision-aiding equipment (e.g., personal computers, spread sheets, computer-based data bases and information systems, e-mail, videoconferencing access to knowledgeable others, and Internet access to information sources). Given these observations, it follows that today's managers are more capable as decision makers than were the managers who came before them.

> Of course, in spite of their greater decision-related capabilities, today's managers are no more likely to make decisions superior to those of their competitors than were managers in the past. Their increased capabilities for making decisions more effectively and more quickly than did their predecessors merely enable them to keep up with—not get ahead of—their competitors (whose decision-related capabilities have also increased).

As we noted earlier, the decision situations with which managers must contend in the future will be more complicated and more time constrained. The implication for firms in the future is obvious—firms that do not devote more effort to selecting, developing, and supporting (with decision-aiding resources) their decision makers will be more vulnerable to misallocations of organizational resources, and thus more vulnerable to being outperformed by their competition. As a consequence, it seems that, in order to maintain or increase the likelihood of their survival, *future firms will direct more effort toward selecting, developing, and supporting managers as decision makers.*[3]

To repeat, "Today's managers are more capable as decision makers than were the managers who came before them." Because the same conditions that led to this outcome will be operating in the future, and because "(all) future firms (and their competitors) will direct more effort toward selecting, developing, and supporting managers as decision makers," it follows that *future managers will be more capable as decision makers.*

This assertion requires an interesting qualification. The quality of a decision is affected by the accuracy of the decision maker's mental model of the decision situation, broadly defined to include beliefs about trends in markets, the organization's strengths, and so forth. In tomorrow's faster changing business environment, it will be more difficult for managers to keep their mental models up to date. To the extent that they do not, the quality of their decisions will suffer.

Maintaining accurate mental models is especially difficult for more senior, upper level managers. One reason is that the mental models of these managers, because they were developed and shaped over a longer time interval, are often "firmer," more resistant to change. A second reason the mental models of these managers are likely to be especially resistant to change is that the beliefs contained in the models have often been reinforced and strengthened by the successes that enabled these managers to reach their firm's upper levels.

Polaroid's apparent failure in the digital camera market has been attributed in large part to the outdated beliefs of its top managers. This example and the quotes in this paragraph are from Tripsas and Gavetti (2000). The firm's long-run success in the instant photograph market led its managers, most of whom had been with Polaroid for many years, to believe that (1) "success came through long-term, large-scale research projects" (p. 1150), (2) "Polaroid's technology and products would create a market" (p. 1150), (3) "Polaroid could not make money on hardware, only on software [i.e. film]" (p. 1158), and (4) "customers valued and wanted an instant print" (p. 1151). In line with these beliefs, "at the beginning of the 1990s, when a market for digital imaging slowly started to emerge, senior management strongly discouraged search and development efforts that were not consistent with the traditional business model, despite ongoing efforts from newly hired members of the Electronic Imaging Division to convince them otherwise" (p. 1158).

That is, the firm's top managers "had a direct influence on activities that did not take place. In particular, there were important areas of capability that Polaroid did not invest in: low-cost electronics manufacturing capability, rapid product development capability, and new marketing and sales capability" (p. 1153). The lack of these capabilities prevented Polaroid from capitalizing on the strong technical capability in digital imaging that it developed in the 1980s. "Polaroid's difficulties in adapting . . . were mainly determined by the cognitive inertia of its top executives" (p. 1159). (Polaroid filed for Chapter 11 protection from its creditors in October 2001.)

INTERIM SUMMARY AND TRANSITION

To determine the nature of decisions and decision-making resources in future firms, we drew on the fact that the future environments will be more dynamic, more complex, and more competitive. From the idea that environmental dynamism will be significantly greater and will be increasing, we surmised that firms will encounter problems and opportunities at an increasingly rapid rate and that they will accordingly be forced to make decisions more rapidly. As a consequence, we concluded that—to avoid putting themselves at risk—firms in the future will either add decision units or create decision units that are faster acting.

Drawing on the fact that environmental complexity will also be significantly greater and increasing, we observed that the problems and opportunities encountered by future firms will be more complicated. Reasoning that the knowledge needed to adequately address these more complicated matters must be either possessed by the firm's decision units or be accessible by these units, we concluded that future firms will ensure that their decision makers individually possess a broader range of knowledge or are readily able to access a broader range of knowledge, or both.

We inferred two different but related consequences of the idea that future firms will face environments where the level of competition will be significantly greater than it is, and will be increasing. One was that, in the future, organizational decisions that arrive late, or that inadequately account for the factors relevant to the situation, will more likely enable competitors to gain advantage and put the firm at risk. The other consequence was that, in the future, organizational decisions that are more timely, or that more adequately account for the multiple relevant factors, will more likely enable the firm to gain advantage and put its competitors at risk. The firm's need for decision makers who are able to grasp the increasing multiplicity of factors, interactions, criteria, and constraints as *effectively* as the situation demands, and yet as *rapidly* as the situation demands, caused us to conclude that future firms will direct more effort to selecting, developing, and supporting their decision makers. Firms that do not do this will have less capable decision makers. Their resources will be allocated less wisely. They will consequently be less competitive. They will not survive in the more competitive environment of the future. They will not be future firms.

Our everyday experiences make clear that organizational decisions are hardly ever made by one person, acting in isolation from the influence of others. Instead, organizational decisions are almost always the outcome of a process where the knowledge, opinions, and recommendations of multiple contributors are drawn upon by the person or small group having the authority to commit the organization's resources. The processes used when obtaining and employing this information to arrive at a decision greatly influence the goodness of fit between the decision situation and the decision taken. Importantly, the processes used also greatly influence the level of commitment (or resistance) to the choice—and thus greatly influence the outcome of the action chosen. Enhancing the *cognitive* capability of their individual decision makers through selection, development, and support is not enough; firms must also act on the fact that the quality of decision outcomes is greatly a consequence of the decision processes used. Better processes lead to better outcomes.

At the intellectual level, managers know this. But the press of other tasks, or the desire to rid themselves of the tension associated with a decision still to be made, often causes managers not to act on this knowledge—a firm's decision processes are often not as carefully managed as after-the-fact reviews suggest they should have been. I explain in the next section why this condition will occur less frequently, and how future firms will manage their decision processes differently and more effectively.

Decision-Making Practices in Future Firms

Most of us believe we are better decision makers than we are. One reason is that we subconsciously tend to avoid recalling our bad decisions while frequently recalling our good ones. Another reason is that we rationalize—we interpret the poor outcomes of our decisions as consequences of unforeseeable or uncontrollable events, and see good outcomes as the result of the quality of our choices. And of course, in organizations, our associates reinforce these self-serving tendencies. That is, while some associates might forthrightly point out our mistakes, most will reinforce our selective recollections and biased interpretations, either because they were part of the decision-making process themselves or because they do not want to offend.

Given these self-serving tendencies and the organizational conditions that reinforce them, we can expect few managers to embrace the ideas that the decision processes they now use will be inadequate in the future, or that tomorrow's firms will manage their decision processes differently than do today's.[d] Recall, however, our earlier conclusions:

1. "In the future, organizational decisions that arrive late, or that inadequately account for the multiple factors relevant to the situation, will be even more likely to enable competitors to gain advantage and put the firm at risk."

2. "In the future, organizational decisions that are more timely, or that more adequately account for the multiple factors relevant to the situation, will be even more likely to enable the firm to gain advantage and put its competitors at risk."

These two ideas make clear that, in the future, the needs for both speed and scope in the making of decisions will be more critical. Because, in general, firms attend to critical matters, it seems reasonable to conclude that, *in the future, firms will more actively manage their decision processes.*

What does this mean? What will future firms do differently? Below we examine decision-making practices that we can expect firms to intentionally employ more frequently in the future—to deal with the needs for both scope and speed.

---

[d]In the course of four studies of organizational decision making (Ullman & Huber, 1973; Huber, 1985; Waller, Huber, & Glick, 1995; and Dukerich, Waller, George, & Huber, 2000), I interviewed nearly a hundred managers, many of them top-level managers, about actual decisions in their organizations. I take away from these interviews the very strong sense that there are few activities where managers are less likely to imagine doing things differently—are less likely to imagine future practices different from present practices—than in their, or their organization's, decision making. This conclusion, based on interviews, would also follow from the argument made above, that most people believe they are better decision makers than they are.

ENSURING SCOPE

In his award-winning book, *Crucial Decisions,* Irving Janis (1989) drew on his decades of experience as a consultant to top executives and policymakers, and on his own extensive research and scholarship, to articulate "an uncommon strategy" for making decisions. He referred to it as a "vigilant" approach to decision making. By this he meant an approach that emphasized the need for vigilance to avoid overlooking critical considerations or superior options. Figure 4.1 describes this process.

In one sense, the process is familiar—it appears to conform to what many managers would recognize as the process prescribed in textbooks. In another sense, it is unfamiliar in the sense that it is not often used—Janis himself labeled it as "uncommon."

Janis challenged himself to see if use of the vigilant approach actually led to superior outcomes. Nineteen strategic decisions concerning international crises encountered by U.S. presidents were studied in considerable depth. Each decision was first scored with respect to how many of seven procedural errors were present in the decision-making process used (see the seven "procedural defects" shown in Figure 4.1). Each decision was also scored on two criteria related to the favorableness of the decision outcome. *The analyses showed a strong negative association between the number of defects in the decision procedure and the favorableness of the decision outcome.*[e]

The conclusion that seems to follow from Janis's rather straightforward study is supported by more elaborate studies as well. In fact, a huge number of studies demonstrate a strong relationship between (1) use of decision processes that ensure consideration of multiple options and broad-scope review of key considerations (as does Janis's approach) and (2) positive decision outcomes such as end-of-process consensus and higher levels of organizational performance).[4] Borrowing Janis's term, let us refer to processes that ensure consideration of multiple options and broad-scope review of key considerations as "vigilant processes." That such processes lead to higher organizational performance motivates the *tentative* conclusion that, in their more competitive business environments, *future firms will more frequently employ vigilant decision processes.*

---

[e]The "favorableness" scoring was carried out separately by two experts who had conducted extensive research on international crises. The two experts were familiar with the 19 crises and their outcomes, but were blind to the nature and purpose of the study. (Space does not permit adequate description of Janis's exemplary research methodology and his safeguards against errors of various sorts.) For one criterion, "the likelihood-of-international-conflict" criterion (reverse scored), the correlation was −.64. For the other, "costly-to-U.S.-vital-interests" criterion (also reverse scored), the correlation was −.62. Given the variation in the number of defects and in the favorableness of the outcomes, these correlations could have occurred by chance alone only 2 times in 1,000.

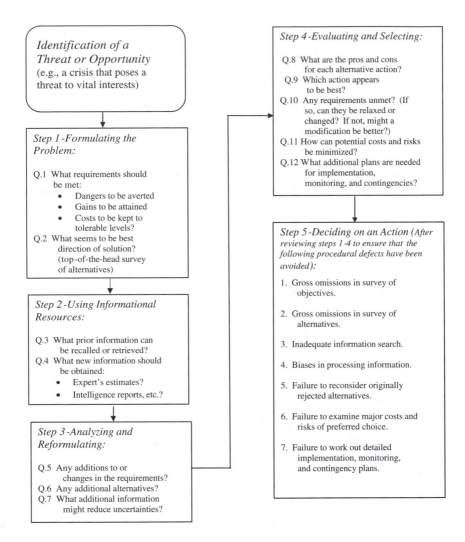

Figure 4.1   Main Steps Characterizing a Vigilant Problem-Solving Approach to Decision Making

NOTE: Feedback loops omitted for purposes of parsimony.

SOURCE: Adapted from Janis, I. *Crucial Decisions*. (New York: Free Press, 1989) 91.

This can be only a tentative conclusion at this point because we haven't yet considered the need for speed, and decision speed will be even more important in tomorrow's more dynamic business environment. We must avoid concluding too quickly, however, that practices for ensuring scope and practices for ensuring speed necessarily preempt each other. Studies of firms operating in very dynamic environments—environments approaching in dynamism the environments described in this book—show that two aspects of vigilant decision processes, the parallel development of multiple alternatives and the extensive use of real-time information, actually increase the speed of decision making.[5] Further, of course, we should recall Janis's finding that more vigilant processes led to better outcomes—*in crises!*

In her research on Silicon Valley firms (described in Chapter 3), Professor Kathleen Eisenhardt found that building and comparing multiple alternatives in parallel enables quick comparative analyses and bolsters confidence that the best alternative has been chosen—thus leading to faster closure of the decision process. In addition, this development of multiple alternatives provides a fallback position if the chosen alternative fails to win subsequent endorsements and in this way, in some instances, speeds the decision process. With respect to acquiring and using information, she found that

> fast strategic decision making is associated with extensive use of real-time information. Executives making fast decisions routinely paid close attention to quantitative indicators such as daily and weekly tracking of bookings, scrap, inventory, cash flow, engineering milestones, and competitors' moves. They preferred these operational indicators to more refined accounting data such as profit. These executives averaged 2.5 regularly scheduled operations meetings per week and indicated a preference for real-time communication via face-to-face conversation or electronic mail rather than through time-delayed media like memos. (Eisenhardt, 1989: 551)

ENSURING SPEED

The fact that, "in the future, firms will encounter problems and opportunities at an increasingly rapid rate," caused us to conclude that "future firms will make decisions more rapidly." Certainly decision speed will be important. It is important even today, but we observe that many business decisions arrive late to the situation they were intended to address. What are the phenomena that account for this and what will future firms do to ensure decision timeliness?

Four common decision-delaying phenomena have little to do with the decision process itself. *One* is a delay in sensing the signals that there may be a need for the firm to act. (Recall from Chapter 3 the example when "the advent of electronic calculators caught Facit's top managers by surprise.") *Another* is a delay in interpreting the sensed signals as indicating the need to act. (Also recall from Chapter 3 the example of Intel failing to correctly interpret the rapid growth in the market for low-end computer chips.)

A *third* phenomenon, *decision-task neglect,* occurs when a manager avoids confronting the decision-making task itself, a behavior sharply noted by one of the most thoughtful and respected of all classical management authorities, Chester Barnard, former President of the New Jersey Telephone Company and of the Rockefeller Foundation:

> The making of decisions, as everyone knows from personal experience, is a burdensome task. . . . Accordingly, it will be observed that men generally try to avoid making decisions, beyond a limited degree when they are rather uncritical responses to conditions. (Barnard, 1938: 189)

The *fourth* source of delay, *decision avoidance,* occurs within the decision process when a manager puts off making a choice because all of the conspicuous options have some negative consequences, consequences that the manager, consciously or subconsciously, wishes to avoid.

Sometimes what seems to be avoidance is really more a matter of a manager attending to tasks more immediately central to his or her responsibilities. In any case, after neglecting the decision task until what may have been a manageable situation becomes a crisis and demands swift action, all too often the manager makes the decision hastily—with the excuse that "we haven't time" to employ a more vigilant process. At this point, of course, a tradeoff between vigilance and speed is necessary. But the tradeoff was not inherent in the decision situation; rather it was the consequence of poor decision management.

An approach that managers sometimes use to excuse their decision avoidance is to claim the need for more information and time to analyze this information. This phenomenon is, of course, the notorious "analysis paralysis."

In contrast with the above four phenomena, *none of which are inherent in the firm's intended decision process,* are phenomena that delay decisions by acting on the decision process itself. These latter phenomena are called *dynamic factors.* Examples of dynamic factors are the arrival of political obstacles, changes in the availability of resources, delays in obtaining information critical to the situation, and competing demands for the time of the decision makers.

Acknowledging the decision-delaying effects of dynamic factors introduces the important but seldom considered matter of clock time versus calendar time.

The *clock time* needed to make a decision is the time actually used by decision unit members to obtain and process the information and knowledge necessary to make the decision. Examples of clock time are the actual time decision makers expend obtaining and exchanging information and opinions and the actual time they spend processing the information and opinions (either alone or in conjunction with others). In contrast, the *calendar time* to make a decision is the time that elapses between when it is recognized that a decision must be made and when the decision is "delivered."[f] *If a careful record were kept of most decision processes, it would be found that the clock time used in making a decision was a very small fraction of the elapsed calendar time.*

Some might argue that the concept of clock time should be broadened. Perhaps it should also include (1) the actual time expended while obtaining a collective interpretation of the situation, (2) the actual time expended in fact-gathering efforts such as surveys or prototyping, and (3) the actual time used to obtain consensus or at least acquiescence among the relevant parties about the decision. Even when these more time-consuming steps are included, *if a careful record were kept of most decision processes, it would be found that the clock time used to make a decision was much less than the elapsed calendar time.*[g]

It seems worthwhile to comment on the matter of competing demands for decision makers' time. Many of the delays that account for the difference between clock times and calendar times occur simply because the managers involved in the decision process focus the great preponderance of their everyday efforts on attending to their operational responsibilities rather than on guiding the decision process. This is understandable. By focusing on their operational responsibilities, managers attain both *extrinsic rewards* and *intrinsic satisfaction.* With regard to extrinsic rewards,

(Continued)

---

[f]Of course some decision processes are truncated due to a change of circumstances, such as the problem or opportunity going away or a powerful entity imposing a preemptive moratorium or action.

[g]I expect that the validity of these two assertions will be self-evident to most readers as they recollect the organizational decisions they've observed or as they read authoritative accounts of actual organizational decisions. I know of no more straightforward study of this matter than the classic study, "The Structure of 'Unstructured' Decision Processes," by Mintzberg, Raisinghani, and Theoret (1976). Although the pace of organizational decision making in business organizations has increased since the time of the study, the conclusions of the study and the model derived from it are still valid.

(Continued)

in their areas of operational responsibility, managers' deadlines and other operational performance measures are explicit and are reliably monitored by higher-level managers who routinely provide extrinsic rewards for high performance (and—generally less obtrusive but still explicit—"punishments" for low performance). With regard to intrinsic satisfaction, in their areas of operational responsibility, managers' familiar skills can be applied to familiar tasks, thus reliably providing intrinsic satisfaction.

As a consequence of all this, managers and others involved in decision processes tend to squeeze decision-related activities in between the activities related to fulfilling their routine responsibilities. Even this "squeezing-in" is done unreliably, perhaps because the decision-related activities are generally less controllable or perhaps because they take time away from performing other activities that are more likely to result in the rewards and satisfaction noted above. While perusal of the business press indicates that managers recognize the importance of decisions, there is little indication that they recognize the importance of managing decision processes.

Recall Herbert Simon's conclusion that "the decision-making process, rather than the processes contributing immediately and directly to the production of the organization's final product, will bulk larger and larger as the central activity in which the organization is engaged." Recall also our earlier conclusion that to survive in the faster moving environments of the future, "future firms will make decisions more rapidly." Given these ideas and yet—in contrast—the understandable predispositions of most managers most of the time to treat decision-making processes as ancillary activities, it seems inevitable that future firms will seek to "more actively manage their decision processes" (a conclusion that we reached earlier through a longer and more thoroughly argued line of reasoning). Exactly how firms will manage their decision processes will, of course, vary with their individual circumstances (e.g., with the firm's industry, its culture, and the preferences of its top management). But given the increased frequency with which decisions will be made, and decreased duration of time windows for exploiting opportunities or dealing with problems, it will be necessary for firms in the future to employ more systematic approaches to ensure the timeliness of decisions.

We can expect to see two approaches applied widely, although with varying degrees of intensity. One is for the firm to act on the idea that decision making is a "central" process and, accordingly, needs to be actively managed. In almost all instances, ensuring active management with particular attention to timeliness means that someone, *one person*, will be made specifically responsible for managing the decision process and for its timely completion. In firms that do not address the issue of decision timeliness by creating specific, personal accountability, a larger proportion of decisions will arrive late, or—at the last minute—will be made hastily, without vigilance. In the more competitive business environments of the future, these firms will not survive to be future firms. *In future firms, for each decision with possibly significant consequences, someone will be more frequently made explicitly accountable for managing the decision process and for the timely delivery of the decision.*[6]

The second approach we can expect to see used for managing decision processes so as to ensure the timely production of their product—the decision itself—is the encouragement of *project-management thinking* among all those accountable for getting decisions made. As decision making becomes more clearly seen as the necessary-to-be-managed integration of knowledge, opinions, and preferences from multiple participants, the similarity between "producing" decisions and producing the intellectual products typically generated by product-design teams, program-review teams, or other "project" teams will become more apparent.

Employing project-management thinking creates a focus on speed and decreases the likelihood that information, people, or enabling authorizations are unavailable when needed. Consequently, given their need to increase the speed and timeliness of decision making, and the high likelihood that they will be explicitly held accountable for the timeliness of decisions for which they are responsible, it seems reasonable to conclude that, *in future firms, managers responsible for the timely delivery of decisions will manage decision processes as projects.*

In especially complex decision situations, framing decisions as projects will frequently contribute to the actual adoption of *project-management procedures*—where the activities integral to making the decision are laid out as a network showing the required activity sequences and where the network is then used for activity coordination and for the allocation and reallocation of resources so as to ensure timely project completion. For example, a manager's use of such a procedure would involve identifying (1) the needed resources—such as experts, cost data, and authorizations, (2) the component activities involved in making the decision—such as efforts to obtain particular information or to develop options, (3) the precedence and temporal relationships among these activities, (4) the estimated times required for completing the individual activities, and (5) the critical path through the network (i.e., the particular activity sequence on which delays would delay project completion).[7]

Use of project-management procedures facilitates understanding of what is generally a complex situation and consequently enables managers to act more preemptively and proactively on dynamic factors that threaten to delay the project and to allocate resources more effectively. Thus it seems reasonable to conclude that, *in future firms, managers responsible for the timely delivery of decisions in especially complex decision situations will more frequently employ project-management procedures.*

Our focus in these last few pages has been on the management of individual decisions. But how will firms deal with the multiplicity of the decisions clamoring to be addressed in the faster moving environments of the future? As is well known, project managers compete for resources, particularly for the time of key personnel. So also do, and will, decision managers. How will future firms allocate resources to deal with the overall flow of multiple decision-making efforts? In particular, will there be centralized prioritization or scheduling? Such coordinative processes are not unprecedented—legislative bodies, for example, centrally manage the flow of decisions, the flow of bills to be voted on. (Although it is not generally recognized by the public, legislative bodies are faced with severe deadlines and prioritization issues—there are many more bills proposed in any session than can be voted on by the body at large, and any bill not voted on dies.)

While the case is not clear, it seems unlikely that the relatively centralized management of decision processes observed in legislative bodies will occur in future firms. Rather, the continuous stream of partially uncontrollable demands for decisions of quite varying natures will cause agreed-upon priorities to shift, resources to be reallocated, and schedules to be altered. In addition, the novelty of many decision situations will force firms to create (rather than select) solutions, thus contributing to the unpredictability of decision-process durations. Thus, although in the future there will be an even greater need for the careful allocation of the organization's decision-related resources, it seems likely that the increased dynamism of the environment will—on balance—cause centralized, mechanistic management of the overall flow of the firm's decisions to be impractical. What is more likely is that the allocation of decision-related resources will be a process of continuous reallocation and will be strongly influenced by lobbying, negotiation, and other informal practices, much as we see today.

In this section, we've emphasized the need for firms to ensure that their decisions are made swiftly, or at least arrive when needed. But, in view of the fact that future environments will be more complex, in the previous section we concluded that future decision situations would be more complicated than those of the past. Addressing complicated situations—such as acquisitions, divestitures, capacity expansions, and new product introductions—hastily, with simplistic processes, in tomorrow's more competitive environment, would be to court disaster. Accordingly, even as they seek to make decisions more rapidly, firms must exercise greater vigilance to ensure that important aspects of the decision situation are not overlooked.

In this regard, it is important to observe that (1) making a specific manager explicitly accountable for managing the decision process and (2) encouraging the use of project-management thinking (and—in the case of especially complex decision situations—the use of project-management procedures) both contribute not only to speed but also contribute to avoiding the procedural errors identified in Janis's vigilant process.

Particularly authorities whose focus is on developing innovative products, or on the benefits of being "first to the market," sometimes strongly emphasize the need to make product-development and marketing decisions rapidly—as contrasted with vigilantly. These authorities often cite as evidence instances where products failed because they arrived late to the market. Of course other instances could be cited to show that products failed because the associated product-development and marketing decision processes were defective. Whatever our personal experience–based bias in this matter, it is important to keep in mind that the firm's intended decision processes are very often *not* the cause of a product's overdue arrival in the marketplace. As we noted above, close scrutiny of instances where products were late to market often shows that the delay was the result of two *pre-decision* phenomena we examined in Chapter 3: (1) a delay in sensing the signals that there may be a need for the firm to act (e.g., "the advent of electronic calculators caught Facit's top managers by surprise") and (2) a delay in interpreting the signals as indicating the need to act (e.g., Intel's failing to interpret the rapid growth in the market for low-end computer chips as an indication that it must adjust its market focus). And then there are the two delays caused by the decision-making manager's shortcomings: (1) decision-task neglect and (2) decision avoidance. Finally, a fifth source of delay frequently encountered in new-product introductions is a *post-decision* phenomenon—difficulty in implementing the decision to proceed with the product. These examples suggest that the late arrival of a product to its market may have nothing to do with the firm's choice between emphasizing scope or emphasizing speed.[8] This is not to say, of course, that speed is not important—it is *very* important—but is rather to call attention to some simplistic, polarized thinking about the matter.

Up to this point we've encountered three quite different means by which future firms will attempt to fulfill their need to increase both the speed and scope of decision making: (1) enhancing the capabilities of their decision makers, (2) creating specific accountability in decision management, and (3) encouraging the management of decisions as projects. We turn now to one more.

EFFECTS OF FORTHCOMING INFORMATION
TECHNOLOGIES ON DECISION SPEED AND SCOPE

During the 1980s and '90s, the availability and use of both *computer-assisted communication technologies* and also *computer-assisted decision-aiding technologies* facilitated changes in the decision structures and processes of U.S. firms.[h] We noted two of these changes earlier in the chapter. *One* was a structural change—the reduction in the number of levels in the hierarchy of many firms. This reduction in levels was enabled in part by using management information systems to capture, organize, and store for direct retrieval and use information that previously was captured, organized, and stored by lower-level units. The reduction in levels was also enabled in part by using communication technologies to efficiently connect units needing "soft" information or up-to-date situational information with the units possessing such information. The *second* change we noted earlier was a process change—the use of communication technology to access the knowledge or views of experts or stakeholders who were not physically present during a decision unit's meeting but whose knowledge or views were needed during the meeting.

These and other uses of IT to enhance decision processes are so familiar that many might wonder whether IT can lead to any further changes in processes or structures. People, seeing so much change, have a hard time imaging more. To the contrary, however, it is highly probable that we do not now foresee certain advances in IT that will appear and be adopted and applied by future decision makers. Such has been the path of science and technology throughout the ages. Here, however, to achieve the benefits of parsimony, we will consider only the effects of some improvements in IT that are at hand or on the near horizon and that will be useful or otherwise appealing to decision makers.

Whether the decision processes and structures of future firms will be different as a result of their employing more advanced IT depends on the answers to two questions:

1. Will future circumstances motivate firms to invest in more IT support for their decision makers?

2. What would be the effects on decision processes or structures if forthcoming IT features were adopted?

It will be convenient to address the questions together.

---

[h]Let us use "communication technologies" to refer to "computer-assisted communication technologies" or "computer-mediated communication technologies" (e.g., electronic mail, image transmission devices, and videoconferencing), use "decision technologies" to refer to "computer-assisted decision-aiding technologies" (e.g., expert systems, decision-support systems, online management information systems, and external information retrieval systems), and use "information technologies" or "IT" to refer collectively to "communication technologies" and "decision technologies."

IT INVESTMENTS FOR ANALYSIS

As we saw earlier, future circumstances will motivate firms to more actively support their decision makers. That is, business environments will be more dynamic, complex, and competitive and, in order to survive in these environments, firms will be forced to make decisions more rapidly and yet with greater vigilance. That's the easy part. Now, is IT relevant to these circumstances? Yes, it is. Experience has already shown that—in many situations at least—even twentieth-century IT enabled decision makers and their advisers to communicate more readily, to access required information more quickly, and to analyze this information more swiftly and yet more thoroughly, and thus to make decisions more rapidly and yet with greater vigilance.[9]

What circumstances would lead firms already fully using IT in support of their decision makers to invest in more IT to provide even more support? *One* would be the availability of decision-aiding IT that would help such firms further increase the scope of important issues and options they could consider without simultaneously sacrificing speed. Two such technologies are currently available and are continuously being improved.

The more common of the two combines *data collection* and *data mining*. Current technologies enable firms to collect and store immense amounts of detailed information about the flows, costs, and durations of even their most minute operations. Analyses of these data lead to finely tuned decisions about staffing, production, and distribution, thus leading to operational efficiencies and economic insights impossible without the information and the computing power to analyze it nearly instantaneously. Other technologies enable firms to collect or purchase huge amounts of information about the actions and attributes of current or potential customers, suppliers, competitors and other relevant entities. Firms can then analyze this data to "discover" previously unknown relationships or to answer important business questions about who? when? where? what? and how much?[10]

Looking to the future, we can expect the combination of (1) advances in IT capabilities and (2) the competition-driven need for decision-related information to lead to the availability of useful data of greater scope and specificity. These conditions, along with advances in the data-processing speed of individual computer chips *or* supercomputers *or* networked computers will enable firms in the future to make such discoveries or to develop better answers to these questions more cheaply and more rapidly. Very few firms exploit such technology to the degree possible. Those that exploit it significantly less than their competitors in the more competitive business environment of the future will not survive.

Data collection and data mining, which together are sometimes referred to as *business intelligence,* have long histories in some companies. But as the competitiveness of the business environment increases, as the cost of the hardware and software declines, and as the proportion of managers who are skilled at exploiting the technology grows, we can expect to see much more widespread use of this tool. Early in the 2000s, its use was sufficiently uncommon that expanded use merited coverage in the business press. For example, an article in *Fortune* first noted that "industrial giants like GE and Procter & Gamble have been slicing and dicing their statistical data for decades; now pharmaceutical manufacturers, retailers, universities, and other institutions are demanding the software" (*Fortune*, 2003: 114+) and then went on to describe applications by retailers as diverse as Ben & Jerry's, Red Robin Gourmet Burgers, Lands' End, and Staples.

The second technology that can increase the scope of issues and options considered, without sacrificing speed, is very closely related to the first—the main difference being the kinds of questions asked and the level of computing power required to answer them. This technology, *computer simulation,* also benefits from the above-mentioned advances in the development of mammoth databases and from advances in the speed with which data inventories can be analyzed.

Computer simulations enable decision makers or their support staff to carry out huge numbers of "experiments" with either real or hypothetical data and to analyze huge numbers of combinations of such experiments. The news that

a severe drought that began in the Great Plains is engulfing the Midwest this winter, snarling the Mississippi River, crippling snow dependent businesses and increasing the likelihood of poor crops (*Wall Street Journal,* January 22, 2003: p. A1)

had major implications for the operations and pricing decisions of cost-sensitive businesses in agriculture, in the food industry, and in transportation. Simulations enable firms to answer questions such as "What will be the possible cost distributions of rail transportation between Minneapolis and Dallas on each day next summer, given the forecasted probability distributions for the germane regions and time periods of (1) the temperature and rainfall and their effects on crop shipments and (2) large-cube and small-cube manufacturing activity in the Midwest?" When used by business organizations, typical outcomes of computer simulations are probability distributions of sales or costs. Typical input data are possible marketing plans, the probability distributions of weather patterns, interest rates, and so forth, and possible actions of the firm's competitors or regulators. As before, ongoing reductions in the costs of acquiring information and of owning or leasing the speed to process it will enable firms in the future to develop better answers to specific questions of the form "What would be the consequences of choosing this action?" more cheaply and more rapidly.

Data acquisition, data mining, and data exploitation using computer simulations and other analyses are, of course, now used to some degree by many firms. As time passes, consulting firms, IT vendors, and new BBA, MBA, and IT graduates will educate more firms and their decision makers about the benefits of employing ever more advanced IT to address ever more challenging business questions. There seems to be no reason to believe that these diffusion mechanisms will become any less effective. Of course they might be replaced by more effective mechanisms, in which case the diffusion would be accelerated. Consequently, as the environmentally driven need to make decisions more rapidly yet more vigilantly continues to grow, it seems reasonable to expect these decision-supporting applications of IT to continue to grow, both the data-capturing applications and the data-processing applications.

From the above discussion, it seems reasonable to conclude that, to deal with environments requiring more decisions to be made with greater vigilance and yet with no loss of timeliness, *future firms will invest more heavily in IT to provide analytic support for their decision makers.*

What will be the effects on decision processes if firms invest more heavily in decision-supporting IT? The answer is that the processes will be broader in scope (i.e., will be more attuned to vigilance) because decision makers will have easier access to decision-relevant facts and to the probable consequences of choosing various actions. Further, due to the speed with which the technologies can access and analyze information, the review of critical facts or the search for superior options will be achieved with very little or no increase in the time to make a decision.

IT INVESTMENTS FOR COMMUNICATION

A *second* circumstance that would lead firms to support their decision makers with more IT would be the availability of communication technology having features that make its use more satisfying and less off-putting to decision makers, and thus more attractive and more frequently used. Availability of such technology seems especially important given the ever-increasing dispersion of decision makers and their advisers and informants. What features would make the use of a communication technology more attractive?

Telepresence is one such a feature. Telepresence is the technology user's assessment of "being there," the sense of being in the physical and social situation that the user has accessed via the technology. The effectiveness of a technology in creating a sense of telepresence is generally greater when (1) the technology provides real-time signals (and thus provides for immediate feedback) and (2) when it exhibits sensory *breadth* and *depth*. *Breadth* refers to the number of the senses that the technology accesses simultaneously. For example, currently available videoconferencing technologies access two senses while currently available teleconferencing technologies access only one. *Depth* refers to the realness of the technology to each sense. For example, a videoconferencing technology with clear images, true color, and high levels of sound fidelity is more effective in creating a sense of telepresence than is a technology with lower levels of realness for sight and hearing.

> Communication technologies that provide high levels of telepresence also provide high levels of *social presence* and *media richness*. With this in mind, in this discussion I mean for social presence and media richness to be subsumed under telepresence.[11]

The importance of telepresence is that it is a significant determinant of the satisfaction of both senders and receivers when the sender's strength of feeling about the message is important or when a sense of social ease is likely to lead to more open communication. Such sensitive conditions characterize a large proportion of important business-decision situations.

Technologies high in telepresence are believed to enhance communication clarity in sensitive communication situations.[12] It seems, then, that having at their disposal technologies that provide high levels of telepresence would appeal to business decision makers, and that firms would provide these technologies if they were available at a reasonable cost. The conclusions of Chapter 2 indicate that we can expect continuing cost reductions in these technologies.

A second feature that would make communication (and decision-aiding) technologies more attractive and used more frequently would be advances in their ease of use and overall *user friendliness*. Managers crave features that will ease and shorten startup and shutdown tasks, shorten the time to learn how to use the technology, reduce the need for technical support, and provide more user-friendly human-machine interfaces. It seems likely that advances in materials science, miniaturization, and human engineering will contribute to the availability of these features and to the attractiveness of the technologies that incorporate them.

Given the increased telepresence and user friendliness that we can expect in future communication technologies, it also seems reasonable to conclude that, *in future firms, (1) more experts and stakeholders will access and be accessed by decision makers, but at the same time (2) fewer experts and stakeholders will be physically present at decision meetings or will be formal members of decision units, and (3) more decisions will be influenced and made by people distributed in time and/or space.*[13]

A consequence of effects (1) and (3) is that decision units will be informed more broadly and more deeply and therefore will be more likely to consider a broader range of alternatives and issues. That is, they will be more vigilant. At the same time, however, the informing messages will encounter fewer of the delays that have historically occurred because the communicating parties were separated in time or space. The overall effect, then, of increased investment in IT is that decision processes will be of a more vigilant nature, and yet will not be less rapid.

INTERIM SUMMARY AND TRANSITION

Earlier we *tentatively* concluded that future firms will more frequently employ vigilant decision processes. Our reasoning was that (1) vigilant processes tend to lead to more satisfactory outcomes than do nonvigilant processes and (2) future firms will face more complicated decision situations, situations that demand vigilant decision processes. Our hesitancy to draw a stronger conclusion followed from our acknowledging the possibility that vigilant processes might not satisfy the need for more speed. But subsequently we saw that some aspects of vigilant decision processes actually speed decision making. We then noted three additional decision-related practices that will simultaneously contribute to both scope and speed and that we can expect to see in future firms. *One* was making a specific manager explicitly accountable for managing the decision process. The *second* was encouraging the use of project-management thinking. The *third* was the adoption and use of more decision-aiding IT. Each of these practices, by contributing to decision speed, makes the use of vigilant processes more viable. It seems reasonable then, given the need for processes well matched to the more complicated nature of many future decision situations, to believe that *future firms will more frequently employ vigilant decision processes.* This is not to say that future firms will never trade vigilance for speed. Rather it is to say that they will do so to a lesser extent than do today's firms—because using the three decision-related practices just noted will enable them to carry out vigilant practices more rapidly.

That these three practices enable vigilant processes to be effectuated more quickly—combined with the fact that *not taking a decision until it must be taken can allow relevant events to unfold and the decision situation to become clearer*—suggests that, in the future more so than today, decision units holding tentative decisions could more rationally delay their final decision until further delay would entail prohibitive risk or be prohibitively costly. While some units might, on occasion, act in this way, two forces will cause such action to be uncommon, even rare. One is the tension people feel when they have unresolved issues. This is the force that often causes decision units to use nonvigilant processes. This tension will, as it has in the past, dispose decision makers to seek closure rather than wait for information that might bring greater clarity. The second force that will work against deliberate delay is the pressure brought to bear on the deciding unit by other units that stand to gain from having the tentative choice be the final choice or that need a final decision so they can begin their tasks that depend on knowing what the choice will be.

In this section we've examined four decision-related practices that will characterize future firms: (1) more frequently employing vigilant decision processes, (2) assigning to a specific manager formal responsibility for getting a decision made by a specified date, (3) managing decisions as projects, and (4) employing more advanced IT in support of decision makers. Adopting these progressive practices will not be easy; certainly today's firms seldom explicitly address the question of how to decide how to decide. The increased competitiveness of future business environments will not permit such a casual approach, however.

Firms are more likely to perform well and survive if their managers make better decisions. And it seems that employing more vigilant processes and managing decisions as projects would contribute to making better decisions. So we would expect performance-seeking *firms* to seek adoption of these practices. But will future *managers* be inclined to adopt them? Won't the press of work in tomorrow's more dynamic decision-requiring environment tempt future managers to use shortcut methods at least as frequently as do today's managers? Let us turn to this question.

Tempting Practices and Firms' Responses

Let us again seek some illumination from Chester Barnard's observation that

> the making of decisions, as everyone knows from personal experience, is a
> burdensome task. . . . Accordingly, it will be observed that men generally try to
> avoid making decisions, beyond a limited degree when they are rather uncritical
> responses to conditions.[i] (Barnard, 1938: 189)

Every manager has encountered instances where someone (perhaps even himself or herself) has avoided making a decision, avoided making a commitment to allocate or not allocate resources. But is decision avoidance really commonplace, even among managers? Barnard's statement that "men" (by which Barnard meant especially managers, and today would be referring to women managers as well) are disinclined to make decisions seems much less likely to be valid today than it was when Barnard expressed it. Barnard's views were developed in a more authoritarian and status-sensitive era (the first half of the twentieth century). People then were more conditioned through their experiences and more led by the culture of the times to expect direction from those of higher status or rank. According to Lyndall Urwick, a highly regarded management historian, Barnard was a very progressive thinker and "was among the first to emphasize . . . the functional and dysfunctional aspects of status systems" (Urwick, 1984: 373). Given the era in which he managed, it seems likely that Barnard was often frustrated when, as an executive, he tried to get subordinates to think for themselves.

Times have changed. People are less inclined than were people in earlier times to let others think for them. In particular, the more dynamic environments of today's businesses have forced more decisions to be made, and have consequently caused managers at all levels to require their subordinates to make some of these decisions. Flatter organizational structures and broader spans of management, too, have forced subordinates to make more decisions themselves, rather than to try to compete for the boss's time. Altogether, these changed conditions have caused managers not to avoid making decisions, but rather to avoid taking (much) time to make decisions.

Today many managers would say, and probably Barnard would say,

> the time for making decisions, as everyone knows from personal experience, is
> difficult to find. . . . Accordingly, it will be observed that managers generally try to
> avoid using much time when making decisions.

---

[i]This tendency to avoid mental exertion has been remarked upon by other keen observers as well. Hear James Bryce, oft-quoted British historian, statesman, and diplomat: "To the vast majority of mankind, nothing is more agreeable than to escape the need for mental exertion. . . . To most people nothing is more troublesome than the effort of thinking" (Bryce, 1901: 7).

The daily work life of managers is hectic and often causes managers not to take the time to think deeply about decision situations. Henry Mintzberg received the McKinsey Award for making this fact so sharply clear in his award-winning 1975 *Harvard Business Review* article. Janis observed the same phenomena, noting that many of the managers he interviewed in his research and consulting

> explain that they are appallingly busy keeping their offices running, carrying out all sorts of daily routine chores, meeting regular deadlines for budget estimates, and putting out all sorts of little as well as big fires that are smoldering and raging concurrently. So when it comes time for making a decision . . . they feel that very little of their time and energy can be devoted to searching for the pertinent information and deliberating about the pros and cons of alternative courses of action. (Janis, 1989: 34)

Of the changes that have occurred in managerial working conditions since Mintzberg and Janis made their observations, one of the most significant is that the pace has quickened. Due to the greater rate with which problems and opportunities appear, there is more to do and less time to do it. How do managers avoid spending much time making decisions? Will tomorrow's managers do differently?

INTUITIVE DECISION MAKING

Many managers claim to use intuition when making some decisions. While intuitive decisions are always made quickly, on other dimensions they vary considerably. Some are of very poor quality. What conditions lead to high-quality intuitive decisions?

Intuitive decisions were studied intensively during the 1960s through the 1980s. One of the most active and respected researchers was Nobel laureate Herbert Simon, whose thinking we encountered earlier and whose appointments at Carnegie-Mellon University included positions in computer science, psychology, and the Graduate School of Industrial Administration.

> In simultaneous play, the professional (chess player) takes much less than a minute, often only a few seconds, for each move. . . . When we ask the grandmaster or master how he or she is able to find good moves under these circumstances, we get the same answer that we get from other professionals who are questioned about rapid decisions: It is done by "intuition," by applying one's professional "judgment" to the situation. A few seconds' glance at the position suggests a good move, although the player has no awareness of how the judgment was evoked. (Simon, 1987: 59)

Scientists have shown that intuitive decision making is a matter of subconscious pattern matching. What is matched is (1) a situation that the expert has seen so many times in the past that he or she holds it in memory as a "chunk," with (2) a solution that the expert has found many times in the past to be well suited to such a chunk. This association between the situation and the solution has been made so many times that the expert has forgotten, and so cannot describe, the connecting logic.

> From . . . research on expert problem solving and decision making, we can draw two main conclusions. *First,* experts often arrive at problem diagnoses and solutions rapidly and intuitively without being able to report how they attained the result. *Second,* this ability is best explained by postulating a recognition and retrieval process that employs a large number—generally *tens of thousands or even hundreds of thousands* of chunks or patterns stored in long term memory. [Italics are mine.] (Simon, 1987: 61)

> Some direct evidence also suggests that the intuitive skills of managers depend on the same kinds of mechanisms as the intuitive skills of chess masters or physicians. It would be surprising if it were otherwise. The experienced manager, too, has in his or her memory a large amount of knowledge, gained from training and experience and organized in terms of recognizable chunks and associated information. (Simon, 1987: 61)

> Organizational decision makers possess a cultural repertoire of possible schemas for the problems and opportunities that have been encountered in the past. . . . Decision makers also possess a cultural repertoire of answers or action alternatives that can deal with a wide variety of issues, problems, and opportunities in the firm. (Ocasio, 1997: 194)

So, an intuitive decision would be one made when a manager (1) encounters a situation he or she has seen a great many times—so many times that it has been stored in memory as a "chunk," (2) subconsciously evokes a solution found a great many times in the past to be well suited to the chunk, and (3) "chooses" the evoked solution because it matches the chunk.

From this description it seems likely that truly intuitive decisions would be uncommon in future firms. That is, while it may be that many decades ago managerial environments were so slow-changing that identical or nearly identical decision situations arose again and again, and were well resolved with the same solutions again and again (such that a subconscious association between the situation and the solution developed), in tomorrow's faster-changing world these conditions will not exist. Decision situations will more often be novel, so chunks that match the situation will be scarcer, and solutions that are still well suited to chunks that evolved in times past will also be scarcer. As a result of these conditions, *in future firms, truly intuitive decision making will be rare.*

In most instances, what managers really mean when they say that they made an intuitive decision is that they made a quick decision using professional judgment.[14] Using professional judgment is good. Who would say otherwise? (Careful examination of Figure 4.1 shows that professional judgment is required in *every* step of Janis's vigilant decision-making process.)

If future conditions will seldom allow a truly intuitive decision process, what processes will enable managers to make decisions with little effort, as anticipated by Barnard, but at the same time will enable them to draw on their professional judgment? There are two, both well-known, *satisficing* and *analogizing*.

SATISFICING AND ANALOGIZING

Satisficing is probably the most common approach to decision making. As contrasted with attempting to identify multiple solutions and then attempting to choose the best of the lot, satisficing means accepting the first of the alternative solutions that meets the minimum requirements of the situation. Often the search for alternatives is simply a mental search, a search of the mind rather than of the environment. Further, the "search" is often subconscious—what is "found" is what spontaneously surfaces when the decision situation is considered.

Satisficing is a very attractive approach in that, by eliminating much of the search for alternatives, (1) it more quickly reduces the tension level of the manager who owns the problem or opportunity and (2) it permits the manager to move on to other tasks. Of course, it also generally leads to lower-quality decision outcomes than would be obtained from more complete searches. Satisficing exemplifies two pervasive human tendencies, tendencies certainly not limited to managers. Specifically, research and experience show that when making decisions, people give more weight than they should, and even more weight than they intend, to *short-term considerations* and to *sure outcomes*. Thus managers are prone to act as if the *quick* and *certain* "sense of relief" that they know they will feel immediately from having "dealt with the situation" is of more value than is the *possibly* more favorable outcome that *might* accrue to the firm if a more thorough search for solutions had been made.

Analogizing occurs when a manager (often subconsciously) searches his or her memory for an analogy to the current decision situation, and acts in accord with the thinking or action that was applied in the analogous situation. For example, if a previous price cut by a competitor was the first step in an all-out price war, then analogizing would result in a manager responding to a new price cut by preparing for a price war, perhaps by preemptively and deeply cutting prices on related products, or undertaking even more drastic actions. Of course the current price cut could be an attempt by the competitor simply to lower inventory or to better position another product in the competitor's portfolio of products, in which case the responses above would be entirely inappropriate. Analogizing has the same attractions as does satisficing—by resolving the problem situation it reduces tension and frees time.

When decision makers "search" for satisficing solutions or for analogies, they usually "find" what is most readily available in their memory. What is most readily available is unfortunately greatly influenced by the strength of the emotions or the vividness of the circumstances surrounding the earlier storage in memory of the solution or analogous situation. As a consequence, the goodness of fit of the satisficing solution or the analogy to the decision situation is often quite poor.[15]

Will managers in future firms use satisficing and analogizing proportionately more, or less, than do managers in today's firms? That is, will the proportion of organizational decisions made using these shortcut methods increase or decrease relative to the proportion made using more vigilant approaches? On the one hand, research confirms the commonsense notion that firms using more vigilant decision processes tend to outperform those using less vigilant processes (see Endnote 4). And earlier we concluded that "future firms will more frequently employ vigilant decision processes." However, *that problems and opportunities will arrive with increasing velocity will be a strong motivator for future managers to use the shortcut methods of satisficing and analogizing.*

The benefits of additional vigilance accrue principally to the firm, generally after a lapse of time. In contrast, the costs of additional effort required to apply the vigilant approach accrue principally to the manager in charge of making the decision, and accrue in real time. In combination, these facts constitute one explanation for why managers use shortcut methods.

Future firms will have a greater need for their decision makers to use vigilant decision processes, but their decision makers will, at the same time, have greater motivation to use shortcut methods. The next section describes approaches firms will employ to address the discrepancy between the firm's needs and the propensities of its decision makers.

FIRMS' RESPONSES TO PERSONAL PROPENSITIES TO USE SHORTCUT METHODS

Many managers would agree that, given the more complex, dynamic, and competitive nature of future business environments, the use of the progressive practices described earlier—especially vigilance-enhancing processes—would be likely *in firms where members adhere to a cultural norm of cooperation in attaining organizational goals.* But many others would argue that use of these progressive practices is unlikely in firms that are highly politicized or burdened with recalcitrant managers. In this regard, let me offer three observations.

The *first* is that the increased competitiveness of future business environments will force firms to adopt and use practices that lead to more appropriate decisions. As margins and profits are squeezed, the need to more optimally allocate resources becomes more critical. If organizational politics or personal preferences interfere with a firm's making effective decisions, these more competitive environments will select the firm out, and it won't be around to be counted as a future firm. This has implications for managers—*in the future, firms will more frequently direct their managers to use more vigilant decision-making processes.*

The *second* observation is that firms must often induce managers to undertake the actions that firms seek. For example, they must deal with managers' understandable propensities to use shortcut decision procedures. It seems reasonable to conclude, therefore, that *in future firms, appraisal and compensation systems and promotion reviews will more heavily weigh managers' choice and management of decision processes.*

As an example of what we might see when organizations require their managers to adopt more appropriate decision-making processes, consider the adoption in the past of "new" information technologies. In its era, the telegraph became a pervasive technology in railroads, as did—in their eras—the calculator in brokerage houses and the radio in armies. If organizations did not adopt these technologies, they could not survive. Recalcitrant managers whose inclinations caused them not to use these technologies in performance of their tasks (such as timely delivery of freight, accurate and comprehensive information for investors, or effective coordination in battle) were converted or purged. Organizations necessarily require that their managers help them compete. If extensive use of vigilant decision processes is necessary to compete successfully, firms will act to ensure that this use occurs, whatever the personal inclinations of individual managers.

The *third* observation is that, by their nature, highly politicized firms are internally highly competitive. Under these conditions, for managers to acquire resources, they must propose actions or projects that satisfy the personal goals of resource controllers. Technical or financial analyses are widely used to persuade resource controllers that the manager's proposals best satisfy the resource controller's goal—credible analyses are weapons in intrafirm battles for resources. Even in firms where power and politics play a significant role in resource allocation, and they do pervasively, so also do analyses.[16]

These last two observations together suggest that, in order to advance their own interests, *in the future, managers will more frequently use more vigilant decision-making processes.*

Chapter Summary and Transition

The complex and dynamic nature of the forthcoming business environments will cause the firm's problems and opportunities to be more complicated and to arrive at an increasingly rapid rate. These conditions, along with heightened competition, will force future firms to make decisions more frequently and more rapidly, and yet to attend to scope (in keeping with the more complicated nature of future decision situations). Accordingly, future firms will ensure that their decision units are more numerous or faster acting, and that they have or can readily obtain the information necessary to make appropriate choices. They will necessarily direct more effort toward selecting, developing, and supporting decision makers.

In particular, we noted that future firms will be those that tend to enhance their decision-making resources through

1. selecting and promoting managers who are able and inclined to employ progressive decision-making practices,

2. developing the decision skills of their managers, particularly by educating their managers about progressive decision practices and when to use them, and

3. using review and reward systems that explicitly weigh the appropriateness of their managers' decision processes.

Enhancing their decision-making resources will help firms deal with their need to make decisions more rapidly and yet with greater vigilance. Beyond this, however, we concluded that future firms will, to a much greater extent than have firms in the past, (1) employ vigilant decision processes, (2) assign to a specific manager formal responsibility for getting a decision made by a specified date, (3) manage decisions as projects, and (4) employ IT in support of their decision makers.

Because of the increased competitiveness both in the business environment and within firms, some decision-making practices historically in common use will be used, relatively speaking, less frequently in future firms. Among these are truly intuitive decision making, satisficing, and analogizing.

The decision-related organizational attributes and management practices described in the chapter as characterizing future firms are more congruent with the complexity, dynamism, and competitiveness of future business environments than are the decision-related features and practices observed in firms today. Firms that do not adopt these attributes and practices will be less well suited to the future. They will be more prone to the misallocation of resources, or to the tardy allocation of resources. They will be at a competitive disadvantage. They will not survive. Adopting the decision-enhancing characteristics described here will not guarantee survival, but—due to the greater and increasing levels of complexity, dynamism, and competitiveness that will characterize future business environments—only firms that possess these characteristics will survive as future firms.

Future firms will have to cope more frequently with threats and opportunities, but a particular environmental challenge will occupy their attention on an ongoing and everyday basis—the need to innovate. Customers want the best quality, the best service, or the best value. To survive, firms must provide one or more of these best-of-class product features on a nearly continuous basis. As we saw in Chapter 2, advances in technology eventually cause any level of quality, service, or value to become outmoded. Thus firms must *innovate*—they must make changes in their products or processes so that at least some portion of the market sees their products as best-of-class. But innovation requires new knowledge (or a new way of combining current knowledge) and new knowledge (or a new way of combining current knowledge) requires learning. Altogether, these ideas and the earlier observation that tomorrow's business environments will be more dynamic and more competitive than are today's, form the motivation for Chapter 5—that to survive, future firms will learn more effectively than do today's.

Endnotes

1. In their classic study, D. Dearborn and H. A. Simon, "Selective Perceptions: A Note on the Departmental Identification of Executives," 1958, concluded that managers possessed perceptual biases, biases that seemed to be associated with the managers' functional responsibilities (and presumably with their functional backgrounds). This conclusion was widely accepted as reflecting current reality, and the matter was apparently not addressed again by organizational scientists for many years. To the contrary, the Dearborn and Simon study was used in hundreds of articles to support the authors' contention that functionally related perceptual biases were pervasive and affected even top management decisions. An important point seemed to go unrecognized—the work experience of the managers studied by Dearborn and Simon occurred in an era when job rotation and business education were uncommon. Subsequent studies by A. Kefalas and P. P. Schoderbek, "Scanning the Business Environment—Some Empirical Results," 1973; and J. Walsh, "Selectivity and Selective Perception: An Investigation of Managers' Belief Structures and Information Processing," 1988, addressed similar (but not identical) issues. Their findings are not easily interpreted as supportive of the Dearborn and Simon conclusion, but neither are they contradictory. A study by N. P. Melone,

"Reasoning in the Executive Suite: The Influence of Role/Experience-Based Expertise on Decision Processes of Corporate Executives," 1994, comparing the reasoning of CFOs and VPs of corporate development, as they made judgments about possible acquisitions, found evidence that the current positions influenced the attention paid to different data but had little effect on overall reasoning. In addition, these executives recognized their functional bias. A recent study by P. Chattopadhyay, W. H. Glick, C. C. Miller, and G. P. Huber, "Determinants of Executive Beliefs: Comparing Functional Conditioning and Social Influence," 1999, found hardly any evidence of a functionally related bias among members of top management teams, and another recent study, by M. Waller, G. P. Huber, and W. H. Glick, "Functional Background as a Determinant of Executives' Selective Perception," 1995, found that CEOs demonstrated no bias related to their primary functional background. I suspect that these later results are primarily the consequence of functionally broadening experiences, such as cross-functional assignments and formal business management education. While this apparent correlation across time, between an increase in functionally broadening experiences for managers and a decline in research support for the idea that managers' views are biased by their current or primary functional background, *is not proof* that such experiences broaden managers' knowledge bases and thereby their perspectives, it is certainly congruent with the logic that drives the widespread use of these experiences and related broadening practices.

2. These data are, respectively, from the Association to Advance Collegiate Schools of Business, 2001, "Number of Undergraduate and Master's Business Degrees Awarded Is on the Upswing; Doctoral Degrees Continue to Decline"; Newsline (Winter 2001), www.aacsb.edu/publications/printnewsline/NL2001/wndoestats.asp; from personal correspondence with the executive director of the Executive MBA Council in Atlanta, GA; from data provided by the Kennedy Information Research Group and published in "DataWatch Consulting by Numbers," *Consulting,* February 2002: 52-53; and from Table 4.1. of "Selected Business and Professional Services," *Official Statistics* (U.S. Census Bureau, 1998); and Current Business Reports SAS/00, Service Annual Survey: 2000 (U.S. Census Bureau). All indicators from the Executive MBA Council point to an accelerating growth in executive MBA programs: (1) In terms of number of programs, the average rate is an increase of 4.7 programs a year between 1963 and 2002, but it actually started at about 2 programs a year, and increased at an increasing rate. (2) In terms of cost, the average rate is an increase of $202,633 a year between 1963 and 2002, but it actually started at about $73,196 a year, and increased at an increasing rate. (3) In terms of revenue, the average rate is an increase of $9,320,472 a year between 1963 and 2002, but it actually started at about $4,789,526 a year, and increased at an increasing rate. (4) In terms of class size, the average rate is an increase of 196 heads a year between 1963 and 2002, but it actually started at about 78 heads a year, and increased at an increasing rate. See also www.usatoday.com/. . .ber/tech/2002/04/30/online-training.htm

3. For an extensive review of what firms can do to overcome the cognitive biases of their decision makers, see C. Heath, R. P. Larrick, and J. Klayman, "Cognitive Repairs: How Organizational Practices Can Compensate for Individual Shortcomings," 1998. For a very readable and yet soundly based tutorial on what individual managers can do to improve their decision making, see J. E. Russo and P. J. H. Shoemaker, *Decision Traps,* 1989.

4. Examples of field research demonstrating connections among the comprehensiveness of decision processes and key outcomes such as strategic consensus, the quality of decision outcomes, and firm performance are A. C. Amason, "Distinguishing the Effects of Functional and Dysfunctional Conflict on Strategic Decision Making: Resolving a Paradox for Top Management Teams," 1996; J. W. Dean and M. P. Sharfman, "Does Decision Process Matter? A Study of Strategic Decision-Making Effectiveness," 1996; K. M. Eisenhardt, "Making Fast Strategic Decisions in High-Velocity Environments," 1989; I. Goll and A. M. A. Rasheed, "Rational Decision-Making and Firm Performance: The Moderating Role of Environment," 1997; A. L. Iaquinto and J. W. Fredrickson, "Top Management Team Agreement About the Strategic Decision Process: A Test of Some of Its Determinants and Consequences," 1997; and D. Knight et al., "Top Management Team Diversity, Group Process, and Strategic Consensus," 1999.

5. See K. M. Eisenhardt, "Speed and Strategic Choice: How Managers Accelerate Decision Making," 1990. Also see K. M. Eisenhardt, "Making Fast Strategic Decisions in High-Velocity Environments," 1989, and "Strategy as Strategic Decision Making," 1999; and W. Q. Judge and A. Miller, "Antecedents and Outcomes of Decision Speed in Different Environmental Contexts," 1991. The relationship between a firm's use of vigilant decision processes and its performance seems to be dependent on the context in nonintuitive ways. For example, in their study of decision making in 645 large manufacturing firms in the United States, Goll and Rasheed (1997) found that the relationship between the "rationality" or vigilance of decision processes and firm performance was much stronger for firms in environments that were *more munificent* and *more dynamic.* Casual speculation might well have led to different predictions.

6. Of course assigning accountability and changing behavior are two different matters, as observed in K. M. Sutcliffe and G. McNamara, "Controlling Decision-Making Practice in Organizations," 2001, and implied in D. A. Garvin and M. A. Roberto, "What You Don't Know About Making Decisions," 2001. We will address this issue later in the chapter.

7. This paragraph draws on ideas from G. P. and R. R. McDaniel, "The Decision-Making Paradigm of Organizational Design," 1986.

8. *The Innovation Journey,* 1999, by A. H. Van de Ven, D. Polley, R. Garud, and S. Venkataraman is an excellent field research–based description and analysis of the product innovation process as it really happens, with good coverage of the later stages. An award-winning book with prescriptions for creating radical product innovations in large firms, also based on field research by its authors, is *Radical Innovation,* 2000, by R. Leifer, C. M. McDermott, G. C. O'Connor, L. S. Peters, M. P. Rice, and R. W. Veryzer. A somewhat similar book is Clayton Christensen's well-known *The Innovator's Dilemma: When New Technologies Cause Great Firms to Fail,* 1997. A very readable yet authoritative book on managing product innovation, especially the early stages of the innovation process, is J. C. Huber's *Managing Innovation: Mining for Nuggets,* 2001.

9. For elaboration, see G. P. Huber and C. B. Crisp, "Effects of Information Technologies on Organizations," 2002. For a review and critique of beliefs about effects of communication technology within and between organizations, see S. O'Mahony and S. Barley, "Do Digital Telecommunications Affect Work and Organization?" 1999.

10. For elaboration and examples of these technologies in use, see K. J. Cios, W. Pedrycz, and R. Swiniarski, *Data Mining Methods for Knowledge Discovery,* 1998; W. H. Inmon, *Building the Data Warehouse,* 1996; and S. Kelly, *Data Warehousing in Action,* 1997.

11. J. Steuer, "Defining Virtual Reality: Dimensions Determining Telepresence," 1992, provides an authoritative description and review of telepresence. Its strong effect was manifested in V. Venkatesh and P. Johnson, "Telecommuting Technology Implementations: A Within- and Between-Subjects Longitudinal Field Study," 2002, where the researchers compared "employee acceptance and sustained use of a traditional system design based on the common 'desktop metaphor,' with a virtual-reality system designed to enhance social richness and telepresence. . . . Results showed much higher telecommuter acceptance and use of the virtual-reality system. Strong support emerged for the hypotheses that higher social richness and higher telepresence lead to higher telecommuter motivation and higher sustained use of the system" (Venkatesh & Johnson, 2002: 661).

"Social presence" (J. Short, E. Williams, and B. Christie, *The Social Psychology of Telecommunications,* 1976) is a concept "linked to the nonverbal signals, including facial expression, direction of gaze, posture, dress, physical appearance, proximity, and orientation" (J. Fulk and L. Collins-Jarvis, "Wired Meetings: Technological Mediation of Organizational Gatherings," 2001). Social presence emphasizes a communication medium's usefulness in developing and maintaining interpersonal relationships.

Some scientists who study communication technologies speak of the technologies (or media) as being "rich" or "lean." These handy adjectives describe points on a dimension called *media richness.* The richness of a communication medium depends on two attributes: (1) the speed with which the medium allows feedback from the message receiver to the message sender, and (2) the ability of the medium to convey multiple cues (such as the sender's physical settings, body language, and tone of voice). From (2) comes the ability of the medium to convey emotions and feelings more accurately than do words alone. Face-to-face communication allows maximum values on both of these attributes and serves as a standard against which other media (especially IT-assisted media) are assessed with regard to their richness. A rough media richness ranking—decreasing from face-to-face—is videoconferencing, animated picture phones, teleconferencing or telephones, voice mail, and asynchronous e-mail. (Online interactive e-mail may rank higher than voice mail, depending on the users' needs. It provides faster feedback, but generally conveys feelings or emotions less precisely.)

Media richness is an important consideration in the communications commonly involved in organizational decision making. On the one hand, richer media tend to be more effective for communicating about decision situations where elaborate explanations of proposals or other ideas are necessary, or where multiple meanings can be attributed to "the facts," or where the strength of feeling of key participants is particularly relevant. On the other hand, leaner media are more efficient if the information is necessarily dense (as in tables of figures, complex schematics, or long passages of text), but is otherwise easily interpreted, and if the issues are relatively straightforward. The classic article on media richness is R. L. Daft and R. H. Lengel, "Information Richness: A New Approach to Managerial Behavior and Organization Design," 1984. Subsequent research by Daft and his associates demonstrates that more successful managers are those who wisely choose the medium to fit the communication situation (R. L. Daft, K. R. Bettenhausen, and B. B. Tyler, "Implications of Top Managers' Communication Choices for Strategic Decisions," 1993; R. L. Daft and R. H. Lengel, "Information Richness: A New Approach to Managerial Behavior and Organization Design," 1984; R. L. Daft, R. H. Lengel, and L. Trevino, "Media Symbolism, Media Richness, and Media Choice in Organizations: A Symbolic Interactionist Perspective," 1987).

Important in the choice of communication technology is the familiarity of the participants with each other and the commonality of their backgrounds, cultures, terminologies, and so forth. Research shows that communicators who are familiar with each other and/or have common backgrounds, cultures, terminologies, and so forth, are considerably more effective using lean media than are participants without these advantages (as noted in the reviews by J. Fulk and L. Collins-Jarvis, "Wired Meetings: Technological Mediation of Organizational Gatherings," 2001; and R. E. Rice and U. E. Gattiker, "New Media and Organizational Structuring," 2001).

12. The literature review by J. Fulk and L. Collins-Jarvis, "Wired Meetings: Technological Mediation of Organizational Gatherings," 2001, casts doubt on the contribution of telepresence to the performance of problem-solving groups where performance is measured objectively and where the task does not require the participants to deal with personally sensitive issues. The reviews note, however, that *studies conducted in real-life settings find participants to be invariably more satisfied with media higher in telepresence.*

13. A more complete rationale for these conclusions is provided in G. P. Huber, "Effects of Advanced Information Technologies on Organizational Design, Intelligence, and Decision Making," 1990.

14. For elaboration on this point, see L. Burke and M. Miller, "Taking the Mystery Out of Intuitive Decision Making," 1999.

15. Experience and research indicate that even modest-size databases of readily retrievable, rich descriptions of previously encountered problems and solutions can be of great use to decision makers seeking to draw on analogous decision situations as guides in choosing actions. When a firm's experiences are captured and inventoried in this way, the result is a decision aid that greatly enhances the quality of decision makers' *case-based reasoning.* For elaboration on the nature and use of this IT-facilitated decision aid, see J. Kolodner, *Case-Based Reasoning,* 1993; and C. Riesbeck and R. Schank, *Inside Case-Based Reasoning,* 1989. More on these matters when, in Chapter 6, we discuss managing knowledge.

16. As the reader may have observed, some data gathering and analysis is symbolic and has as its primary purpose creating a favorable impression of the person engaging in these processes. Early and rich elaborations of this practice were provided by P. Sabatier, "The Acquisition and Utilization of Technical Information by Administrative Agencies," 1978; and M. Feldman and J. G. March, "Information in Organizations as Signal and Symbol," 1981.

5

Organizational Learning and Knowledge Acquisition[1]

Organizational learning first claimed recognition as a critical organizational function during the 1990s. No one denies, however, that organizational learning has long been active in influencing organizational survival.

Learning and Survival

Consider American LaFrance, a classic example of an established, market-dominating firm that failed to survive because it failed to learn. In 1985, after 153 years of production, the last fire truck rolled off the quarter-mile-long assembly line at American LaFrance in Elmira, New York. American LaFrance once ruled its marketplace as well as any American company ever dominated a business. Why does a company like American LaFrance fail? What happened that a preeminent organization came to fall so woefully behind its competition that it could not survive?

The answer is Emergency One, then only 11 years old, an upstart manufacturer of fire trucks that tried and succeeded with a technological innovation—making the bodies of fire trucks out of aluminum rather than steel. Because aluminum doesn't corrode and is consequently cheaper in the long run, this change in product design made Emergency One the market leader. Emergency One also revolutionized the assembly process for fire trucks. While American LaFrance took 6 months to manufacture a basic fire truck, using more advanced manufacturing management techniques, Emergency One took one-fourth as long. And while American LaFrance spent a week hand-drafting blueprints for each order, Emergency One learned to do the same thing in a few hours by drawing on a (then) new technology, computer-aided design. Thus Emergency One learned about, and learned how to exploit, both product-relevant technology and process-relevant technology.

Executives directly in charge at LaFrance offered no explanation for its demise. Executives at the conglomerate that had owned LaFrance since 1966 cited LaFrance's dated truck designs, high overhead, and a string of heavy losses. But they missed the basic issue—American LaFrance failed to survive because it failed to learn.[2]

Organizations are failing today exactly as American LaFrance failed—they are failing to learn as fast as their competitors.

What about the future? Is the importance of learning to a firm's survival likely to be any different than its importance today? The answer follows from considering three dependencies:

1. Survival in a dynamic and competitive business environment requires innovation.

2. Innovation requires new knowledge, or a new way of combining current knowledge.

3. New knowledge, or a new way of combining current knowledge, requires learning.

Putting these ideas together and recalling from Chapter 2 that tomorrow's business environments will be more dynamic and more competitive than today's, it follows that, *in the future, a firm's survival will require more learning than in the past.*

Learning, Knowledge, and Innovation

"Organizational learning" is given different meanings by different users of the term. I have treated this technical and somewhat tedious matter elsewhere.[3] Here let us use the term as it is most commonly understood:

Organizational learning occurs when an organization's members revise their beliefs in ways that, when the beliefs are acted upon, improve the organization's performance.

Professor Bo Hedberg of the University of Stockholm, long known as an authority on organizational learning, articulated very early in the development of the organizational learning concept the relationship between individual learning and knowledge on the one hand and organizational learning and knowledge on the other:

Although organizational learning occurs through individuals, it would be a mistake to conclude that organizational learning is nothing but the cumulative result of their members' learning. . . . Members come and go, and leadership changes, but organizations' memories preserve certain behaviors, mental maps, norms and values over time. (Hedberg, 1981: 6)

Let us use "knowledge" broadly to include, for example, information, know-how, and understanding. Further, to avoid the confusion that sometimes arises when "learning" is used as an outcome, let us view "learning" as a *process* and "knowledge" the *outcome* of learning. When the learning (the belief revision) concerns changes in the certainty of facts, we call the result "new information." When the revision concerns changes in beliefs about how something can be done, we call the result "new know-how." When the revision concerns changes in beliefs about the appropriateness of the content and limits of one's mental map or worldview, we call this "new understanding."

Customers want either the best quality, the best service, or the best value. To survive, firms must provide one or more of these best-of-class product features on a nearly continuous basis.[a] As we've seen, advances in technology eventually cause any level of quality, service, or value to become outmoded. Thus firms *innovate*—they make changes in their products or processes so that at least some portion of the market sees their products as best-of-class.

How do firms achieve best-of-class products? There is only one way—they integrate into their products, or into the processes used to provide their products, *knowledge* not previously so used. *All products contain knowledge,* usually a great deal of it. For example, embedded within a service, such as a physician's diagnosis, are thousands of days of learning by the physician, tens of thousands of days of learning by his or her teachers, and hundreds of thousands of days of learning by the scientists who provided the knowledge that the teachers and textbook writers conveyed to the physician. Clearly, services contain knowledge. Likewise, embedded in a product such as an airplane are millions of workdays of knowledge creation and acquisition by scientists, engineers, managers, and skilled workers.

Frequently the value-adding knowledge contained in a firm's products is scientific or technical in nature, such as that employed by a pharmaceutical company when providing a more potent vaccine with fewer side effects. Sometimes it is new marketing knowledge, such as that used to improve advertising or packaging and thereby enhance the visibility or attractiveness of a product. Often it is new knowledge about how to produce or distribute a product (either a good or a service) more reliably, more rapidly, or more cheaply, thereby adding value or permitting a decrease in price.

Putting together the ideas of these three paragraphs, we see what has always been true, but has seldom been articulated—any increases in the performance

---

[a]By product I mean to include both goods and services. Two caveats apply to the statement: (1) Just as beauty is in the eye of the beholder, so also are quality and value in the mind of the customer. As a result, multiple products with only small differences can each be viewed by different buyers as "best" and thus be successful in a single product category. (2) Customer ignorance, inertia, or loyalty sometimes allows firms to maintain a survival-permitting market share during periods when the firm does not offer the best product or service.

or value of a product or class of products can be achieved only by applying knowledge not previously applied in the product's design, production, or marketing.[b] Similarly, any increases in a firm's effectiveness can be achieved only by successfully applying knowledge not previously so applied by the firm.

Like today's firms, future firms will need to innovate—will need to change and improve their products and the processes, structures, and other features that determine their ability to provide best-of-class products. Indeed, given the higher levels of dynamism and competition they will face, future firms will have to innovate more rapidly than today's firms. How will they acquire the new (to them) knowledge needed to do this? How will they learn?

Organizational Learning: A Practice Whose Time Has Come

In 1965, William Dill was IBM's program director of education, research, and development. Vincent Cangelosi was an associate professor in the business school at the University of Texas. Their article, "Organizational Learning: Observations Toward a Theory," published that year, came before its time.[4] In 1965, organizational learning was not the high-fashion topic that it later became. It was not a concept in use by either managers or academics. There was little need for it. Scientific and technical information was being generated at a rate that was only a fraction of what was soon to be the case. For example and as we noted earlier, during the 15 years following Cangelosi and Dill's article, the number of scientific articles published per day rose from 3,000 to 8,000 (Huppes, 1987). Alvin Toffler had not sounded his wake-up calls, *Future Shock, The Third Wave,* and *Power Shift.* GM, Ford, and Chrysler were not worrying about the Honda Accord possibly becoming the best-selling car in the United States—in 1965 Honda didn't make automobiles. There seemed to be little reason to expend valuable resources on learning (except for what we would view today as meager budgets for training and R&D).

More than a third of a century later, things are decidedly different. Organizational learning is receiving a good deal of attention in the business press and management literature. Many firms are seeing it as a function deserving of

---

[b]This conclusion holds in this context of an organization's learning and its use of acquired knowledge. Working in a broader context, however, we would say that any increases in the performance or value of a product or class of products can be achieved only by applying knowledge not previously applied in the product's design, production, marketing, *or use.* That is, we would acknowledge that users can sometimes increase product performance by applying knowledge that they possess.

considerably increased attention. Early organizational actions are just what we would expect—someone is put "in charge" of the organization learning function. So we saw in the 1990s the creation in many firms positions having titles such as Chief Learning Officers (CLOs) and Chief Knowledge Officers (CKOs). In other firms, Chief Information Officers (CIOs) are having organizational learning added to their responsibilities.

Whether these titles and the distinctive organizational units formed to manage learning will endure is uncertain. Either in spite of the importance of organizational learning or because of it, CLOs and CKOs might be out of business when, as will occur in future organizations, the learning activity becomes broadly diffused and incorporated into organizational cultures and practices. Such happened in the 1980s, when the short-lived position of Director of Decision Support Systems became commonplace, served well, and disappeared (as line managers bought desktop computers, hired away the Director's MBAs, and took control of the data). Also in the 1980s, the longer-lived Directors of Operations Research, whose empires were founded in the 1960s, saw their tools and personnel appropriated by line managers wanting faster response and more control. But in their day, these special-function managers and their units created foci and taught practices that are still with us. Because these actions led to line management's adoption of the tools and practices of decision support and operations modeling, the success of these missionaries led to the demise of their titles and units.

Firms in the future are likely to pursue a pattern similar to the above as they actuate organizational learning—i.e., first an awakening and awareness of a new need, then focused responsibility (perhaps in the form of the CLOs and CKOs), then distributed implementations, and finally diffused and generalized responsibility. Whether or not the exact pattern repeats itself in all cases, it is certain that firms will direct significant effort toward increasing the effectiveness and timeliness of organizational learning. Increased environmental complexity, dynamism, and competitiveness, and the accelerating arrival of threats and opportunities reviewed in Chapter 2, will force this. Because threats and opportunities will be generated at an increasing rate, firms will necessarily become increasingly vigilant. This increased vigilance will cause firms to be confronted with information overload, but at the same time the increasing numbers of threats and opportunities will cause firms to need information they do not have. Further, their faster paced and more competitive environments will decrease the likelihood that firms will be able to recover from learning that is belated or incorrect. Thus the effectiveness of their learning processes will influence which firms fail and which firms survive to be counted among the future firms.

Said differently, a necessary feature of future firms will be learning processes more effective than those we see today. The existence and performance of learning processes will not be left to chance. Instead, actions will be taken to ensure that effective processes are in place and active. More actively managed learning processes will, of course, not guarantee survival. But in a more competitive future, where near-continuous improvement is a necessity, not managing learning processes more actively than have firms in the past will guarantee a firm's demise. *The learning processes of future firms will be more actively managed.*

What will be the nature of the learning-related structures and practices that will characterize future firms more than they characterize today's? This chapter is directed at answering this question.

Managerial and academic writings show that three learning modes encompass most activities that might be regarded as organizational learning. Each is familiar to us, either from our personal observation or from our acquaintance with the experiences of others. The three modes are not mutually exclusive in either definition or practice, but treating them separately is useful for expository purposes.

Learning from experience, *experiential learning*, is a form of first-hand learning. In contrast, organizations also learn by acquiring knowledge from others, as when they rent or hire outside experts with specialized knowledge or engage in technology-exchanging alliances. This process of learning what others have learned is called *vicarious learning*. The third learning mode, *intelligence gathering*, is also a form of first-hand learning. Having discussed intelligence gathering in some depth in Chapter 3, we need not examine it again. Experiential learning and vicarious learning are examined in this chapter. We begin with experiential learning.

Learning From Experience

The increased complexity of future business environments, combined with the faster arriving penalties for poor decisions, will cause firms without adequate decision-relevant knowledge to fail more frequently and more quickly. The most useful knowledge for a decision situation is often the product of the firm's own experience, as when the choice among marketing strategies is informed by the firm's experience with different strategies for its particular products and market competition. Hence we can expect future firms to attempt to learn more effectively from their experiences than do today's firms. How will they do this? The next sections describe four approaches to experiential learning that future firms will employ more intensively than did their predecessors.

HIGHLY EFFECTIVE LEARNING
EXPERIENCES: DESIGNED EXPERIMENTS

Designed experiments—such as those commonplace in research and development practices, in the test marketing of new consumer products, and in the management of product quality—are particularly fruitful learning experiences. Due to the forethought involved in planning them, the diagnostic value of the information obtained is usually high. More generally, because experiments are specifically designed to eliminate or greatly reduce the uncertainties and ambiguities that might interfere with correctly determining cause-effect relationships, the results of designed experiments tend to be interpretable and therefore contribute to fast, correct learning.[c]

In spite of these positive features, designed experiments—other than those that are routinely employed in an industry—are only infrequently authorized. In some cases this is because key managers are concerned that the research results might not favor their personal agendas. (I once heard a university president—one well schooled in social science research methods—say, *in his capacity as president,* "I never authorize a survey unless I know what the results will be.") Another reason designed experiments are seldom authorized is that managers' need to project an image of confidence and decisiveness sometimes causes them not to admit to the uncertainty that would justify an experiment. So in the past, and even today, we see a trade-off, and sometimes a standoff, between the need for diagnostic, decision-aiding learning on the one hand and the reality of organizational politics and image management on the other.

What will be the case in the future, with respect to the use of designed experiments as learning tools? Will rationality (as defined by an outside observer) become more prevalent, or will politics and image management maintain their place? In support of the idea that designed experiments will be more commonly used in the future is the following reasoning. Although the suboptimal decisions associated with personal agendas are tolerable in benign environments, or when the organization has a large reserve of slack resources, these conditions will be infrequent in the future. To the contrary, the future environments of business organizations will be more competitive and thus more demanding of rational decisions than are today's environments. The usefulness of objective and diagnostic information will consequently be greater, and designed experiments—because they tend to provide such information—will consequently be used more often. It seems reasonable, then, to expect that *future firms will use designed experiments more frequently than do today's firms.*

---

[c]For a very readable elaboration and an interesting acknowledgment of the value of research, see the *Harvard Business Review* article, "Boost Your Marketing ROI With Experimental Design" (Almquist & Wyner, 2001).

HIGHLY EFFECTIVE LEARNING
EXPERIENCES: NATURAL EXPERIMENTS

Another approach to effective learning that is especially efficient is the use of *natural experiments*. Natural experiments can be used to learn in situations where possible determinants of performance vary naturally among a firm's subunits, products, or processes.

As a consultant to the U.S. Department of Labor in the 1970s, I advised the department in its use of a natural experiment to improve organizational performance. The department had recently provided funding for a new computer-based operating system for the multiple Employment Service (ES) offices in each of 18 states. The system greatly facilitated an office's core operations. All offices had the same task and, before implementing the new technology, all had the same operating procedures and structures. Some offices did not change their procedure or structures when they implemented this new technology. Most did, but in a variety of ways. We viewed this as a natural experiment, where characteristics of the post-implementation office procedures and structures were the independent variables and the changes in performance of the ES offices were the dependent variable. Statistical analyses and interviews with agency managers and operating personnel enabled us to determine which of the various new procedures and structures were associated with (and logically causal to) positive and negative changes in Employment Service office performance. Thus a natural experiment led to learning.[5]

Because natural experiments are less costly than designed experiments—the delays or resources needed to start natural experiments are generally less than those needed for designed experiments—and because they are often more feasible, they tend to meet less resistance. But these features are in effect today. Why would future firms employ natural experiments more than do today's firms? The answer follows from our earlier conclusions that the future environments of business organizations will be more competitive, and thus more demanding of more informed decisions, than are today's environments, and that this will cause the usefulness of objective and diagnostic information to be greater. Thus, as is the case with designed experiments, these facts will force future firms to be more attentive to opportunities to use natural experiments to obtain such information.[d] It seems safe to conclude that *future firms will use natural experiments more frequently than do today's firms.*

> CIGNA Corporation's introduction and continued use of business reengineering is a good example of how a firm learned by treating its own performance-focused changes as a natural experiment. The early part of CIGNA's learning curve occurred in the early 1990s when it completed over 20 reengineering initiatives. Both failures and successes were analyzed, and each project team was responsible for publishing its learning in the company's reengineering database. Lessons learned were then applied to subsequent projects. (Failures occurred in about half of the initiatives, but several of these were revamped after being analyzed and subsequently became successes. Altogether, these 20 initiatives cumulatively saved CIGNA over $100 million, with a payback of $2-3 for each $1 invested.)[6]

Firms frequently fail to recognize when a natural experiment opportunity confronts them. Chains such as nursing home chains and some hotel and restaurant chains seem particularly blind to learning opportunities. Chains destroy natural experiments when they impose their "best practices" on the enterprises they acquire for incorporation into the chain or when they retard natural experiments by allowing no deviation from the firm's "standard practices."[7] When all variations are eliminated and suppressed, the firm's individual sites cannot learn through their own experimentation and, further, the chain itself cannot learn by analyzing the effects of variations within and among its units. *Firms can learn by experiencing variation, but they cannot learn by experiencing standardization.* This is not to say that some level of standardization is not needed for certain practices—adhering to governmental regulations, for example, or reporting performance. The benefits of standardization are obvious. The costs of standardization, especially the opportunity costs of not learning from variation, tend to be overlooked, however, and so benefit-to-cost comparisons are seldom made.[e]

---

[d]Designed experiments provide more valid information than do natural experiments because they control more adequately for unmeasured factors that might affect the results. But natural experiments tend to be less costly and are often more feasible. We can expect more frequent use of both approaches. Which will be employed will depend on the situation.

[e]It is interesting to note that in some instances what a firm learns from experience can serve not only to improve the firm's operations but—when codified into a "best practice"—can be marketed as intellectual property. Ford, for example, "has already pulled in about $1 million by teaching other companies how to use its method of 'best practices replication'—a way of ensuring that efficiencies at one plant are used system-wide" (Deutsch, *New York Times*, 2002: C4).

To emphasize the usefulness of retaining variation, let me return to the Department of Labor's natural experiment described above. As a result of this experiment, the department had learned "the one best way" to organize an employment service office so as to fully exploit the computing technology for matching job applicants with employer interviews. Approximately half of the Employment Service offices chose not to adopt the recommended "standard procedures and structure" but instead either to keep their old structure or to adopt one of their own making. Rather than attempting to force the issue, the department chose to *maintain the resulting variations in processes and structures as a continuous natural experiment,* one where the performance of every office was reported and shared on a monthly basis—so all could learn who chose to learn. Allowing and monitoring these ongoing variations for the purpose of future learning made sense because what worked best during one period in the nation's economy and at one location might not work as well in another period or in a different location.

HIGHLY EFFECTIVE LEARNING EXPERIENCES: LEARNING FROM ACTION PROBES AND OPERATIONS

Firms often use probes to obtain more information about environmental events or conditions that they have identified through scanning. *Action probes* are particularly effective for learning how competitors, customers, suppliers, or other stakeholders will react if the organization were to take a particular action. Experiments in packaging, pricing, and advertising are examples of action probes. By generating information-rich responses from the environment, action probes can lead to learning that is much more specific and valid than that obtainable through more passive approaches. Certainly a competing airline's actual response to another airline's fare reduction is much more informative to the fare-reducing airline than is a hypothesized response to a hypothetical price cut.

Some action probes are a form of designed experiments, such as are many local gasoline station price reductions. Although the term is unfamiliar to most managers, use of *action probes* is not uncommon. We can expect, however, that the demands for timelier and more informative data will cause future firms to more clearly see action probes as learning mechanisms and to use them more frequently.

Emergency One, the fast-learning manufacturer of fire engines described at the beginning of the chapter, was especially creative in its use of action probes to learn from experience. It lent new fire trucks to the Boston Fire Department and obtained feedback on them from fire department personnel. Its sales executives lived at a Boston firehouse and went out on 60 fire calls, thus creating the opportunity for intense learning from these "probes."

Most organizational actions, of course, are not intended as experiments. Price cuts, for example, are often actions launched in reaction to declines in demand, and changes in production procedures are generally intended to improve quality or reduce costs. Experiential learning includes learning from feedback about the effectiveness of changed operations, whether or not they were intended as learning probes. Consequently, all forms of audits, analyses, and evaluations can be framed, in part, as components of a firm's program of learning from its experience. The increasing effectiveness of information technologies as tools for quickly obtaining and interpreting the results of action probes will contribute to making action probes a more frequent and effective form of organizational learning.[8]

It is interesting to consider that any of an organization's operations can be viewed as an action probe. Hear, for example, the director of marketing for the division responsible for marketing Dell Computer Corporation's products and services through the Internet as he describes a new-product introduction as an action probe:

The important thing is to "develop the best products we can, put them in front of the customer [and] expand aggressively on the things that work. To a very large extent we don't know what our customers want. There is no market research better than letting customers vote with their dollars" (Bentzin, 1999).[9]

The uncertainty reflected in these remarks reflects the complexity and dynamism of the environment of the late 1990s for Internet marketing. As business environments increase in complexity and dynamism at an increasing rate, firms will necessarily be more active in attempting to learn about them and from them. At the same time, the increasing competitiveness of business environments will cause firms to make more changes in their operations and products. These changes, intended to influence the firm's internal or external environments, can also serve as action probes. Due to the greater frequency of such changes, and the greater need for information about the environment's responses to these changes, we can expect that *future firms will more frequently treat changes in their operations or products as action probes from which to learn.*

The outcomes of a firm's action are always specific to the action context. Consequently, correctly learning from a specific change, action, or event often requires a good deal of interpretation. Why, exactly, did we lose in court? How is it that we invested all that money in developing this product and have nothing to show for it? These are the kinds of questions where formal efforts to manage the interpretation process can have major learning benefits. Indeed, multiple (different) interpretations of a single event can sometimes lead to a higher level of understanding than can a single interpretation of multiple events. Interpretations stored in memory and subsequently retrieved can help avoid future mistakes and can help identify useful future actions. Sometimes the resultant "lessons learned" can be framed as a positive payoff from an otherwise negative outcome—a framing useful when attempting to build an organizational culture where people are willing to take risks.[10]

Given the attractiveness of interpreting feedback from individual organizational actions or information about individual environmental events—to develop knowledge not otherwise obtainable—we can expect future firms to adopt practices that will cause interpretation efforts to be more effective. What might these be?

HIGHLY EFFECTIVE LEARNING EXPERIENCES: LEARNING BY OBSERVING SAMPLES OF ONE OR FEWER

Professor James March of Stanford University is the most influential scholar in the field of experiential learning in organizations. From him and his associates comes the idea that organizations can learn a good deal from single events and from "near events," that is, from samples of one or fewer. Let us first consider single events.

Organizations also enhance the richness of history by focusing intensively on critical incidents. For example, when a large section of the metal skin of an Aloha Airlines aircraft peeled away in mid-air, the event attracted considerable attention and triggered a major modification in FAA-mandated maintenance programs. Close examination of what happened revealed significant features of aircraft engineering and maintenance that had not been noted earlier. By identifying those features and their implications, the organizations learned. Similarly, when a computer science graduate student propagated a "virus" among many computer networks, producing breakdowns in hundreds of systems, and considerable publicity, the incident stimulated analyses that identified weaknesses in the underlying computer code and in how people and systems were organized to respond to such events. (March, Sproull, & Tamuz, 1991: 2-3)

Stepping back for a moment, we realize that—once having "gotten into" an event—those analyzing the event are well positioned to learn much more. Entry costs are largely behind them, so the benefit-to-cost ratio of attempting to learn beyond what was initially required is high. Conclusions with respect to the original mandate—to learn quickly what happened—must be provided as rapidly as possible, of course, to satisfy concerns of external and internal stakeholders. But further study of other aspects of the event will often provide useful knowledge not otherwise obtainable or even identified as existing.[11]

Of course these learning opportunities need not follow only from failures. For example, hear John Browne, former CEO of British Petroleum, describe how BP reaped "fantastic gains" in deep water drilling efficiency while drilling in the Gulf of Mexico. "In 1995, we spent 100 days on average drilling deep water wells. Now we spend 42. How did we do it? By asking every time we drilled a deep water well, 'What did we learn the last time and how do we apply it the next time?'" (Prokesch, *Harvard Business Review*, September-October 1997: 151).

The second practice is to learn from near-events:

If a basketball game is decided by one point, one team wins and the other team loses, with consequences that may be vital for a championship. But the outcome will normally be interpreted by experts as a draw from some probability distribution over possible outcomes rather than simply as a "win" by one team and a "loss" by the other. In general, if a relatively small change in some conditions would have transformed one outcome into another, the former will be experienced to some degree as having been the latter. In such a spirit, the National Research Council (1980) has defined a safety "incident" as an event that, under slightly different circumstances, could have been an accident.

Air traffic systems illustrate how organizations learn from near-histories or "incidents" (Tamuz, 1987). By collecting information about near-accidents from pilots and air traffic controllers, air safety reporting systems considerably enlarge the sample of events that can be treated as relevant to understanding aviation safety. Information on near-accidents augments the relatively sparse history of real accidents and has been used to redesign aircraft, air traffic control systems, airports, cockpit routines, and pilot training procedures. (March, Sproull, & Tamuz, 1991: 4-5)

Single events or near-events are often highly vivid and, by their nature, are not "balanced" by other events. A danger in these instances is that the observer might associate in his or her mind the event with a prior or subsequent event, and then imagine a line of causal reasoning connecting the events—when in fact no causal connection exists. The "learning" that takes place in such

instances is called "superstitious learning." Superstitious learning, even when
based on samples of one, can lead to both strongly held beliefs and ill-directed
actions.[f] As an example,

> Sewell Avery, as head of Montgomery Ward, believed that there would be a depres-
> sion at the end of World War II. *The basis for this belief was the fact that there had
> been such a depression after World War I.* His belief was so strong that it influenced
> his decision not to allow Ward to expand to meet competition from Sears. This
> decision led to a permanent loss of market share to Sears. (Hartley, 1976: 8-9)

Although today's firms sometimes appoint ad hoc teams to analyze individual instances of the firm's success and failure, or to analyze recent events in the
firm's environments, the increasing competitiveness of future business environments will motivate firms to learn more effectively from these experiences and
events.[12] This inclination will be reinforced by the availability of greater numbers
of experiences and environmental events generated by tomorrow's more
dynamic event-generating environment. As a result, it seems reasonable to expect
that—as an approach to acquiring knowledge—*future firms will more frequently
and more systematically analyze naturally occurring events and near-events.*

If this were so, we would expect firms in industries where high-stakes
events repeat themselves to engage in such analyses. An example instance
was Boeing's effort to avoid its difficulties with the 737 and 747 plane
programs. Both planes had serious problems when introduced. A
high-level employee group was established *to compare the development
processes of the 737 and 747 with those of the 707 and 727, two of the firm's
most profitable planes.* The group's 3-year analysis resulted in hundreds
of "lessons learned" and recommendations, captured and communicated in a one-inch-thick document. "Several members of the team were
then transferred to the 757 and 767 start-ups, and guided by experience,
they produced the most successful, error-free launches in Boeing's
history" (Garvin, *Harvard Business Review,* July-August 1993: 85).

---

[f]People have a strong propensity to imagine or "see" connections between events even when
no connection exists. Further, they are prone to interpret connections as causal connections when
the "connections" are actually only coincidental. Especially in more complex environments, an
event imagined to have been caused by another particular event is often more likely, in fact, to have
been caused by any of a number of events that were unnoticed or less clearly linked in time or
space. Thus we can speculate that the increasing complexity of future environments will make
superstitious learning more frequent and correct learning less frequent.

An advantage of a firm's learning from its own experience is that the knowledge acquired can be unique to the firm. Unique knowledge can lead to new-to-the-market or new-to-the-industry innovations, innovations that can offer a significant competitive advantage. In contrast, knowledge acquired vicariously is already known outside the firm. Thus, *unless there is a unique integration with other knowledge,* vicariously acquired knowledge—generally being at least somewhat available to a firm's competitors—is less likely to lead to competitive advantage than is unique knowledge generated within the firm. Why, then, do firms search their environments for knowledge, rather than seek to acquire it through experience? The answer is that in many situations, useful knowledge can be acquired from the environment more quickly, more reliably, and at lower cost than it can be acquired from experience, and can then be used to leverage the knowledge the firm has acquired through its own experience.

Also, of course, by scanning their environments firms can encounter knowledge that they recognize as useful but that they had not thought about before encountering it. For both of these reasons, firms search their environments for knowledge to improve their performance, knowledge they can use to leverage their existing knowledge.

Learning From Others—Vicarious Learning

Managers and other personnel are intensely aware of innovations in their firm. The vividness of an innovation, and the intensity of a firm's actions in moving an innovation forward, tend to give the firm's members a distorted picture of the innovation's origin, a biased view that the source of the information or knowledge leading to the innovation originated in the firm itself.[g] Studies show, however, that for most firms most of the time, their innovations are prompted or enabled by information or knowledge originating outside the firm.[13] This follows in part from the fact that, even though any one external source (e.g., competitor, supplier, university) is unlikely to generate a particular element of knowledge needed by a firm, there are so many such sources in the environment that the probability that *no* external source generates the knowledge before the firm does is necessarily very small. This idea has been captured in the maxim, "the industry learns faster than the firm."[h]

---

[g]I mean to include as innovations changes in practices, processes, and products that are new only to the firm as well as those that are without precedent anywhere.

[h]In the future, increases in the use and effectiveness of communications technology will undoubtedly increase the effectiveness of vicarious learning. The human genome project is a dramatic example of how the Internet facilitated industry-wide learning. Early developments, especially, in this project were the result of widespread knowledge sharing, with researchers publishing their results on the internet for others to build on. This enabled researchers in different organizations to acquire knowledge without having to discover it in-house.

Firms possess knowledge, but the amount they possess is minuscule compared with the knowledge already residing in their industry, in adjacent industries, in the business world, and in society in general. Consequently, when a firm needs knowledge, it often finds it to be faster, more certain, and less expensive to obtain the knowledge from the environment (for example, from a firm already possessing the knowledge or possessing the expertise necessary for quickly developing the needed knowledge) than to acquire it through experience.[14]

One practice for acquiring knowledge from outside the firm (specifically, knowledge possessed and used by competitors in their products) is called "reverse engineering." A vivid instance of reverse engineering occurred in 1944 when equipment failures forced three American B-29s to land in the Soviet Union. Soviet dictator Joseph Stalin ordered these advanced aircraft copied—to provide his military with an aircraft far superior to any it had at the time. One of the planes was used as a model. One was used for test flights. The third was disassembled and replicated—in just 2 years. The Soviet Union eventually built 850 of these clones (Associated Press, January 27, 2001).

Even when the key knowledge element prompting an innovation originates inside the firm, the large and rapidly growing stock of world knowledge will, more so in the future than in the past, virtually guarantee that a large proportion of the knowledge the firm will use to flesh out and bring to fruition the innovation will originate in the firm's environment.

Stanford University Emeritus Professor of Organizational Behavior Harold J. Leavitt makes the point forcefully:

In the 2000s, the technology/organizational relationship has become intensely symbiotic. Organizations are caught up in technology's thrall. . . . S & T has become so huge and speedy, with so many tentacles snaking into so many aspects of organizational life, that all organizations . . . must stay sharply focused on it. . . . Unless they keep up, technologically, with all their competitive neighbors, modern organizations cannot hope to survive the violent, ever-hanging mix of inter-organizational warfare and collaboration that has become their normal milieu. (Leavitt, 2002: 131)

In the more competitive future, the need to capture and exploit knowledge from the environment will be even more apparent and compelling. It seems safe to conclude, therefore, that *future firms will more actively attempt to acquire knowledge from their environments.*[i]

How will they do this? How will firms "more actively attempt to capture knowledge from their environments"? Of course practices will vary from firm to firm due to differences in firm strategies, features, and circumstances, but it seems likely that most firms will pursue to some degree each of three practices. One of these practices has to do with enhancing the firm's capacity to absorb knowledge from its environment.

ABSORPTIVE CAPACITY

The ability of a firm to recognize the value of new, external information, assimilate it, and apply it to commercial ends is critical to its innovative capabilities. We label this capability a firm's *absorptive capacity* and suggest that it is largely a function of the firm's level of prior related knowledge. (Cohen & Levinthal, 1990: 128)

The more knowledge a firm possesses, the more effectively it can learn. Firms having within themselves a high level of intellectual capital in the form of knowledge workers (e.g., market analysts, R&D personnel, and managers) are more able to assimilate and exploit customer suggestions, new scientific and technological advances, improved operating processes, or performance-enhancing management practices. The depth of a firm's knowledge is not the only variable that determines the firm's ability to absorb new knowledge, however. The breadth or diversity of its expertise is also a determinant. This is especially true with regard to knowledge that leads to highly innovative products, as such products appear to come disproportionately from cross-discipline and cross-industry endeavors.[15]

A firm's strategy and other features and circumstances will determine its relative needs for knowledge depth versus breadth, and thus will determine the design of the firm's approaches to vicarious learning. In any case, however, their greater need for external knowledge as a fuel for innovation will force firms in the future to increase their absorptive capacity. *Future firms will more intentionally staff themselves so as to assimilate environmental knowledge relevant to their current and currently imagined products, processes, and markets.*

This is not to say that any of the firm's members will necessarily have environmental monitoring as their primary or sole responsibility. For the most

---

[i]Particularly firms with a first-mover, "break-through-products" strategy will also more actively attempt to generate knowledge internally. This fact in no way diminishes the fact that they will also attempt to capture more knowledge from their environments, as it is often the externally acquired knowledge that (1) prompts or enables the generation of radically new knowledge, and/or that (2) enables the firm to exploit its internally developed, experientially acquired knowledge. In the context of firms' innovation strategies, in Chapter 7 we will examine the contexts where developing knowledge inside the firm is faster and more appropriate than is acquiring it from outside the firm.

part, responsibility for assimilating relevant knowledge into the firm will continue to rest with experts employed primarily to contribute directly to the firm's operations (e.g., engineers, market researchers, R&D personnel) or to manage the firm's assets (e.g., financial analysts, human resources specialists). Needed in the future, however, will be a much greater capacity to recognize and draw into the firm unfamiliar or not-previously-available technologies or other relevant product-altering knowledge. To achieve this absorptive capacity will require future firms to possess expertise broader or deeper than what they currently use.

In many firms, this requirement will be met by (1) employing people having expertise beyond that normally required for their everyday work, and (2) arranging that these personnel employ this excess expertise by initiating assimilations and utilizations of relevant environmental knowledge not currently possessed by the firm. Employing (and financially compensating) people possessing more expertise than they routinely use in their work is, of course, commonplace without being intentional. It is commonplace because it is nearly unavoidable—almost everyone possesses more knowledge than his or her job requires. Employing people with more expertise than they routinely use in their work is also, however, inefficient. But, because future environments will be characterized by an accelerating growth of potentially useful-to-the-firm knowledge, the possession and employment of this "excess expertise" will be necessary to maintain an adequate absorptive capacity. As an example, their study of developments in aircraft engine control systems led researchers at the University of Sussex to conclude that

> multi-technology firms need to have knowledge in excess of what they need for what they make, to cope with imbalances caused by uneven rates of development in the technologies on which they rely and with unpredictable product-level interdependencies. By knowing more, multi-technology firms can coordinate loosely coupled networks of suppliers of equipment, components, and specialized knowledge and maintain a capability for systems integration. (Brusoni, Prencipe, & Pavitt, 2001: 597)

This idea, that a firm must employ appropriate expertise to capture knowledge from its environment, is especially germane given the growing practice of outsourcing. If a firm outsources much of the R&D function to its suppliers or alliance partners, the firm must nevertheless maintain an absorptive capacity relevant to its product line or it will be unable to recognize or correctly grasp the knowledge that the supplier or alliance partner provides. If the firm is unable to do these things, over time it will become less capable—perhaps incapable—of making knowledgeable decisions about how to create and produce leading edge products, and may even lose out to its newly competent suppliers. The United States "lost" the black-and-white TV market to Japan in exactly this way.[16]

IMPORTING KNOWLEDGE IN THE FORM OF EXPERTISE[j]

Drawing into itself people who possess knowledge not already available in the firm not only increases a firm's absorptive capacity but also ensures that the knowledge so acquired will be available when it is needed. In particular, having the knowledge at hand increases the likelihood of successful innovation, as the innovation process often depends on having ready access to the relevant knowledge resources so that the innovation's momentum or timeliness is not lost.[17] As a result, firms sometimes acquire for later use the mind-resident knowledge of knowledge workers by hiring in advance of an immediate need. For example, from a *BusinessWeek* article on Microsoft's acquisitions:

> Microsoft is as anxious to get the masterminds behind the companies as the companies themselves. . . . For instance, Microsoft isn't certain it will keep all of the products that come with its Nov. 20 purchase of Macintosh software maker ResNova Software Inc. But it sure wants Resnova's five developers. Says Microsoft Senior Vice-President Brad A. Siverberg: "New blood brings in exciting new ideas."[18] (*BusinessWeek*, 1997: 35)

In the future, the frequency with which firms need to have new knowledge *ready at hand* and the frequency with which new knowledge is generated *in the environment* will both be increasing. In combination, these phenomena will tempt firms in the future to more frequently hire knowledge workers possessing knowledge different from that possessed by the firm's current personnel, and to make room for these new employees by discharging current employees.[k]

As contrasted with situations where a firm might want to have knowledge on hand for future use, in other situations the knowledge acquired is intended for more immediate use, to solve a problem or exploit an opportunity. Example processes include hiring management consultants or other experts or forming technology-transfer alliances with other firms. Thus we can also expect that, *in future firms, the use of temporarily employed experts and temporary technology-transfer alliances will be greater.*[l]

---

[j]This short section introduces some controversial and complex issues relating to firms' employment practices. Be assured that we will examine these issues and practices in depth in Chapters 7 and 8.

[k]A large-scale implementation of this practice occurs when a firm acquires a new-to-it business (with the business's employees) from another firm and sells a business (with the business's employees) in which it has less interest to obtain the funds to make the acquisition.

[l]Additional support for this conclusion appears in Chapter 7.

If this were true, we would already expect to see firms employing, for example, consultants at an increasing rate. We do. "Global consulting revenue had a healthy 8% compound annual growth rate throughout the 1970s, which grew to over 21% in the 1980s and averaged 18% in the 1990s," according to the Kennedy Information Research Group (2002: 53). Further, as we noted in Chapter 4, during the 1990s, the amount spent in the United States on management, scientific, and technical consulting grew by over 200%.[19]

ENHANCING ORGANIZATIONAL LEARNING
BY ENHANCING INDIVIDUAL LEARNING

Finally, a third practice we can expect to be carried out more extensively in future firms is the active facilitation and encouragement of employees' attempts to increase their own knowledge. Firms gain knowledge when their members gain knowledge. Today, common examples of employer-sanctioned employee learning processes include reading technical journals, attending training programs involving outside instructors, and attending university courses or programs. A less common practice is that of lending personnel to other firms, to suppliers, or to research consortia—in order for the personnel to acquire knowledge embedded in these sources and then subsequently to share or employ this knowledge on behalf of the firm. Recent research on the microchip and pharmaceutical industries demonstrates the competitive advantage that can be gained through this practice and other practices directed at opening up to the environment, even at the risk of having competitors learn what the firm knows.[20]

Increased competition in the market for customers will force firms in the future to facilitate and promote employee participation in knowledge-acquiring activities. Increased competition in the labor market for knowledge workers will also cause firms to aid and encourage employee training. As a consequence of either of these conditions, we can expect that *future firms will more actively facilitate and encourage employee learning than did their earlier counterparts.*

Although the fast-changing external environments of firms are causing all processes directed toward employee learning to be more commonplace, perhaps none is growing more rapidly than formal job-related learning (e.g., continuing professional education and executive education). Originally intended as a means of ensuring that the firm's workforce was adequately productive, job-related and especially field-related training have increasingly become part of the employment package for knowledge workers. Many employees interpret such training as a means of maintaining job security or, more generally, employment security. Many employers view providing such training as both a means of maintaining and increasing the intellectual capital of the current employees and a means for attracting new employees who demand such learning opportunities. Because both the development and recruitment of intellectual capital are growing in importance, and because both are facilitated by providing job-related training, we can expect that *future firms will be more active in providing formal job-related learning opportunities.*

In a growing number of fields, knowledge is growing so rapidly that the most effective way for firms to capture it is to hire people who have recently acquired this knowledge through formal schooling. Compatible with this but perhaps independent of it, fear of obsolescence, or the desire to acquire knowledge that is more specialized, deeper, or more leading edge, will cause some experts, and other experts as well, to seek new-to-them knowledge through career-related schooling. This will occur more frequently in the future than in the past because the growth in knowledge that motivates knowledge acquisition will be occurring at a more rapid pace. Overall, then, it seems safe to conclude that, *in the future, the proportion of experts who more frequently engage in career-related schooling will be greater.*

For the most part, except when we discussed the need to innovate so as to capture markets, we've focused on firms responding to changes in their environments. Here we should note that this need for schooling will raise the issue of who should pay for occupational schooling—the firm, the employee, or the public at large. Because increased environmental competitiveness will encourage firms to hold down the costs of education, and especially because post-employment occupational education increases the ability of employees to find other and perhaps more attractive employment, we can expect firms to attempt to transfer much of the cost of post-employment education by acting on their environment. We can expect more of what we've seen in recent decades—businesses lobbying colleges and government bodies to provide technical and professional education at convenient times and inexpensively. *Future firms will attempt to increase opportunities for their employees to be occupationally educated at publicly supported institutions.*

It is clear that, because they must, future firms will engage in a variety of new-to-them learning practices or will intensify and systematize learning practices already in place. How will firms initiate these changes? The next section addresses this question.

Introducing Learning Practices

Two issues need to be addressed. *One* has to do with improving current learning practices versus adopting new learning practices. "Doing things better" is an approach to learning that would often suffice in a new—but not very different—environment. This approach is attractive whenever the environment does not render the practice irrelevant. However, a danger is that "doing better what we're doing" will absorb all of the effort that management chooses to direct toward improving the firm's learning, and consequently "doing better things" will never happen.

A second danger associated with "doing better what we're doing" is that what is being done better (and better, and better still) can become a "competency trap"—a practice continued and fine-tuned largely because the firm is already competent at it rather than because the practice is the most appropriate for current or oncoming conditions. A well-known instance of a firm falling into the competency trap is Digital Equipment Corporation's early attempts to enter the microcomputer market:

> DEC was highly successful in the mid-1980s pursuing the VAX strategy—it had a line of computers ranging from workstations to near-mainframes all running the same software on the same operating system employing the VAX minicomputer architecture. . . . DEC seemed to offer *a seamless networking solution* [where its different machines could all talk to each other]. . . . [In keeping with this very successful strategy] in September 1986, DEC introduced an AT-class microcomputer called the VAXmate. Priced far above the usual AT price range, it featured a built-in ability to network with a VAX. However, it appeared just as Compaq propelled high-end computing into the 32-bit generation. DEC missed the entire 80386 generation by offering only an expensive 80286 machine *with networking capabilities that few wanted*. . . . DEC failed in microcomputing, but for precisely the same reasons that drove its success in the minicomputer arena. [Italics are mine.] (Anderson, 1995: 56-57)

Competency traps curtail the search for or adoption of new practices that have the potential to significantly enhance organizational performance. (Only) when these two dangers—(1) allowing managerial attention to be deflected from "doing better things" and (2) being blinded by competency traps—are recognized and guarded against is "doing better what we're doing" a useful and safe approach.

While "doing things better" meets less resistance from a firm's members, it is "doing better things" that is invariably necessary to adequately adapt to a significantly different environment. So, one issue that firms must grapple with is the question of what to do—which practices to discard, which practices to improve, and which new practices to take on. Adoption by future firms of at least some new-to-the-firm learning practices seems inevitable, given (1) that new knowledge is necessary to provide new best-of-class products, (2) that such products are necessary to compete, and (3) that competition in the future will be greater and increasing.

Besides the matter of adopting new practices versus improving current practices, a *second* issue is one of process. How will transitions to learning practices congruent with the demands of future environments come about? In some cases, these transitions will evolve incrementally and without central direction. This will occur, often without fanfare, when there is a general and widespread recognition within the firm of the need to be more alert to new knowledge. More often than not, however, such a bottom-up change will be too slow to match the firm's changing needs, and we will instead see some variant of managed change. That is, we can expect most firms to act on the idea that a comprehensive learning system should be centrally conceptualized and articulated. In some cases, the firm's executives (e.g., the CIOs, CLOs, or CKOs) will design and actuate the learning systems. In other instances, firms will use design teams involving both area experts and potential users of the knowledge needed. Still other firms will merely, but still intensely, coordinate the knowledge-gathering systems that have already evolved in the firm's component units, and attempt to fix any gaps in the integrated composite of these component systems.

A firm's strategy, environment, culture, history, and management preferences will determine which approach(es) it uses. But, one way or another, in the future it will be necessary for firms to develop and manage learning systems more actively. Those that do not will be less able to provide best-of-class products. As the buffers that protect firms from competition erode more completely, firms not providing such products will not survive.

Chapter Summary and Transition

To be survivors, future firms will necessarily be more actively engaged in learning than are today's firms. Two factors forcing this more proactive approach are (1) the need to provide best-of-class products in the more competitive environment firms will face and (2) the accelerating growth of knowledge that enables firms and their competitors to provide such products. The accelerating obsolescence of the knowledge currently contributing to their performance will force future firms to undertake learning initiatives. Philosopher and longshoreman Eric Hoffer made the point sharply: "In a time of drastic change, it is the learners who inherit the future. The learned usually find themselves equipped to live in a world that no longer exists" (1973: 22).

Because the learning function will be more critical to survival, future firms will, *because they must,* engage more actively in managing it. Some practices that today are rarely or seldom encountered will be more widespread. Many of today's learning practices will be continued, but will be carried out more intensely and in a more coordinated manner. The combination of these changes will cause the learning systems of future organizations to be much more visible, and more recognizable for what they are. The appearance of high-ranking executives with titles such as CLO and CKO is an early indication of this.

All future firms will be more active learners. Depending on the maturity of their industry and its technologies, and on their strategy and other features and circumstances, individual firms may emphasize experiential learning or vicarious learning. Nevertheless, the increased need to acquire and exploit knowledge in the provision of best-of-class products, in conjunction with the fact that combinations of knowledge from inside and outside the firm are often the synergistic basis of innovations, strongly suggests that most firms will put into place practices that enhance both their experiential and their vicarious learning.

The outcome of learning is knowledge. Firms that manage their knowledge well, particularly its storage and distribution, outperform those that manage it less well. In the next chapter, Chapter 6, we will examine some ways future firms will manage their acquired knowledge differently than do today's firms. In Chapter 7 we will examine how future firms will exploit their knowledge in the pursuit of improved performance, and in Chapter 8 we will examine how future firms will manage knowledge workers.

Endnotes

1. Parts of this chapter draw on, and greatly extend, G. P. Huber, "Synergies Between Organizational Learning and Creativity & Innovation," 1998; G. P. Huber, "Organizational Learning: A Guide for Executives in Technology-Critical Organizations," July-August 1996; and G. P. Huber, "Organizational Learning: The Contributing Processes and the Literatures," 1991.

2. This case description draws on J. Merwan's report on LaFrance's demise in "The Limits of Tradition," *Forbes,* May 20, 1985; and on R. L. Daft and G. P. Huber, "How Organizations Learn: A Communication Framework," 1987.

3. G. P. Huber, "Organizational Learning: The Contributing Processes and the Literatures," 1991.

4. V. E. Cangelosi and W. R. Dill, "Organizational Learning: Observations Toward a Theory," 1965. Apparently it wasn't until more than a decade later that prominent organizational scientists all at once began to address organizational learning in depth. See C. Argyris and D. A. Schön, *Organizational Learning: A Theory of Action Perspective,* 1978; R. Duncan and A. Weiss, "Organizational Learning: Implications for Organizational Design," 1979; and R. E. Miles and C. C. Snow, *Organizational Strategy, Structure, and Process,* 1978, 155-167. P. Senge, *The Fifth Discipline: The Art and Science of the Learning Organization,* 1990, was a major stimulus to the currently high level of attention and interest given to the subject. An anthology of works relating organizational learning to

competitive advantage, especially interesting because some of the contributors are nonacademics, is that of B. Moingeon and A. Edmondson, *Organizational Learning and Competitive Advantage,* 1996. See K. E. Weick and S. Ashford, "Learning in Organizations," 2001, for insightful commentary on several aspects of learning in organizations.

5. For a more complete description of this natural experiment and its organizational consequence, see G. P. Huber, J. C. Ullman, and R. Leifer, "Optimum Organization Design: An Analytic-Adoptive Approach," 1978.

6. See J. R. Caron, S. L. Jarvenpaa, and D. B. Stoddard, "Business Reengineering at CIGNA: Lessons Learned From the First Five Years," 1994.

7. This issue is well analyzed by S. G. Winter and G. Szlanski, "Replication as Strategy," 2001. See also the discussion of knowledge flows in "infinitely flat" organizations by J. B. Quinn, P. Anderson, and S. Finkelstein, "Leveraging Intellect," 1996.

8. Early interest among organizational scientists about the action-probe approach to learning can be gleaned from W. H. Starbuck, "Organizations as Action Generators," 1983; K. E. Weick, "Managerial Thought in the Context of Action," 1983; and "Enacted Sensemaking in Crisis Situations," 1988.

9. For elaboration of this idea, see J. C. Huber, *Managing Innovation: Mining for Nuggets,* 2001.

10. In part because they do not know how, most organizations do not maintain a culture that is supportive of risk taking. For some very solid ideas on how to make failure something to be avoided but not so intensely feared that people go to extreme ends to avoid it (including avoiding endeavors that might fail), see B. M. Staw and J. Ross, "Behavior in Escalation Situations: Antecedents, Prototypes, and Solutions," 1987. For ideas on building a risk-taking culture, see T. Peters, "Support Fast Failures," 1987.

11. The organization that is perhaps best known for the practice of "After Action Reviews" is the U.S. Army, particularly as these are conducted after war gaming sessions. See R. Cross and L. Baird, "Technology Is Not Enough: Improving Performance by Building Organizational Memory," 2000, for a brief summary of the procedure. See T. E. Ricks, "Army Devises a System to Decide What Does, and Does Not, Work," *Wall Street Journal,* May 23, 1997, for examples of where business firms have adopted the procedure. For rich elaborations of how organizations can and do learn by analyzing small numbers of events or experiences, see J. S. Carroll, J. W. Rudolph, and S. Hatakenaka, "Learning From Experience in High-Hazard Organizations," 2002; S. B. Sitkin, "Learning Through Failure: The Strategy of Small Losses," 1992; and K. E. Weick, *Sensemaking in Organizations,* 1995.

12. Organizational learning from experience can be inhibited when discussion of errors is frowned upon (A. C. Edmondson, "Learning From Mistakes Is Easier Said Than Done: Group and Organizational Influences on the Detection and Correction of Human Error," 1996) and when certain forms of accountability are present (M. W. Morris and P. C. Moore, "The Lessons We (Don't) Learn: Counterfactual Thinking and Organizational Accountability After a Close Call," 2000). For an in-depth examination of learning from negative outcomes, see S. B. Sitkin, "Learning Through Failure: The Strategy of Small Losses," 1992.

13. This commonly accepted view may follow from the early research by J. M. Utterback, "The Process of Technological Innovation Within the Firm," 1971; and

E. von Hippel, *The Sources of Innovation,* 1988. At the present time the view is inaccurate for firms that are knowledge-intensive, huge, and heterogeneous, such as 3M and GE. However, it seems likely that the view will be even more generally valid in the future than at present, as the rate at which the world's knowledge will grow in the future virtually guarantees that a large proportion of the knowledge a firm will ultimately use will appear first in the firm's environment rather than within the firm itself.

14. Very different studies supporting this reasoning are those by A. Hargadon and R. I. Sutton, "Technology Brokering and Innovation in a Product Development Firm," 1997; and L. Rosenkopf and A. Nerkar, "Beyond Local Search: Boundary-Spanning, Exploration, and Impact in the Optical Disk Industry," 2001.

15. With respect to the relationship between cross-discipline and cross-industry endeavors and innovativeness of products, see A. Hargadon and R. I. Sutton, "Technology Brokering and Innovation in a Product Development Firm," 1997; and M. Kotabe and K. S. Swan, "The Role of Cooperative Strategies in High Technology New Product Development," 1995. For elaboration of the idea that diversity of expertise is a determinant of the firm's ability to absorb knowledge, see W. M. Cohen and D. A. Levinthal, "Absorptive Capacity: A New Perspective on Learning and Innovation," 1990; and S. Zahra and G. George, "Absorptive Capacity: A Review, Reconceptualization, and Extension," 2002. Studies examining other factors affecting interorganizational learning are those of A. K. Gupta and V. Govindarajan, "Knowledge Flows Within Multinational Corporations," 2000; P. J. Lane and M. Lubatkin, "Relative Absorptive Capacity and Inter-organizational Learning," 1998; B. L. Simonin, "Ambiguity and the Process of Knowledge Transfer in Strategic Alliances," 1999; T. E. Stuart, "Interorganizational Alliances and the Performance of Firms: A Study of Growth and Innovation Rates in a High-Technology Industry," 2000; and F. A. J. Van den Bosch, H. W. Volberda, and M. de Boer, "Coevolution of Firm Absorptive Capacity and Knowledge Environment: Organizational Forms and Combinative Capabilities," 1999.

16. For a detailed account of how this occurred, see R. A. Bettis, S. P. Bradley, and G. Hamel, "Outsourcing and Industrial Decline," 1992.

17. Several of the cases described by A. H. Van de Ven, D. Polley, R. Garud, and S. Venkataraman in *The Innovation Journey,* 1999, make this clear. This book is an outstanding elaboration of the complex and demanding nature of the innovation process.

18. For an early but still relevant discussion of this phenomenon of purchasing companies for their knowledge workers, see O. Granstrand and S. Sjolander, "The Acquisition of Technology and Small Firms by Large Firms," 1990. Also see F. Vermeulen and H. G. Barkema, "Learning Through Acquisitions," 2001.

19. See Table 4.1 of "Selected Business and Professional Services," Official Statistics (U.S. Census Bureau, 1998) and Current Business Reports SAS/00, Service Annual Survey: 2000 (U.S. Census Bureau).

20. See, for example, L. D. Browning, J. M. Beyer, and J. C. Shelter, "Building Cooperation in a Competitive Industry: Sematech and the Semiconductor Industry," 1995; and R. Henderson and I. Cockburn, "Scale, Scope, and Spillovers: The Determinants of Research Productivity in Drug Discovery," 1996.

6

Leveraging Learning by Managing Knowledge

Georgetown University's Robert Grant reflects the belief of many of those who conduct research in the area of strategic management when he states that "knowledge has emerged as the most strategically-significant resource of the firm" (1996b: 375). As would be expected, and as the examples of this chapter will make clear, beginning in the 1990s many firms realized the need to more formally manage this resource. In Chapter 5, we saw that the rapid growth in the world's stock of knowledge, combined with the heightened need to innovate in response to the increasing competitiveness of the business environment, will lead firms to acquire knowledge at unprecedented rates.[a] How will future firms deal with this blessing and burden? How will they leverage it? I attempt to answer these questions in this chapter.

> Knowledge management is nothing new. For hundreds of years, owners of family businesses have passed their commercial wisdom on to their children, master craftsmen have painstakingly taught their trades to apprentices, and workers have exchanged ideas and know-how on the job. But it wasn't until the 1990s that chief executives started talking about knowledge management. As the foundation of industrialized economies has shifted from natural resources to intellectual assets, executives have been compelled to examine the knowledge underlying their businesses and how that knowledge is used. At the same time, the rise of networked computers has made it possible to codify, store, and share certain kinds of knowledge more easily and cheaply than ever before. (Hansen, Nohria, & Tierney, *Harvard Business Review*, March-April 1999: 106)

---

[a] As before, we will use "knowledge" broadly to include, for example, information, know-how, and understanding.

This long quote introduced three important facts: (1) much of "knowledge management" is "knowledge sharing," (2) knowledge management shot upwards in prominence during the 1990s, in response to changes in the business environment, and (3) in the 1990s, computer-assisted information technology enabled organizations to manage knowledge to a much greater extent than ever before.

Sematech

Perhaps no instance of technical *knowledge sharing* has had greater international economic impact than that which occurred in the U.S. semiconductor research consortium, Sematech, during the late 1980s and early 1990s. Founded within a national culture where interfirm competition is highly valued, and in an industry where interfirm and manufacturer-supplier relations were at the time pervasively acrimonious, Sematech's creation was a consequence of a national crisis. From owning 85% of the world market in semiconductors at one point, in 1985 the U.S. share fell to 43%—surpassed for the first time by the Japanese. By 1987, the U.S. share had fallen to 39%. Based on these trends, industry analysts predicted that by 1993, the U.S. share of semiconductor sales would shrink to around 20%.

To counter this threat, in 1988, 14 U.S. chipmakers and the U.S. Department of Defense founded Sematech to do pre-competitive research, development, and testing on a *cooperative* basis. It accomplished this in spite of the cultural obstacles and the industry's traditions of secrecy. Sematech met its technical goals on time, and sometimes early. Most important, by 1994 the U.S. share of semiconductor sales was 48% of the world market to the Japanese share of 36%.

How was this accomplished? To a large extent the answer is that Sematech's "research, development, and testing" resulted in knowledge that Sematech's member firms were able to transform into innovations in manufacturing technology, innovations that led to more efficient, more internationally competitive plants.

Sematech had to learn extremely quickly—its members were in a survival crisis. But to initiate its key experiential learning processes, of research, development, and testing, Sematech needed to possess a significant level of prior knowledge (because speed and effectiveness of learning are related to the level of prior knowledge). Of considerable importance in understanding Sematech's success is the fact that, as an entirely new organization, *Sematech itself had no "prior knowledge."* It had to obtain and integrate a body of prior knowledge swiftly, as a foundation from which to generate new knowledge.

The knowledge Sematech needed to launch its research, development, and testing processes existed in a disaggregated form within Sematech's member firms. But to get these firms to share their proprietary knowledge was—early on—extremely difficult, due to the industry's culture and traditions of secrecy and competitiveness. According to Deepak Randive, the first manager of Sematech's fabrication plant, "Before Sematech there was no communication on something as simple as what equipment firms were using" (Browning & Beyer, 1999: 225). Largely through the example and leadership of Sematech's first CEO, Robert Noyce, and other early influential officers, *at Sematech a culture of knowledge sharing was intentionally and successfully created.*[1]

Knowledge sharing by its member firms was critical to Sematech's success, and very likely to its survival. And Sematech's success in creating and transferring leading edge semiconductor manufacturing technology to its member firms was likewise critical to the success, and very likely the survival, of the chip manufacturing business of most of its members.

In Chapter 5 we saw that "any increases in a product's performance or value can be achieved only by applying knowledge not previously applied in the product's design, production, or marketing" and, further, that "any increases in a firm's effectiveness can be achieved only by applying knowledge not previously so applied." These observations bring into sharp focus why knowledge is a critical resource for business organizations. The widening recognitions in the 1990s of two facts—that knowledge was valuable and that increased competition required firms to leverage knowledge by making it available to all units that could use it—led to the idea that a firm's knowledge was a resource that needed to be actively managed. Hence came the concept and practice of *knowledge management.*

This chapter deals with how future firms will manage their knowledge. It will be useful to have in mind, here and in subsequent chapters, the forms and loci of the firm's knowledge.

The Four Repositories of Organizational Knowledge

To really understand what it means for a firm to "manage" its knowledge, we must first be clear about where a firm's knowledge is held. A firm's knowledge is located in four repositories. *One,* of course, is the minds of its members. People carry in their minds not only explicit and tacit knowledge about their work and area of expertise but also knowledge about how their firm works (e.g., its workflows and decision rules). They also have in their minds the culture of the firm—the commonly accepted values, beliefs, expectations, and norms that govern member behavior. A firm's members are an important repository of much of a firm's knowledge and are, in most cases, the nearly exclusive repository of the firm's most current knowledge.

A *second* locus of knowledge is the firm's documents and data files, broadly defined. A software firm's reusable code, a consulting firm's computer-based records of client engagements, or a construction firm's archived analyses of the differences between estimated and actual project costs are examples of data files that can provide competitive advantage by retaining organizational knowledge for later use.[2]

Recalling that all products contain knowledge, it follows that a *third* form of a firm's knowledge is the knowledge embedded in its products (e.g., in the computer chips or potato chips that it manufactures). The fact that components of many products are patented—the patents protecting the knowledge used and contained in the components—sharpens the observation that some of a company's knowledge is resident in its products. Of course patents and copyrights are themselves marketable knowledge-containing products.

Fourth and finally, a great deal of a firm's experience-acquired knowledge is incorporated in its work flows, office layouts, operating equipment, machine settings, decision-support systems, business practices and other processes, artifacts, and routines. For example, by no later than the mid-1990s, Dell Computer could combine vendor-supplied components into personal computers faster than could most of its competitors. Knowledge about how to integrate the components of a system (e.g., a computer, a factory, or an army) is called *integrative knowledge.* Dell possessed and employed, in the whole of its design and assembly processes, unique and valuable integrative knowledge about how to do this.[b]

Some examples of integrative knowledge uncovered in Arthur D. Little's research on organizational learning are given it its publication, *Prism.*

We know how to manufacture compact discs of the highest quality at competitive cost.

We know how to enter emerging markets and gain market share rapidly without losing significant amounts of money.

We know how to acquire companies and integrate them swiftly, painlessly, and effectively.

We know how to make strategic alliances work.

We know how to induct new employees into the company and integrate them so that they are highly productive within a month.

We know how to select people for key management positions. (Arthur D. Little, 1995: 16)

---

[b]Integrative knowledge, comprised of interdependent elements of diffuse knowledge, tends to provide a sustainable competitive advantage because it is difficult for other firms to replicate. In some contrast to its exploitation of its difficult-to-copy integrative or systemic knowledge was Dell's practice of selling directly to customers, a practice more easily and quickly copied by Compaq and other Dell competitors.

With this understanding of the repositories of organizational knowledge in mind, let us turn to the topic of knowledge management and its treatment in this book. The term has been used broadly to include a wide variety of organizational processes, from organizational learning to developing patenting strategies to managing databases to influencing the turnover of knowledge workers. Without in any way attempting to restrict the meaning of the term, in this chapter we focus on knowledge distribution and, in particular, on knowledge sharing.[c]

The Need to Manage Knowledge[3]

The 1960s and 1970s saw an acceleration in efforts directed toward under-standing the sharing and diffusion of scientific and technical knowledge within organizations and in the larger scientific and technical communities. In the 1990s, a similar acceleration took place but was broadened in scope (i.e., it was directed also toward understanding the diffusion of commercially useful knowledge). This interest in commercially useful knowledge followed from the recognition that knowledge, properly exploited, resulted in profits for firms and economic growth for nations.

> Knowledge has become the key economic resource and the dominant—and perhaps even the only—source of competitive advantage.
>
> Peter Drucker, from *Managing in a Time of Great Change* (p. 271)

Experts were also in agreement that the intra-organizational diffusion of such knowledge was much less effective than was desired.[4] Executives, too, seemed in agreement that knowledge-related processes were not fulfilling organizational needs or management expectations.

"If TI only knew what TI knows," lamented Jerry Junkins, the late chairman, president, and CEO of Texas Instruments. Lew Platt, chairman of Hewlett-Packard, echoed this with "I wish we knew what we know at HP" (O'Dell & Grayson, 1998a: 154).

In a 1997 study of 431 U.S. and European organizations conducted by the Ernst and Young Center for Business Innovation, "only 13% of the responding executives thought that their firms were adept at transferring knowledge held

---

[c]In other chapters we examine other knowledge-related issues: in Chapter 5 we examined organizational learning, in Chapter 7 we will examine structures and processes for rapidly inte-grating knowledge for product and process innovation, and in Chapter 8 we will discuss practices future firms will use in their management of knowledge workers.

by one part of the organization to other parts" of the organization. Few executives were satisfied—94% agreed that "it would be possible, through deliberate management, to leverage the knowledge existing in my organization to a greater degree" (Ruggles, 1998: 81).

What basic business conditions would cause these executives to be concerned about and dissatisfied with their firm's knowledge management, and perhaps motivate them to direct their firms to more actively manage knowledge sharing and storage? In Chapter 2, we encountered two answers to this question: (1) increased and accelerating levels of knowledge and (2) an increasingly competitive business environment. As these conditions evolve, they will make even more apparent that knowledge is critical to a firm's performance. Firms that do not act on this fact will not be as effective or competitive as firms that do, and hence will not survive to become future firms. Thus it seems reasonable to conclude that *future firms will more actively manage the sharing and storing of their knowledge.*

How will they do this? Answers to this question are set forth in the next three sections having to do with, respectively, (1) direct and informal knowledge sharing, (2) Knowledge Management Systems, and (3) knowledge sharing across teams.

Direct, Informal Knowledge Sharing

Before knowledge is deposited in a firm's files or embedded in its products or operating systems, it is almost always contained in the minds of the firm's employees. It follows that a great deal of the firm's newest knowledge is possessed by its knowledge workers. It is very much to the firm's advantage that this knowledge be shared with other of the firm's employees—so that it can be maximally leveraged and exploited. Although articulation of this fact was endlessly fashionable during the 1990s, insightful executives have long been aware of it:

> The only irreplaceable capital an organization possesses is the knowledge and ability of its people. The productivity of that capital depends on how effectively people share their competence with those who can use it. (Andrew Carnegie, as quoted in Stewart, 1997: 128)

Firms where knowledge is shared will outperform firms where it is not. However, as we saw earlier, knowledge distribution in organizations is far less than what is desirable; and what it seems to be is less than what can be achieved. Although we will shortly consider infrastructure solutions to this problem, as if the problem was that those who possess knowledge and those who need knowledge had no timely and effective access to each other, we begin here by considering the fact that in many situations motivation seems to be the primary determinant of whether knowledge is conveyed. We must keep in mind that

> for many people, sharing their bright ideas with the rest of the company involves not only laboriously transferring their knowledge to the management system; it also means handing over their most valuable asset for general corporate use. (*The Economist*, April 22, 2000: 61)

AN EXAMPLE OF HOW MOTIVATION CAN NEGATIVELY AFFECT DIRECT, INFORMAL KNOWLEDGE SHARING

Of the obstacles to getting knowledge shared, motivation stands out in terms of the attention it has received.[5] To make this clear, let us draw on a study of knowledge sharing in a university where businesslike practices were being introduced in response to an increasingly competitive and hostile environment, an environment that was becoming more like the environment of future firms. As we will see, the context of the study makes it very appropriate for gaining insight into the effects of motivation on knowledge sharing among highly trained professionals.

As we review the context and results of this study, it is important to keep in mind that it was conducted in a research-oriented university and that very relevant to the findings are two facts:

1. Academics self-select into a profession where sharing their knowledge is the primary task, whether through lecturing to classes or publishing in scholarly journals, and

2. sharing knowledge with colleagues has long been a social norm in academia.

Full and free knowledge sharing has been commonplace and culturally supported in academic institutions. Without outside intervention, we would expect the centuries-long tradition to continue. But then comes another fact:

3. Increasing pressures for accountability and efficiency are leading managers in many academic institutions to adopt objective performance-assessment methods and pay-for-performance practices more characteristic of business firms.

What resultant effect on knowledge sharing can we expect from this intervention? Is the long-standing academic culture strong enough that full and free knowledge sharing will continue at historical levels? In many firms, knowledge is readily shared. But the management practice of pay-for-performance, especially as manifested in bonuses-for-performance, has been steadily increasing in the United States for over a decade.[6] What might be the consequences if bonuses were paid for sharing knowledge? Will future firms provide rewards for sharing knowledge and penalties for not sharing knowledge?

A single case study cannot definitively answer these important questions. But it can suggest some possibilities, clarify some key issues, and make tangible some important concepts.

The (Australian) university studied was facing increasing governmental pressure to generate a greater part of its income from commercial activities (the target set was 65% of funding to be derived from nongovernmental sources).[7] Research and consulting were to be the primary means of achieving this—Australian law clearly allows universities to compete on equal terms with corporate entities. Further, it was national policy for the universities to be "benchmarked against each other with respect to 'productivity' and income" (Standing & Benson, 2000: 340). To compete, the university aggressively undertook three "businesslike" processes:

1. "Corporatisation"—performance appraisal for each academic in the form of measuring research output and teaching performance. "As a result, many (faculty) see themselves as autonomous workers and their colleagues as competitors" (p. 344). Hear one speak:

   It is a very competitive situation, as we are all evaluated individually and recognised and promoted individually. I have seen a league table of researchers in our School and I have heard comments about my position! Sharing knowledge is seen as giving away power and status. (p. 343)

2. "Rationalisation"—reductions in the number of administrative staff. "Specialist knowledge in this environment provides some security for employees and sharing it is often perceived as against their best interests" (p. 344). For example,

   People are afraid to share their knowledge and experiences as they feel their positions might be taken away from them by their opponents. (p. 343)

3. "Marketisation"—"The commercialisation and commodification of knowledge has been a driving force in Australian universities in the nineties. [Faculty] see their knowledge as a commodity for bargaining purposes" (p. 344). For example,

   Look, why would I share knowledge that has some value to me? It is my competitive advantage, it puts distance between me and others. If I share my latest knowledge others may take advantage of that. Will they do the same for me? (p. 343)

The disturbing lesson to be learned from this study is that even in an organization where knowledge sharing can be expected as a consequence of occupational norms, all but minimal knowledge sharing can disappear if the organization creates a strongly competitive environment. And, of course, full knowledge sharing is voluntary—no one can know all that someone else knows. So, accurately assessing the degree to which someone shares his or her knowledge is impossible. The more competitive or otherwise threatening the organization's internal environment, the more likely it is that the organization's members will not share with others their most valuable knowledge, as it is the resource most likely to provide them with employment security and organizational rewards.

A moment's reflection makes clear that this university has been "rewarding A while hoping for B."[8] What is A? A is individual performance—on dimensions (teaching and research) where an individual's knowledge is a competitive advantage. What is B? B is organizational performance, which is certain to be greater if faculty share with each other their best teaching techniques or help each other with the difficult problems that all researchers encounter. The university is rewarding A—high levels of individual performance—while hoping for B—high levels of organizational performance. But by rewarding individual performance, it is curtailing the organizational performance that it hopes to achieve.[9]

It is well established that compensation and other incentive schemes that reward individual achievement often interfere with cooperation among work-team members. The derivative idea that individual pay-for-performance schemes may interfere with knowledge sharing, as indicated in the above study and in other studies as well, seems just as valid and is receiving the attention of researchers and consultants.[10] (We will examine this idea further in this chapter's section on Knowledge Management Systems and will explore it further still in Chapter 8.) Associated with this realization is the growing recognition that in many situations an effective approach to ensuring knowledge sharing is to create and maintain a culture that specifically supports the practice.

ORGANIZATIONAL CULTURE: AN ACHIEVABLE SOLUTION TO THE PROBLEM OF MOTIVATION?

Organizational culture is the set of values, beliefs, norms, and expectations that are widely held in an organization. It can positively influence knowledge sharing in that it leads to organizational members being subjected to strong social pressures to conform to the prevailing cultural norms (for example, to share knowledge).[11]

To a great extent, organizational cultures are maintained through signals and symbols. These often occur in the form of public recognitions for exemplary actions or individuals. 3M is itself an exemplar of a firm that uses such recognitions, with its designation of "Corporate Scientists"—whose salaries equal those of 3M's division managers and who are given wide latitude to take on tasks of their choosing, but who are expected to share their knowledge with others and so leverage it on behalf of the firm. Similarly, 3M publicly recognizes with its Inventors Hall of Fame those who have been important creators of knowledge. Membership in this honorary society is limited to those who have made a substantial contribution to the technology and sales of more than one division. Another of 3M's honorary societies, the Carlton Society, uses similar selection criteria.

> If a firm wants to create a culture where knowledge sharing is commonplace, then those responsible for knowledge management need to (a) ensure that none of the firm's policies and no features of the firm's reward systems discourage knowledge sharing, (b) articulate the *expectation* that people will engage in knowledge sharing because it is the right thing to do—thus communicating organizational *values*, (c) set the example by sharing their knowledge and by getting other influential organizational members to do so, (d) publicize and celebrate instances where sharing knowledge benefited the organization and its members— thus creating the *beliefs* that knowledge sharing has effects, is recognized, and is a norm, and (e) encourage laggards to share.

Creation of organizational cultures as a means of motivating knowledge sharing is, of course, not new. As a notable example, William McKnight, longtime president and chairman of the board at 3M, established a policy early on that became part of 3M's culture: "technology is free." Technology developed by a division for its own products and markets must be shared with other divisions for use in their products and markets. But in the 1990s, organizational culture became widely articulated and discussed in the business press and management literature. As more is learned about how to create particular cultures, perhaps through experience and certainly through the ongoing research into how compensation systems create and destroy and interact with organizational cultures, we can expect organizational cultures to be more intelligently used as a means of encouraging knowledge sharing. As managements become more effective in using organizational culture, and as the need to manage knowledge becomes even more apparent, we can expect that *future firms will more actively attempt to create organizational cultures where free and full knowledge sharing is actively pursued as a matter of course.*

The fact that it has a strong culture of knowledge sharing has been used to explain GE's success as a conglomerate.

> GE has got around the traditional objection that a conglomerate cannot allocate capital better than the market can. Capital, he (GE's CEO Jack Welch) points out, is not a scarce resource, but knowledge is. GE's success is rooted in the way that it circulates more ideas and management talent faster than smaller specialists ever could. (Micklethwait & Wooldridge, 2000: 135)

> GE's success is rooted in its movement of ideas and management talent around the group. It not only excels at using knowledge and experience within a business, but also does something the specialist cannot, by transferring it over the whole company. . . . At GE the culture is built in. Pay and promotion, for instance, are tied to "boundaryless behaviour." (*The Economist*, 1999: 24)

It appears that not only does such a culture mitigate the negative effect of competition on knowledge sharing, but it also tends to result in knowledge sharing between firm members who are unacquainted.[12]

STRUCTURAL APPROACHES FOR FACILITATING DIRECT, INFORMAL KNOWLEDGE SHARING

Our everyday experiences remind us of the fact that actions are often a consequence of motivations meeting opportunities. Just as some firms are actively attempting to motivate knowledge sharing, some of these same firms and other firms as well are actively facilitating knowledge sharing with infrastructures and other resources that create opportunities for knowledge sharing. 3M is well known as an exemplar in this respect. For example, its Technical Forum, organized by 3M Laboratories and having technically specialized "chapters" or "communities of practice" and an annual county fair–like show where selected new technologies are showcased, is actively supported by the firm.

Hitachi is another firm that has actively encouraged and supported informal knowledge sharing:

If there are any heroes within the loosely knit organization, they are Hitachi's elite corps of more than 1200 PhD engineers. Their advanced degrees, mostly earned after joining the company, win them a place in a shadow society at Hitachi called Henjinkai, or oddball club. The group was created years ago to forge stronger links among gifted researchers at Hitcachi's scattered facilities. Members fraternize at technical conferences, swap ideas, and informally advise Hitachi's board on important technology developments. . . . On a 51-acre refuge west of Tokyo, they contemplate micro-machines and virtual reality as they stroll on pathways through natural forest and manicured gardens or work out in the Olympic-sized swimming pool. Such collegiality also helps Hitachi tap the vast expertise housed across the company's dozens of divisions. (*BusinessWeek,* September 28, 1992: 92)

Of course, few firms provide as much active support for informal and direct knowledge sharing as 3M and Hitachi. Most firms today are much more passive in this regard. But we are speaking here of past practices. In tomorrow's business environment, competition will be significantly greater and knowledge will be a significantly more critical resource. Firms that manage their knowledge more effectively will be able to compete more effectively, and will be more likely to survive to be counted as future firms. The necessity to manage their knowledge, combined with the penchant that organizations have for structured approaches to directing behavior, strongly suggests that *future firms will more frequently develop and activate processes and practices that facilitate and promote informal knowledge sharing.*

While few firms facilitate knowledge sharing on scales so grand as those of 3M and Hitachi, many firms facilitate ad hoc intra-organizational knowledge sharing on a small scale. Some firms, for example, put "chat rooms" on the firm's intranet and "white boards" at the intersection of worksite hallways. We might expect that these hallway work surfaces will soon electronically record and distribute their contents as their users desire, just as is the case today for the work surfaces of some conference rooms. Communication-facilitating infrastructures such as these, and the even more effective infrastructures that will undoubtedly appear (such as those alluded to when discussing telepresence), are part of a fashion that will not pass. Their usefulness is too great. Further, in addition to facilitating knowledge sharing, such infrastructures facilitate creativity and camaraderie, both valuable organizational resources.

Many organizational actions intended primarily for other purposes can be structured to facilitate knowledge sharing, especially those that create or provide for interaction. Consider one of Shell's practices as described by Arie de Geus, employed 38 years as a professional with Royal Dutch/Shell, much of it in long-range planning, and author of the best-selling book *The Living Company* (1997):

> Shell, for instance, spends about $2400 per employee each year on training that helps employees advance in their fields, move into new endeavors, and develop new skills. Even more significant, most of the training is collaborative. It is very important for teams of disparate people to undergo intensive training together at regular intervals. Such an experience helps disseminate knowledge across an organization and brings together people from various cultural backgrounds and professional and academic disciplines. The flocking is intensive. Course attendees nearly always report afterward, "It was not so much what I learned in the official sessions but what I picked up from my colleagues during the breaks that was important." (De Geus, *Harvard Business Review,* March-April 1997: 57)

I cannot help but include De Geus's relevant and interesting example of how the processes and practices of another "living system" led to learning:

> In the late nineteenth century, milkmen left open bottles of milk outside people's doors. A rich cream would rise to the tops of the bottles. Two garden birds common in Great Britain, titmice and red robins, began to eat the cream. In the 1930s, after the birds had been enjoying the cream for about 50 years, the British put aluminum seals on the milk bottles. What happened? By the early 1950s, the entire estimated population of one million titmice in Great Britain, from Scotland to Land's End, had learned to pierce the seals. The robins never acquired that skill.
>
> Why did titmice gain the advantage in the interspecies competition? Remember that Wilson (a University of California–Berkeley zoologist) identified the conditions necessary for learning to take place in a population: numerous mobile individuals, some of whom are innovative, and a social system for propagating innovation. The red robins lacked such a social system. Of course, robins sing, have color, and are mobile—they can communicate. But they are fundamentally territorial birds. Four or five robins live in my garden, and each has its own small territory. There's a lot of communication among them, but what they usually have to say to one another is, Get out. Titmice also love my garden. They live together in pairs in May and June. By the end of June and July, you see the titmice in flocks of 8, 10, and 12. They fly from garden to garden, and they play and feed.
>
> Birds that flock learn faster. So do organizations that encourage flocking behavior. (De Geus, *Harvard Business Review,* March-April 1997: 56)

INTERIM SUMMARY AND TRANSITION

Here we've examined informal, direct sharing of knowledge in today's firms, and we've drawn some conclusions about how it might be different in future firms. Considering that the competitiveness of future business environments will be greater and increasing, and that knowledge is the key resource that enables firms to provide best-of-class products or otherwise increase their effectiveness, we concluded that future firms will more actively manage knowledge sharing. Specifically, we concluded both that future firms will more actively attempt to create organizational cultures where free and full knowledge sharing is actively pursued as a matter of course and that, in parallel with this, they will more frequently develop and activate processes and practices that facilitate informal knowledge sharing.

Communicating knowledge informally and on a person-to-person basis generally results in distribution to a relatively small set of users. As a result, the leveraging of the knowledge is limited. Recognizing that leverage could be increased by making the knowledge available to many users, and across time, many firms have brought information technology to bear on the task of collecting, storing, and distributing knowledge. Some firms have done this in an aggressive and systematic way, implementing what are generally known as Knowledge Management Systems. In these systems, organizational members enter their knowledge into a computer-based document storage and retrieval system, and other members access this knowledge. Knowledge Management Systems have the advantage of making available ready access to stored knowledge by members of the firm who may not even know of the existence of the members who originally possessed the knowledge, or who may have difficulty in contacting these members because of differences in time, place, or hierarchy. Indeed, those who originally possessed the knowledge may have left the firm. Knowledge Management Systems were the most publicized and studied knowledge-sharing practice in the 1990s.

While this is the essence of Knowledge Management Systems, some firms extend the concept considerably. Some, for example, create units that draw on the contents of the stored documents to develop "best practices," and then enter these into the system as knowledge documents.[13] We might expect that some firms will rotate certain types of personnel—such as their internal consultants—through these units, so as to broadly diffuse what the firm has learned. And, of course, some firms today develop computer-resident personnel directories that enable knowledge seekers to identify those who possess certain types of knowledge. We will discuss these "people-finder" directories in the next section.

As we examine the use by today's and tomorrow's firms of this less direct and more formal approach for managing knowledge sharing (and storage), we will encounter issues and practices that might also apply to the attempts by future firms to motivate the direct, informal knowledge sharing discussed earlier. The issue of how to motivate knowledge sharing takes on particular significance in the case of Knowledge Management Systems, however, for two reasons. *One* is that the immediate social reward that people can commonly expect when they share their knowledge person-to-person is generally not available as a motivator when they insert their knowledge as a document into a computer. The anticipated unavailability of this common reward has negative consequences on knowledge sharing. The *second* reason motivation takes on added significance in the case of Knowledge Management Systems is that computers can remember and they can count—thus instances of contributing or accessing contents of a Knowledge Management System can be more readily monitored than in the less structured knowledge-sharing situations discussed above. As a result, extrinsic rewards can be more readily tied to participation in Knowledge Management Systems, as can penalties for nonparticipation.

Knowledge Management Systems

Knowledge Management Systems provide storage for some of the firm's knowledge, especially knowledge developed through its experience. Often the storage time is long—leading to use of "reusable" as a descriptor of what is stored, as in reusable computer code and "best practices." But Knowledge Management Systems are first and foremost a communication technology, one—like voice mail—where knowledge-containing records are stored *en route* to their users. As with other communication technologies, and with document storage and retrieval technologies, we can conclude that Knowledge Management Systems will become technologically more effective and more user friendly. Given this, and the fact that knowledge sharing and leveraging will be more critical to firms' survival in the future, we can expect that *the proportion of firms employing Knowledge Management Systems will be greater in the future than it is today.*[d] But what proportion this will be and how greatly these systems contribute to firm performance will depend on whether and how the human participants in the systems are motivated.

At least since the time of the Luddites, motivation has played a key role in the adoption of man-machine technologies. In particular, in the 1970s and 1980s the motivational issues associated with the man-machine technology

---

[d]It also seems reasonable to believe that, because the volume of knowledge stored must be large to justify the costs associated with both managing and using Knowledge Management Systems, the use of Knowledge Management Systems in future firms will be more frequent in large- and medium-size firms than in small firms—just as it is today.

labeled "information systems" was a subject of considerable concern and interest. Many conferences on information systems and a significant portion of the research on information systems focused on the motivations of the human components of these systems. Articles in the business press and management research literature addressed the reluctance of individuals to use information technology. Others addressed the reluctance of electronic data processing departments to share "their" information with line managers. Aided greatly by improvements in the user-friendliness of information technologies, firms won their battles with the reluctant individuals and departments. By the early 1990s, these particular motivational "problems" were seldom observed.

At about this same time, some firms began to act on their growing recognition that their members' knowledge was a key resource and that considerable benefits could be gained if the firm could get this knowledge shared and thereby gain leverage. One action taken was to employ information technology to create an electronic repository into which members could contribute knowledge-containing documents and from which other members could retrieve these documents. Hence came Knowledge Management Systems.

The consulting industry is a leader in knowledge management. Most large consulting firms include as part of their Knowledge Management System an archive of consultant-deposited information about specific engagements. A large proportion of such information is impossible to codify, but can still be very useful if it is interpretable. The director of Arthur Andersen's knowledge management system, *KnowledgeSpace*, describes how such a system can be used:

> When a client calls for help with a proposal, we can browse over other engagements where we have helped clients get educated, and by looking at each individual's story and gleaning a sense of how he went about the process, we can gain the confidence to recommend an approach. We can piggyback off prior stories, and put the project in context. (Rappleye, 2000: 63-64)

With Knowledge Management Systems, however, firms ran into the problem that some members were not inclined to contribute their knowledge. Other members were not inclined to bother tapping into the system to see what useful knowledge might be there. In the next section we will see that attempts to benefit from Knowledge Management Systems have met with mixed success, and we speculate about what future firms will do to make the systems more successful.

MOTIVATIONAL ISSUES IN
KNOWLEDGE MANAGEMENT SYSTEMS

Xerox's *Eureka* is a well-publicized example of a Knowledge Management System. *Eureka* is an enormous knowledge base that helps Xerox's service representatives solve particularly difficult problems. It is a resounding success. An article in the July 24, 2000, issue of *Fortune* reported, "Used by 15,000 Xerox tech reps on a quarter-million calls a year, the shared knowledge in *Eureka* will save Xerox some $11 million this year." And an article in the March 23, 2002, issue of *PC Magazine iBiz* reported that "last year it helped solve 350,000 service problems and saved Xerox approximately $15 million in parts and labor." Xerox's director of corporate strategy knowledge initiative describes the stimulus for *Eureka*'s development:

> Once in about a thousand service calls, there is a problem nobody has ever seen before. The service rep is out there trying to fix it at the customer site. That takes a long time and costs a lot. We don't want to have anybody have to do that again. So, the question becomes: How do we capture that solution, from the service rep who is the only one who knows, into a knowledge base they all can use? (Rappleye, 2000: 60)

The answer to this question was obtained from a series of studies by a team of behavioral scientists:

> In these communities whose world is their work team—five to 10 people in a local geographical area—the opportunity to become known as a thought leader, to have solved a difficult problem that nobody else had ever seen, and to be personally identified with the solution, before all Xerox reps, all over the world, was enough to incent them to take the time to write up their solution, and put their name to it, and put it into the knowledge base. (Rappleye, 2000: 60)

Assuming that these findings are representative of the situation in which they were obtained, what insights can we draw from this example that we might be able to use as we think about Knowledge Management Systems in future firms? It seems there are two:

1. *Extrinsic rewards were not used as motivators.* "It is personal pride, and recognition by peers, that makes *Eureka* work—motivation far beyond money, or promotion, or any other conventional rewards" (Rappleye, 2000: 60).

2. *Knowledge stickiness was not a problem.* Indeed, *Eureka* seems a perfect example of the fact that

> when communicators share similar knowledge, background, and experience, they can more effectively communicate knowledge via electronically mediated channels. For example, by means of a central electronic repository, an organization can disseminate explicit, factual knowledge within a stable community having a high degree of shared contextual knowledge. (Zack, 1999: 59)

Note that, due to a high level of shared contextual knowledge, communication effectiveness was high. But knowledge sharing among these service reps could still have been a problem—if the service reps had not been motivated to share their hard-earned knowledge. Did they share their knowledge because they sought recognition as experts? Or did they share it out of more altruistic, "we're a team" motivations? Or did they share it out of a felt need for equity and reciprocity—they were benefiting from the knowledge contributions of others and felt a need to "give back"? Or did they share it because doing so might prompt others to share—in order to maintain social equity—and thereby provide themselves and other service reps with solutions that would make their jobs easier? Or, finally, did they share because it was "the right thing to do" (i.e., because it fit the culture, was the organizational norm)? For future reference, let us use the term "social-psychological forces" to refer to the need for recognition, the need to serve, the need for equity, the need to adhere to organizational norms, and also the potential intrinsic satisfaction associated with fulfilling certain of these needs through knowledge sharing.[14]

Knowing that sharing took place, these forces—these hypothesized explanations—seem commonsensical and highly valid as predictors of sharing. But sharing does not always take place. To the contrary, it is often the case that valuable knowledge is not freely and fully shared. How, then, should we view the reliability of these forces as determinants of knowledge sharing?

Xerox's *Eureka* is a widely discussed knowledge management success story. But contrast the *Eureka* story with the concluding observation from another study of knowledge workers involved in equipment repair in a service organization *just as were the Xerox workers*:

> Most of the individuals we talked to had an existing responsibility that was measured, . . . and a responsibility [to contribute to the firm's Knowledge Management Systems] on top that was not formally measured. These individuals obviously knew that [this second, more general, collective responsibility] was important, but if the compensation and reward system favored their existing responsibilities, it was very clear which part of their work would get neglected when time was short. (Moore & Birkenshaw, 1998: 90)

So we have two situations involving workers doing essentially the same type of work, but *in one situation the sharing of knowledge is highly reliable and in the other it is highly problematic.* Why did the social-psychological forces not cause sharing in the second situation? Or, for that matter, why did they not cause sharing among the faculty and staff in the situation of the Australian university discussed earlier?[e]

---

[e]Of course we do not have the contextual specifics of these latter two situations, but I strongly suspect that—even if we did—our hypothesized answers to the questions would not stand up to an aggressive challenge. What we know about knowledge sharing is exceeded by our ignorance about knowledge sharing. Relatively few systematic studies are available, and the conclusions of some of these seem questionable due to problems of measurement or informant bias.

At least two important issues are raised by these contrasting examples of knowledge sharing in Knowledge Management Systems:

1. How will future firms bring specific social-psychological forces into play to counter or overwhelm opposing forces, such as a knowledge holder's need to fulfill other responsibilities or desire to maintain a personal competitive advantage? How will firms motivate more than minimal participation in their Knowledge Management Systems?

2. What are the effects on knowledge sharing of interactions between extrinsic rewards to share knowledge, on the one hand, and the various social-psychological forces on the other, and how will future firms account for these interactions?

These questions are critical. Careful thought makes clear that, in a great many situations, only the possessors of knowledge know what they know. It is at their discretion whether they identify what they know or share what they know. And certainly the amount of effort they put forth to make complete and clear what they share is under their influence. Thus, even when knowledge sharing is a formal responsibility, a necessary activity for fulfilling an organizational role, the sharing might be less than complete, either because the knowledge holder is reluctant to share or because full sharing is effortful. Full knowledge sharing is a voluntary behavior. Given this reality, what makes the above questions critical is the large body of research showing that extrinsic motivators (such as salaries and bonuses) can adversely affect the positive effects of social-psychological forces on an "extra-role" behavior like knowledge sharing.[15]

Two streams of studies help explain the negative effects that extrinsic motivators have on the social-psychological forces that encourage knowledge sharing. *One* stream demonstrates the "crowding-out effect," which refers to the fact that the extrinsic rewards—being as conspicuous as they are—become focal. By distracting attention from the social-psychological forces, they reduce the positive influence of these forces. The crowding-out effect motivates people to perform the behaviors that are explicitly measured and extrinsically rewarded—to the exclusion of behaviors that might be more beneficial (such as providing an extensive

(Continued)

(Continued)

and well-designed knowledge document—rather than a terse but "countable" one—that is not rewarded in proportion to the effort required to accomplish it). The *second* stream of research demonstrates the "control effect," which refers to the resistance that people—especially highly educated people—exhibit when they feel manipulated. "If I share, is it because I want to or because 'they' want me to?" "If they have to pay me to do this, maybe there's a reason why I shouldn't."[16]

MANAGING MOTIVATION IN KNOWLEDGE MANAGEMENT SYSTEMS

The issue we are examining here is the problematic nature of the relationships between extrinsic motivators and the various social-psychological forces that may operate in the context of knowledge sharing. Extrinsic rewards can deflect attention from the social-psychological motivators that may, in the long run, be more effective at prompting knowledge sharing. Especially for personnel steeped in a culture of knowledge sharing, the use of extrinsic rewards for sharing expertise can be seen as demeaning. And in some circumstances it can create competition among people who should be—for the sake of the organization—in a highly cooperative mode.

Of course bonuses for participating in the firm's Knowledge Management System have a place in some situations. One is when potential knowledge contributors and knowledge users do not communicate directly, and thus social rewards for contributing knowledge are weak or nonexistent. Another situation is when use of the system requires learning efforts that interfere with performance on the potential participant's primary task, and these "start-up" efforts are likely to be put forth only if they are rewarded. The March 19, 2001, issue of *BusinessWeek* reports, for example, that "Siemens offered incentives such as free trips to those who contributed expertise or used the knowledge of others" (Ewing, 2001: EB 36).

Tangible penalties for not participating may have a place in situations where resistance is high and rewards are not sufficiently effective, particularly if they are combined with rewards to create a carrot-and-stick approach. Hear, for example, the international CKO of KPMG speaking of dealing with a "significant cultural impediment" in creating a shift from a knowledge-hoarding culture to a knowledge-sharing culture: "It takes time to convince people that they will be penalized if they continue previous behavior, and rewarded if they embrace the new one" (Rappleye, 2000: 60).

An interesting version of the carrot-and-stick approach implied in this quote has been used in IBM's consulting organization, where the within-the-firm sharing of knowledge (about clients and consulting tactics and tools) is clearly of high value to the firm. This approach involves the require-ment that consultants "re-qualify" every few years in order to be eligible for future compensation increases, promotions, or even to retain status as a consultant. Re-qualification depends in part on earning a certain number of re-qualification points since the previous re-qualification. Contributing to the firm's computer-resident knowledge base, or successfully using this knowl-edge base, are important means of acquiring re-qualification points. In some circumstances, a minimum number of re-qualification points must be earned in this way.

What will be the posture of future firms with respect to motivating par-ticipation in their Knowledge Management Systems? *First*, we should recall our earlier conclusions: (1) that future firms will more actively manage the sharing and storing of their knowledge, (2) that they will more actively attempt to create organizational cultures where free and full knowledge sharing is actively pursued as a matter of course, and (3) that they will more frequently develop and activate processes and practices that facilitate informal knowledge sharing. Firms in the future will take these actions irrespective of how they address the matter of motivating participation in their Knowledge Management Systems.

With respect to how future firms will motivate this participation, it seems certain that the approaches will vary, as they do now and for the same reason—some situations favor one approach and some situations favor another approach, and these situations will vary in the future, just as they do today. Some future firms will directly reward participation in the firm's Knowledge Management System and be successful. Others will forego the use of extrinsic motivators and instead rely entirely on social-psychological forces (as, appar-ently, did Xerox with *Eureka*) and be successful. Which of these—or other—approaches is chosen is likely to vary reasonably systematically with the industry norms, with the occupational norms, and with the nature of the knowledge (e.g., its explicability, its availability elsewhere, and its criticality).[f] That is, *the use of rewards and penalties to motivate participation in Knowledge*

---

[f] It may also vary, especially in the short run, idiosyncratically with the wishes and biases of the firm's upper level managers.

Management Systems will be more uniform within industries than across industries, more uniform within occupations than across occupations, and more uniform within types of knowledge than across types of knowledge.[8]

The rapid propagation of previously uncommon management practices tends to occur first in narrow domains where the contexts favor use of the practice, and then to diffuse to other industries. For example, beginning during and shortly after the middle of the twentieth century, the use of matrix structures emerged in the U.S. defense industry and then became commonplace in other industries. The heightened need for faster decision making and product development that hit many industries worldwide in the last third of the twentieth century hit the U.S. defense industry earlier and at a time (a national crisis) when resistance to change was low.

The use of Knowledge Management Systems propagated rapidly through the U.S.-based consulting industry in the 1990s. The practice was well suited to the particular context of this industry during this period—rapidly increasing competition, clients who were becoming much more demanding, recognition that explicit knowledge was a critical resource, and deep understanding of information technology. Because these contextual factors will become more characteristic of many, or all, industries in the future, we can expect to see Knowledge Management Systems adopted widely (although the label "Knowledge Management" may go out of style).

SITUATIONAL INFLUENCES FAVORING THE USE OF EXTRINSIC MOTIVATORS

Let us refer to combinations of industry, occupation, and type of knowledge as "situations." What kinds of situations favor the use of extrinsic motivators to induce full participation in Knowledge Management Systems?

---

[8]This follows from a combination of three facts: (1) organizational characteristics, such as the nature of their Knowledge Management Systems, are determined in part by rational analysis of circumstances, (2) organizational characteristics are also determined in part by a need to adhere to prevailing norms and practices, and (3) circumstances, norms, and practices are less likely to vary within than across industries, occupations, and types of knowledge.

Long-Lived Traditions and Cultures

Some industries and occupations have traditions or cultures where social-psychological forces have traditionally operated to motivate knowledge sharing within the work group. (Both K-12 and higher education may be such industries.) Recalling that extrinsic motivators can diminish the positive effects of social-psychological forces as motivators, it may be that in these industries introducing extrinsic motivators to induce participation in the firm's Knowledge Management System would be counterproductive. In contrast, other industries have cultures that attract people who are especially motivated by extrinsic rewards. (Management consulting may be such an industry, and sales is such an occupation.) In these industries or for these occupations, it might be disastrous for a firm to attempt to not provide extrinsic rewards for an activity that is commonly extrinsically rewarded in the industry or occupation. Such an attempt would be counter to employee expectations and would very likely meet with low performance on the "unrewarded" task. Consequently, it seems likely that future firms in industries characterized by the use of extrinsic rewards to motivate individuals will more likely employ extrinsic rewards as motivators for individuals to participate in Knowledge Management Systems.

Two situations more prevalent in the business environments of the future appear to conflict in their impact on the use of incentives for individuals to contribute to Knowledge Management Systems. We will first examine the two situations and then consider how future firms will deal with their combined and conflicting effects.

Increased Use of Teams and of Incentives for Team Performance

As we will see in Chapter 7, future increases in environmental complexity and dynamism will require even more use of group structures than we see today, and will also contribute to higher levels of interdependence within groups. Because group-level incentives motivate cooperative behavior (such as knowledge sharing) when group performance is dependent on cooperation,[17] we can expect that, due to these changed environmental conditions, future firms will more frequently use team- or group-based incentives.

What will be the effect of using incentives for group performance on the effectiveness of incentives as motivators for individuals to contribute to the firm's Knowledge Management System? The answer follows from our earlier discussion of the motivational effects of social-psychological forces. These forces motivate knowledge sharing when they contribute to the group's welfare. If the group's welfare—its bonus for high performance on its primary task—is enhanced by individuals' sharing their knowledge, we would expect groups to reinforce knowledge sharing with whatever social rewards or punishments are under their control. In general, the effect of social rewards from the work group would be to diminish the need for firms to use extrinsic rewards to encourage individuals to participate in their Knowledge Management Systems. Altogether this reasoning suggests that future firms would rely less frequently on extrinsic motivators to encourage knowledge sharing. But this lessened need for extrinsic motivators might be offset by another change forthcoming in the business environment—decreased employee identification with the work group and the firm.

Lower Levels of Organizational and Group Identification

Cooperative behavior in groups and organizations tends to be motivated most strongly by the social-psychological factors discussed earlier when members "identify" with the group or organization, that is, when members see the group or organization as manifesting the same values that they see themselves as holding. Such organizational identification tends to be stronger among long-tenured members.[18] Unfortunately for the sharing of knowledge, long-tenured members of groups or organizations will be less common in the future, as through various mechanisms the heightened levels of environmental dynamism will lead to higher personnel turnover. (More on this in Chapter 8.) Thus group and organizational identification will be less frequently available to motivate participation in Knowledge Management Systems. Similarly, higher turnover will reduce the effectiveness of organizational cultures as positive influences on knowledge sharing, as employees will—on average— be subjected for shorter periods of time to the firm's enculturation processes. As a consequence of this reduction in. the positive influences of organizational identification and culture on knowledge sharing, we might expect that future firms would rely more frequently on extrinsic rewards to motivate individuals to enter their knowledge into their firm's Knowledge Management Systems.

Net Effects

What will be the net effects of (1) the environmental forces that increase firms' use of groups and group-incentive systems and (2) the environmental forces that—by inducing turnover—decrease the within-group social-psychological forces that motivate participation in Knowledge Management Systems? The answer to this question is more straightforward than it might appear. The matter hinges on the level of social influence. If within-group influence is low, due to the short tenures that follow from rapid turnover or because the group members expect to complete their task quickly and have no further interactions, then the positive contribution of social-psychological forces to participation in the Knowledge Management System will be very small. Without this source of motivation, it is reasonable to expect that participation levels will be intolerably low unless some alternative source of motivation is provided. Some firms will not see this. Other firms will come to see this and will act on their insight, will gain advantage, and will survive to become future firms. This leads to the conclusion that future firms will be more likely to (1) analyze work-group situations for their strength of social influence, (2) use extrinsic rewards to motivate individuals to participate in Knowledge Management Systems when social influence in the work group is low, and (3) rely on other enculturation processes and on the social-psychological forces described earlier when social influence in the work group is high.

The knowledge provided by the Xerox service reps is rather highly codi-fied, as in "if-then" instructions. In contrast, the engagement narratives stored in the Knowledge Management System repositories of consulting companies are not nearly so structured or codified. It is easy to imagine situations in any industry where narratives and other loosely structured, noncodified knowledge would not be fully informative or interpretable. What can be done when differences in the backgrounds of knowledge providers and potential users cause archived narratives and other information not to be fully inter-pretable or otherwise useful? The solution is to enable potential users to query those who authored the archived knowledge documents. This returns us to direct, person-to-person, informal knowledge sharing discussed earlier in the chapter.

PERSON-TO-PERSON KNOWLEDGE SHARING FROM A DISTANCE

In Knowledge Management Systems, a computer serves as a repository of knowledge-containing documents. Its main function is to allow potential users to access material at any time, thus avoiding situations where the original knowledge holder is temporarily or permanently unavailable or has forgotten the details of what he or she once knew. In addition, the computer's data-management and indexing capabilities enable it to serve as an efficient "knowl-edge finder."

In situations where certain knowledge is difficult to understand or to interpret outside of the context in which it was developed, and thus is not amenable to the use of computers as repositories and communication channels for accessing this knowledge, firms use computers, software, and information about knowledge workers to develop and maintain a "people-finder" directory.

In these situations, the information technology is used either to broadcast the knowledge seeker's query to those likely to be able to respond effectively, or to search for and identify individual experts likely to possess the needed knowledge and to whom a personal query can be made. In these systems, just as the role of the computer changes, so does the role of those who possess knowledge. Rather than entering their knowledge into the computer, they serve as informants, as responders to queries.

The nature of the interaction between the knowledge seeker and the knowledge owner can vary widely. The knowledge seeker might query a directory of experts to find one or more who are likely to possess the needed knowledge and ask the more likely expert(s) for help. Sometimes the query is a request for an elaboration of the content of a narrative contained in the computer-resident archive, a narrative containing knowledge that is hard to make explicit and that can be communicated only with a good deal of interaction. On other occasions, the query is a broadcasted request for over-the-phone or e-mail technical assistance about a situation that the potential user does not understand or is having trouble articulating or is finding not treated in any known archive.[19]

A published example of this last situation is that of a partner in an international consulting firm who was confronted with a client's difficult strategy problem. Drawing on her own "mental directory," she identified several of the firm's partners who possessed relevant expertise. But she also used her organization's computer-resident "people-finder" database to identify even more contacts and eventually put together an internationally based team of experts in the problem from her firm. During the course of the engagement, she and her team "consulted with expert partners regularly in meetings and through phone calls and e-mail. In the process of developing a unique growth strategy, the team tapped into a worldwide network of colleagues' experience" (Hansen, Nohria, & Tierney, 1999: 108).

The increased need for knowledge sharing within firms, and the ongoing and forthcoming advances in technologies associated with document management, virtually guarantee that *the proportion of firms employing computer-based, people-finder systems will be greater in the future than it is today.*

In this and the previous sections, we focused primarily on knowledge sharing by individuals. We must, however, not neglect the important process of direct knowledge sharing between organizational units. This process is perhaps most clear in the context of knowledge sharing between project teams, the topic to which we turn next.

Planned Knowledge Sharing Across Teams

Hardly ever do project teams initially possess all the knowledge they need to carry out their task. Frequently teams must invent the knowledge they need. In other instances, they unintentionally discover knowledge they were not seeking but that is useful. Teams learn while doing. This experience-based learning can be leveraged if it can be captured and distributed to other of the firm's teams or units. Successful leveraging makes a difference.

> Some companies excel at transporting knowledge between teams and then capitalizing on it, while others do not. Motorola built on its portable pager business to develop portable cellular telephones, Searle built on its technical core competency in drug research to develop NutraSweet, and Corning used its expertise in glass technology to develop optical fibers (Lynn, Morone, & Paulson, 1996). Xerox, however, failed to apply its copier technology to the personal copier market until competitors were firmly entrenched, Firestone and Goodyear resisted the shift to radial tires, and Seagate waited to develop 3.5" computer disk-drives until other companies had secured an insurmountable lead. (Bower & Christensen, 1995, as reported in Lynn, 1998: 74)

CAPTURING AND SHARING TEAM LEARNING[20]

All teams have experiences. Whether or not they learn from these experiences is another matter. Whether they learn correctly from these experiences and capture what they learn for later use by others is another matter still.

The obstacles to learning in organizations are most acute when units encountering a learning opportunity focus entirely on completing their primary tasks and allocate no resources to capturing and sharing their learning. This fact, and the fact that leveraging unique experience-derived knowledge will be even more critical in the more competitive business environments of the future, will lead firms to institutionalize practices for capturing and sharing team learning. Firms that do not in this way leverage what they learn will be less competitive. Because leveraging newly developed knowledge by distributing it to teams and other units having a potential need for it contributes to a firm's effectiveness and viability, it seems reasonable to conclude that *future firms will more frequently institutionalize practices for sharing and explicating knowledge as the knowledge evolves within the team and for subjecting it to examination, critique, and revision as it takes form.*

Firms today capture and explicate their experience-based knowledge for later use, but aside from firms in the consulting industry, such capturing and explication tend to be ad hoc. For example, consider again from Chapter 5 the instance of Boeing, faced with the challenge of avoiding—in the development of its 757 and 767 planes—the difficulties it encountered in its development of its 737 and 747 planes.

> A high-level employee group was established to compare the development processes of the 737 and 747 with those of the 707 and 727, two of the firm's most profitable planes. The group's three-year analysis resulted in hundreds of "lessons learned" and recommendations, captured and communicated in a one-inch thick document. (Garvin, 1993: 85)

Establishing the high-level employee group was an ad hoc action, necessary in part because the "lessons learned" in developing the 707 and 727 had not been captured and documented. In contrast, and certainly not an ad hoc action, was the creation of the "one-inch-thick document" by the high-level group.

The increased need to exploit project-team learning will cause firms in the future to make explication and distribution of team learning a more standard practice (just as do consulting firms with their Knowledge Management Systems and as did Boeing's high-level group). We can expect that *future firms will more frequently institutionalize the practice of having their teams create and deliver "lessons learned" documents to those with a need to know, and to the firm's archives.*

OBSTACLES TO WITHIN-FIRM KNOWLEDGE SHARING, AND SOLUTIONS

Many managers are quick to attribute the notorious lack of intra-organizational knowledge sharing to lack of motivation on the part of the potential knowledge-using unit or potential knowledge-sharing unit, or both. For example,

> Porter (1985) blames both the recipient, who can "rarely be expected to seek out know-how elsewhere in the firm," and also the source, who "will have little incentive to transfer [know-how], particularly if it involves the time of some

of their best people or involves proprietary technology that might leak out" (p. 368). . . . Unless the motivation system reflects these differences [in perspective], it will be extremely difficult to get business units to agree to pursue an interrelationship and to work together to implement it successfully (p. 386). (Porter, 1985, quoted in Szulanski, 1996: 37)

It has long been established that most people, including managers, overweight motivation explanations when attempting to analyze or deal with the poor performance of others, and underweight the important effects of ability and circumstances.[21] In contrast, research conducted in the context of knowledge sharing indicates that knowledge-related barriers can dominate motivation-related barriers in explaining the inability of firms to share best practices within themselves.[22] Given the benefits to the firm of leveraging team learning, what practices can we expect from future firms as they attempt to get their teams' learned knowledge shared?

Two especially potent obstacles to team-to-team knowledge sharing are *absorptive capacity* and *causal ambiguity*. Recall from Chapter 5 that a team's absorptive capacity refers to the team's ability to recognize the value of new, external information, assimilate it, and apply it. This capacity of a team or other unit is largely a function of the unit's level of prior knowledge. Given this, it seems likely that firms will use at least two approaches to enhancing a team's prior knowledge more frequently in the future than in the past.

One will simply be the more frequent use of a practice now used when the need to ensure sharing is clear and considerable. As an example, recall Boeing's need to ensure that its lessons learned were absorbed by the 757 and 767 design and development teams. How did Boeing enhance the capacity of these teams to absorb the lessons learned by the high-level group? "Several members of the team (that discovered and codified the lessons) were then transferred to the 757 and 767 start-ups, and guided by experience, they produced the most successful, error-free launches in Boeing's history" (Garvin, 1993: 85). Clearly these transferred members of the teams that had discovered and codified these lessons enhanced the absorptive capacity of the 757 and 767 teams. The need to rapidly leverage lessons learned in the more dynamic and competitive environments of the future strongly suggests that *future firms will more frequently transfer members of knowledge-generating teams to teams or other organizational units with a need to absorb the knowledge learned.*

A key benefit of this practice is that the transferred members are not simply carriers of knowledge but are also teammates in the team needing to absorb the newly found knowledge. That is, the transferred members enhance the absorptive capacity of the unit needing to learn. This reframing of the transferred person's role, from "alien messenger" to "teammate," can help to reduce the not-invented-here source of resistance to new ideas.

The second fruitful practice that we can expect to see—when the need to ensure sharing is clear and considerable—has been less common. It tends to overcome a low or uncertain absorptive capacity in the need-to-know unit. At the same time it increases the likelihood that the causal relationships discovered by the knowledge-generating unit will be effectively conveyed to the need-to-know unit. *Future firms will more frequently temporarily assign to the knowledge-generating unit a member of the need-to-know unit who, as an individual, seems to have a high level of absorptive capacity for the kind of knowledge being generated.*[h]

Chapter Summary and Transition

As the rate of knowledge generation accelerates, and as the competitiveness of the business environment grows, future firms will compete more on their ability to exploit knowledge. As a consequence, they will necessarily attempt to manage their knowledge more effectively. One aspect of knowledge management, knowledge sharing, enables firms to leverage the knowledge possessed by only one or a few of their members or units. This chapter dealt with knowledge sharing between individuals and between project teams or other work groups.

Because knowledge leveraging will be more critical in the more competitive environments of the future, we can expect future firms to motivate knowledge sharing with extrinsic rewards in some situations and with a cultural norm of sharing in all situations. We can also expect that they will enhance knowledge sharing with infrastructures wherever possible. In order to increase the leverage of their knowledge, we can further anticipate that future firms will employ Knowledge Management Systems to distribute and reuse their knowledge. In the form of both Knowledge Management Systems and people-finder systems, the use of information technology to facilitate knowledge sharing will be more widespread in the future than it is today.

To successfully compete and thus survive, firms in the future must exploit their knowledge rapidly. As we will see in the next chapter, their ability to do this will depend on their structures and processes.

---

[h]This practice can change the labeling of the to-be-transferred knowledge from "Not invented here" to "It's our invention now." Involving this temporary assignee in the codification of the knowledge-generating team's "lesson learned" can greatly increase the chances of successful interteam knowledge sharing.

Endnotes

1. The culture of cooperation at Sematech was studied intensely during the 1990s. See, for example, L. D. Browning, J. M. Beyer, and J. C. Shelter, "Building Cooperation in a Competitive Industry: Sematech and the Semiconductor Industry," 1995; L. D. Browning and J. M. Beyer, "The Structuring of Shared Voluntary Standards in the U.S. Semiconductor Industry: Communicating to Reach Agreement," 1998; J. M. Beyer and L. D. Browning, "Transforming an Industry in Crisis: Charisma, Routinization, and Supportive Cultural Leadership," 1999; and L. D. Browning and J. C. Shelter, *Sematech: Saving the U.S. Semiconductor Industry,* 2000. The structures and staffing processes that Sematech used to ensure knowledge sharing within Sematech and between Sematech and its member firms are noted in T. H. Davenport, *Information Ecology: Mastering the Information and Knowledge Environment,* 1997; and T. H. Davenport and L. Prusak, *Working Knowledge: How Organizations Manage What They Know,* 1998. Although it is widely agreed that Sematech played a major role in reversing the decline in the U.S. semiconductor industry, L. D. Browning, J. M. Beyer, and J. C. Shelter, "Building Cooperation in a Competitive Industry: Sematech and the Semiconductor Industry," 1995 (p. 119), note that "this reversal of fortune for the semiconductor industry has (also) been attributed to several factors, including U.S. trade restrictions, the increasing impact of Korean manufacturing on the Japanese, the recession in Japan in the 1990s, and the efforts of Sematech (*Financial Times,* 1993)." They also quote Intel CEO Craig Barret as saying, "I judge Sematech by results. The organization set out to recover market share from Japan; five years later, market share has been recovered. At Intel we call that a results-oriented, successful project."

2. Experience and research indicate that even modest-size files of readily retrievable, rich descriptions of previously encountered problems and solutions can be of great use to decision makers seeking to draw on an analogous decision situation as guides in choosing actions. When a firm's experiences are captured and inventoried in this way, the result is a decision aid that greatly enhances the quality of decision makers' *case-based reasoning.* For elaboration on the nature and use of IT-facilitated case-based reasoning, see J. Kolodner, *Case-Based Reasoning,* 1993; and C. Riesbeck and R. Schank, *Inside Case-Based Reasoning,* 1989.

3. Parts of this section draw on and extend G. P. Huber, "Transfer of Knowledge in Knowledge Management Systems: Unexplored Issues and Suggested Studies," 2001.

4. Regarding early work on knowledge sharing and diffusion, see T. J. Allen, *Managing the Flow of Technology,* 1984; and D. C. Pelz and F. M. Andrews, *Scientists in Organizations,* 1996, and references therein. Regarding later work, see C. O'Dell and C. J. Grayson, *If Only We Knew What We Know: The Transfer of Internal Knowledge and Best Practices,* 1998; and E. M. Rogers, *Diffusion of Innovations,* 1995, and references therein. Concerning the generally unsatisfactory state of knowledge sharing and diffusion in firms, see the entire Special Issue on Knowledge and the Firm of the *California Management Review,* Spring 1998.

5. See, for example, J. Berry, "Employees Cash In on KM—Knowledge Management Programs Pay Rewards to Share Ideas," May 22, 2000; S. Koudsi, "Actually, It's Like Brain Surgery," March 20, 2000; W. C. Rappleye, "Knowledge Management: A Force Whose Time Has Come," January 2000; and C. Standing and S. Benson, "Knowledge Management in a Competitive Environment," 2000.

6. See *Salary Increases 1999-2000 (United States)* (Lincolnshire, IL: Hewitt Associates LLC, 2000).

7. This example is taken from C. Standing and S. Benson, "Knowledge Management in a Competitive Environment," 2000.

8. This common conundrum has been closely examined by Steve Kerr, former academic at Ohio State University and the University of Southern California, then CLO at GE, and now CLO and managing director at Goldman Sachs, in his classic article "On the Folly of Rewarding A, While Hoping for B," 1975, subsequently reprinted in the *Academy of Management Executive*, 1995.

9. For a study of hundreds of university faculty and administrative personnel and the factors that influence them to share or not share information and knowledge within their organization and within their professional association, see S. L. Jarvenpaa and S. Staples, "Exploring Perceptions of Organizational Ownership of Information and Expertise," 2001.

10. J. Pfeffer, "Six Dangerous Myths About Pay," 1998, provides a very readable but still well-grounded review of the idea that incentives for individual performance can reduce cooperation in work groups. Important, relevant research studies and summaries are those of J. R. Deckop, R. Mangel, and C. C. Cirka, "Getting More Than You Pay For: Organizational Citizenship Behavior and Pay-for-Performance Plans," 1999; R. Drago and G. T. Garvey, "Incentives for Helping on the Job: Theory and Evidence," 1998; E. E. Lawler III, "Reward Systems in Knowledge-Based Organizations," 2003; J. Pfeffer, *The Human Equation: Building Profits by Putting People First*, 1998; and R. Wageman, "Interdependence and Group Effectiveness," 1995. A. K. Gupta and V. Govindarajan, "Knowledge Flows Within Multinational Corporations," 2000a; "Knowledge Management's Social Dimension: Lessons From Nucor Steel," 2000b; and G. P. Huber, "Transfer of Knowledge in Knowledge Management Systems: Unexplored Issues and Suggested Studies," 2001, examine this idea in the context of knowledge sharing.

11. D. Constant, L. Sproull, and S. Kiesler, "The Kindness of Strangers: The Usefulness of Electronic Weak Ties for Technical Advice," 1996; S. L. Jarvenpaa and S. Staples, "Exploring Perceptions of Organizational Ownership of Information and Expertise," 2001; and W. J. Orlikowski, "Learning From Notes: Organizational Issues in Groupware Implementation," 1993, report studies demonstrating the effects of organizational culture on knowledge sharing.

12. See the article by D. Constant, L. Sproull, and S. Kiesler, "The Kindness of Strangers: The Usefulness of Electronic Weak Ties for Technical Advice," 1996. Whether weak ties lead to the sharing of highly complex knowledge is unclear—see M. T. Hansen, "The Search-Transfer Problem: The Role of Weak Ties in Sharing Knowledge Across Organization Subunits," 1999.

13. Examples and elaboration of this practice are provided by K. Moore and J. Birkenshaw, "Managing Knowledge in Global Service Firms: Centers of Excellence,"

1998; and M. Sarvary, "Knowledge Management and Competition in the Consulting Industry," 1999.

14. See D. Constant, L. Sproull, and S. Kiesler, "What's Mine Is Ours, or Is It? A Study of Attitudes About Information Sharing," 1994; "The Kindness of Strangers: The Usefulness of Electronic Weak Ties for Technical Advice," 1996; and M. Osterloh and B. S. Frey, "Motivation, Knowledge Transfer, and Organizational Forms," 2000, for reviews and studies of such forces in the context of knowledge sharing.

15. That extrinsic motivators frequently have a negative effect on desirable extra-role behaviors (such as knowledge sharing) is documented in R. Eisenberger and J. Cameron, "Detrimental Effects of Reward: Reality or Myth," 1996; S. Kerr, *Ultimate Rewards: What Really Motivates People to Achieve*, 1997; A. Kohn, "Why Incentive Plans Cannot Work," 1993; M. Osterloh and B. S. Frey, "Motivation, Knowledge Transfer, and Organizational Forms," 2000; and J. Pfeffer, *The Human Equation: Building Profits by Putting People First*, 1998.

16. See especially M. Osterloh and B. S. Frey, "Motivation, Knowledge Transfer, and Organizational Forms," 2000; and also C. O'Dell and C. J. Grayson, *If Only We Knew What We Know: The Transfer of Internal Knowledge and Best Practices*, 1998, for reviews of these studies.

17. For elaboration, see J. S. DeMatteo, L. T. Eby, and E. Sundstrom, "Team-Based Rewards: Current Empirical Evidence and Directions for Future Research," 1998; B. Graham-Moore and T. L. Ross, *Gainsharing and Employee Involvement*, 1995; E. E. Lawler III, *Rewarding Excellence: Pay Strategies for the New Economy*, 2000; E. E. Lawler III and S. G. Cohen, "Designing Pay Systems for Teams," 1992; S. L. Rynes and B. Gerhart, *Compensation in Organizations*, 2000; and R. Wageman, "Interdependence and Group Effectiveness," 1995.

18. R. M. Kramer, "Intergroup Relations and Organizational Dilemmas: The Role of Categorization Processes," 1991, provides an excellent discussion of group and organizational identification. The field studies of J. E. Dutton, J. M. Dukerich, and C. V. Harquail, "Organizational Images and Member Identification," 1994; and F. Mael and B. E. Ashforth, "Alumni and Their Alma Mater: A Partial Test of the Reformulated Model of Organizational Identification," 1992, demonstrate the importance of identification in affecting behavior.

19. For a review of the state of design of people-finder systems in organizations, see D. Yimam-Seid and Al Kobsa, "Expert-Finding Systems for Organizations: Problem and Domain Analysis and the DEMOIR Approach," 2003. T. L. Griffith and M. A. Neale, "Information Processing in Traditional, Hybrid, and Virtual Teams: From Nascent Knowledge to Transactive Memory," 2001; and T. L. Griffith, J. E. Sawyer, and M. A. Neale, "Virtualness and Knowledge in Teams: Managing the Love Triangle of Organizations, Individuals, and Information Technology," 2003, provide rich examinations of what is known about knowledge sharing in virtual teams.

20. This section draws on and extends G. P. Huber, "Facilitating Project Team Learning and Contributions to Organizational Knowledge," 1999.

21. See R. Nisbett and L. Ross, *Human Inference: Strategies and Shortcomings of Social Judgment*, 1980, for a review of studies of this particular attribution tendency. While the tendency is broad-based, it seems to be most apparent in the case of managers whose ideology is "authoritarian-conservative" (P. E. Tetlock, "Cognitive Biases and

Organizational Correctives: Do Both Disease and Cure Depend on the Politics of the Beholder?" 2000).

22.   See, for example, G. Szulanski, "Exploring Internal Stickiness: Impediments to the Transfer of Best Practices Within the Organization," 1996; parts of C. O'Dell and C. J. Grayson, *If Only We Knew What We Know: The Transfer of Internal Knowledge and Best Practices,* 1998; and especially L. Argote and P. Ingram, "Knowledge Transfer: A Basis for Competitive Advantage in Firms," 2000.

7

Innovation:
The Integration and
Exploitation of Knowledge

Product innovations dominate the popular press, but *process* innovations are often an important source of product success. An example of such a process innovation is Dell Computer's Morton L. Topfer Manufacturing Center, opened in 2000 to replace a nearby factory opened in 1997. The early design specifications for the new plant were straightforward: "We told them (the facilities planners) to basically double the output per employee and the output per square foot" (John Egan, Dell's Director of Desktop Operations, quoted in Jones, 2003: D1).

The space saving was achieved by eliminating in the new facility the 250,000-square-foot "sorting center" where, in the 1997 facility, orders were batched for shipping. The increase in employee productivity—it was five times greater at the new facility in 2002 than at the previous facility in 2000—was achieved through a combination of changes. One was the reallocation of transportation and storage tasks between Dell and its suppliers, a change greatly enabled by information technology—key elements of which were obtained from an outside contractor. Other changes involved designing the factory and the computers themselves to reduce by about 50% the number of times a computer is touched by employees during its assembly and shipping. Because sales of desktop computers are very price sensitive, this highly efficient innovation clearly contributes to the success of the computers it produces.

Close consideration of this example makes clear that *innovation requires a new integration of knowledge.* As a first step, knowledge is integrated in a way that is new—to the innovator at least and perhaps to the industry or

177

world.[a] As a second step, the resulting product or process is brought "into effect," perhaps as a product that is selling in the marketplace or a process that is functioning in the firm. This step, too, requires at least some new integration of knowledge, as the particular product or process has never before been brought into effect in the context where it appears.

Because it is uncommon to frame innovation as a new integration of knowledge, it may be useful to recall from our chapter on organizational learning that

> customers want either the best quality, the best service, or the best value. To survive, firms must provide one or more of these best-of-class product features on a nearly continuous basis. As we've seen, advances in technology eventually cause any level of quality, service, or value to become outmoded. Thus firms *innovate*— they make changes in their products or processes so that at least some portion of the market sees their products as best-of-class. How do firms achieve best-of-class products? There is only one way—they integrate into their products, or into the processes used to provide their products, *knowledge* not previously so used. *All products contain knowledge,* usually a great deal of it. For example, embedded . . . in a product such as an airplane, are millions of workdays of knowledge creation and acquisition (and application) by scientists, engineers, managers, and skilled workers.[1]

These thoughts make clear that innovation requires a fresh integration of knowledge, integration either of knowledge already existing in the firm or integration of this knowledge with knowledge new to the firm (this latter obtained either experientially or vicariously). So, what will be different about innovation in the future? A straightforward answer and perhaps the most obvious difference is that the future's faster rate of technological change and higher levels of environmental dynamism and competitiveness will require that, to survive in the marketplace, *future firms will innovate more frequently.*[b]

---

[a]Allow me to explain how I'll be using some terms. In this book, an *invention* is something new, useful, and non-obvious. An *innovation* is an invention that is "in effect" (e.g., a product that is selling in the marketplace or a process that is functioning in the firm). Depending on the context, inventions and innovations can be new to different entities (e.g., to the organization, to the industry, or to the world). *Product development* is the process of transforming a new product idea into a marketable product.

[b]While innovating more frequently may be hard to fathom, given how difficult it is to imagine that today's firms could innovate more often than they do, both logic and observation of a decade-long trend of company behaviors lead to this conclusion. Recall from Footnote e in Chapter 2 that, in their recent *Harvard Business Review* article, top officers of Cap Gemini Ernst & Young's Center for Business Innovation report that "in 2001, companies introduced 35,000 new consumer products, up from 15,000 ten years ago" (Meyer & Ruggles, 2002).

In some respects innovation is like crime solving. The outcomes often make headlines, and after-the-fact reviews make liberal use of "discover" and "discovery." But perhaps the most interesting parallel is that, while both processes have a sense of drama, close scrutiny shows that a large proportion of what goes on is mundane. Small routines play a big part. Some involve acquiring knowledge. We encountered them in Chapter 5. Some involve sharing and storing knowledge. We encountered them in Chapter 6. Others, numerous and diverse, but all contributing to knowledge integration, we will examine in this chapter.[c]

The less obvious differences between innovation in the past and innovation in future firms follow from the forthcoming growth in the world's stock of knowledge. As we will see, this growth will force changes in the ways knowledge is integrated, will force changes on how firms innovate. These differences between how things have been done and how they will be done are quite varied, and thus this chapter deals with a wide range of topics. The next section highlights the fact that occupational specialization will increase. This fact introduces the issue addressed in the chapter's second section—the challenge of integrating the knowledge of many much more specialized knowledge workers. The third, fourth, and fifth sections of the chapter examine new issues related to integrating knowledge from outside the firm with knowledge already in the firm.

Occupational Specialization

In 1903 the two brothers Wilbur and Orville Wright knew nearly everything they needed to know to design their biplane and make the first ever manned flight (of 120 feet). But certainly the knowledge of more than two "experts" was involved in designing the customized Wright Aeronautical Corporation monoplane that enabled Charles Lindberg's *Spirit of St. Louis* flight across the Atlantic 24 years later. And certainly many hundreds of kinds of expertise were employed in designing the mammoth, twice-as-fast-as-the-speed-of-sound Concorde that first crossed the Atlantic in 1971. Thus, as the century progressed and the amount of aircraft-relevant knowledge grew, so too did the variety of experts required to create new and better products. At the same time, any one of the individual experts involved in the industry came to possess proportionately less of the knowledge needed to design the next new aircraft.

---

[c]Some topics from Chapters 5 and 6 are examined again in this chapter, but in more depth and with an emphasis on their contribution to innovation.

This story about aircraft experts is an example of a widespread change that has taken place in the environment of business organizations—the increased specialization of experts. As we will see later in the chapter, this increase in specialization will continue and will become a more potent determinant of (1) structures for managing innovation, (2) the employment practices of firms, and (3) the employment strategies of experts.[d]

To attain their sustenance-providing niche within the tribe, and then within the town, and now, for some, in the global labor marketplace, people have specialized occupationally. As a consequence of the long-occurring growth in knowledge, specialization has moved from being based on natural physical assets, to being based on skill, and now, today, to being based largely on type and depth of knowledge. But besides the growth of knowledge, another factor also plays a role in the movement to occupational specialization—our cognitive limitations, our limited ability to absorb knowledge. Certainly since the Renaissance, and perhaps before, an individual's ability to absorb new knowledge has been increasing much less rapidly than has the growth in the world's knowledge.[e]

Interesting observations concerning an individual's dwindling capacity to know all there is to know:

Renaissance man—the typical educated, cultured man of the Renaissance, who, because the knowledge of the world was generally limited, was able to know everything there was to know about a great variety of given subjects.

Webster's Encyclopedic Unabridged
Dictionary of the English Language, 1999.

(Continued)

---

[d]We've seen repeatedly how practices of firms are strongly influenced by the actions of other entities in the business environment—customers, competitors, regulators, and so forth. Especially as knowledge becomes a more important resource, and especially as the newest, potentially most valuable knowledge resides in the minds of experts, the employment strategies of experts will become more of a factor in the employment practices of future firms.

[e]However little knowledge we may absorb, for example, from the content of an article about subatomic particles or about mental disorders, in almost all cases we can absorb more than our grandparents could. This is because we have more background about these and many other matters, from our schooling and from our everyday media perusal and social discourse. The more we know about a subject, the more effectively we can learn about the subject. Because people in each generation are exposed to more knowledge throughout their lives than were their ancestors, they are more able to absorb knowledge about most subjects more effectively. Thus it is true that the ability of individuals to absorb knowledge has been increasing—but quite slowly relative to the tremendous growth in the amount of knowledge available to be absorbed.

(Continued)

England in the 1770s . . . when it was quite possible for a man of (Adam) Smith's intellectual stature virtually to embrace the great body of knowledge of his times.

Heilbroner, R. L., 1992. *The Worldly Philosophers*, p. 52.

Gentlemen, you are probably the most distinguished gathering of intellectuals to have dined at the Executive Mansion, with the possible exception of when Mr. Thomas Jefferson dined here alone.

President John F. Kennedy, to a group of Nobel Prize winners, 1962.

To a great extent, increases in occupational specialization—especially in recent decades—are the consequence of people being confronted with a tremendous growth in the body of knowledge relevant to their occupation. Faced with this, a large and growing proportion of the labor force has had to specialize, has had to forego achieving a breadth of knowledge in order to achieve or retain mastery over a smaller range of knowledge that has grown in depth. *One consequence of past growth in the world's knowledge is today's specialized workforce.*

As we saw in Chapter 2, the world's knowledge in the future will be much greater than it is today. Just as the average person today possesses more knowledge than did the average person decades ago, individuals in the future will know more—in an absolute sense—than do individuals today. But in a relative sense they will know less. That is, *individuals in the future will know a smaller proportion of all that is known.* Even with improvements in learning methods and learning aids, growth in the world's stock of knowledge combined with limits on human cognitive abilities will force individuals in the future into ever narrower realms of expertise.

There is an alarming increase in the number of things I know nothing about.

(commonly attributed to Berkeley "street philosopher" Ashley Brilliant).

Recall from Chapter 5 that "any increases in the performance or value of a product or class of products can be achieved only by applying knowledge not previously applied in the product's design, production, or marketing." It follows that firms seeking to provide products superior to those available will—with only rare exceptions—need to incorporate *ever larger quantities* of knowledge into these products.[2] For example, just as previous generations of aircraft embodied within themselves more knowledge than did their predecessors, the aircraft that supersede today's commercial aircraft will have incorporated within them more knowledge than do the Airbus 380 and the Boeing 777. At the same time, drawing on the reasoning of these several pages, the individual experts that firms employ will know an *ever smaller amount* of the knowledge necessary to generate these new, superior products.

From these ideas, it seems reasonable to conclude that, in the future, any one expert will tend to know an ever decreasing portion of what a firm needs to know in order to create a given percentage improvement in a current product or in a new product that serves the same market need.

Because each type of expert will be able to contribute a smaller portion of the total knowledge needed, it follows that achieving an improvement equal in significance to previous improvements will require a greater variety of experts. *In the future, a greater variety of experts will be necessary to create a given percentage improvement in a current product or in a new product that serves the same market need.*

Among the ways that the specialization of knowledge workers has affected the structure of firms is that along with knowledge specialization comes the need for knowledge integration. That is, while an *invention* can be produced by a single individual, in contrast almost all *innovations* require integration of the knowledge of several or many people. As John Kenneth Galbraith, Harvard economist and adviser to Presidents Kennedy and Johnson, once observed,

> The real accomplishment of modern science and technology comes in taking ordinary men, informing them narrowly and deeply and then, through appropriate organization, arranging to have their knowledge combined with that of other specialized but equally ordinary men. This dispenses with the need for genius. (Galbraith, 1971: 60-61)

Robert Grant, George Washington University business school professor and authority on the strategic value of knowledge to the firm, more recently put the matter into a business context:

> If the strategically most important resource of the firm is knowledge, and if knowledge resides in specialized form among individual organizational members, then the essence of organizational capability is the integration of individuals' specialized knowledge. . . . The primary role of the firm, and the essence of organizational capability, is the integration of knowledge. (Grant, 1996b: 375)

> The critical source of competitive advantage is knowledge integration rather than knowledge itself. (Grant, 1996b: 383)

This is what firms do. Firms arrange for the knowledge, expertise, and skills of specialized men and women to be combined and integrated into products. This is what firms will do in the future. But organizational processes and structures for combining the knowledge of specialized individuals have changed during the last few decades as a result of increases in the world's stock of knowledge. And they will change further, as the growth in knowledge accelerates.

As a foundation for examining the effects of *future knowledge growth* on the *forthcoming knowledge integration structures* of future firms, it will be useful first to see with some clarity the structures now in use. The following brief review is intended to help in this regard. It might also suggest to some readers that *today's knowledge integration structures are merely a temporary mix in a continually changing aggregate of structural forms*, as contrasted—for example—with being the high point on some truncated graph of organizational evolution. We will return to this rather challenging idea later in the chapter.

Within-Firm Approaches for Speeding Knowledge Integration: A Brief Recounting

Instances of unacceptably slow aggregation of knowledge are a part of almost everyone's experience. In his 1998 *Sloan Management Review* article, Harvard Business School professor David Garvin reports a study of white-collar processes *for integrating information and decisions* where it was found that "value-added time (the time in which a product or service has value added to it, as opposed to waiting in a queue or being reworked to fix problems caused earlier) is typically less than five percent of total processing time" (p. 35). While research yet to come may find less (or more!) extreme values, this finding does suggest why firms are motivated to search for alternative approaches to more rapidly combine the information and other forms of knowledge contained in the minds of their employees.

The problems associated with integrating knowledge rapidly have long been discussed in the management literature and have been attacked in industry with gradually increasing success.[3] Wartime pressure for speed contributed to the development and diffusion of matrix structures (to replace the functional structures discussed in Endnote 3) in the U.S. defense industry during the third quarter of the twentieth century. That competitors would introduce new and improved products before the firm did was a universal threat that forced the proliferation of team-based structures (again, to replace functional structures) during the fourth quarter of that century. At the beginning of the twenty-first century, the three most fashionable practices for combining expert knowledge to generate new products were cross-functional project teams, concurrent engineering, and use of modular architectures.

PROJECT TEAMS

Project teams are composed of individuals working interactively to bring to bear their individual functional or technical expertise on a project.[4] Typically the team members have different functional responsibilities or different types of expertise. The team's typical task is to integrate its members' knowledge, as when a consultancy team develops a plan for dealing with a client's declining market share. Project teams are sometimes self-managed, with no hierarchy, but more often have a project manager or team leader who does some coordination of team members and is the primary link to the larger organization. (As used here, "team" refers to a group that is coordinated by no more than one "leader" or manager. When more than one leader or manager is required to coordinate the efforts of subgroups, we will think of the structure as having multiple teams.)

When the sought-after innovation is of *high complexity* (such as the first-of-its-kind computer factory described earlier), more varieties of expertise are required. The structure becomes one in which multiple project teams, each producing a different knowledge module needed in the innovation, are coordinated by a *program manager* working with the team leaders. Especially when the knowledge modules are difficult to understand, or when downstream teams in the knowledge integration process can greatly benefit from information about the evolving nature of knowledge modules from upstream teams, much of the interteam coordination is done by the team leaders themselves rather than by the program manager. This *network of team leaders* serves as a *virtual* layer of management. It speeds horizontal communication. Its mixed effects on vertical communication have apparently not been studied.

The benefit, under these conditions, of intermodule coordination by team leaders is that team leaders tend to be technically more proficient than is the program manager in the specific areas of interface between their project and the projects of immediately adjacent teams. As a consequence they are more able to coordinate expertise, a critical component of the overall coordination task. For example, in their 2000 study of "Coordinating Expertise in Software Development Teams," Samer Faraj of the University of Maryland and Lee Sproull of New York University found that "expertise coordination (knowing where expertise is located, where it is needed, and bringing it to bear) shows a strong relationship with team performance that remains significant over and above team input characteristics, presence of expertise, and administrative coordination" (p. 1554).

Combining the knowledge modules is a difficult task. The modules are not always as compatible as was planned, so integrating them can be technically difficult. In addition, pride of ownership and reluctance to rework what has been done create fertile ground for conflict. While integration is often achieved by the project team leaders, it is also frequently the case that conflicts cannot be resolved by the team leaders in a timely manner. As a result, the next level of management (e.g., the project manager) gets involved. Managers at this level possess more organizationally relevant knowledge (e.g., the relative priorities assigned to various product attributes and the current budgetary situation) and also, if necessary, can call on uninvolved (and consequently more objective) experts who possess the knowledge needed to resolve technical disagreements.

> The principal driving force behind the evolution of teams for integrating specialists' knowledge was the need to compete on the basis of speed. The ongoing growth of egalitarianism in the workplace may have played a role as well, particularly as knowledge workers increasingly sought to influence the nature of their work and work environment and as firms were forced to compete for knowledge workers with attractive working conditions. We will examine this and other changes in the firm's human resources environment later in this chapter and in Chapter 8.

This review concludes with a brief discussion of two procedures, concurrent engineering and the use of modular architecture, that in the 1990s began to receive much wider recognition and implementation than they had in the past.

CONCURRENT ENGINEERING AND MODULAR ARCHITECTURE

When the knowledge integration task is fairly well understood, as are many instances in the design-development-manufacture-marketing of hard goods, the rather formalized process of concurrent engineering is often used. The central concept in concurrent engineering is to make the steps in the knowledge integration sequence overlap as much as possible, but—at the same time—to avoid the need for downstream teams to revise their work (as would be the case when the knowledge modules from upstream teams are different from what was anticipated). For example, the downstream engineering design of a personal pager could begin sooner if it overlapped with the pager's upstream industrial design. The risk of needing to later change engineering design features could be reduced if the final "maximum block dimensions" of the industrial design were frozen and communicated to engineering—even though the industrial-design group had not finished determining the pager's precise shape.[5]

The high need for accurate, precise, and timely transfer of information about the evolving nature of the knowledge products to be contributed by the several teams causes much of the coordination to be carried out by the *project-execution team*. The members of this team are liaisons, members themselves of the teams of specialists whose work is upstream or downstream from the work of the other specialized teams. These liaisons are generally the team leaders of the specialized teams. They coordinate the flow of knowledge products from one team to another, but under the close direction of the program manager who is intimately involved in coordinating the overall effort.[6]

When the firm's or industry's experience with the innovation puts the firm high on the learning curve (i.e., when the firm is well learned about the knowledge modules and the manner of their integration into a process or product architecture), *modular architectures* are used to design the knowledge-containing modules. As with concurrent engineering, modularization and modular architectures are more commonly used in the development of hard goods, but also in the development of intellectual products that can be assembled from modules, such as software and sequences of operations.[7]

A system's architecture is the scheme by which the system's components are interconnected. It is also a way in which the functionality of a system is partitioned or allocated among components. In an *integral architecture*, changes in components frequently force changes in other components. In a modular architecture, the components are not tightly coupled. This allows changes in some components not to affect the design of other components.

Modularity is created in an architecture when the interfaces between functional components are standardized (i.e., not allowed to change over some period of time) and specified to allow the substitution of a range of variations in components into the product architecture without requiring changes in the designs of other components. (Sanchez, 1995: 95)

INTERIM SUMMARY AND TRANSITION

Let us summarize these last several pages. We began with the observation that the world's stock of knowledge has grown enormously. We observed that this growth has led to increases in occupational specialization. Greater specialization has in turn increased the need for knowledge integration, the means through which firms innovate as they attempt to produce ever superior goods and services. At the same time, this growth in knowledge has led to the advances in the effectiveness of communication and transportation technologies that increased the rate at which competitors could create and introduce new products. Thus firms have been forced to compete on the basis of speed. We saw that one consequence of these environmental changes has been the proliferation and diffusion of team-based structures and the expanded recognition and implementation of concurrent engineering and modular architecture.

Given that firms have invented in the past approaches such as these for dealing with the need for speedy knowledge integration in the pursuit of rapid innovation, it seems unlikely that the nature or mix of knowledge integration structures and procedures in use will not change in keeping with the increases in environmental dynamism and competitiveness that will cause the need for rapid innovation to rise to heretofore unseen levels. In this regard, we should remind ourselves that *new and newly commonplace organizational forms have been appearing at an increasing rate*. For example, during the twentieth century

1. the multidivisional corporate form was invented and became commonplace,
2. the assembly line and the administrative machinery for its control were invented and became commonplace,
3. the matrix and project team structures evolved and became pervasive,
4. the virtual organizational form and other arrangements of autonomous firms increased greatly in number and in the range of their application,
5. firms divested themselves of components not directly related to their core competence, and
6. firms delayered and became flatter.[8]

Finally, we might remind ourselves that systematic studies continue to uncover factors that contribute to successful innovation.[9] It seems likely that the findings of these studies will find their way into the structures and practices of innovation-seeking firms.

These observations of a century of evolution of structural forms in firms serve as a strong indication that today's knowledge integration structures are merely a temporary mix in a continually changing aggregate of structural forms. Said differently, it seems certain that future firms will employ structures and procedures for integrating knowledge different in nature or mix from those employed in the past. Let us turn to examining some knowledge integration approaches that future firms will use.

Knowledge Integration Structures in the Future

Earlier in this chapter, Galbraith and Grant reminded us that firms create value in their products or increases in the effectiveness of their operations by combining knowledge. Bearing on this are the facts that, in the future,

1. any one expert will tend to know an ever decreasing portion of what needs to be known to create a given percentage improvement in product performance,

2. a greater variety of experts will be necessary to develop and produce a new product of a given type, and

3. there will be an increasing demand for speed in the development of products, and thus an increasing demand for speed in the integration of knowledge.

These thoughts, and our earlier example concerning the increasing variety of experts needed to create generations of aircraft, make clear that producing a new product in the future—equal in market attractiveness and impact to a new product introduced to serve the same general market need in the past—will mean combining the knowledge of more experts from more varied domains. This will pose organizational-design challenges for future firms greater than those faced by today's firms. More specifically, the task of combining the knowledge of more individuals, each more narrowly specialized, is more complicated than is the present task of combining the knowledge of fewer, more broadly knowledgeable individuals. And, of course, adding to this is the fact that increased competition and faster changes in products and markets will require this knowledge integration to be accomplished more rapidly. Altogether, these facts portray an environment for innovation different from what we see today. As a consequence, keeping in mind the need for organizations to be congruent with their environments, we must conclude that, *in the future, firms will invent and employ structures and processes for integrating knowledge that were unknown or not yet common near the beginning of the twenty-first century.*

Further, given that the integration task will be more complicated and yet the pressure for rapid integration will be greater, it also seems reasonable to conclude that, *in the future, structures and processes for integrating knowledge will be employed with relative frequencies different from those apparent today.*

New organizational structures and processes proliferate when current forms are ineffective in meeting major threats or in exploiting new opportunities.[10] What processes and structures will future firms employ to more rapidly integrate the knowledge of larger numbers of ever more highly specialized individuals? Let us turn to possible answers. We begin with within-firm structures and processes. In subsequent sections we will examine structures and processes for bringing external knowledge into the firm and combining it with knowledge already present.

Changes in Within-Firm Structures and Processes

We saw earlier that producing a product-improving module of knowledge—equal in terms of its proportional impact to the module used to improve a previous product serving the same market need—has meant combining the knowledge of more experts. And so it will be in the future. Significantly increasing the number of experts and support staff involved in an innovation effort will necessarily result in changes in the firm's structures or processes or both.

STRUCTURES

From this need for the knowledge of more individuals, it follows that in an increasing proportion of instances, the number of experts necessary to develop or produce a new product *of a given type* will more frequently exceed the manageable size of a team. As a consequence, we can expect that, *in the future, the proportion of product improvements or new products created with a single team will decline.*[f]

Similarly, given that more knowledge will be required, but that team size is constrained, we can also conclude that, *in the future, the number of project teams required to achieve a given percentage improvement in a current product, or in a new product that serves the same market need, will increase.*

Knowledge that is newly created, as is the knowledge generated by project teams, tends to be tacit and ill-structured and consequently difficult to communicate. Transferring such "sticky" knowledge accurately, precisely, and rapidly can be achieved more effectively through team-to-team contacts than it can using a program manager as a go-between. This becomes increasingly the case as the number of project teams increases (and nearly exponentially increases the program's coordination load on the program manager). We can expect, therefore, that the team-to-team knowledge transfer described earlier will more often be used to satisfy the demands created by tomorrow's innovation-demanding environment. *The structures of future firms will more frequently include networks of teams.*

As we just saw, when the number of specialists needed to create an innovation increases, as will more often be the case, the number of teams also increases. Coordinating large numbers of specialized teams is difficult, just as is coordinating large numbers of specialized experts. So, the aggregate of teams is organized into groups of teams. The individual teams produce team-knowledge modules that are later combined to create group-knowledge modules. These in turn are integrated in producing the innovation. Coordination of these groups of teams is achieved through the same mechanisms as is coordination of teams (networks of team leaders and superordinate managers) and, again, another level of management—real or virtual—is added. Thus forthcoming increases

---

[f]Recall that, as used in this book, "team" refers to a group coordinated by no more than one leader or manager.

in specialization will lead to increases in the number of people involved in creating innovations, and—through the integration-of-knowledge processes just examined—these increases in the number of people will lead to increases in the number of managerial levels.

Unless effective offsetting mechanisms are employed, the number of managerial levels in innovative firms will increase. How will firms resist the growth in the number of managerial levels that would follow from the ever growing number of specialists and support staff required to create innovations?

PROCESSES

Let us be clear about the particular issue we are addressing. This potential increase in the number of managerial levels is driven by the real increase in the number of specialists required to create a given percentage improvement in a current product or in a new product intended to supplant the current product. Attempting to integrate ever larger amounts of expert knowledge leads to involvement of ever larger numbers of specialists and teams, and ultimately leads to unwieldy organizations. More specifically, attempting to incorporate more mind-resident knowledge into products causes increases in the number of employees and in the firm's horizontal and vertical dimensions.

The potential rise in the number of managerial levels due to increases in the number of personnel can be lessened if team-to-team coordination is made more effective. In this regard, it seems reasonable to believe that use of tomorrow's more advanced communication technologies will have positive effects on team-to-team knowledge integration and conflict resolution, especially technologies high in telepresence. One particular outcome of using such technologies would be to bring coordination communication among teams distanced in space or time closer to the higher levels of communication frequency and effectiveness obtained by collocated teams that can meet face to face.[8] Thus, to minimize the potential rise in the number of managerial levels that follow from increases in functional or technical specialization, we can expect that *future firms will more intensely employ high-telepresence communication technologies for coordinating knowledge integration.*

---

[8]Recall from Chapter 4 that telepresence is the communication technology user's assessment of "being there," the sense of being in the physical and social situation that the user has accessed via the technology. Higher levels of telepresence more closely approximate the face-to-face communication that people tend to prefer when communicating about complex or sensitive matters, such as communications involving the transfer of tacit knowledge or the reduction of disagreement.

We arrived at this conclusion by examining the effect of the growth in the world's stock of knowledge, which will increase the level of occupational specialization, which in turn will increase the number of specialists involved in creating innovations, which in turn will increase the need for coordination and the number of managerial levels. It seems important to recognize that the use of more effective communication technology will not only retard the potential rise in the number of managerial levels but more generally will increase the effectiveness of the whole innovation enterprise. As experience makes this apparent, we can expect to see the use of communication technology high in telepresence become commonplace. Of course people will continue to convey easily communicated or more routine information using technologies low in telepresence (low in richness), such as e-mail and even hard-copy mail.

Let us return for a moment to the greater requirement for speed that will face future firms in their development and introduction of innovations. Given the heightened demand for speed when attempting to satisfy the market's demands for the best products or the best values, we can anticipate that more firms will more often attempt to overlap the efforts of their project teams. As a result of the learning that follows from these experiences, the firms will become more adept at the task and will increasingly be able to adhere to the concepts and practices of concurrent engineering. Thus we can expect that *future firms will more frequently employ the concepts and procedures of concurrent engineering and modular architecture.*

In this section we examined differences between today's and tomorrow's firms in the structures and processes they will use to exploit their knowledge in the pursuit of innovation. But, as documented in Chapter 5, in most firms most of the time, innovations are prompted or enabled to a significant extent by information or knowledge originating outside the firm. In the next two sections, we will continue with our focus on integrating the mind-resident knowledge of specialists, but will consider how firms will draw on the expertise available in the external labor market and how experts will position themselves in this market. In the last topical section of the chapter we will examine future firms' approaches to acquiring knowledge from other autonomous firms.

Changes in Firms' Employment Practices

Earlier we concluded that, "in the future, any one expert will tend to know an ever decreasing portion of what a firm needs to know in order to create a given percentage improvement in a current product or in a new product that serves the same market need," and that, "in the future, a greater variety of experts will be necessary to create a given percentage improvement in a current product or in a new product that serves the same market need."[h] These two conditions, along with other factors to be considered shortly, will force future firms to engage in employment practices different from those we see today. These differences will involve changes in how firms approach workforce resizing, management of turnover, staffing, and compensation. We will examine how future firms will alter their workforce size and manage their turnover and compensation in Chapter 8. Here we examine future staffing practices.

DRAWING ON EXPERTISE

As noted earlier, the growth in the world's stock of occupationally relevant knowledge has forced people to become more highly specialized in the knowledge that they possess and sell. At the same time, more dynamic business environments have made the need for any particular specialized knowledge more fleeting. In combination, these circumstances have diminished the likelihood that any particular firm is able to keep highly specialized experts fully occupied *in their areas of specialization*. This has created problems for specialized experts and for the firms that need their expertise. Specialists dislike working outside their specialty, at least for long periods—one reason being fear of obsolescence. And firms cannot afford to pay for expertise seldom used. These two realities, combined with the fact that, in the future, an ever increasing variety of specialists will be needed to develop, produce, and market an improved product, will cause future firms not to retain in-house

---

[h] It may be worthwhile at this point to note the dimensions of expertise that might be of value to a firm, depending on the firm's current requirements. As used here, "experts" are experts who are especially learned in a specific field. Some possess *deeper* knowledge, and can accordingly accomplish tasks other experts cannot. Some experts possess new, *leading edge* knowledge. They, too, can accomplish what others cannot. It will sometimes be convenient when speaking collectively of experts possessing special, deeper, or leading edge knowledge, to refer to them collectively as "particularly qualified," or "highly qualified," or "specialized" experts.

cadres of experts whose specialized knowledge is needed only on occasion. Instead, *future firms will more frequently employ specialized experts on a temporary basis.*[i]

While working for a small software company, I once observed a prototypical example of this practice of renting expertise. The company had been doing well for several years making incremental improvements on its single product. Then it suddenly developed a very different product, one believed to have high market potential. The company's marketing personnel were experienced at marketing the current commodity-like product and its variations, but were inexperienced and ill prepared to introduce a new and quite different product to a new and different market. The solution to this "employment problem" was to find and hire an independent contractor whose specialty was the *introduction* of new business software. The one (and only) such person found made it clear to the company that after the product was "in the market" (he estimated 9 months), he would be bored, no longer drawing on his expertise, and ready to move on. So a 9-month contract it was, and the expectations of all parties were fulfilled within that time window.

The use of temporary workers expanded greatly during the 1990s. But adoption of this practice was generally more a matter of managing overall labor costs than it was a matter of managing the availability of expertise. In contrast, note that here we are not speaking about outsourcing work to reduce costs or to unload tasks not associated with the firm's core competencies. Rather we are talking about temporarily employing specialized experts solely because their knowledge is needed quickly and not available within the firm.

---

[i]This conclusion may seem less valid for firms that are knowledge-intensive, huge, and heterogeneous, such as 3M and GE. But, due to the forthcoming increases in the levels of specialization that will characterize future experts, it will nevertheless become valid even for firms such as these. It may also seem less valid for firms that employ highly specialized experts so that the firm can provide highly specialized knowledge to other firms. But, for the same reason—future increases in specialization—the conclusion will be more valid in the future for these firms as well. More on these matters later in the chapter.

The above paragraphs dealt largely with the change in duration of employment relationships between firms and specialized experts. Another change in the staffing practices of future firms involves how the expertise of such experts is integrated into the firm's products or processes. This second change is driven by the nature of new knowledge. Specifically, the new, leading edge knowledge most likely to contribute to new-to-the-market innovations is often still tacit or at least, because it is still not well understood, difficult both to convey and to assimilate. In a word, it is "sticky." Integrating and instilling such knowledge into products or processes generally requires a degree of intense personal interaction among those involved in the innovation.[11] Such interaction is not commonly found in outsourcing relationships. The necessary knowledge transfer occurs most effectively when specially qualified experts are able to interact with the firm's experts frequently and intensely, as they could if they were on-site members of a project team.[j]

What we are talking about, then, is the temporary bringing into the firm of specially qualified experts, not so much to learn from them— although this will always be attempted—but rather to get work done in the near term that the firm could not get done without their particular knowledge. What we are speaking of is the temporary "insourcing" of particular expertise. This is not to say that outsourcing of certain tasks, even knowledge-intensive tasks, will diminish. Rather it is to emphasize the effect on employment practices of the greater need in the future for the firm to import and absorb the sticky knowledge possessed by specialized experts. To get such knowledge effectively transferred, *future firms will more frequently bring temporarily employed, specially qualified experts deep into the intellectual operations of the firm.*[12]

Some of these temporarily employed experts will be taken on as employees with specific-duration contracts, as was—for example—the temporarily hired marketing expert described above (whose specialty was the introduction of new business software). Others will work on a project basis with indefinite duration contracts. Some will be borrowed or leased from other firms, as when—due to the highly irregular pattern of workloads—the interfirm borrowing and lending of experts became commonplace among collocated U.S. defense firms in the 1950s and 1960s.

---

[j]Although it is not often discussed in the management or technology transfer literatures, a specially qualified expert's contribution and value to the firm is greatly a function of the ability of the expert and the firm's regular employees to work together in getting the expert's knowledge brought to bear on the firm's task. This "ability" includes both a sufficient level of interpersonal competence on the part of both parties and a sufficient level of absorptive capacity on the part of the firm's employees.

The temporary employment relationship between a firm and a specialized expert is often characterized by a balance of power, by mutual respect, and by a lack of specificity regarding working hours, hours worked per day, term of employment, and specific deliverables. Further, mutual adjustment of whatever understandings were agreed to on such matters often takes place as the work unfolds. (It is not unusual, in fact, for a fixed-term contract to evolve into an indefinite-term contract.)

The interparty cooperation that characterizes these relationships, and that makes such flexibility as much the norm as not, follows from one or more of three conditions frequently found in these relationships: (1) the expert and the manager responsible for getting the task accomplished have similar professional backgrounds and values, (2) both parties recognize that they may want either to extend or repeat their relationship, and (3) the parties are operating in a "small world," where a favorable or unfavorable reputation can greatly affect the success of their future participation in the labor market.[13]

FINDING EXPERTISE

A *thin* labor market is one where, for a given task or occupation, there are few job openings and few job candidates. The labor market for highly qualified experts is just such a market. Further, because the forthcoming growth in knowledge will force increases in occupational specialization, *the labor market for highly qualified experts will be thinner in the future.* How will future firms find such experts when they need them? One way will be to do what firms do now—rely on word-of-mouth searches. Phone calls are made to a few people likely to know of someone having the required knowledge. These calls result in referrals to other people even more likely to know of such an expert, and so on until the required expert is located. Experience shows that this *traditional* approach, while low cost, is somewhat tedious and tends not to generate a very large pool of candidates—with resultant questions about whether the firm got the best expertise it could afford. It is especially inadequate in a thin market, as is the labor market for specialized experts. Another traditional approach is to "search" by seeking responses to advertisements posted in print media.

As increases in environmental dynamism and competition heighten the need for experts with particular qualifications, firms will seek more effective and efficient *nontraditional* approaches to finding them. Starting from the near-zero base level of the early 1990s, the absolute growth in hires resulting from Internet searches will be considerable.[k] That is, because future labor markets will be more global than they are today, and because the Internet is a global communication medium, we can expect that future firms will more frequently use Internet searches to identify possible employees, especially employees with particular expertise. Of course, one advantage of the word-of-mouth search and referral system described above is that a certain amount of goodness-of-match screening takes place, by all parties and in both directions. So we can expect that both firms and experts will continue to use this personal reference system, while at the same time taking advantage of the Internet or its successors to increase the number of possible contacts. We can expect, too, that improvements in the Internet and other communication media and increased availability of media high in tele-presence, in combination with further learning by both firms and experts about the effective use of these media, will cause the media to become more useful screening aids and therefore used more often.

We can also expect another mechanism to more commonly serve part of the expert-for-rent labor market. Brokers performing the same function in the specially qualified expert labor markets that executive search firms now perform in the executive labor market will appear and act as referral agents. Use of this mechanism will be limited, however, as in many fields it will be unlikely that aspiring brokers will have the expertise needed to correctly assess the exact nature of a firm's technical needs or the exact nature of an expert's qualifications.

Here we've examined the effect on recruiting practices of an important change in the future environments of business organizations—the thinning of labor markets for certain types of experts. Because the more dynamic nature of forthcoming business environments will cause firms to suddenly need expertise they don't have, it seems reasonable to conclude that *future firms will more frequently employ nontraditional approaches to finding specially qualified experts.*

INTERIM SUMMARY AND TRANSITION

In this section on the staffing and compensation practices of future firms, we drew three conclusions. One was that firms will more frequently employ

---

[k]The early *percentage* growth, as contrasted with *absolute* growth, has already been considerable—as we would expect. See Harvard Professor Peter Cappelli's "Making the Most of On-Line Recruiting" in the March 2001 issue of the *Harvard Business Review*. As firms and experts learn to use such media more effectively, they will tend to use it more frequently.

experts on a temporary basis. Another was that firms will more frequently bring temporarily employed, specially qualified experts deep into the firm. The third conclusion was that higher levels of specialization among experts will lead to ever thinner labor markets, a condition that will cause firms to more frequently use the Internet and other more effective information technologies to find the expertise they need to create and exploit a competitive advantage.

The nature of the labor market is, of course, determined jointly by firms and workers. The actions that firms take in the market affect workers, and the actions workers take affect firms. Let us turn now to the combined effects on experts, and particularly on specialized experts, of (1) increases in the rate at which knowledge grows and (2) changes in experts' employment practices.

Changes in Experts' Employment Strategies

The effect of the increased specialization of experts, along with the reluctance of firms to suffer the ongoing costs of experts whose specialization is not fully utilized, is that the likelihood that a highly specialized expert *can* find full-time employment with any one firm has begun to decline from what it was during most of the twentieth century. A second consequence, to be explained shortly, is that the likelihood that such experts *want* full-time employment with any one firm has also begun to decline. In response to these conditions, an employment strategy adopted by a growing number of experts is to become independent contractors and thereby—if their special expertise is in sufficient demand—work when and how and as much as they choose.

> While working as an independent contractor for a consulting firm, I once observed a prototypical example of just such an expert. The firm had a contract to help a defense agency choose among companies bidding on a proposal to design a very advanced "electronic warfare system." While the consulting firm was well-known for its expertise in decision aiding, it was not especially knowledgeable about electronic warfare systems. The firm solved this problem by finding a contractor who was reputed to be the world expert on electronic warfare. This man was employed as a contractor on average about one day a week, at an extraordinary daily rate. The other days of his workweek he read scientific, technical, and military literature and attended conferences dealing with matters both closely and tangentially related to electronic warfare.

FACTORS PROMPTING GROWTH IN INDEPENDENT CONTRACTING

Three evolving conditions will lead a larger proportion of experts to adopt this *independent contractor employment strategy* (hereafter referred to as the *independent contractor strategy*). *One* is that, for those experts who are inclined to this strategy, implementing it will be increasingly facilitated by two technological advances: (1) forthcoming increases in the effectiveness of the information systems that experts and expertise-seeking firms will use to find each other (as noted earlier), and (2) forthcoming increases in the speed of transportation systems that facilitate the personal contact and intense interaction that will enable specially qualified experts to bring their sticky knowledge to bear on complex problems. Aside from whatever motivations there may be to adopt it, *implementing the independent contractor strategy will be more feasible in the future.*

A *second* condition favoring greater use of a contractor strategy has to do with the expert's need for continuous learning. On the one hand will be the growing threat of obsolescence driven by the rapid growth in knowledge. As knowledge in all fields will be increasing at an increasing rate, *in the future, experts' concerns about their possible obsolescence and future employability will be greater.*

One approach experts can use to buffer themselves from obsolescence is to engage continuously in work that is within their area of expertise or that is developmental to it. Because the demand for a particular expertise tends to be more continuous in the labor market as a whole than in any one firm, this approach to maintaining special competence at a high level is more easily enacted with an independent contractor strategy. Similar will be the desire of some experts to compete in the labor market by extending their knowledge, as contrasted to deepening it. This can be accomplished by taking on tasks that provide access to leading edge knowledge or other valued knowledge adjacent to the knowledge they already possess. Such developmental engagements also tend to be more available in the labor market than in any one firm. Another approach to buffering themselves from obsolescence is to engage in nonemployment learning experiences, such as taking advanced academic work or engaging in research or other independent learning activities (as did the electronic warfare expert described above).

Third and finally, for those interested in maximizing their income, a factor favoring use of the contractor strategy will be the availability of disproportionately high rewards in many fields and industries for very high levels of talent, expertise, and other marketable attributes.[1] *The increased availability of disproportionately*

---

[1] Chapter 8 explains and documents the disproportionately high rewards for individuals possessing very high levels of attributes valuable to the firms in an industry.

large premiums for talent will, in the future, make income maximization a more salient consideration when highly qualified experts choose among employment strategies. As we noted earlier, in many firms specialized experts can be fully utilized and afforded only occasionally. Thus, to receive full value for their expertise, many highly qualified experts will choose to sell to the highest bidder, and—in a turbulent business environment—the most needy and highest bidding firm will change frequently. The independent contractor strategy exploits this labor market condition.

To summarize, in these last few pages we reasoned that, in the future, (1) implementing an independent contractor strategy will be more feasible and (2) conditions likely to motivate an independent contractor strategy will become more intense. Each of these circumstances will contribute to the attractiveness of the independent contractor strategy. Consequently, it seems reasonable to conclude that, *in the future, the proportion of experts who use the independent contractor strategy will be greater.*[14]

Review of the reasoning supporting the ideas that (1) the independent contractor strategy will become more feasible, (2) the conditions that motivate a contractor strategy will become more intense, and (3) firms will more frequently employ specialized experts on only a temporary basis, makes clear that the reasoning applies just as well to a sister employment strategy, *job hopping.* Consequently, we can expect that, *in the future, the proportion of experts who choose to frequently change employers will be greater.*[m]

If it were true that firms believe that an effective way to capture leading edge knowledge is to hire people who have recently acquired that knowledge through formal schooling, we would expect that compensation for new graduates with this knowledge was already increasing faster than was compensation for previous but recent hires. Peter Cappelli, Codirector of the U.S. Department of Education's National Center on the Educational Quality of the Workforce, and Professor of Management and Director of the Center for Human Resources at the Wharton School, gives a nice example of an evolving pattern:

(Continued)

---

[m]While the italicized conclusions of the chapter are set forth straightforwardly, the degree to which we see them manifested in any particular time window will of course vary with the labor market conditions existing at the time. Further, given the overall set of forces bearing on this conclusion, it may be that the conclusion is less valid for experts who work for expertise-providing service firms. But, due to the forthcoming increases in the levels of specialization that will characterize future experts, it will nevertheless be valid even for these firms. More on this shortly.

(Continued)

In fields such as information systems, where the demands are constantly changing, the wage structure within the firm may have little apparent order: older skills may suddenly have virtually no market value, since new programming skills do not build on old ones. Young programmers find that their wages may be highest when they first enter the labor market because their skills are on the cutting edge. From that point on their value and market compensation erodes, and they may well find themselves unemployable unless they update their skills regularly. (Cappelli, 1999: 7)

If it were true that the growth in knowledge will cause more experts to more frequently engage in career-related schooling, we would already expect to see more adults engage in vocational or professional schooling. We do.[15]

The increased use of the independent contractor strategy that we might expect—given the arguments made earlier—will be lessened somewhat by the same three factors that modulate it today. In the interest of a balanced analysis, let us briefly review these factors.

FACTORS CURTAILING GROWTH IN INDEPENDENT CONTRACTING

Three factors will lessen—but not halt—the forthcoming growth in independent contracting by experts. *One* is the near universal need that people have for association and affiliation. For many, ongoing association with a group of coworkers contributes to fulfilling these needs. As a consequence, some experts will trade off their desire for higher income, or their desire to determine where, when, how, and on what tasks they work, for the opportunity to participate in an ongoing work group. They will forgo the independent contractor strategy and instead adopt the *enduring-relationship employment strategy* that was so pervasive during most of the twentieth century. But for those whose social needs are not so great or, more likely, whose social needs are fulfilled through relationships with family members or friends, the independent contractor strategy may be the more attractive of the two.

A *second* factor that will attenuate growth in the proportion of experts who adopt the independent contractor strategy is the tendency most people have to avoid high levels of uncertainty about their income stream. Holding layoffs aside for the moment, independent contracting often results in a more variable income stream than does employment with a single employer. But highly qualified experts tend to have high income levels, and the increasing premium paid for expertise by future firms will make this more universally true than it is today. Thus the possible variations in income associated with periods of unemployment will tend to sit on top of a high base of financial assets. For this reason, possible uncertainty about periods of unemployment is of less consequence for many experts than might be imagined, and is likely to be of less consequence still in the future.

A *third* factor that will retard the growth of independent contracting will be the simultaneous growth in the number of firms that provide specialized, deep, or leading edge knowledge to other firms. This growth in the number of expertise-providing service firms will be driven by the same need for expertise that will cause firms to use independent contractors, that is, the need for temporary access to specialized, deep, or leading edge knowledge. These specialized firms will compete with independent contractors and, at the same time, will themselves employ some specialized experts who otherwise might choose the independent contractor strategy.

Some experts will join these specialized service firms. But such firms necessarily place very high demands on their employees. One of these demands is to take on the type of work that the firm contracts to do, rather than what the particular expert prefers to do. Another is to be available when "the firm needs you." These requirements restrict the expert's autonomy (i.e., they constrain choices about when, where, how, and on what tasks he or she works). Total congruence between what the firm needs to do to stay in business and what the expert wants to do to enhance a career is often not attained, even in specialized firms. Finally, the firm's overhead costs can work to reduce the expert's income.

On the other hand, working for a firm whose specialty is congruent with the expert's special capability can provide collegial interaction with coworkers in the same general field (which fulfills both social needs and expertise-building needs) and can also provide some degree of income certainty. That is, "opportunities for training, advancement, and employment security conceivably might be greater at a specialized provider—and their employees might also reap distinctive psychological benefits from being around others doing the same kinds of jobs" (Baron, 2000: 91).

What we can expect to see, then, is a knowledge market containing three interacting parties: (1) firms temporarily needing expertise they don't possess, (2) highly qualified experts working as independent contractors, and (3) specialized firms that both provide expertise to other firms and employment to highly qualified experts. Of course, we already see each of these parties in today's labor market. What will be different in tomorrow's? The difference will be that the forthcoming and accelerating growth in the world's knowledge will increase the numbers of each of these three parties and will decrease the proportion of (1) firms employing on an ongoing basis all the expertise they need and (2) highly specialized experts working within a single firm on an ongoing basis.

Thus the joint actions of firms and experts, particularly highly qualified experts, will create a more *fluid* labor market, a market where individual pairings of firms and highly specialized experts will be short-lived relative to what we've observed in the past.

On an everyday basis, future firms will obtain more expert knowledge from individual independent contractors and from specialized service firms than do today's firms. Let us examine further the means by which future firms will obtain the knowledge needed to leverage their own special competence.

Acquiring and Integrating Expert Knowledge From Other Autonomous Firms

In our Chapter 5 discussion of experiential versus vicarious learning we noted that "firms possess knowledge, but the amount they possess is minuscule compared with the knowledge already residing in their industry, in adjacent industries, in the business world, and in society in general. The chances are often very large that much of the knowledge a firm needs already exists in its environment."[16] One common way for firms to obtain knowledge from other firms is to buy it. Let us turn to examining how this will come about in future firms.

THE MAKE OR BUY DECISION IN FUTURE FIRMS

Firms whose core competence is component integration and product assembly acquire a great deal of the knowledge embedded in their final products from other firms. A well-known example is Dell Computer. Dell buys computer components from other firms. These supplier firms possess deep technical knowledge about designing and manufacturing the components they sell. This knowledge is embedded in their products. When Dell assembles computers from these purchased components, it is integrating the deep knowledge of its suppliers by applying its own knowledge about which components are compatible and synergistic and how they can be efficiently assembled in Dell's factory.

In this way, Dell and other product assembly specialists (such as automobile and appliance manufacturers) regularly produce routine innovations by drawing on new knowledge from outside the firm, knowledge embedded in new, higher-performing or otherwise more attractive components. They exploit their core competence, their special knowledge about assembly (often embedded in their routines), by integrating knowledge from outside the firm.[n]

When, in producing the new manufacturing plant described earlier, Dell reallocated—between itself and its suppliers—tasks associated with transporting and storing components, "key elements" of the facilitative information technology were obtained from a firm specializing in this area. Some of this firm's expert knowledge was embedded in the technology it sold to Dell. Dell's purchase of this product is an example of what we noted in Chapter 5, that "in many situations, useful knowledge can be acquired from the environment more quickly, more reliably, and at lower cost than it can be acquired from experience, and can then be used to leverage (to exploit) the knowledge acquired through experience."

Will firms in the future do differently? Will the relative frequency of making versus buying knowledge change for situations where the knowledge needed is embedded in products readily available in the market? Will the processes involved in acquiring such embedded knowledge change?

The answer to the last question is "Yes." The primary processes involved in acquiring such off-the-shelf products are "search" (for the best value component) and "transport" (the component to the appropriate location). We have from Chapter 2 that, "in the future, the effectiveness of information and transportation technologies will be greater, and will be increasing." As a consequence of this important fact, in the future the search for knowledge-containing products will be more efficient and transport will be faster and less costly.

For situations where the knowledge needed is embedded in products available in the market, will the relative frequency of make versus buy change in the future? Here, too, the answer is "Yes." The proportion of instances where knowledge for leveraging the firm's special competence will be acquired from outside rather than developed inside will increase, for three reasons:

1. search for the best product or the best value will be more efficient due to advances in information technology;

2. transport of the product will be faster and less costly due to advances in transportation technology; and

---

[n]In this context, let me draw on an article appearing in the *Los Angeles Times* for an example of "core competence" and "special knowledge about assembly." "Dell is a master of . . . order-to-delivery: taking a customer's order and very quickly producing the requested product. It takes Dell only five days—sometimes less—to assemble a computer to a customer's specifications and ship it out the factory door" (T. Y. Jones, 2003: D1).

3. from Chapter 2, the variety and number of products and suppliers from which to choose will be greater.

For these reasons, when the knowledge needed to exploit their special competence in the pursuit of innovation is embedded in products available in the market, future firms will be more likely than are today's firms to buy this knowledge rather than to develop it internally.

What about knowledge that the firm needs and that is not available in the firm but, while not available in off-the-shelf products or services, could be made available by purchasing it from a firm specializing in providing such knowledge products or services? Examples of such knowledge products are advertising campaigns and unique product components. Will the processes involved in acquiring such knowledge change? Will the relative frequency of make versus buy change? Some of the same forces examined earlier will operate in these situations as well—products and suppliers will be greater in variety and number, and candidate suppliers will be more easily found. Particularly when the knowledge needed is embedded in the expertise of vendor firms, the greater effectiveness of forthcoming information and transportation technologies will contribute to increased purchasing of knowledge rather than in-house development. *When the customized knowledge needed to exploit their special competence can be bought from other firms, future firms will be more likely than are today's firms to buy this knowledge rather than to develop it internally.*

Firms acquire knowledge from other firms through structural arrangements as well as through purchases. Let us consider how readily future firms will acquire and integrate knowledge from other firms using structural arrangements.

ACQUIRING AND INTEGRATING EXPERT KNOWLEDGE USING STRUCTURAL ARRANGEMENTS

Much of what was said above supports the idea of firms acquiring knowledge for leveraging their core competence from external sources rather than developing the knowledge internally. In the 1990s and the early 2000s, arguments in the management literature encouraged the use of interorganizational arrangements with other firms as the preferred means for drawing on the knowledge of these firms, arrangements such as alliances, joint ventures, equity investment, or through outright acquisition of another firm.[17] Many firms complied with these admonitions, to their advantage.

Several powerful counterarguments and cautions to this practice are offered by Henry Chesbrough of Harvard University and David Teece of the University of California–Berkeley.

> Champions of virtual corporations are urging managers to subcontract anything and everything. All over the world, companies are jumping on the bandwagon—decentralizing, downsizing, and forging alliances to pursue innovation. . . . But, while there are many successful virtual companies, there are even more failures that don't make the headlines. . . . Although networks, with their high-powered incentives may be effective over the short run for an unchanging technology, they will not adapt well over the long run as technology develops and companies must depend on certain internal capabilities to keep up. . . . The lesson is that companies that develop their own capabilities can outperform those that rely too heavily on coordination through markets and alliances to build their businesses. (Chesbrough & Teece, 2002: 127-134)

The relative merits of seeking and integrating capability-leveraging knowledge through structural arrangements involving other firms, and the relative merits of these alternative arrangements, depend on several factors, including

1. the capability of the firm to advance and employ the technology relative to the speed with which the firm's competitors are able to advance and employ the technology,

2. the financial strength of the knowledge-seeking firm,

3. the bargaining power of the firm possessing the knowledge sought,

4. the expected difficulty of communicating and integrating the knowledge,

5. the firm's experience with the various arrangements,

6. the firm's ability to curtail the use of its knowledge by the other firm in ways harmful to the firm, and

7. the firm's ability to curtail the loss of its intellectual property and other forms of its valuable knowledge through the other firm to the firm's competitors.

A good deal of thought and research has been directed toward determining which structural arrangement is superior under which combination of factors.[18] Recalling our earlier conclusions that, in the future, (1) the need to compete on the basis of speed will be greater, (2) the variety and number of knowledge-seeking and knowledge-selling firms will be greater, (3) our understanding of the situation-dependent effectiveness of these knowledge integration arrangements is growing, and (4) the effectiveness of communication technologies for managing knowledge transfer will be greater, we can expect that *future firms will more frequently use structural arrangements to acquire and integrate expert knowledge from other firms, rather than develop this knowledge internally.*

Entering into any of these arrangements is a significant move involving major resource commitments. Establishing an arrangement with a new partner generally requires weeks or months of fact gathering and negotiation, and months or years for successful implementation and knowledge integration to take place. While individual firms in the future will be involved in more of these interfirm relationships than are firms today (due to the facilitating nature of experience if for no other reason), limitations to managerial attention and other problems of coordination make fruitfully benefiting from any one relationship increasingly difficult as the number of relationships grows. So, what will future firms do to minimize these problems?

Reasoning set forth in Chapter 6 and earlier in this chapter supports the idea that, to minimize inter-organizational problems of knowledge transfer and integration, firms will take actions very similar to those taken by firms attempting to minimize intra-organizational problems of knowledge transfer and integration. That is, paraphrasing Chapter 6 conclusions regarding how firms will deal with their need to rapidly and effectively transfer knowledge within the firm, we have that, as actions to facilitate their acquisition and integration of knowledge from other firms,

1. *future firms will more frequently transfer members of the knowledge-possessing firm to the knowledge-seeking firm*, and that

2. *future firms will more frequently temporarily assign to the knowledge-possessing firm a member of the knowledge-seeking firm who, as an individual, seems to have a high level of absorptive capacity for the kind of knowledge needed. Overall, to facilitate knowledge transfer, there will be more commingling of personnel.*

Similarly, paraphrasing earlier conclusions from this chapter regarding how firms will deal with their need to integrate the knowledge products of project teams, we have in the context of acquiring and integrating knowledge from other firms that

3. *future firms will more intensely employ high-telepresence communication technologies for coordinating knowledge transfer and action integration,*[o] *and*

4. *future firms will more frequently employ the concepts and practices of concurrent engineering when coordinating interfirm knowledge integration.*

As we have noted, transferring and integrating mind-resident knowledge about complex matters is difficult. It is especially difficult when the knowledge must move across organizational boundaries. Managing the transfer and integration of such knowledge will require high levels of skill in relationship building, in multiple business functions, and in multiple technical areas. Some who take on the task will have acquired these skills without design. Others will manage their work experiences so as to acquire them. It appears that some firms will go so far as to intentionally develop managers with the required set of skills.

Consider, for example, the findings of Geoffrey Parker and Edward Anderson, business school faculty at Tulane University and the University of Texas at Austin respectively. These researchers studied how a large personal computer manufacturer changed its supply-chain management after outsourcing the majority of its design and manufacturing to a network of suppliers. They found that, "to cope with this new structure, this firm developed a cadre of highly-skilled generalists, 'supply-chain integrators,' who coordinate product development, marketing, production, and logistics from product concept to delivery across firm boundaries" (Parker & Anderson, 2001: 75). They also found that the skill set of these integrators differed from the skill set of supply-chain personnel in the pre-outsourcing era. If this finding is replicated in other contexts, it will indicate that the evolving growth of inter-organizational knowledge integration will lead to another specialized occupation.

Chapter Summary and Transition

Chapter 5 focused on acquiring knowledge and Chapter 6 focused on leveraging knowledge by making it available across time and organizational units. Building on these chapters, this chapter focused on how future firms will integrate

---

[o]For well-known reasons, knowledge transfer and action coordination between firms is more difficult than within firms. As a result, firms in the future will be more prone to support their interfirm coordinators with a wide spectrum of communication technologies, including those high in telepresence.

knowledge when developing innovative products and processes. In it we saw that forthcoming increases in occupational specialization, driven by forthcoming increases in knowledge, will make knowledge integration more difficult in the future, as "the task of combining the knowledge of more individuals, each more narrowly specialized, is more complicated than is the present task of combining the knowledge of fewer, more broadly knowledgeable individuals."

The chapter dealt with three broad topics. One was structures and processes for integrating the firm's knowledge. The particular issue that surfaced was that future increases in specialization will force increases in the number of specialists and support staff required to achieve a given percentage improvement in a current product, or in a new product that serves the same market need. This fact will, in turn, force increases in the number of teams needed and—unless offsetting mechanisms are emplaced—increases in the number of managerial levels. Use of communication technologies high in telepresence and increased employment of the concepts and procedures of concurrent engineering and modular architecture were identified as mechanisms that will see more use in future firms.

The second topic examined was changes in employment practices of firms and in experts' employment strategies. To deal with the fact that the expertise of highly specialized personnel is useful to any one firm only occasionally, a fact becoming all the more relevant as specialization increases, future firms will more frequently employ specialized experts on a temporary basis. To deal with the fact that the knowledge possessed by specially qualified experts is often sticky, future firms will necessarily bring these experts deep into the intellectual operations of the firm, thus increasing the likelihood that their sticky knowledge will be effectively integrated with that of the firm's own knowledge workers.

The third and last topic examined was acquiring and integrating knowledge from other autonomous firms. Because the availability, accessibility, and affordability of externally available knowledge useful for leveraging the firm's special competence would be increasing in the future, we concluded that firms in the future will more frequently buy knowledge with which to leverage their competence rather than develop it internally. For these same reasons, we also concluded that future firms would more frequently use structural arrangements to acquire expert knowledge rather than develop it internally.

Its own innovations require a firm to make changes, as do the innovations of its competitors. And, as we saw in Chapter 2, entities other than competitors, such as suppliers and regulators, will more often confront firms with the need to change. As a consequence, future firms will attempt to ready themselves for rapid and efficient change with structures and processes that ensure flexibility. But such structures and processes generally interfere with the repeated experiences and routinization that leads to high levels of efficiency. Further, many of the firm's efforts to change or to increase efficiency reduce employee commitment. We examine how future firms will deal with the resulting dilemmas in Chapter 8.

Endnotes

1. Whether a particular firm focuses on innovations that provide the best quality or the best value depends on the economy, on the life cycle stage of the relevant technologies, and on the firm's strategic place in its industry. For example, when the economy is up and when the benefits of each advance in technology are still significant, customers tend to buy the best quality. When the economy is down and when the benefits of technological advances are marginal, customers tend to buy the best value. For elaboration, see "Coming of Age: A Survey of the IT Industry," *The Economist*, May 10, 2003. In a competitive environment filled with fast-arriving technological advances, both large and small, firms will have to innovate more frequently to attain or retain market share whichever the case (i.e., whether the market is seeking the best quality or seeking the best value).

2. There will be rare occurrences when a new insight exploits a small quantity of knowledge in the creation of a new product or process, a quantity less than the quantity incorporated in the product or process being supplanted. (Note that the new insight itself is an element of knowledge that is part of the total quantity of knowledge incorporated within the new product or process.) While it is often the case that some knowledge previously needed will no longer be needed (few aircraft manufacturers employ knowledge about propeller design), this doesn't negate the validity of the assertion—the amount of new knowledge needed almost always exceeds the amount no longer needed.

3. One of the culprits that in times past contributed to delays in new product development and other innovations was the "functional" or "silo" structure. During the middle of the twentieth century, knowledge integration in the development and market introduction of goods and services tended to be, in large- and medium-size firms, decidedly sequential in nature. In large manufacturing businesses especially, the knowledge from units having the particular functions of (1) research, (2) development, (3) engineering, (4) production, (5) distribution, (6) marketing, and (7) sales was sequentially integrated in the development and commercialization of both hard and soft goods. In large service businesses (retirement communities or insurance companies, for example), the knowledge integration sequence was some variant of (1) concept formation, (2) market research, (3) development of the standard product, (4) marketing, (5) sales, (6) product customization, and (7) service. During the latter part of the twentieth century this *functional structure* came to be increasingly inadequate, especially in manufacturing firms. Gradually, but at an accelerating rate, organizational structures and procedures that enabled faster knowledge integration began to displace purely functional structures. Conspicuous among these were matrix structures and project-team structures.

4. As is well-known, in some industries the project-team structure evolved out of the matrix structure. Indeed, the functional structure and the project-team structure bracket a continuum of different types of matrix structures. See, for example, E. W. Larson and D. H. Gobeli's *functional matrix, balanced matrix,* and *project matrix* in their article, "Matrix Management: Contradictions and Insights," 1987. For further analysis of the relationships between these structures, see R. C. Ford and W. A. Randolph's review and integration of matrix organization and project management ("Cross-Functional Structures: A Review and Integration of Matrix Organization and

Project Management," 1992). Project teams are the predominant structural units of adhocracies, a structural form that became increasingly popular toward the end of the century (for elaboration, see H. Mintzberg, *The Structuring of Organizations: A Synthesis of the Research*, 1979; "Organization Design: Fashion or Fit," 1981; *The Structuring of Organizations*, 1993).

Project teams generally disband upon completion of the team's project. In contrast, particularly during the 1990s, another team-based structure also became more common— a structure where the personnel in traditional, permanent departments were organized as teams for the purpose of more quickly integrating their individual information or knowledge in the production of either goods or services, especially services. This structural change was essentially a change in the responsibility for coordination from a structure where department managers directed, coordinated, and controlled the tasks of their subordinates to one where the department's operations-level personnel assumed primary responsibility for combining and coordinating their work. High-fashion terms like "employee empowerment" and "self-managed teams" were often used when describing this change to a structure that might be called *permanent* or *departmental teams*.

An interesting example of the possible benefits of moving to a departmental team structure is reported by Caron, Jarvenpaa, and Stoddard, "Business Reengineering at CIGNA Corporation: Diffusing a New Way of Thinking," 1994. As part of its introduction and use of business reengineering, CIGNA was very proactive in transforming its traditional departmental structures into team structures. Whereas departmental personnel had previously acted on customer cases by combining their specialized information, knowledge, quality checks, and approval decisions sequentially (with many handoffs and much time in queues), afterward, departmental teams took charge of cases and integrated their knowledge and information in a much more simultaneous manner. For example, in one reported instance, "Six functions were consolidated into two processes. The functional hierarchy was flattened by pushing decision making to self-managing teams as cross-functional teams of 6 to 8 members delivered an end-to-end service to a customer" (Caron, Jarvenpaa, & Stoddard, 1994: 238). Here, as in almost all uses of departmental teams, the team structure was used to quickly aggregate knowledge for operating purposes rather than for innovation.

5. For elaboration of this example as well as a tutorial on the type of economic analysis that can be used to determine the appropriate degree of overlap between adjacent processes, see V. Krishnan, S. D. Eppinger, and D. E. Whitney, "A Model-Based Framework to Overlap Product Development Activities," 1997.

6. For elaboration, see K. H. Bowen et al., "Regaining the Lead in Manufacturing," 1994; K. B. Clark and S. Wheelwright, "Organizing and Leading 'Heavyweight' Development Teams," 1992; and S. Wheelwright and K. Clark, *Revolutionizing Product Development: Quantum Leaps in Speed, Efficiency, and Quality*, 1992. R. P. Smith, "The Historical Roots of Concurrent Engineering Fundamentals," 1997, provides a historical review of the evolution of concurrent engineering. For studies of the effect of concurrent engineering in different contexts, see K. M. Eisenhardt and B. N. Tabrizi, "Accelerating Adaptive Processes: Product Innovation in the Global Computer Industry," 1995; V. Krishnan, S. D. Eppinger, and D. E. Whitney, "A Model-Based Framework to Overlap Product Development Activities," 1997; and C. Terwiesch and C. H. Loch, "Measuring the Effectiveness of Overlapping Development Activities," 1999.

7. C. Y. Baldwin and K. B. Clark, "Managing in an Age of Modularity," 1997, called attention to the fact that "a growing number of industries are poised to extend modularity from the production process to the design stage" (p. 85). A specific application of modular architecture in process development is described in R. Sanchez, "Marketing Architecture in the Marketing Process," 1999.

8. For more on the development of new organizational forms, see H. Mintzberg, *The Structuring of Organizations,* 1979, and *Structure in Fives: Designing Effective Organizations,* 1993; J. B. Quinn, *Intelligent Enterprise,* 1992; and J. B. Quinn, P. Anderson, and S. Finkelstein, "Leveraging Intellect," 1996.

9. Perhaps the content of this paragraph needs no elaboration, but for those interested in but not familiar with "what we think we know," let me offer some references. The first four are sequenced in accord with the breadth of the definition of innovation (from organizational renewal to new-product creation) and inversely sequenced in accord with the focus on the specificity of the guidelines stated or implied: M. L. Tushman and C. A. O'Reilly III, *Winning Through Innovation,* 1997; R. L. Leifer et al., *Radical Innovation,* 2000; P. G. Smith and D. G. Reinertsen, *Developing Products in Half the Time,* 1991; and J. C. Huber, *Managing Innovation,* 2001. Perhaps no studies have more clearly demonstrated that many important innovations evolve without a carefully scripted process than those traced in the Minnesota Innovation Research Program. See A. H. Van de Ven, H. L. Angle, and M. S. Poole, *Research on the Management of Innovation,* 1989; and A. H. Van de Ven, D. E. Polley, R. Garud, and S. Venkataraman, *The Innovation Journey,* 1999. Examples of studies identifying determinants of successful innovations in particular industries are M. Iansiti, "Technology Integration: Managing Technological Evolution in a Complex Environment," 1995 (mainframe computer industry); and R. Henderson and I. Cockburn, "Scale, Scope, and Spillovers: The Determinants of Research Productivity in Drug Discovery," 1996 (pharmaceutical industry).

10. An interesting example was the development of the *chaebol* organizational form in Korea. Beginning at least in the 1970s, Korea aspired to replicate Japan's economic miracle with one of its own. The then-pervasive private-sector organizational form in Korea was a small-to-medium firm serving the domestic market. This form was ill equipped to meet international competition and thus satisfy the nation's aspiration of becoming a rich economy. With the financial and political support of a series of Korean governments, a "new"—for Korea—organizational form was evolved, the kinship-based large conglomerate of unrelated businesses called a "chaebol." During the late 1970s and throughout the 1980s, just over a dozen chaebols came to dominate the Korean economy. Chaebols were allowed and encouraged to grow because they were able and willing to support fledgling or otherwise temporarily weak member firms and thereby help the growth of the economy and the stability of employment. Their financial success during this period caused them to be perceived by many as a major contributor to Korea's justifiable label as one of Asia's young tigers and its ability to thrive in the international marketplace. (This example taken from S. M. Lee, S. Yoo, and T. M. Lee, "Korean Chaebols: Corporate Values and Strategies," 1991.)

When in the 1990s the environment of Korea's business organizations turned hostile—when international competition became more acute and when the "Asian crisis" shrank markets—the performance of large, global, and highly diversified chaebols plummeted.

Suddenly, from having been viewed as a highly regarded institution, chaebols became scapegoats. Questions arose about problems of coordination and paternalism. The government switched from encouraging the growth of chaebols to encouraging their downsizing through the spinning off of unrelated businesses and the shutting down of noncompetitive firms. By the end of the century, the "new"—for Korea—organizational forms were large- and medium-size global firms and conglomerates less diversified than they had been for a decade or more. (This discussion draws on M. L. Clifford, "Showdown in Seoul: Can President Kim Finally Get the Chaebol to Change?" 1998.)

11. For elaboration and evidence on this important point, see G. Szulanski, "Exploring Internal Stickiness: Impediments to the Transfer of Best Practices Within the Organization," 1996; M. T. Hansen, "The Search-Transfer Problem: The Role of Weak Ties in Sharing Knowledge Across Organization Subunits," 1999; and parts of C. O'Dell and C. J. Grayson, "If Only We Knew What We Know: Identification and Transfer of Internal Best Practices," 1998.

12. This raises the issue of the firm's need to protect its intellectual property. But the protection of intellectual property from theft by temporarily employed experts will not, of course, be a new problem; theft of intellectual property by consultants and exiting employees occurs today. Certainly the possibility of theft will be an important consideration. But the increased speed at which new knowledge must be exploited both reduces the opportunities for the firm's competitors to gain from theft and increases the need for the firm to exploit leading edge knowledge not currently available within the firm—by bringing experts with leading edge knowledge deep into the firm's intellectual operations. We can expect today's safeguards (e.g., covenants not to compete and written confidentiality/nondisclosure agreements) to be used in the future, and perhaps new ones as well. In addition, it is worth noting that the matter of theft is self-limiting because even the suspicion of theft can end a career. For more on the matter of loss of intellectual property through use of temporarily employed experts, see S. Matusik and C. Hill, "The Utilization of Contingent Work, Knowledge Creation, and Competitive Advantage," 1998, especially page 687.

13. This form of employment relationship is seldom studied—or even discussed—in depth (but see M. Carnoy, M. Castells, and C. Brenner, "Labor Markets and Employment Practices in the Age of Flexibility: A Case Study of Silicon Valley," 1997; S. R. Cohany, "Workers in Alternative Employment Arrangements: A Second Look," 1998; A. Kalleberg, "Nonstandard Employment Relations: Part-Time, Temporary and Contract Work," 2000; and S. Matusik and C. Hill, "The Utilization of Contingent Work, Knowledge Creation, and Competitive Advantage," 1998).

While evidence identifying certain dysfunctional consequences of firms' use of temporary workers and contractors is growing (e.g., A. Davis-Blake, J. P. Broschak, and E. George, "Happy Together? How Using Nonstandard Workers Affects Exit, Voice, and Loyalty Among Standard Employees," 2003; A. Davis-Blake and P. P. Hui, "Contracting Talent for Knowledge-Based Competition," 2003; and A. Kalleberg, "Nonstandard Employment Relations: Part-Time, Temporary, and Contract Work," 2000; it appears that these consequences apply minimally or not at all in the case of the employment relationships described here (a fact noted by A. Davis-Blake, J. P. Broschak, and E. George, "Happy Together? How Using Nonstandard Workers Affects Exit, Voice, and

Loyalty Among Standard Employees," forthcoming; and S. Matusik and C. Hill, "The Utilization of Contingent Work, Knowledge Creation, and Competitive Advantage," 1998).

Contradictory arguments have been proposed regarding the "small world" effect. On the one hand, economists' "transaction cost theory" (Williamson, 1975, 1981) argues that open-end contracts such as those discussed here are dangerous in small worlds because, without much competition around to discipline them, suppliers might choose to cheat their buyers. In contrast, when there are many suppliers, cheaters tend to be driven out because buyers have options and will refuse to buy again from the unscrupulous. Sociologists' "social reputation theory," on the other hand, argues that small-world situations blunt incentives to cheat. Buyers can more easily learn the reputation of candidate suppliers and can communicate to other buyers their experience with suppliers. Sociologists, then, say that small worlds are good at driving out cheaters through reputation effects while economists say that large worlds are good because they approximate the conditions of perfect competition in which dishonest suppliers are removed by the competitive conditions of the market. (I am indebted to Andy Henderson for putting me onto these alternative lines of reasoning.)

14. I've seen no data to support the idea that this is already occurring, and I would question what data I did find if it were from the 1990s, as the tendency may well be influenced by the state of the labor market during those years. Nevertheless, holding labor market conditions aside, the conclusion seems to follow from the evolving circumstances just noted. In this regard, I call attention to the very thoughtful pieces by R. E. Miles and C. C. Snow, "Twenty-first Century Careers," 1996; and by K. Inkson and M. B. Arthur, "How to Be a Successful Career Capitalist," 2001; and also the book *The Boundaryless Career,* edited by M. B. Arthur and D. M. Rousseau, 1996.

15. S. Creighton and L. Hudson, *Participation Trends and Patterns in Adult Education: 1991 to 1999,* 2002, shows widespread increases in the percentage of various groups participating in non-baccalaureate education from 1991 through 1999. An interesting exception is "professional and managerial" workers, but this seems readily explainable as a consequence of the labor market for this group in these years. In 1991 the U.S. economy was down—unemployment was 6.8%. In 1999, at the peak of the computer and communication technology boom, unemployment had declined to 4.2%, a huge proportional decline. The 1990s was a period of job growth for many technical and business professionals. Workers in these groups were in great demand and working many hours per week. The year 1999 was hardly a time for participating in continuing education.

16. Very different studies supporting this reasoning are those by A. Hargadon and R. I. Sutton, "Technology Brokering and Innovation in a Product Development Firm," 1997; and L. Rosenkopf and A. Nerkar, "Beyond Local Search: Boundary-Spanning, Exploration, and Impact in the Optical Disk Industry," 2001.

17. Influential books were those by W. H. Davidow and M. S. Malone, *The Virtual Corporation,* 1992; and J. B. Quinn, *Intelligent Enterprise,* 1992. A particularly well-informed and well-reasoned short piece is that by D. L. Deeds, "Alternative Strategies for Acquiring Knowledge," 2003.

18. E. B. Roberts and W. K. Liu offer a set of guidelines in their *Sloan Management Review* article, "Ally or Acquire? How Technology Leaders Decide," 2001. Examinations of the influence of small combinations of the factors are those by B. Harrison and M. R. Kelley, "Outsourcing and the Search for 'Flexibility,'" 1993; B. L. Simonin, "Ambiguity and the Process of Knowledge Transfer in Strategic Alliances," 1999; T. E. Stuart, "Interorganizational Alliances and the Performance of Firms: A Study of Growth and Innovation Rates in a High-Technology Industry," 2000; H. K. Steensma and K. G. Corley, "On the Performance of Technology-Sourcing Partnerships: The Interaction Between Partner Interdependence and Technology Attributes," 2000; and W. Tsai, "Knowledge Transfer in Intraorganizational Networks: Effects of Network Position and Absorptive Capacity on Business Unit Innovation," 2001. Two of the most sophisticated and thorough discussions of this matter are J. B. Quinn, *Intelligent Enterprise*, 1992; and C. H. Fine, *Clockspeed*, 1998. O. Granstrand and S. Sjolander, "The Acquisition of Technology and Small Firms by Large Firms," 1990, arrive at the interesting finding that acquisitions of technical firms are often made in a seller's market.

8

Dealing With the Conflicting Needs for Change, Efficiency, Flexibility, and Employee Commitment

Technologies advance, products change, markets change, firms change to survive. The changes firms make generally affect productivity. They always affect employees.

In 1986, IBM employed 406,542 people. By 1994, it employed only 219,839. A 46% drop in its workforce is a momentous event for any firm, and was especially momentous for such a large firm.[a] Of perhaps more significance than this percentage change was the absolute magnitude of the downsizing—in 1986, only six U.S. firms employed more people than the 186,703 people that IBM shed in those 8 years.

In 1994, IBM began to ramp up again. By 2000, 6 years after the bottoming out at 219,839, IBM's workforce was up to 316,303. This 44% employment growth in 6 years was also a momentous event. Other large organizations, for example, AT&T, Intel, General Motors, Microsoft, Sears, and the U.S. Postal Service, also had huge (unidirectional) changes in size during the 1980s and 1990s. Smaller firms, of course, had greater percentage changes, especially immediately after the turn of the century when the "dot com bubble" burst and

---

[a]It is of some significance and interest that IBM's huge downsizing actually happened—it was an *actual* downsizing—in contrast to many *announced* downsizings that never materialize in the numbers announced (and that perhaps were never intended to materialize in such numbers).

when travel-industry firms coped with the decline of their environment following the 9/11 terrorist attack. During these times, firms changed not only in *size*. Many changed in *shape*, as they flattened to speed decision making or as they made acquisitions and divestitures to change their direction or scope.

IBM's adaptations to its changing environment and circumstances were made in accord with top management's perceptions of threats or opportunities in IBM's environment. Of course top management's perceptions of environmental changes sometimes lag reality, or are otherwise askew, so firms' workforce sizes are often not optimal. Attaining and maintaining the firm's "right size" is one of upper management's never-ending tasks. So also is attaining the "right shape" (i.e., adding and deleting lines of business and components of the value-adding chain as the firm adjusts its strategies and business models).

We saw in Chapter 2 that the future environments of business organizations will change more frequently and be more competitive. These conditions will require firms to initiate changes more frequently and to carry out these changes more rapidly. A firm that doesn't make timely and appropriate changes will, over time, become increasingly less well aligned with its environment and will consequently obtain an even smaller share of the environment's resources. As a result, its performance will decline on some dimension. Especially when the performance decline is in earnings or market share, the firm's resources tend to decline on other dimensions as well—shareholders sell, employees with the most marketable skills leave, lenders become reluctant, and suppliers demand faster payment. As its resources decline, the firm becomes less able to compete and its competitors drive it to extinction. As the dynamism and competitiveness of future business environments increase, this scenario will progress more quickly. It follows that, because they must to survive, *future firms will change more frequently and more rapidly than have firms in the past.*

Because environmental dynamism will be significantly greater in the future, and will be increasing at an increasing rate, a plausible argument can be made that in many instances the rate at which a firm can adapt cannot match the rate of change in its environment. In this regard it seems useful to remind ourselves of the story about the two hikers who, looking back across a bend in the trail, saw that a grizzly bear was following them. "We'd better run for it," said one. The second hiker didn't answer but sat down and proceeded to take off his hiking boots and put on his running shoes. "Don't be absurd," said the first hiker, "you can't outrun that bear!" "I don't have to," said the second, "I only need to outrun you."

(Continued)

(Continued)

Future firms will need to adapt to threats and opportunities more rapidly than have firms in the past, but the standard they must meet is not necessarily the rate of change in the environment—the speed of the bear. In many cases, the standard they must meet is merely a level of adaptability—trail-running speed—that is no less than that of their competitors.

This fact may not greatly reduce the need to adapt rapidly, as all surviving competitors will be faster moving and moving faster. The bear will have eaten the slow ones and the remaining ones will have changed shoes.

Among the obstacles to change are those that delay the decision to change. We discussed these in our chapters on sensing, interpreting, and decision making. We also discussed there the organizational attributes and management practices future firms will put into place to minimize these obstacles or their effects. Here we discuss another class of obstacles to change, the more-than-occasional conflicts among the different actions a firm might consider implementing to satisfy its need to change and its simultaneous needs for efficiency, for flexibility, and for committed employees. The next section summarizes these conflicts. The succeeding three sections of the chapter describe how the conflicts might influence a firm's inclination to change or its approach to change.

Let us not lose sight of the fact that today's firms must make changes, or they will not survive to be future firms. My purpose in this chapter is simply to call out some not always recognized or fully understood tradeoffs associated with organizational changes. Understanding these tradeoffs can help managers make changes that are less detrimental to their firms' efficiency, flexibility, and employee commitment.

More-Than-Occasional Conflicts

CHANGE-EFFICIENCY CONFLICT

Forthcoming increases in environmental competitiveness will drive firms in the future to be more efficient, to produce their products at lower cost. At the same time, increases in environmental dynamism and competitiveness will together drive firms to change their products and markets more frequently and more rapidly. Unfortunately, the impermanence associated with frequent change interferes with obtaining experience and with the associated efficiency that follows from such experience. While changes directed specifically at increasing efficiency often increase it in the long run, more generally *changes force learning, but interfere with mastering.* As a result, they frequently interfere with attaining high levels of efficiency.

CHANGE-COMMITMENT CONFLICT

Firms are more likely to surpass their competitors in providing best-of-class products if they have employees committed to the firm and its goals, committed not only to fulfilling their assigned tasks but also committed to going beyond their formal responsibilities in serving the interests of the firm and of their coworkers.[b] But, when—in response to environmental change—firms discontinue lines of business, break up established work groups, or assign employees to new and unwelcome (to them) jobs, a frequent consequence is a loss of employee commitment to the firm.

CHANGE-FLEXIBILITY CONFLICT

People get married, go on trips to strange places, change jobs to advance their careers. People choose change, often. But people resist change when it interferes with maintaining their self-image or in achieving other of their personal or career goals. Acceptance of, or resistance to, change is greatly affected by the person's readiness for change. If people have successfully experienced changes at work and have become familiar with changes at work, then they tend to be accepting of changes at work, and their units are seen as "flexible." But if their work-related change experiences have been bad, or if the changes have come at such a fast pace that the people involved have not had time to gain control of their changed situation, then people are resistive or apathetic. The collective inertia they exhibit and the issues they collectively raise make their units appear "inflexible." Thus changes can help a firm become more flexible or can cause it to become less flexible.

EFFICIENCY-COMMITMENT CONFLICT

Firms' efforts to increase their efficiency often include layoffs or the rationalization of work processes into jobs that provide little variety, autonomy, or

---

[b]Going beyond formal responsibilities in serving the interests of the organization and coworkers is called *organizational citizenship behavior.* Research studies confirm what we might suspect, that these actions do lead to increased firm performance.

opportunity to interact with other employees. Efficiency needs can also work against use of worker-friendly practices such as flexible work hours. Job situations such as these are at odds with maintaining high levels of employee commitment.

FLEXIBILITY-EFFICIENCY CONFLICT
AND FLEXIBILITY-COMMITMENT CONFLICT

Firms seek flexibility to make future changes more quickly and at less cost. One way is to use temporary rather than (intendedly) permanent employees. But as we will see, use of temporary workers can have unexpected adverse effects on the performance and commitment of permanent workers.

INTERIM SUMMARY AND TRANSITION

These conflicts exist today, of course. But they will be more intense in the future. That is, because the firm's needs for change, efficiency, flexibility, and employee commitment are driven by environmental dynamism and competitiveness, and because these two environmental conditions will be greater, these four needs of all firms will also be greater. Because the needs will be greater, the intensities of the conflicts among them will be greater and will pose greater challenges than they do today. In the remainder of the chapter, we examine these conflicts and consider how future firms might deal with them differently than do today's firms.

In previous chapters, we drew conclusions about organizational characteristics that all future firms will possess to a greater degree than do their counterpart firms today. In this chapter, we will depart, at times, from this form. Instead we will identify goal conflicts that will be more important to firms in the future, conflicts that will receive more consideration as firms address the difficulty of simultaneously satisfying their greater needs for change, efficiency, flexibility, and employee commitment. We must proceed in this way for three reasons:

1. because approaches to satisfying these four needs vary so greatly with a firm's operations (for example, approaches to increasing efficiency or to changing the firm's core technology depend greatly on whether the firm is in a heavy-manufacturing industry or a service industry),

2. because trade-offs among approaches to satisfying the needs are complex (as noted above), and

3. because the relative importance of satisfying the needs depends greatly on the immediate threats and opportunities facing the firm.

Let us first examine how future firms are likely to manage these conflicts in the context of downsizing. Downsizing—as much as does any other organizational change—manifests most if not all of the issues involved in the conflicts noted above. After examining downsizing in some depth, we will pivot from it to two other changes that involve a high level of complexity and conflict: (1) use of temporary workers and (2) attempts to manage the culture of the firm.

Downsizing

During the first two decades after World War II, many U.S. firms acquired excessively large workforces. Worldwide circumstances allowed this—at the end of the war, U.S. firms accounted for more than 60% of the value of all manufactured goods produced in the world, and for some time afterward the U.S. gross domestic product was roughly 40% of that of all nations combined. In addition, due to the devastation wrought on other industrialized nations, the United States had enormous advantages in production and distribution capability and in resources available for research and development. In this munificent business environment, U.S. firms hired huge numbers of employees. As the capacities of other major national economies recovered and moved toward their pre–World War II levels, the huge advantages held by U.S. firms gradually disappeared. The resulting global competition forced many U.S. firms to downsize during the 1960s, '70s, and '80s. By the 1990s, the downsizings that followed from the economic distortions of World War II had run their course. But other downsizing-prompting forces were in place, were growing, and will be more intense in the future.

COMPETITION AS A DRIVER OF DOWNSIZING

All else equal, when a firm has a workforce of the exact size needed to meet the current production requirements for its market, the firm is maximally productive. When production requirements decline, firms are obliged to consider reducing the size of their workforce (i.e., downsizing).[c] Downsizing sometimes follows from a decline in a firm's *market,* as when consumers

---

[c]For purposes of precision, let us use "downsizing" in a narrow sense, to mean intentionally reducing the workforce associated with a line of business that the firm plans to continue, as contrasted with eliminating a line of business and its associated workforce. Using this narrow definition distinguishes between (1) attempting to maintain or increase the productivity of the workforce associated with a product line planned for some level of continuation and (2) strategically changing the portfolio of the firm's product lines, as in divesting or otherwise discontinuing product lines—strategic actions that also lead to reduction in the firm's workforce. Further, for competitive reasons, firms outsource non-core functions. This action results in a smaller workforce but generally doesn't result in the conflicts noted above. The following discussions are not intended to apply to outsourcing of non-core functions, although in some cases they might apply.

change their tastes or when governments ban unsafe products. More often, downsizing follows from a decline in a firm's *market share*, a decline precipitated by a competitor introducing a product superior in performance or value.

As we saw in previous chapters, future increases in the rate at which knowledge is generated will lead to advances in technology, and these advances will lead to increases in the rate at which new products will appear. Some of these new products will be superior to the firm's current products. If the differences between the competitor's improved product and the firm's current product are small, and if the firm has an oncoming flow of improvements in the product line (or is gaining in related product lines such that redundant employees can be easily shifted to these related product lines), downsizing is unlikely. But if the market sees the competitor's new product as significantly superior or as a significantly better value, firms often downsize to reduce workforce costs in accord with their reduced revenues.

We saw in our discussion of organizational learning that "the industry learns faster than the firm." As a result, all firms will more frequently be confronted with competitors' products superior to their own. In the future, the more frequent arrival of such products will prompt the firm to more frequently search for and evaluate cost-reducing responses to the decline in its revenues, including possibly downsizing; *in the future, firms will more frequently consider downsizing.*

COMMON ORGANIZATIONAL PHENOMENA AS CAUSES OF DOWNSIZING

The conclusion that "future firms will more frequently *consider* downsizing" followed from the rather direct effect of forthcoming environmental changes. Before we draw conclusions about whether firms will *actually* downsize more frequently, we should ask ourselves whether there are non-environmental forces that might affect the propensity to downsize, perhaps forces more inherent in the nature of organizations themselves. Let us examine this possibility.

Dramatic downsizings are sometimes consequences of the extreme optimism that Federal Reserve Board Chairman Alan Greenspan labeled "irrational exuberance." Speaking about this phenomenon in the context of the U.S. stock markets (as was Chairman Greenspan), Laura D'Andrea Tyson, former dean of the Haas School of Business at the University of California at Berkeley and currently dean of the London School of Business, noted that

(Continued)

(Continued)

> During the past six years, the Internet phase of the IT revolution has succumbed to this pattern (of irrational exuberance). Supportive capital markets . . . and the suspension of norms of due diligence and valuation sent share prices of New Economy companies to unprecedented heights. (*BusinessWeek*, April 30, 2001: 26)

The extreme optimism about the future role of IT in the economy not only raised share prices but also dramatically raised firms' workforce sizes—as firms staffed up rapidly to put products into what were expected to be extraordinarily large markets. These massive hirings contributed to the massive layoffs seen in the IT industries during the years just before and after the turn of the twenty-first century. The issue was not one of market decline but rather one of reducing employment levels that were excessive because they'd been created to serve markets that hadn't developed.

Understandable motivations cause workforces to grow even when positive changes in markets have not occurred and are not anticipated. For example, all other matters the same, the larger the number of a manager's subordinates, the greater are the manager's compensation, status, and resources for making a positive contribution to the firm. So, if they have access to the necessary funds, managers are often motivated to increase the number of employees under them—even when the cost of the additional employees might not be justified from the perspective of the firm. These same motivations also encourage managers not to terminate employees even when markets decline. In other instances, managers choose not to terminate because they believe they can reclaim the lost market and will need the employees.[1] And, of course, sympathy and empathy also contribute to managers' reluctance to terminate "good" employees—even though the firm cannot currently afford these employees. The cumulative effect of these understandable motivations is an excess of personnel, an excess that must be pared for the firm to offer "best value" products.

In aggregate, the cumulative effect of (1) overly optimistic managerial judgments, (2) commonplace managerial motivations, and (3) reasonable undertakings that required hiring new employees for which there is no longer a need, is an excess of personnel. None of these three forces or events is likely to become less frequent in the future. Indeed, increasing environmental dynamism is likely to increase the frequency with which new endeavors are initiated, fulfill their mission, and must be dismantled. Our earlier conclusion, then, still seems valid even after examining a wider range of forces and events related to downsizing: "In the future, firms will more frequently be forced to consider downsizing." But will they choose to downsize?

Casual review of the business press (which, admittedly, is a questionable process using a questionable database!) suggests that the most frequent response to a market decline is a workforce reduction, and an in-depth study of manufacturing firms found this to be the case during the 1980s. An interesting finding of the study was that firms that first focused on improving work processes (especially with heavy involvement of their workforce) achieved performance superior to those firms that moved directly to downsizing.[2] Assuming that this finding is repeated in manufacturing and in other industries in the future and that upper level managers learn of it, we would be tempted to conclude that, in the future, firms will more frequently consider other alternatives before deciding whether or how much to downsize.

This possible conclusion conflicts so greatly, however, with the apparent inclination of top managers to adopt downsizing as a first response that we must postpone its further consideration until we've examined the possible effects of forces that might inhibit downsizing in the future.

FORCES INHIBITING DOWNSIZING

Decisions to downsize are generally made at the highest levels of the firm. Although top managers recognize and often assert that employees are their most valuable resource, their press announcements suggest that workforce reductions are the first action considered when profits plunge. These announcements generally indicate that two numbers determine the size of workforce reductions: (1) the out-of-pocket expenses associated with the buyouts and, after taking these expenses into account, (2) the net savings to the firm from employing a smaller workforce. These two numbers are estimated from accounting data. Both tend to be viewed as valid and authoritative, and the latter often results in a temporary uptick in the value of the firm's stock. Research has shown, however, that downsizings are notoriously unreliable predictors of positive changes in a firm's future financial performance; future profits are often much less than what would be expected given the announced net savings. Their extensive examination of the research literature led Stanford University Professors James Baron and David Kreps to conclude that the research evidence to date is mixed, to say the least. A recent survey of over 1000 companies by Watson Wyatt, a consulting firm, found that only one third of companies that had downsized saw profits increase after the layoff as much as expected; fewer than half reported that the cuts reduced expenses as much as expected; and only a small minority reported a satisfactory increase in shareholder return on investment as a result of the layoff. Similarly, a 1997 survey of HR managers in large U.S. companies by the AMA found that companies that had eliminated jobs in the 1990s were slightly more likely than other firms to report short-term profit increases, but they were also somewhat more likely to report profit *declines* afterward. . . . Although some econometric studies have uncovered modest positive effects of white-collar downsizing on financial performance, in general the studies suggest the financial effects of downsizing in the short- and longer-term are negative.[3] (Baron & Kreps, 1999: 424)

> In my view, this conclusion may be misleading. What research has not determined is what would have happened to the downsizing firms had they not downsized. Even though their performance was poor for some time after the downsizing, it may have been poorer still if the downsizing had not taken place. Perhaps the firm would have failed. It may be that studies of surviving firms would show that many, such as IBM, downsized in each of several adjacent years and had ongoing performance declines in subsequent years. But their subsequent performance declines in these years would not indicate that these firms were wrong to downsize. To the contrary, the reduction in workforce costs may have enabled the firm to "weather the storm" or to make the changes that led to its eventual survival.

Many authorities argue that the reason these projected savings are poor predictors of future financial performance is that neither the firm's analysts nor its top executives take into account the full costs of downsizing. That is, when estimating the savings to be achieved through workforce reduction, some sizable "soft costs" associated with layoffs are ignored because they can't be satisfactorily estimated or because the analysts or decision makers are unaware of them. If these costs have often been ignored in the past, is there any reason to expect that they will more often be considered in the downsizing decisions of future firms? The answer may be "Yes." If these soft costs are greater in the future, then firms in the future will be more likely to consider them than have firms in the past.

Systematic studies have identified four consequences of downsizing that negatively influence firm performance, sometimes directly and sometimes through their effect on employee commitment. As we will see, it appears that these consequences will be greater in the future. To the extent that they are, they may serve to inhibit downsizing in either frequency or magnitude or both. In the next four sections, we examine these consequences, these soft costs, in the following order:

1. loss of "the firm's knowledge" that the departing employees take with them (e.g., the loss of organizational memory),

2. lower productivity of the remaining employees,

3. loss of "personal" connections with the firm's customers, suppliers, and knowledge sources, and

4. increases in unwanted turnover.

As we proceed, we will examine the possibility that, in view of the increasing magnitude of these four soft costs, future firms—when considering whether to downsize—will choose to downsize less frequently.

Loss of Organizational Knowledge

Let us use "organizational knowledge" to mean knowledge to which the firm has easier access than does any other organization. Among other kinds of knowledge, this includes the mind-resident knowledge of the firm's employees. When employees leave a firm, they often take with them—in their minds— some of the firm's knowledge. An example of downsizing resulting in the loss of organizational knowledge is reported by University of Michigan Professor Kim Cameron in his 1994 article "Strategies for Successful Downsizing," based on his study of change in 30 U.S. firms:

> Quick-hit, across the board cuts (in the firm's workforce) get attention. On the other hand, the harm caused by workforce reduction strategies may offset the positive effects of unfreezing the organization. This is illustrated in one organization where a purchasing agent was offered an incentive to retire early. This individual was the primary agent for ordering steel, and over the years, modifications in the types of steel and alloys being ordered had been made. Unfortunately, commensurate changes in the written specifications had not kept pace. Shortly after this purchasing agent accepted the early retirement option, an order was placed for steel following the precise written specifications. This produced a $2 million loss for the organization in downtime, rework and repair. The organizational memory, as well as the expertise needed to do the work, left with the purchasing agent. (p. 198)

Would good management have prevented this loss? Yes, if by "good management" we mean that, as a standard operating procedure, managers *reliably* checked to make sure that their knowledge-worker subordinates *continually* updated into the company's files *all* of the company-related information that the subordinates used in their work. Has this been standard practice in the recent past? No. Rather it has been, at most, a "sometimes practice." Can we expect it to be a standard practice in the future? No, we cannot—tomorrow's managers will be even more burdened with fast-arriving problems and opportunities. They will be even more focused on meeting deadlines than on maintaining records.

Of course "good management" may also mean that downsizing-directing management (1) was able to identify all of the potentially critical knowledge that employees at lower levels in the firm held in their heads and (2) captured most of this knowledge before the discharged employees departed. Is this realistic? No, it isn't—for two reasons. *One*, well-known but seldom articulated, is that firms don't know what they know, so identifying their critical knowledge—in order to retrieve it—is problematic. This is particularly true of soft knowledge. For example,

> During an interview, one senior manager of a Fortune 100 company described a situation where a bookkeeper making $9 an hour was let go in a downsizing effort. However, the company later discovered that it lost valuable institutional memory in the process, for the bookkeeper knew "where's, why's, and how-to's" that no one else apparently did. The result? The former bookkeeper was hired back as consultant at $42 per hour! (Cascio, 1993: 99)

These paragraphs and examples indicate that, in general, management's understandable unawareness of who knows what that isn't recorded makes it infeasible to avoid the loss of mind-resident knowledge during layoffs. *Another* reason it is infeasible to avoid this loss is that people in the process of being laid off are not inclined to be diligent about putting what they know into the firm's memory banks—knowledge sharing is a voluntary behavior.

Customers want the best quality, the best service, the best value, or some combination of these features. How do firms achieve best-of-class features in their products? There is only one way—they integrate into their products, or into the processes used to provide their products, knowledge not used by their competitors. The minds of their employees are the major repositories of most firms' most valuable knowledge. Hear again, Georgetown University's Professor Robert Grant, an authority on strategic management:

> Sustainability of competitive advantage therefore requires resources which are idiosyncratic (and therefore scarce), and not easily transferable or replicable.

These criteria point to knowledge (tacit knowledge in particular) as the most strategically important resource the firm possesses. (Grant, 1996b: 376)

If the firm continues in the business of the unit being downsized, the cost of the lost knowledge will be significant.[d] This cost will generally be greater than is recognized, as in many instances the firm will not know that the knowledge that disappeared with the departed employees ever existed.

But ignorance of what the firm knows seems to be more general than ignorance of only soft knowledge. Recall the comments of executives speaking in the broader context of "knowledge, know-how, and best practices":

"If TI only knew what TI knows," lamented Jerry Junkins, the late chairman, president, and CEO of Texas Instruments. Lew Platt, chairman of Hewlett-Packard, echoed this with "I wish we knew what we know at HP." (O'Dell & Grayson, 1998a: 154)

The above analysis serves as a preamble to an important question: What will be different about the future that might cause future firms to give greater consideration to the loss of their knowledge during downsizing? The answer is linked to the fact that the more competitive environments of the future will require firms to provide best-of-class products on a nearly continuous basis. Consequently, knowledge (the resource that—when absent—prevents firms from providing best-of-class products) will be even more valuable than it has been, and the loss of knowledge through downsizing will be all the more costly to the firm's bottom line. Thus the answer to the question about what will be different in the future is that, *in the future, heightened levels of competition and the resultant increase in the firm's need to provide best-of-class products will cause the cost of losing the firm's knowledge to be greater.*

Some firms will be quicker to recognize this and account for it in their decision making. (This will especially be the case for firms positioning themselves to capitalize quickly on rebounding markets, or on new markets that require knowledge similar to the knowledge residing in the minds of current employees.) Firms that do recognize and account for the value of the knowledge contained in the minds of their employees will be more likely to survive in the long run, to be future firms. *Future firms, when choosing whether or how much to downsize, will give greater consideration to the cost of losing the knowledge of the employees they might discharge.*[4]

---

[d]Recall that we are using "downsizing" to mean intentionally reducing the workforce in a line of business the firm intends to continue, as contrasted with eliminating a line of business and its workforce.

Lower Productivity of Retained Employees

If the least productive members of a firm's workforce are identified and discharged during downsizing, casual thinking would lead us to expect that the average productivity of the individual retained workers would increase. This might occur either because the workers discharged were the least productive or because the retained workers were motivated to work harder if they believed further layoffs were imminent and wanted to avoid being among those discharged. Studies of downsizing show, however, that this expected result is often not obtained; productivity is often unchanged or is even less than it was before the downsizing.[5] Findings from this research have identified four reasons.

One reason is associated with the increased post-layoff workload of the surviving employees. If employee motivation and work methods had been equivalent to those at the firm's competitors, we might expect that the number of employees discharged during a downsizing would be proportionate to the decrease in demand associated with the shrinkage of the market. In practice, however, firms typically seek not only to adjust to the change in market size but also to regain sales by decreasing their employee cost per unit produced, thus enabling them to lower prices. To achieve lower employee costs, they often reduce the number of employees further than they reduce the amount of work. They do this in the belief that, as the remaining employees do their previous work plus that of departed employees, the average productivity per employee will increase.

In support of this belief, reason would suggest that productivity per employee would increase in the short run, as individuals put forth extraordinary effort to keep their jobs. On the other hand, reason would also suggest that in the longer run productivity per employee would decrease, due to burnout, increased error rates, and the mistakes and accidents associated with ongoing high workloads. Similarly, we would expect that, when employees are faced with greater workloads, in the short run latent ideas about more efficient ways to work would be forthcoming and productivity would increase. Again, however, we would expect that in the longer run, higher workloads and fear of personal failure would inhibit process innovations and hence curtail productivity improvements. The fact that the validity of these arguments probably varies from context to context may explain the mixed findings of studies examining the effects of downsizing on productivity.[6] Let us turn from this idea— that added workloads have mixed effects on productivity of individual retained employees—to examining other factors whose effect on productivity is more certain.

A *second* reason that the productivity of downsized workforces is sometimes less than was the productivity of the original workforce is associated with the *reduction in knowledge sharing* that often follows downsizings. All else the same, firms that leverage the knowledge of their employees—by having this knowledge shared with other employees who can exploit it on behalf of the firm—will be more effective than firms that do not. Consequently, low levels of intrafirm knowledge sharing can put the firm at such a competitive disadvantage that it will not survive. This makes critically important the fact that downsizings and downsizing announcements can cause employees to withhold knowledge that they otherwise would share. Oftentimes this "withholding" of knowledge is merely a matter of employees not putting forth the effort to share what they know with someone who might be able to use this knowledge (perhaps because the "knowledge-owning" employee had to take on extra tasks as a result of the departure of discharged employees). Knowledge sharing is an effortful behavior.

Other times not sharing knowledge is more intentional. Recall from Chapter 6 the comments from professionals in an organization where people were being encouraged to put their knowledge into the organization's Knowledge Management System, but who—at the same time—saw themselves in danger of being laid off as a result of new pressures on the organization to be more competitive:

> Look, why would I want to share knowledge that has some value to me? It is my competitive advantage, it puts distance between me and others. (Standing & Benson, 2000: 343)

> Specialist knowledge in this environment provides some security for employees and sharing it is often perceived as against their best interests. (Standing & Benson, 2000: 344)

Professors Theresa Amabile of Harvard University and Regina Conti of Colgate University encountered a similar concern about information sharing in their study of a Fortune 500 high-tech firm that was downsizing. For example,

> Communication is not as open and honest. . . . Trust within the group has deteriorated because people are worried about their jobs. (Amabile & Conti, 1999: 636)

All managers are aware of the importance of trust as a determinant of cooperation. Fewer recognize the adverse effect of downsizing on inter-employee trust within the firm. Still fewer managers keep in mind the causal pathway:

1. downsizing leads to lower inter-employee trust,

2. lower employee trust leads to less knowledge sharing, and

3. less knowledge sharing leads to lower productivity per retained employee.

In this regard, let us draw on the scholarship of Professor Paul Adler of the University of Southern California:

> Effective sharing of knowledge . . . depends on and engenders a sense of mutual trust. Firms . . . attempt to create high levels of community and trust by providing material and nonmaterial *expressions of commitment to their employees* . . . (e.g., by avoiding layoffs, I add). Building on many decades of research on the critical role of informal organization in innovation, community—particularly in the form of communities of practice—is increasingly recognized as the organizational principle most effective in generating and sharing new knowledge.[7] (Adler, 2001: 220)

But community, communities of practice, and inter-employee trust are all undermined when established relationships are eliminated, as when parties to the relationship are let go during downsizing.

Whether not sharing knowledge is a matter of consciously withholding knowledge or is merely a matter of not proactively sharing what might be useful to other members of the firm, reduced knowledge sharing reduces the productivity of downsizing survivors who "make do" without the unshared knowledge (whether or not they recognize its absence).

A *third* reason that the productivity of downsized workforces is sometimes less than was the productivity of the original workforce is that layoffs create disconnects in the social networks and social relationships that enable employees to solve nonroutine problems and successfully undertake difficult tasks, such as innovation. Successful resolution of nonroutine problems and successful completion of difficult tasks in organizations generally require the cooperation of many people. But after downsizing, many employees will be called upon to cooperate with strangers, or at least with other employees with whom they have no established ties. Their full cooperation in facilitating the initiatives of these others is less likely. This is especially true when helping with the initiative is not one of their formal obligations. In all organizations, it is informal relationships—established over a history of interactions—that "make the system work." When layoffs eliminate people, they eliminate these relationships. As a result, it is more difficult to "get things done," and productivity suffers.[8]

The *fourth* reason that the average productivity of the remaining employees is often less than was the average productivity of the original workforce members is that the productivity of the work teams to which the remaining employees belong is often less than what it was. This loss in team productivity occurs even when a discharged team member is replaced. The issue being addressed is not one of maintaining the size of teams, but rather it is the evolved "fit" and synergy of the team's members. When one or more group members is eliminated, as might be the case in downsizing, the experience-acquired, work-related knowledge the members have about the departed member is lost, and the group and its individual members become less effective.

Through their interactions, work group members learn which other members know what and which members can and will do what; members learn which tasks other members are prone to perform well and which they are prone to perform poorly. This knowledge (called "transactive memory") enables the optimal task allocation that increases the average productivity of the individual group members. It also, over time, heightens the specialization of team members—as they repeatedly are informally "assigned" the tasks at which they are best. These repetitions of experience result in individual members learning to do "their jobs" better. This increases the work group's productivity, as other members come to know on whom they can rely for what—thus enabling these other members to focus on developing and employing their own special skills.[9] Let us listen to two authorities on knowledge management at Boston University's School of Management, Rob Cross and Lloyd Baird, as they describe how a history of working together has positive influences on productivity by enhancing knowledge sharing, cooperation, and transactive memory:

> First, time spent interacting on work tasks establishes a sense of reciprocity and trust among colleagues. This social capital encourages employees to turn to colleagues to get useful assistance or advice about future initiatives. For example, we spoke with one manager who remarked, "Just because [a team member] knows something that I may need to know does not mean that he is going to share it with me in a helpful way. This is not because he is hoarding the information, but because he is busy and doesn't have the time to share what he knows at the level of detail that I need. The only reason that he will take the time to tell me is because we have worked together, fought through a tough project, and developed a relationship that we each know we can rely on." Second, by working closely together, colleagues build an understanding of each person's particular knowledge and skills. This understanding allows employees to seek out the right peers for information in the future. (Cross & Baird, 2000: 71)

In these last few pages we've seen four reasons why downsizing can, and almost always will, have an adverse effect on the productivity of the individual retained employees. Whether the cumulative loss in productivity, when summed across the retained employees, will be less or greater than the gain in the firm's productivity achieved by decreasing the workforce to be more congruent with current demand for the firm's products will depend on several factors. Some reflect consumer-market and labor-market conditions, but several are idiosyncratic to the firm. As we will see, it will be useful to withhold our conclusions about the overall effect of these matters until we've reviewed the two remaining soft costs of downsizing, costs which are also idiosyncratic to the firm.

Decreased Effectiveness of Interfirm Relations

One of the greatest needs in achieving the hoped-for synergies in technology transfer alliances—or in virtual organizations created to exploit the strengths of the member companies—is to develop, between the boundary-spanning employees who interface across the organizations, both social comfort and cross-understanding of each other's job-related responsibilities and knowledge. These features of relationships are also important to the effectiveness of workings between sales or service personnel and their clients and between representatives of firms and their subcontractors. Research and everyday experience make clear that these features of relationships develop over time. Downsizings (or any other human-resource program that causes turnover among incumbents) breaks these relationships and can lead to breaks in interfirm relations or to short-term losses in interfirm effectiveness.[10]

Will the effectiveness of interfirm relations be a more important issue in the future? It seems inevitable that this will be the case. The anticipatable increases in specialization among firms (that we noted in earlier chapters) will force the number of linkages among firms to grow, thus increasing the dependence of the firm's productivity on the effectiveness of its boundary-spanning personnel.

Increases in Unwanted Turnover

A large number of systematic studies are unambiguous in their findings that downsizing leads to less trust in management, less identification with the firm, and less loyalty to the firm. Through these attitudinal changes, downsizing increases the likelihood that retained employees will leave the firm of their own volition. In addition, of course, downsizing dismembers work groups and workplace friendships, and in this way breaks the social bonds that have long been known to retard turnover.[11] Finally, as we've just seen, downsizing leads to increased workloads and to reduced trust and information sharing in the workplace.

Overall, downsizing creates a more aversive, less satisfying workplace environment for the employees that the firm chose to retain. Among employees who have opportunities elsewhere, the resultant job dissatisfaction leads to turnover. In general, of course, those who leave will be the employees who are most marketable, who are most skilled, who possess the most knowledge, and who are therefore potentially the most productive. Replacing these employees is very costly to the firm. Will unwanted turnover be of greater concern in downsizing decisions in the future?

In view of our earlier conclusion that knowledge will be more valuable in the future, especially the mind-resident knowledge of the firm's employees, it seems reasonable to conclude that firms will attend more to the cost of unwanted turnover than have firms in the past. *Future firms, when choosing whether or how much to downsize, will more frequently consider the possibility and costs of losing—from among the employees not discharged—those employees who possess knowledge most critical to the firm.*

INTERIM SUMMARY AND TRANSITION

In this section we examined four adverse consequences of downsizing: (1) the loss of mind-resident organizational knowledge, (2) lower productivity of the remaining employees, (3) loss of "personal" connections with the firm's customers, suppliers, and knowledge sources, and (4) increases in unwanted turnover. We are now confronted with the question of whether two actions—(1) considering the soft costs when determining the optimum workforce reductions and (2) minimizing these costs when implementing downsizings—are efforts more likely to be undertaken by future firms. In this regard, it seems appropriate to review two conclusions drawn in the chapter on decision making:

> In the future, organizational decisions that . . . inadequately account for the multiple factors relevant to the situation, will be even more likely to enable competitors to gain advantage and put the firm at risk.

> In the future, organizational decisions . . . that more adequately account for the multiple factors relevant to the situation, will be even more likely to enable the firm to gain advantage and put its competitors at risk.

Because the need to consider downsizing will occur more frequently in the future, firms that consider the soft costs examined here when deciding whether or how much to downsize, and/or that attempt to minimize these costs, will have more opportunities to outperform competitors that do not deal with these matters. These firms will more likely survive. The survivors will be the future firms. With this in mind, it seems reasonable to expect that *future firms will more frequently consider the soft costs of downsizing when deciding whether or how much to downsize and/or will more frequently attempt to minimize these costs when downsizing.*

I expect that most readers have encountered instances or anecdotes where middle managers complied with directives to downsize their units but, in order to simultaneously comply with strong urgings to maintain previous production levels, had to hire back the discharged employees as contract workers (who were not counted as employees and so didn't

(Continued)

(Continued)

adversely affect the managers' net headcount reductions). I encountered an instance of this when teaching a weekend executive MBA class. I found that some software engineers in the class—who had been laid off by a prominent local firm—had been hired back by the same firm as full-time contract employees, *at three times the hourly rate they'd been paid previously.* (This led to some understandable friction between them and other software engineers in the class who were still employed as permanent employees by this firm.)

Earlier we concluded that, "in the future, firms will more frequently be forced to consider downsizing." Just now, after reviewing many supporting arguments, we concluded that "future firms will more frequently consider the soft costs of downsizing when deciding whether or how much to downsize." It seems inevitable that the rising importance of these soft costs in the future will exert an attenuating effect on the frequency with which firms, after considering these costs, will actually downsize. We can expect that, *in the future, the greater magnitude of the soft costs of downsizing will either cause downsizing to be less frequently implemented, relative to the increased frequency with which it will be considered, or will cause the extent of the downsizing to be less.*

Further, drawing on these arguments concerning the growing importance of soft costs, it seems reasonable to conclude that, *in the future, firms will more frequently consider other alternatives before deciding whether or how much to downsize.*

The propensity for firms to downsize will undoubtedly continue to vary considerably. The reasons are three:

1. the actual importance of soft costs will vary across firms;

2. the awareness of soft costs and the perceived importance of soft costs will vary across top managers; and

3. the availability and desirability of alternatives to downsizing will vary across firms.

As is well known, some companies are loath to downsize. When they anticipate that the current market shrinkage will not be long lasting, or when they expect soon to roll out products requiring workforce skills

(Continued)

(Continued)

similar to those required of the operations being curtailed, these companies first reduce costs other than their workforce costs and then employ one of two tactics. If they have sufficient cash reserves, they temporarily assign their "redundant" employees to other useful tasks, albeit tasks of less importance, such as preemptive maintenance or undertaking special projects. If they do not have sufficient cash reserves to employ this first tactic, they instead often reduce their workforce costs by going to shorter workweeks or mandatory sabbaticals. For specific examples of companies using these tactics and for elaborations of arguments for resisting downsizing, see the articles by M. Conlin (2001), "Where Layoffs Are a Last Resort," and R. Levering and M. Moskowitz (2002), "The Best in the Worst of Times." Other alternatives to downsizing, *albeit actions that risk losing the firm's better employees*, include reducing bonuses, freezing salaries, eliminating merit payments, and lending employees to other firms.

As we've seen, downsizing is a change generally made to bring workforce costs into line with revenues. The next topic need not be a change—often it is an ongoing staffing strategy. Although sometimes used to minimize workforce costs, more often and more importantly it is used to maintain workforce flexibility.

Use of Temporary Workers

In his article in the *Annual Review of Sociology*, University of North Carolina Sociology Professor Arne Kalleberg describes the forces that led to the growth in the use of temporary workers:

Changes beginning in the mid-1970s created conditions that led countries, organizations, and workers to search for greater flexibility in employment. Consequently, the standard employment relationship began to unravel. Global economic changes increased competition and uncertainty among firms and put greater pressure on them to push for greater profits and to be more flexible in contracting with their employees and responding to consumers.[e] (Kalleberg, 2000: 342)

---

[e]For our present purposes, what Kalleberg describes is the key causal history. For our more global understanding, however, it is worthwhile to recognize that "the history of employment relationships in the United States makes clear that what we think of as the 'traditional' model of long-term attachment, internal development, and mutual obligations likely existed for little more than a generation. The current move to a more market-mediated employment relationship is in some ways a return to earlier arrangements" (Cappelli, 1999: 12).

MOTIVATIONS TO USE TEMPORARY WORKERS

Congruent with Kallenberg's "greater pressure" are three separate motivations that have pushed firms to increase their use of temporary and subcontract workers. *One*, the need for efficiency, has caused some firms to reduce their workforce costs by employing temporary and subcontract workers rather than permanent workers.[f] Will this same motivation lead to more use of such workers in the future? As a result of increases in competition, we might think so.

Because temporary employees tend to be younger, less experienced, and sometimes more willing to trade off compensation for autonomy or fewer working hours per week, in some situations firms can employ them at lower wages and—due to less regulation—can provide lower levels of benefits. These potential cost savings, however, are not obtained when these employees are leased from a temporary employment agency, where the markups of 50 to 100% on the wages of leased employees exceed the wage and benefit savings obtainable by directly employing the temporary workers in place of permanent employees. Hear the conclusion of Susan Houseman and George Erickcek, senior researchers at the Upjohn Institute for Employment Research, sum the case with regard to low-skill employees:

> Unless an organization's low-skilled employees are earning above market compensation, management will have little to gain in terms of wage and benefits cost savings from the use of agency temporaries and contractors. Where we observe such use, the organization's motivation is something else. (Houseman & Erickcek, 2002: 2)

Besides the desire to reduce wage and benefits costs, what else might Houseman and Erickcek have in mind? What other motivations bear on this issue? One, the *second* of the motivations that have increased the use of temporary and subcontract workers is the "administrivia" necessary to carry out some of the human resources functions.

Peter Drucker makes the argument that, *in the United States*, a motivation for the growth in the use of temporary employees is that firms are less constrained by government regulation in how such employees are managed. In particular, associated with government regulation of all jobs, he asserts, are two problems especially vexing to small- and medium-size businesses. One is the complexity of many of the regulations and the other is the onerous reporting requirements. It appears that many firms, in response to the growing number of regulations and the associated problems of interpretation and reporting, are

---

[f]"Permanent" worker (or employee) does not imply employment that is for life or until voluntary termination. Rather, it is meant to indicate that the relationship is not explicitly limited in duration and thus could be of unlimited duration.

going to what Drucker calls "professional employee organizations" or "PEOs." These firms specialize in dealing with the legal and reporting aspects of managing a firm's employees, often including traditional human resources tasks such as payroll and benefits.

> The driving force behind the steady growth of temps and the growth of PEOs, I would argue, is the growing burden of rules and regulations for employers.... Between 1980 and 2000, the number of U.S. laws and regulations regarding employment policies and practices grew by about 60%, from 38 to 60. (Drucker, 2002: 72-73)

Whether governmental regulations concerning the relationship between employees and employers will continue to grow is uncertain. Certainly a projection of current trends indicates that it will, but the burden of regulations may be nearing the point where counterforces will arise to truncate these trends. What does seem certain is that growth in competitive pressures will increasingly cause firms to focus on their core competence and to outsource support functions, particularly those that are burdensome relative to their contribution to core competence. To this end, even today, some firms have gone so far as to make *all* of their employees, *including their top managers,* leased employees of an employee-leasing firm (while retaining a role in the hiring and retention decisions).[12] The greater competitive pressures of the future seem likely to further this approach to the human resources function. This discussion leads to two conclusions:

1. *Future firms will more frequently outsource some or all of their human resource functions.*

2. *In the future, more firms will lease some or all of their employees from employee-leasing firms.*

We've just seen that the reduction of workforce costs and avoidance of the hassle associated with certain aspects of the human resource function are two of the three separate motivations that have pushed (and will push) greater use of temporary and contract workers. But a *third* motivator, the need for flexibility in workforce configuration brought on by the growth in environmental dynamism, has also been the overwhelmingly important motivator for the use of such workers.[13] That environmental dynamism will be greater in the future will cause the need for flexibility in workforce size, shape, and skill level to also be greater in the future.

But will firms act to fulfill this need? Or are there forces that work against the use of temporary and contract workers and that will be stronger in the future and perhaps offset a concern for maximum flexibility? Let us turn to this question.

FORCES INHIBITING USE OF TEMPORARY WORKERS

As with the use of downsizing, use of temporary employees to achieve lower costs and greater flexibility often results in adverse consequences to the firm that we will again refer to as "soft costs." *One* of these, not so soft, can be lower productivity—when the temporary employees are less well qualified than are permanent employees. This condition is, of course, short-lived. A *second* soft cost is the lower level of employee commitment to the firm that typifies temporary workers. And why not, as the firm clearly avoids a commitment to them? Except where temporary employees wish to become permanent employees and hope that by exhibiting commitment to the firm they increase their chances, the lack of commitment is generally associated with lower levels of organizational citizenship behavior. This results in lost opportunities. For example, it seems less likely that temporary employees would exert much effort to put into any of the firm's repositories methods or knowledge that they had developed.

Systematic research supports the idea that these costs are real, that they are observable. For example, both of these costs and a generally lower level of commitment to the firm were observed in the study of 10 companies in five industries carried out by Hong Kong University of Science and Technology Professor Anne Tsui and her associates at the University of California–Irvine and the University of Dublin: "[Permanent] employees performed better on core tasks, demonstrated more citizenship behavior, and expressed a higher level of affective commitment" (Tsui et al., 1997: 1089) than did employees working on a "quasi-spot contract" (i.e., temporary employees).

The effect of temporary employees on the *productivity* of permanent employees varies. If permanent employees can off-load lower-skill tasks to temporary employees, then their productivity increases. But if they become heavily involved in the training or coordination of the temporary employees— which is often the case—the personal productivity of the permanent employees declines. It also appears that use of temporary employees leads to decreases in the commitment of permanent employees.[14] Importantly, the positive and negative effects of these two work groups on each other depend in complex ways on the extent to which the groups interact with each other and on whether the temporary employees work directly for the firm or work for a subcontractor.[15]

What will be the effects on decisions—about the use of temporary employees—of (1) lower levels of commitment of temporary employees or (2) lower levels of permanent employee productivity and commitment? I think not much. The decision to have work done by temporary employees is generally made by higher-level managers who don't observe firsthand these soft costs. In contrast, these upper level managers do hear—firsthand—from their staff advisors about the lower costs and fewer regulatory issues that result when temporary employees rather than permanent employees are laid off. There appears to be little reason to believe that these conditions will greatly change. Thus it may be that the influence of soft costs will not increase significantly, even though the costs themselves will. With soft costs remaining unobserved and therefore as impotent in their effects in the future as in the present, it seems likely that, to respond to their increased need for flexibility, *future firms will more frequently make greater use of temporary workers.*

We must not misinterpret this conclusion. In nearly all firms, certain high-skill knowledge workers are central to maintaining and exploiting the firm's core competence. The cost of employing these workers is considerable, but the contribution they make to the firm's performance is a large multiple of their cost. Accordingly, firms attempt to keep a core of these workers by providing them with permanent employment insofar as is possible. As the competitiveness of firms becomes even more based on their ability to exploit knowledge quickly (as discussed in Chapter 7), the need to employ on a permanent basis a cadre of workers with a high level of skills central to firms' core competencies will increase. Future firms will not use temporary workers to replace permanent knowledge workers whose high skill levels are central to maintaining and exploiting the firm's core competence (and who can maximally use their knowledge on the firm's behalf because they know the firm's culture, history, and ways of getting things done, and know who in the firm knows what and does what). The increased use of temporary workers will be at the expense of workers other than these.

We've seen that decisions to reduce the workforce significantly and to employ a significant number of temporary workers have important side effects. They are strategic decisions that both address and cause some of the conflicts discussed early in the chapter. We turn now to two other matters of strategic importance that interact and that also involve conflicts, organizational change, and organizational culture.

Change and Culture

Let us define an organization's culture as "the set of beliefs and values that is widely shared and strongly held throughout the organization." *Strong* cultures are those that are widely shared and strongly held; *weak* cultures are those that are not.

This definition is not restrictive regarding how the beliefs and values came to be. Some authorities argue that an organization's culture is the unique set of beliefs and values that has been collectively learned by the organization's members through their experiences *in the organization*. In this sense, each organization's culture is unique to some degree.

It will be useful to remind ourselves of some of the reasons why its culture is important to a firm:

1. Congruence between the firm's culture and its strategy determines how effectively the strategy will be implemented.

2. The strength of a firm's culture influences the firm's changeability; firms with strong cultures tend to be resistant to change.

3. Organizational cultures influence the choices employees make about how much effort to put into fulfilling assigned responsibilities, whether to engage in organizational citizenship behaviors, what to do in ambiguous situations, whether to believe management's statements, and so forth.

4. Congruence between the employee's values and the firm's culture influences voluntary turnover and other manifestations of employee commitment; the nature of the firm's culture partially determines the nature of the employees it can expect to retain.

5. Congruence between potential employees' values and the firm's culture influences the firm's recruiting success; the nature of the firm's culture partially determines the nature of the employees it can expect to hire.

From this it is clear that the nature and strength of the firm's culture are important to top management because they affect the firm's ability to satisfy the needs for change, efficiency, flexibility, and employee commitment.[g] Consequently, top managers attempt to influence their firm's culture.

The firm's environment also influences its culture—the environment influences the beliefs and values people bring with them to the firm, and changes in the environment affect the firm in ways that influence what

---

[g]By the "nature" of an organization's culture I mean the nominal levels of its belief-or-value-laden attributes. For example, a firm's culture could reflect that its members value *integrity* or *expediency, risk-taking* or *risk-avoidance,* and *merit* or *seniority* or *egalitarianism* as a basis for compensation.

employees believe and value. Let us first examine how future environments will affect the cultures of future firms. Then we will examine how future environments will affect top managers' actions and success with regard to managing their firms' cultures. Third, we will review some unintended effects on firms' cultures that are brought about by management actions. Finally, we will examine how cultures affect the firm's ability to change or be changed.

ENVIRONMENTAL EFFECTS ON THE CULTURES OF FUTURE FIRMS

Future environments will be more dynamic, causing the need for certain types and numbers of employees to fluctuate. Future information and transportation technologies will be more effective, enabling people to move and still stay connected with people and places they value. Knowledge workers, especially, will be more motivated to relocate to upgrade their knowledge and increase their opportunities. These and other ideas led us to conclude earlier that, in the future, employee turnover will be greater. Greater turnover will cause the firm's members to have fewer common experiences and interactions *in the firm,* and in this way will retard development of a particular widely shared and strongly held set of beliefs or values that would be unique to the firm. Thus, *the cultures of future firms will be less unique.*

On the other hand, for reasons already reviewed, future firms will tend to be more specialized with regard to their products, processes, markets, and knowledge. As a consequence, the employees attracted to and hired by any particular firm will be more similar on some dimension(s) (e.g., expertise, education, interest) than they would be if the firm were less specialized. More similar employees will bring to the workplace their more similar beliefs and values. And when these employees leave, they will be replaced by similar employees having similar beliefs and values. This will result in a strong culture. But this *imported* culture will be a set of beliefs and values linked to the knowledge, products, processes, and markets in which the firm specializes, not a set of beliefs and values learned by the organization's members through their experiences *in the organization.* So, future firms will have strong cultures, but the cultures will be less unique to the firm. Altogether, the reasoning in these two paragraphs indicates that *their higher levels of specialization will cause future firms to tend to have strong cultures, but cultures that are less unique.*

ENVIRONMENTAL EFFECTS ON MANAGEMENT'S CULTURE-MANAGING ACTIONS AND SUCCESS

If for no other reason than that their employees know what to expect from each other, firms with strong (but not dysfunctional) cultures outperform firms with weak cultures.[16] Accordingly, when the firm is performing well, management generally attempts to strengthen the culture with rewards, stories, rituals, symbolic and exemplary actions, and descriptions of the benefits of adhering to the currently held beliefs and values. To be successful, of course, these "treatments" require that they be repeatedly observed by the firm's employees. But, as we noted above, in the future, employee turnover will be greater, perhaps much greater. Employees who have learned the firm's culture will leave more often, and new employees will enter the firm more often. Consequently, we can expect that, *in the future, management's efforts to strengthen or maintain the firm's culture will be less effective.*

Let us move from attempts to *strengthen* or *maintain* culture to attempts to *change* culture. This is a critically important matter when top management is attempting to change the firm's strategy or a process involving a high level of employee discretion. For example, when the effectiveness of a firm's strategy depends on employee actions that are not easily monitored or measured, or that must be created "on the spot" because the circumstances are not precisely anticipatable, the nature and strength of the firm's culture will determine the firm's performance.

Examples of employee actions that are generally more governable with culture than with either direct supervision or explicit incentives are (1) interacting with customers or other stakeholders—especially when the interactions take place off the firm's premises, (2) cooperating with other employees, (3) acting in the firm's interests when choosing what to do in ambiguous situations, and (4) fully sharing expertise. When the need to change the firm's strategy is apparent, and when employee actions such as these are important to the strategy, top management will generally attempt to change employee actions by changing the firm's culture.[h]

As an example, top management might see the need for the firm to begin to offer best-of-class service (as contrasted with a commodity-level service), as did British Airways during its dramatically successful turnaround in the 1980s. (British Airways' top management went to great lengths to change the service-related actions of its frontline employees by changing employee *beliefs* about what was important and by reinforcing employees' socially-induced *values* of respect for others (i.e., by changing the firm's culture.)[17]

As another example, top management—sensing that the firm's rates of adaptation and innovation are less than those of its competitors—might see the need for the firm's employees to begin proactively obtaining and passing on information useful to units other than their own, or proactively sharing their

---

[h]Management might instead choose to change employee actions by changing the system of rewards and penalties. In a subsequent section, we will examine the circumstances under which changing the firm's culture will be more effective and the circumstances under which changing the firm's bases for rewards and penalties will be more effective.

expert knowledge. Such employee actions are most effectively governed with culture. Given that threats and opportunities will arrive at a faster rate in the future, firms will have to change their strategies and processes more frequently. From this it follows that *future firms will attempt to change their cultures more frequently.*

Using well-known methods and avoiding well-known (but commonly repeated) mistakes, over time and with intense effort, top management can influence employees' everyday choices (about what to do and what not do) by changing the firm's culture.[18] But efforts to change widely shared and strongly held beliefs and values in an organization do not succeed quickly. (Even the extensive and intensive multiyear effort to change British Airways' culture was not entirely successful.) Further, such efforts are particularly unfruitful when employee turnover is high, and, as we've noted, employee turnover will be greater in the future. It follows that, *in the future, top management's efforts to change the firm's culture will be less successful.*[i]

ADVERSE EFFECTS OF CHANGE ON THE FIRM'S CULTURE

Strong cultures are generally associated with high levels of performance. But two common strategic actions weaken a firm's culture (and employee commitment). One is downsizing. Let us recall from our earlier discussion that "community, communities of practice, and inter-employee trust are all undermined when established relationships are eliminated, as when parties to the relationship are let go during downsizing" and that "a large number of systematic studies are unambiguous in their findings that downsizing leads to less trust in management, less identification with the firm, and less loyalty to the firm." Whatever levels of belief employees had about the degree to which they could trust other employees to "do the right thing" or the firm to "do them no harm," these levels are diminished when the firm downsizes. Downsizing reduces the "trust" component of a firm's culture.

The second strategic action that weakens a firm's culture is use of temporary workers. Their social remoteness from the firm's long-term employees, the fact that they frequently work at sites other than the firm's physical facility, and the fact that they are often short-timers are factors that tend to cause temporary workers to absorb to only a small degree the beliefs and values that are more widely shared and strongly held by the firm's permanent employees. For

---

[i]Of course, the widely shared set of beliefs and values of the firm's employees can be changed by firing current employees and hiring new employees who have the sought-after beliefs and values. But this approach is generally infeasible and, further, there seem to be no strong arguments that it will be much more feasible in the future than at present.

244 THE NECESSARY NATURE OF FUTURE FIRMS

the most part, the beliefs and values of temporary workers are more influenced by forces and entities outside the firm than are the beliefs and values of permanent employees. To the extent that they do interact with the permanent employees, while this may result in their absorbing some of the firm's culture, their presence dilutes the strength and uniqueness of the firm's culture. Thus, recalling our earlier conclusion that "future firms will more frequently make greater use of temporary workers," we must now conclude that *their greater use of temporary workers will cause future firms to have weaker and less unique organizational cultures.*

In contrast, recall our earlier conclusion that "their higher levels of specialization will cause future firms to tend to have *stronger* organizational cultures, but their cultures will be less unique." So, greater use of temporary workers will lead to weaker cultures while higher levels of specialization will lead to stronger cultures. Both phenomena, greater use of temporary workers and higher levels of specialization, will characterize future firms. What, then, can we say about the strength of the cultures of future firms? Will they be weaker or stronger?

Two facts are pertinent to the matter. One is that firms will vary in the extent to which they specialize. The other is that they will also vary in the extent to which they use temporary employees. Together these observations restrict us to the conclusion that *the strength of the cultures of future firms will be influenced by the extent to which they specialize relative to the extent to which they employ temporary workers.*

HOW CULTURES AFFECT THE ABILITY OF THE FIRM TO CHANGE

Beliefs and values are developed through experiences and interpretations. Subsequent experiences and interpretations that challenge these beliefs and values are threatening. The desire to avoid such threats causes individuals and groups to avoid experiences different from those that led to their current beliefs and values. In this way, strong organizational cultures are inertial to change, and firms possessing strong cultures are resistant to change. As observed by eminent social psychologist Karl Weick, "A coherent statement of what we are makes it harder for us to become something else" (Weick, 1985b: 385).

Two things we'd like to know but don't know: we don't *know* whether it is possible for firms to have a culture that embraces major change, and we don't *know* whether a culture that embraces change in general would influence an employee's tendency to embrace *a particular change*. Do changes that are successful from a firm's perspective have sufficiently positive effects on the lives of employees that they truly cause work-related *change in general* to be widely and strongly valued? We don't know this, although—understandably—change-needing managers would like for it to be so. If work-related change in general is widely and strongly valued, does this mean that employees will believe that every particular change is one that they should embrace? Or do the salient features of a particular change dominate employees' evaluation of it? How strongly will valuing change in the abstract influence the evaluation of particular changes? About these matters we are far from certain.

Because, over time, people come to value and "believe in" what they do, and because what people do can be influenced by rewards, the values and beliefs of people can be shaped with appropriately designed compensation systems. Thus a firm's compensation system can be helpful in changing the firm's culture to make it more congruent with the firm's needs. But well-intentioned compensation systems can also be incongruent with desirable organizational cultures, as when rewarding or retaining knowledge workers based on their expertise-enabled performance curtails the norm of knowledge sharing. So, in keeping with this chapter's focus on dealing with conflicting needs, let us examine some of the relationships between culture and compensation.

Culture and Compensation

Organizations attempt to influence the performance (and otherwise control the actions) of their members in three ways: (1) monitoring and measuring performance and subsequently giving rewards and penalties, (2) directly supervising, and (3) inculcating and reinforcing certain beliefs and values (i.e., creating and maintaining an organizational culture).

The common manifestation of (1) is *pay-for-performance*. This approach to influencing performance became more commonly used in white-collar, professional, and managerial jobs in the latter decades of the twentieth century, as the competitiveness of the business environment increased and firms sought higher levels of employee productivity. It became very fashionable in the 1990s—often in the form of performance bonuses or stock options. Pay-for-performance for individual employees is particularly well suited for the following conditions:

1. performance can be accurately measured,

2. performance is largely under the employee's control,[j]

---

[j]Violation of these first two conditions led to much of the criticism of the high levels of executive compensation early in the 2000s, as when in vivid instances corporate performance was found to be inaccurately reported and when increases in executive compensation were viewed as incongruent with the absolute declines in firm performance. (Relative-to-competitor declines seem not to have been considered.)

3. the employee's focus on the performance dimension being rewarded doesn't result in significant negative effects on coworkers, on cooperation and teamwork, on the performance of other employees, or on the organization's stakeholders, and

4. its use doesn't violate the norms associated with the employee's occupational culture.

Example occupations that tend to satisfy these conditions especially well are soloist entertainers, soloist athletes, soloist writers, soloist artists, and certain salespeople, as well as certain executives, where account can be taken of conditions in the industry and where the performance of the executive's unit is measured in the longer run. We will discuss pay-for-performance for teams later in this section.[19]

Direct supervision is a viable approach to controlling employee actions when the appropriate actions are well-known and easily observed and when its use doesn't violate the norms associated with the employee's occupational culture.

Creation and maintenance of *organizational culture* is the third approach to influencing performance and employee behavior and is used, either alone or in conjunction with other approaches, in the huge proportion of situations when other approaches are not wholly satisfactory. Let us consider whether the relative usefulness, and frequency of use, of these three approaches will change in the future.

CHANGES IN CONDITIONS FAVORING DIRECT SUPERVISION

In the industrialized nations, direct supervision has become unfashionable and violates the expectations of many employees. As other nations industrialize and as the levels of their citizens' education increases, direct supervision will tend to violate worker expectations in these nations as well. Direct supervision is resented by specialists, who tend to question whether their supervisor knows more about their work and the task at hand than they do. As occupational specialization increases, and we noted earlier that it will, direct supervision will be tolerated by a smaller proportion of the workforce. Direct supervision is less useful in situations where mind-resident knowledge must be transferred or integrated, because the degree of transfer or integration *relative to its potential transfer or integration* cannot be adequately assessed. As we noted, these situations will become increasingly common. In light of these facts, and the fact that there seem to be no compelling arguments suggesting that its use will increase in the future, we can expect that, *in the future, direct supervision will be used less frequently.*

CHANGES IN CONDITIONS FAVORING PAY-FOR-PERFORMANCE

We saw in Chapter 2 that future business environments will be even more competitive than are today's. As communication and transportation technologies become more effective and enable competitors to break through buffers of location or of customer ignorance or loyalty, a firm's survival will be more tenuous and more problematic. But even where survival is virtually guaranteed, a firm's profitability varies with its performance against its competition. Thus an effect of the future's higher level of competition will be an increase in the need to produce best-of-class products. In many industries, the resource most critical to producing best-of-class products will be the talent level of the firm's personnel.

Given these increases in the competitiveness of the business environment, we can expect that—out of necessity—firms will compete more strongly for top talent in talent categories important to the firm's performance. This has important implications for the firm's compensation practices. In particular, when differences in talent are critical determinants of the performance of firms and their competitors, firms will be forced to pay disproportionately large premiums for high levels of such talent.

In his recent book on the impact of globalization on local and national economies, *The Lexus and the Olive Tree* (2000), Pulitzer Prize–winning author Thomas Friedman makes this point in an interesting way. Friedman highlights the fact that rewards are disproportionately large for those firms whose products are superior to their competitors' products. He also highlights that rewards are disproportionately greater for employees whose impact on the firm's performance is greater than that of their near peers. After authenticating these points using economic data, he goes on to tell us about Joe Klein, Michael Jordan's teammate on the Chicago Bulls' 1997 NBA championship team, whose

> shooting skills were only marginally less effective (than Jordan's), whose jump shot was only slightly less accurate, whose free-throw shooting was only slightly less consistent, whose defensive skills were only slightly less intense. But he (Klein) was still a great basketball player. After all, he was in the NBA and he was on the championship Chicago Bulls. . . . Same game, same league, same team, same bench! (p. 313)

But Michael Jordan's salary was more than 100 times that of Joe Klein's, and his endorsement income was greater still. Why? Because Jordan's *impact* on the outcome of games, and at the box office, was off-the-scale greater than Klein's. His talent justified his market-based salary, and—Friedman notes—led to his huge *impact* on the markets for the products he endorsed.

> Jordan's value was underscored upon his return to the NBA in March 1995, after an eighteen-month hiatus in baseball. The stock market value of [his] five

endorsees—McDonald's, Sara Lee, Nike, General Mills and Quaker Oats—soared $3.8 billion within two weeks. (p. 313)

The Chicago Bulls had a continuous need for Michael Jordan's talent and were willing to pay his high salary because it was justified by his considerable impact on the Bulls' profits. But hasn't this always been the situation? Hasn't the condition of disproportionate rewards always been in effect? The answer to these questions is, of course, "Yes." But the more relevant question is "Are disproportionate rewards for given increments of ability likely to be greater in the future?" The answer to this question, too, is "Yes." One reason is spelled out in Friedman's chapter "Winners Take All," where he makes clear that customer ignorance, government regulation, transportation costs and time, and almost all buffers to Darwinian competition are falling, and will fall farther in the future (a conclusion we drew in Chapter 2). Because interfirm competition for both customers and talent (or other customer-attracting attributes such as Michael Jordan's persona during his heyday) will be greater in the future, *future firms will more frequently pay disproportionately large premiums for higher levels of talent, expertise, or other attributes useful to the firm.*[k]

If it were true that future increases in interfirm competition will cause competitively useful employee attributes to command greater premiums, we would expect that past increases in interfirm competition would have caused higher levels of expertise to command greater, even disproportionately greater, premiums. Is this the case? Has it happened? To answer requires compensation-distribution data in a highly competitive industry where both firm performance and employee performance have reasonably valid metrics associated with them. Given that competition for audiences among professional sports teams has been increasing (because television has created larger advertising markets and sponsorship revenues have accordingly increased), given that there is a positive association between team performance and revenues, and given that team performance and player performance are subject to assessment with commonly accepted metrics, professional sports is an industry where we might get some inkling of the association between expertise and premiums for expertise. In accord with the reasoning set

(Continued)

---

[k]The above reasoning and data suggest that in the case of rare and useful attributes, such as highly specialized expertise, pay-for-performance will be broadly construed to include pay for *time-on-task*.

(Continued)

forth earlier, we would expect to see the salaries paid to the higher-salaried (more talented) athletes to have diverged rather considerably from the salaries paid to lower-salaried (less talented) athletes. We do.

Consider first the firms in the National Basketball Association, where Michael Jordan worked. In 1968, the average salary of the highest-paid 20% of the players was 5 times as great as the average salary of the lowest-paid 20%. By 1999, the ratio of the average salaries of these two groups of employees had increased from 5 to 24. Turning to baseball, in 1964 the average salary paid to the highest-paid 20% of the major league baseball players was 6 times as great as the average salary paid to the lowest-paid 20%. By 2000, the ratio of the average salaries had increased from 6 to 42. Throughout this period the ratio of the average salaries increased at an increasing rate (a fact congruent with the idea that competition for audiences was increasing at an increasing rate). In major professional sports, where multiple measures of talent are available to firms, and where salary data for the whole range of players are available to researchers, it appears that the premium that firms pay for talent is increasing.[20]

The same is likely to be true for managerial talent, but reliable compensation data for managers below the top two executive levels is unavailable. Further, "social capital" and "symbolism," as contrasted with performance, predict some of the variation across companies in CEO compensation. Finally, reliable performance data for managers at any level is also unavailable, as (1) their unit's performance is often greatly determined by events beyond their control and (2) valid cross-industry comparisons are also unavailable.[21]

Of course, increasing competitiveness will not only cause firms to pay premiums within a talent category[1] but will also cause firms to compete more strongly and pay higher wages in those labor markets where the types of talent

---

[1]My colleague Reuben McDaniel brought to my attention the possibility that, much more so in the future, the criticality of technical expertise to a firm's endeavors could lead to a particularly qualified expert demanding extraordinary compensation to continue participating in a key project. Such an action would parallel the holdout or other strategy of some professional athletes before the season starts. What we don't see is *individual* athletes or other performers going on strike *during* the season. Whether this is because it would be a gross violation of social norms or because it could be a career-ending action is unknowable, but these same two hindrances would also be present in the context in which most experts are employed in firms. For this reason I expected that such an action will occur only very rarely if at all but, at the same time, acknowledge that the future criticality of expertise heightens the possibility.

most critical to improving the firm's products or operating effectiveness are found. Recent trends document that this is already happening:

> Over the past two decades, wage inequality has grown significantly in the United States. The total effect has been large, as the gap between wages at the seventy-fifth percentile of the distribution and the twenty-fifth percentile has increased by nearly 50 percentage points. . . . The main cause . . . appears to be a shift in the demand for workers of different kinds. Demand is growing for workers with exceptional talent, training, autonomy, and management ability much faster than for workers in low- and middle-wage occupations. (Bresnahan, Brynjolfsson, & Hitt, 2000: 145)

The above arguments and data, associated with variation in compensation across occupations rather than within occupations, reinforces our earlier conclusion that "future firms will more frequently pay disproportionately large premiums for higher levels of talent, expertise, or other attributes useful to the firm."[22]

CHANGES IN CONDITIONS FAVORING PAY-FOR-PERFORMANCE FOR TEAMS

When the contributions of individual team members are difficult to measure and where team-member actions can greatly influence the performance of other team members, firms often pay bonuses to team members based on team performance rather than individual performance. Besides being more feasible under these conditions than would be paying bonuses based on individual performance, team performance–based bonuses promote intrateam cooperation, knowledge sharing, and citizenship behaviors.

The importance of sharing knowledge and cooperating in knowledge integration efforts follows from much of what was said in Chapters 6 and 7. The greater pressures for faster innovation and the higher levels of competition that will characterize future environments will cause knowledge sharing and other forms of proactive behavior to be even more important than they are today. Accordingly, we can expect that *future firms will more frequently use team performance–based bonuses.*[23]

CHANGES IN CONDITIONS FAVORING USE OF ORGANIZATIONAL CULTURE

When the beliefs and values of a firm's employees positively contribute to high levels of employee effort, the firm is in a very advantageous position. But we saw earlier that higher levels of environmental dynamism and competitiveness will lead to (1) more use of temporary workers, (2) perhaps more use of downsizing (certainly more frequent consideration of downsizing as an approach for dealing with declines in revenues), and (3) higher levels of unwanted employee turnover. These conditions will make it more difficult for top management to count on use of a strong and favorable organizational culture for achieving high levels of employee effort. So, will organizational culture be employed more frequently or less? Let's look at the firm's alternatives.

While pay-for-performance for teams will be used more frequently, because it motivates within-team knowledge sharing and other forms of cooperation, it is not useful for influencing employee behavior in either of two situations. *One* is when the individual whose knowledge-sharing or full cooperation is needed is unacquainted with or is not a member of the same unit as the person who needs this help. Here, because "social control" is lacking and because the extent of knowledge sharing and cooperation, *relative to what they could be,* are impossible to measure, individual pay-for-performance is an unreliable approach for obtaining high levels of effort from the person whose knowledge or cooperation is needed. Use of organizational culture seems to be the more satisfactory approach in this increasingly important circumstance.[24]

The *second* situation where pay-for-performance for teams is not useful is when the team's contribution to the firm's success is not readily measurable or is significantly influenced by factors outside the team's control. An example would be when the team's contributions are supporting efforts for a network of teams working on a large product and are, therefore, not measurable, as would be the case if the team provided some form of "technical support." Another example would be when the teams in a network of teams were so interdependent that the relative performance of individual teams could not be quantitatively assessed. In these situations, the motivation for employees to contribute as well and as much as they can toward the overall effort would seem to depend on what they value and believe to be appropriate behaviors. As discussed earlier, such situations will be more common in the future.

Altogether, this discussion indicates that the circumstances are increasing when direct supervision and use of pay-for-performance (for either individuals or teams) will be limited as approaches for influencing the actions of knowledge workers. But forthcoming changes in the business environment will increasingly prompt top management to seek more or different efforts from the firm's workforce. As a consequence, organizational culture will be increasingly relevant for influencing employee effort, even if only by default. Thus it seems reasonable to expect that *the top managements of future firms will more frequently attempt to actively manage their firm's culture.*

Chapter Summary

While fully acknowledging that firms must make changes to survive, this chapter dealt with the trade-offs firms must make as they attempt to fulfill their simultaneous needs for change, efficiency, flexibility, and employee commitment. In it we focused especially on the adverse effects on fulfillment of one need that result from actions taken to fulfill another need. After reviewing the conflicts firms encounter when attempting to satisfy these needs, we examined three actions in depth, *downsizing*, using *temporary workers*, and *managing organizational culture*. We saw that downsizing leads to several soft costs, costs that will be more significant in the future, and that it also decreases the strength of the firm's culture. We saw that use of temporary workers, employed to increase the firm's flexibility, often leads to some inadvertent outcomes (e.g., reduction in the productivity and commitment of permanent workers and dilution of the nature and strength of the firm's culture).

In the last sections of the chapter we examined alternative approaches to motivating employees—pay-for-performance, direct supervision, and management of the firm's culture. We concluded that future firms will more often provide very high levels of compensation for very high levels of talent, expertise, or other employee attributes useful to the firm, and that they will more often use pay-for-performance for teams. While we concluded that forthcoming environmental conditions will cause firms' cultures to become less unique and will cause them to be more difficult to manage, we also concluded that their need for more or different efforts from their firm's workforce will nevertheless cause top managements of future firms to more actively attempt to shape and manage the firm's culture.

Endnotes

1. The classic 1975 article by J. Freeman and M. T. Hannan, "Growth and Decline Processes in Organizations," *American Sociological Review*, 40: 215-228, elaborates and documents this point.

2. This study is reported in K. S. Cameron, "Strategies for Successful Organizational Downsizing," 1994; and K. S. Cameron, S. J. Freeman, and A. K. Mishra, "Downsizing and Redesigning Organizations," 1993.

3. As an interesting example study, see the review and empirical results in the article by W. F. Cascio, C. E. Young, and J. R. Morris, "Financial Consequences of Employment-Change Decisions in Major U.S. Corporations," 1997. While downsizing might delay a firm's demise, these researchers found that it doesn't seem to improve profitability—stable employers and downsizing employers had the same (essentially zero) return on assets during the 12-year period covered by the study. It is interesting to

note, however, that the firms that divested of hard assets, as in giving up a line of business, had improved profitability. Overall, the literature on the effect of downsizing on productivity is inconclusive. Few studies include longitudinal data, few compare downsizing firms with stable firms in the same industry, and few account for the fact that ongoing and continuing declines in market share might be forcing downsizing and maintaining productivity at low levels. Further, those based on surveys of managers—because their conclusions differ so greatly from studies where firm performance was assessed using publicly available measures—seem to suffer from the well-known problems of self-serving perceptions and biased recollection and reporting. E. H. Bowman, H. Singh, M. Unseem, and R. Bhadury, "When Does Restructuring Improve Economic Performance," 1999, note that the diversity of outcomes is to be expected partly because firms vary greatly in the effectiveness of their initiatives. One important issue that seems not to have been studied is the possibility that, if it hadn't downsized, the firm may have failed, or failed more quickly.

4. Executives with IBM's Institute for Knowledge Management, Eric Lesser and Laurence Prusak, provide an articulate elaboration of the costs of losing the firm's knowledge as a result of downsizing. See E. Lesser and L. Prusak, "Preserving Knowledge in an Uncertain World," 2001.

5. For examples of recent studies supporting this conclusion concerning the effect of downsizing on productivity, see D. Dougherty and E. H. Bowman, "The Effects of Organizational Downsizing on Product Innovation," 1995; and T. M. Amabile and R. Conti, "Changes in the Work Environment for Creativity During Downsizing," 1999. For reviews of earlier studies of productivity changes or surveys of managers' perceptions that support the conclusion that downsizing often has either no significant effect or has a negative effect, see W. F. Cascio, "Downsizing: What Do We Know? What Have We Learned?" 1993. In contrast to these findings, J. Brockner et al., "Threat of Future Layoffs, Self-Esteem, and Survivor's Reactions: Evidence From the Laboratory and the Field," 1993, found in their study of retained workers that those low in self-esteem reported that they were more motivated after the layoff. This finding was not observed for those high in self-esteem.

6. For research and commentary bearing on the validity of these lines of reasoning see T. M. Amabile and R. Conti, "Changes in the Work Environment During Downsizing," 1999; J. Brockner et al., "Threat of Future Layoffs, Self-Esteem, and Survivors' Reactions: Evidence From the Laboratory and the Field," 1993; J. Brockner et al., "Interactive Effect of Job Content and Context on the Reactions of Layoff Survivors," 1993; W. F. Cascio, "Downsizing: What Do We Know? What Have We Learned?" 1993; and M. Conlin, "Where Layoffs Are a Last Resort," 2001.

7. Adler calls attention to the "Special Topic Forum on Trust in and Between Organizations" in the July 1998 *Academy of Management Review*. Also note the emphasis given to the importance of enduring relationships in the development of trust in the June 2001 *Harvard Business Review* article, "How to Invest in Social Capital," by longtime researchers and consultants Laurence Prusak and Don Cohen.

8. Although this line of argument seems sound, only a few authorities have developed it. S. R. Fisher and M. A. White, "Downsizing in a Learning Organization: Are There Hidden Costs?" 2000, use a social network frame to consider the impact of

downsizing on organizational learning and propose that the effects can be viewed as a nonlinear function of learning-network size. From this perspective, the potential damage to a firm's learning capacity is greater than headcount losses imply. Also see D. Dougherty and E. H. Bowman, "The Effects of Organizational Downsizing on Product Innovation," 1995.

9. Both laboratory and field research show that transactive memory has positive effects on team performance (D. Liang, R. Moreland, and L. Argote, "Group Versus Individual Training and Group Performance: The Mediating Factor of Transactive Memory," 1995; R. L. Moreland, L. Argote, and R. Krishnan, "Socially Shared Cognition at Work: Transactive Memory and Group Performance," 1996). K. Lewis, *The Impact of Interpersonal Relationships and Knowledge Exchange on Group Performance: A Field Study of Consulting Project Teams* (unpublished doctoral dissertation, University of Maryland at College Park, 1999), for example, found that transactive memory explained consulting-team performance above and beyond "input" variables (member demography, familiarity, and prior experience) and "process" variables (good social relationships, functional communication, and willingness to disclose information).

10. The study by N. Bendapudi and R. P. Leone, "Managing Business-to-Business Customer Relationships Following Key Contact Employee Turnover in a Vendor Firm," 2002, provides empirical support for this assertion. For a review of the literature on this matter, see S. Lovett, D. Harrison, and M. Virick, "Managing the Boundary Spanner-Customer Turnover Connection," 1997. See also the anecdotal support in A. Markels and M. Murray, "Call It Dumbsizing: Why Some Companies Regret Cost-Cutting," *Wall Street Journal*, May 15, 1996.

11. See J. L. Price, *The Study of Turnover*, 1977. Although Price's book was written over a quarter of a century ago, the findings of the studies it reviews still seem valid. Certainly they are supported by the recent research of T. R. Mitchell, B. C. Holtom, T. W. Lee, C. J. Sablynski, and M. Erez, "Why People Stay: Using Job Embeddedness to Predict Voluntary Turnover," 2001. This shouldn't surprise us—basic human needs don't change with time. See also L. Prusak and D. Cohen, "How to Invest in Social Capital," 2001.

12. An interesting instance of this form of employee leasing is described in K. Tyson, "Working One Job for Two Companies; Employee Leasing Gains Popularity," 1998.

13. See, for example, R. S. Belous, *The Contingent Economy: The Growth of the Temporary, Part-Time and Subcontracted Workforce*, 1989; A. Davis-Blake and B. Uzzi, "Determinants of Employment Externalization: A Study of Temporary Workers and Independent Contractors," 1993; B. Harrison and M. R. Kelley, "Outsourcing and the Search for 'Flexibility,'" 1993; and B. Uzzi and Z. I. Barsness, "Contingency Employment in British Establishments: Organizational Determinants of the Use of Fixed-Term Hires and Part-Time Workers," 1998.

14. From A. Davis-Blake, J. P. Broschak, and E. George, "Happy Together? How Using Nonstandard Workers Affects Exit, Voice, and Loyalty Among Standard Employees," 2003, we have "The few case studies of blending (of temporary and permanent employees) suggest that using nonstandard (temporary) workers reduces standard (permanent) employees' loyalty and worsens relations between peers (Geary, 1992; Pearce, 1993; Smith, 1994)."

15. See, for example, the reviews and empirical studies by E. George, "External Solutions and Internal Problems: The Effects of Employment Externalization on Internal Workers' Attitudes," 2003; and by A. Davis-Blake, J. P. Broschak, and E. George, "Happy Together? How Using Nonstandard Workers Affects Exit, Voice, and Loyalty Among Standard Employees," 2003; and the review by A. Davis-Blake and P. P. Hui, " Contracting Talent for Knowledge-Based Competition," 2003.

16. See J. P. Kotter, and J. L. Heskett, *Corporate Culture and Performance,* 1992; G. G. Gordon, and N. DiTomaso, "Predicting Corporate Performance From Organizational Culture," 1992; and R. S. Burt, S. M. Gabbay, G. Holt, and P. Moran, "Contingent Organization as a Network Theory: The Culture Performance Contingency Function," 1994.

17. See, for elaboration, *BusinessWeek,* "From 'Bloody Awful' to Bloody Awesome," 1989; A. Corke, *British Airways: Path to Profitability,* 1986; and D. Campbell-Smith, *The British Airways Story: Struggle for Take-Off,* 1986.

18. See C. O'Reilly, "Corporations, Culture, and Commitment: Motivation and Social Control in Organizations," 1989; C. O'Reilly and J. A. Chatman, "Culture as Social Control: Corporations, Cults, and Commitment," 1996; and E. H. Schein, *Organizational Culture and Leadership,* 1992.

19. For an authoritative but easily read critique of common beliefs about compensation, including pay-for-performance, see J. Pfeffer, "Six Dangerous Myths About Pay," 1998b.

20. The data underlying these statistics are from R. D. Fort's Web site, *MLB Salaries* (2001), http://users.pullman.com/rodfort/SportsBusiness/MLB/Salaries/MLBSalaries.htm. The R-squared from our multiple regression model predicting the ratio of the salary of the top and bottom 5ths of the distribution, using time and time-squared as the predictors, was .89. This value could have occurred by chance alone less than one time in one thousand. Time was not statistically significant, but time-squared was significant at the .001 level. The concave upward curve had an intercept at 1964 of 5.78 and at 2000 had an intercept of 41.92. When the Coefficient of Variation was used as the predicted variable (i.e., when the standard deviation of the whole distribution of salaries for a given year divided by the mean of the salaries for the same year was used as the predicted variable), the R-squared was .81. This value could have occurred only one time in 20. Time was not statistically significant, but time-squared was significant at the .05 level. The concave upward curve had an intercept at 1964 of .70 and had an intercept at 2000 of 1.44. While not as impressive as the ratio data, these latter data still show a doubling of the spread after accounting for the growth in the mean. See also http://users.pullman.com/rodfort/SportsBusiness/BizFrame.htm.

21. Studies demonstrating these effects are those of M. A. Belleivieau, C. A. O'Reilly III, and J. B. Wade, "Social Capital at the Top: Effects of Social Similarity and Status on CEO Compensation," 1996; J. D. Westphal and E. J. Zajac, "Substance and Symbolism in CEO's Long-Term Incentive Plans," 1994; and "Accounting for the Explanations of CEO Compensation: Substance and Symbolism," 1995.

22. The conditions favoring extreme levels of compensation (and the consequent dispersion of compensation) are authoritatively described in E. E. Lawler III *Rewarding Excellence: Pay Strategies for the New Economy,* 2000. See also the study by J. D. Shaw, N. Gupta, and J. E. Delery, "Pay Dispersion and Workforce Performance: Moderating Effects of Incentives and Interdependence," 2002.

23. It is important to recognize that the conclusion, "future firms will more frequently pay disproportionately large premiums for higher levels of talent, expertise, or other attributes useful to the firm," is *not* incongruent with the conclusion just stated. Consider, for example, that in the National Football League teams pay premium salaries to higher performers, but at the same time the bonuses from winning in the postseason games are shared equally among the team's players. For elaboration of the subtleties associated with achieving effective outcomes and avoiding dysfunctional outcomes when using team-based bonuses see E. E. Lawler III and S. G. Cohen, "Designing Pay Systems for Teams," 1992; J. S. DeMatteo, L. T. Eby, and E. Sundstrom, "Team-Based Rewards: Current Empirical Evidence and Directions for Future Research," 1998; and R. Wageman, "Interdependence and Group Effectiveness," 1995.

24. For elaboration of this statement and empirical evidence supporting it, see M. S. Granovetter, "The Strength of Weak Ties," 1973; M. T. Hansen, "The Search-Transfer Problem: The Role of Weak Ties in Sharing Knowledge Across Organization Subunits," 1999; and D. Constant, L. Sproull, and S. Kiesler, "The Kindness of Strangers: The Usefulness of Electronic Weak Ties for Technical Advice," 1996.

9

Recapitulation: The Necessary Nature of Future Firms

As a partial foundation for later chapters, this book began with an articulation of some self-evident truths and some assertions that seem to follow from these truths. For brevity, allow me to paraphrase these several ideas:

A firm's survival depends on its ability to attain and maintain congruence with its environment. Top management's primary responsibility is to ensure that the firm possesses the capabilities needed to attain and maintain this congruence. To achieve these capabilities requires that managers at all levels make commitments, that they choose and implement organization design features and management practices well matched to their firm's environment. Wise commitments, even for the purpose of achieving the flexibility needed for dealing with unforeseeable events, require that managers make or accept predictions about future business environments. Prediction is necessary in a non-benign world.

These were the ideas of Chapter 1. In total they made obvious that, to determine the necessary nature of future firms, we must first determine the nature of the environments with which the firms must be congruent—not a determination based on extrapolations of recent short-term trends, nor one based on assessments made by experts currently caught up in the enthusiasm of their specialty, but one based on trends possessing three characteristics:

1. their existence must be explainable;
2. they must have a substantial history, and their future courses must be explainable with current information; and
3. they must be logically antecedent and causally linked to the environmental features that might influence the nature of future firms.

Two trends, advances in scientific knowledge and advances in the effectiveness of technologies, satisfied these requirements. A broad-ranging analysis of these trends led to the conclusions that, in the future, both the world's stock of scientific knowledge and the effectiveness of business-relevant technologies will be greater, and will be increasing at an increasing rate.

Additional analyses made clear that these scientific and technological advances will lead to increases in the variety and number of environmental entities—such as suppliers, customers, and competitors—and to increases in the interdependencies between the firm and these entities. Succinctly said, in the future, environmental *complexity* will be greater and increasing. Further analyses made clear that the forthcoming scientific and technological advances will cause future levels of environmental *dynamism* and *competitiveness* also to be greater than today's, and to be increasing. In several cases, we encountered evidence that these advances in science and technology and increases in complexity, dynamism, and competitiveness had already begun, but at present were still developing at rates lower than what we can expect in the future. These conclusions concerning science, technology, and environmental complexity, dynamism, and competitiveness were the primary outcomes of Chapter 2 and, along with the assumptions from Chapter 1, constituted the foundation for the remaining chapters of the book.

Drawing on the conclusions concerning the higher levels of environmental complexity, dynamism, and competitiveness that will be forthcoming, we went on to conclude in Chapter 3 that future firms will be confronted with threats and opportunities greater in number and complexity than those encountered by today's firms. A large proportion of these events will not have been previously encountered and, for this reason or due simply to their greater complexity, will be difficult to understand. Thus, in the future, the speed and appropriateness of a firm's actions, and hence its performance and survival, will depend more than in the past on the firm's ability to rapidly and effectively sense and interpret environmental changes.

In response to this situation, future firms will adopt structures and processes different in degree or kind from those of today's firms. While some large firms will create staff units to monitor and probe environmental events, the great majority of firms will seek less expensive approaches to obtaining environmental intelligence, such as purchasing intelligence-gathering services from vendors specializing in this function. In general, future firms will be more active in supporting and encouraging all of their members to serve as environmental sensors and, to this end, will employ in some form the environmental sensing practices we labeled *specialized accountability* and *eclectic responsibility*.

In firms and other organizations, interpretation is often a social process, involving a significant portion of the organization's upper echelon. With this in mind, Chapter 3 went on to explain why, in addition to their commonplace informal discussions, the top managers of future firms will more frequently meet to intensively review the firm's operations and performance and to exchange information and interpretations of new environmental events. While recognizing that the intended purpose of these review sessions is to enhance firm performance, the chapter noted three additional benefits of these intense interactions: (1) the top managers will tend to develop rich and overlapping understandings of their firm's context; (2) they will tend to develop cross-understandings of each other's mental models; and—as a consequence of these two outcomes—(3) they will tend to be more able to interpret new situations quickly and appropriately.

Thus, a firm's sensing and interpretation processes have two important consequences. *One* is that the interpretation of a situation largely determines the subsequent decision process, which in turn influences the decision taken. The *second* important consequence of interpretation processes is that they often lead to changes in the mental models of the firm's top managers, models that the managers will use to interpret future events. In these ways, interpretations exert important influences on both current and future organizational decisions.

That the dynamic and complex nature of forthcoming environments will cause decision situations to be thrust upon the firm at an increasingly rapid rate and also to be more complicated has, of course, implications for decision making. Chapter 4 explored how future firms will cope with this state of affairs, adopting structures and processes that enable them to make decisions more frequently and more rapidly and that, nevertheless, account for the broader scope of issues that will characterize future threats and opportunities. We saw in the chapter that decision speed and scope are not nearly so incompatible as is commonly believed and noted structures and processes that future firms will adopt to ensure that decisions are both timely and appropriate to the decision situation's complexity. For example, we examined the facts that future firms will ensure that their decision units are more numerous or faster acting and that the units will have or can readily obtain the information necessary to make appropriate choices. Also examined was the idea that future firms will direct more effort toward selecting, developing, and supporting their decision makers.

Beyond describing these structural features and developmental processes, Chapter 4 described why and how future firms will, to a much greater extent than have firms in the past, more often (1) employ "vigilant" decision processes, (2) assign specific and formal responsibility for getting a decision made, (3) manage decisions as projects, and (4) employ specific forms of information technology in support of their decision makers. The chapter closed by explaining why, in spite of the heightened pressures managers will face to make decisions rapidly, some decision-making practices historically in common use (i.e., truly intuitive decision making, satisficing, and analogizing) will see less use in future firms.

While future firms will have to cope more frequently with threats and opportunities, a particular environmental challenge will occupy their attention on an ongoing and everyday basis—the need to innovate:

Customers want either the best quality, the best service, or the best value. To survive, firms must provide one or more of these best-of-class product features on a nearly continuous basis. As we've seen, advances in technology eventually cause any level of quality, service, or value to become outmoded. Thus firms (must) *innovate*—they (must) make changes in their products or processes so that at least some portion of the market sees their products as best-of-class.

We also concluded that "(1) innovation requires new knowledge, or a new way of combining current knowledge, and (2) new knowledge, or a new way of combining current knowledge, requires learning." Altogether, these ideas and the earlier observation that tomorrow's business environments will be more dynamic and more competitive than are today's, formed the motivation for Chapter 5—that, to survive, future firms will learn more effectively than do today's. This chapter described why and how future firms will more actively attempt to learn from their experiences (i.e., through designed experiments, natural experiments, action probes and operations, and in-depth analyses of infrequent events). It also described how they will learn vicariously, by attending to their absorptive capacity, by importing knowledge in the form of expertise, and by enhancing the learning of their members.

But learning alone will not sufficiently prepare firms for the task of innovating at a level that assures survival in the more competitive environment of the future. In addition to acquiring knowledge (a process that is, in reality, accomplished by individuals or small groups), firms must leverage what their members and groups learn. They do this by causing the acquired knowledge to be shared, perhaps at a later time, with other members and groups that may be able to use it to create innovations on the firm's behalf. Thus we can expect that future firms will more actively manage the storage and sharing of the knowledge their members and groups acquire.

Chapter 6 described several structures and processes that future firms will use to facilitate knowledge sharing, including building supportive cultures, creating processes and structures that enhance direct, informal sharing, employing information technology in Knowledge Management Systems and people-finder systems, and transferring individuals with high capacity for absorbing and communicating the pertinent knowledge across units. An important message in Chapter 6 was that "full knowledge sharing is a voluntary behavior," one for which there are strong disincentives. Accordingly, the chapter elaborated on these disincentives and discussed multiple approaches for blunting their effects.

Knowledge acquisition and knowledge leveraging facilitate innovation, but innovation itself requires knowledge integration. Chapter 7 focused on how future firms will integrate knowledge in pursuit of innovative products and processes. It explained how the firm's knowledge integration efforts will be greatly and adversely affected by forthcoming increases in occupational specialization (increases that are inevitable given the forthcoming increases in the world's stock of knowledge), as "the task of combining the knowledge of more individuals, each more narrowly specialized, is more complicated than is the present task of combining the knowledge of fewer, more broadly knowledgeable individuals."

The chapter dealt with three broad topics. *One* was structures and processes for integrating the firm's knowledge. The particular issue surfaced was that future increases in specialization will force increases in the number of specialists and support staff required to achieve a given percentage improvement in a current product, or in a new product that serves the same market need. This will, in turn, force increases in the number of teams needed and—unless off-setting mechanisms are emplaced—increases in the number of managerial levels. Use of communications technologies high in telepresence, and increased employment of the concepts and practices of concurrent engineering and modular architecture, were identified as mechanisms that will see more use in future firms.

The *second* topic examined was changes in firms' employment practices and in experts' employment strategies. To deal with the fact that the expertise of highly specialized personnel is useful to any one firm only occasionally—made all the more relevant as specialization increases—future firms will more frequently employ specialized experts on a temporary basis. To deal with the fact that the knowledge possessed by such experts is often sticky, future firms will necessarily bring these experts deep into the intellectual operations of the firm, thus increasing the likelihood that their knowledge will be effectively integrated with that of the firm's own knowledge workers.

The *third* and last topic examined was the acquisition and integration of knowledge from other autonomous firms. Here the chapter elaborated on the fact that both the availability and accessibility of externally available knowledge will be increasing in the future and concluded that, as a consequence, future firms will more frequently buy knowledge that leverages their special competence rather than develop this knowledge internally. Drawing on the same reasoning, the chapter also concluded that future firms would more frequently use structural arrangements, such as alliances and acquisitions, to acquire expert knowledge rather than develop it internally.

The innovations of their competitors will push firms to innovate more frequently and more rapidly in the future, and entities such as suppliers and regulators will also more often confront firms with the need to change. As a result, future firms will attempt to ready themselves for rapid and efficient change with structures and processes that ensure *flexibility*. But such structures and processes are generally incompatible with the repeated experiences and routinization that leads to high levels of *efficiency*. Further, many of the firm's efforts either to change or to increase productivity reduce *employee commitment*. Chapter 8 dealt with how future firms will deal with these dilemmas, these incompatibilities among what must be goals of all future firms. The chapter also described how future environments will influence firms' cultures and compensation practices, and will attenuate management's ability to influence firms' cultures.

The environments of future firms will be different from the environments firms face today. Future firms will, therefore, necessarily be different from today's firms. Firms will be able to survive future threats and effectively exploit future opportunities only if their top managers have put into place organizational attributes and management practices well suited to the environments of the future.

References

Academy of Management Review. 1998. Special topic forum on trust in and between organizations. 23(3).

Ackoff, R. L. 1983. Beyond prediction and preparation. *Journal of Management Studies,* 20: 59-70.

Adler, P. S. 2001. Market, hierarchy, and trust: The knowledge economy and the future of capitalism. *Organization Science,* 12(2): 214-234.

Adler, P. S., Goldoftas, B., & Levine, D. I. 1999. Flexibility versus efficiency? A case study of model changeovers in the Toyota production system. *Organization Science,* 10(1): 43-68.

Albert, S., Ashforth, B. E., & Dutton, J. E. 2000. Organizational identity and identification: Charting new waters and building new bridges. *Academy of Management Review,* 25: 13-17.

Aldrich, H. 1999. *Organizations Evolving.* Thousand Oaks, CA: Sage.

Allen, T. J. 1984. *Managing the Flow of Technology.* Cambridge: MIT Press.

Almquist, E., & Wyner, G. 2001. Boost your marketing ROI with experimental design. *Harvard Business Review,* 79(9): 135-141.

Amabile, T., & Conti, R. 1999. Changes in the work environment for creativity during downsizing. *Academy of Management Journal,* 42(6): 630-640.

Amason, A. C. 1996. Distinguishing the effects of functional and dysfunctional conflict on strategic decision making: Resolving a paradox for top management teams. *Academy of Management Journal,* 39(1): 123-148.

Ambrose, S. E. 1996. *Undaunted Courage.* New York: Simon & Schuster.

American Productivity & Quality Center. 2001. Developing rewards and recognition for knowledge sharing. Retrieved March 2003 from www.apqc.org/free/articles/dispArticle.cfm?ProductID=1406

Anand, V., Glick, W. H., & Manz, C. 2002. Thriving on the knowledge of outsiders: Tapping organizational social capital. *Academy of Management Executive,* 16(1): 87-101.

Anderson, P. 1995. Microcomputer manufacturers. In G. R. Carroll & M. T. Hannan (Eds.), *Organizations in Industry.* New York: Oxford University Press.

Anderson, P., & Tushman, M. L. 1990. Technological discontinuities and dominant designs: A cyclical model of technological change. *Administrative Science Quarterly,* 35(4): 604-633.

Appelbaum, E., & Berg, P. 2000. High-performance work systems: Giving workers a stake. In M. M. Blair & T. A. Kochan (Eds.), *The New Relationship: Human Capital in the American Corporation.* Washington, DC: Brookings Institution Press.

Argote, L. 1999. *Organizational Learning: Creating, Retaining and Transferring Knowledge*. Boston: Kluwer.

Argote, L., Beckman, S., & Epple, D. 1990. The persistence and transfer of learning in industrial settings. *Management Science*, 36(2): 140-154.

Argote, L., & Ingram, P. 2000. Knowledge transfer: A basis for competitive advantage in firms. *Organizational Behavior and Human Decision Processes*, 82(1): 150-169.

Argyres, N. 1999. The impact of information technology on coordination: Evidence from the B-2 "Stealth" bomber. *Organization Science*, 10(2): 162-180.

Argyris, C., & Schön, D. A. 1978. *Organizational Learning: A Theory of Action Perspective*. Reading, MA: Addison-Wesley.

Arthur D. Little. 1995. The learning organization: Making it happen, making it work. *Prism*, Third Quarter.

Arthur, M. B., & Rousseau, D. M. (Eds.) 1996. *The Boundaryless Career: A New Employment Principle for a New Organizational Era*. New York: Oxford University Press.

Ashby, W. R. 1956. *An Introduction to Cybernetics*. New York: Wiley.

Ashby, W. R. 1960. *Design for a Brain: The Origin of Adaptive Behavior* (2nd ed.). New York: Wiley.

Austin, J. R. 2003. Transactive memory in organizational groups: The effects of content, consensus, specialization and accuracy on group performance. *Journal of Applied Psychology*, 88(5).

Balachandra, R., & Friar, J. H. 1997. Factors for success in R&D projects and new product innovation: A contextual framework. *IEEE Transactions on Engineering Management*, 44(3): 276-287.

Baldwin, C. Y., & Clark, K. B. 1997. Managing in an age of modularity. *Harvard Business Review*, 75(5): 84-93.

Barnard, C. I. 1938. *The Functions of the Executive*. Cambridge, MA: Harvard University Press.

Baron, J. 2000. "Comment" on Market-mediated employment, by P. J. Cappelli. In M. Blair & T. Kochan (Eds.). *The New Relationship* (pp. 90-99). Washington, DC: Bookings Institution Press.

Baron, J. N., & Kreps, D. M. 1999. *Strategic Human Resources: Frameworks for General Managers*. New York: John Wiley.

Barr, P., Stimpert, J., & Huff, A. 1992. Cognitive change, strategic action, and organizational renewal. *Strategic Management Journal*, 13(Summer): 15-36.

Bell, D. 1976. *The Coming of Post-industrial Society: A Venture in Social Forecasting*. New York: Basic Books.

Belleivieau, M. A., O'Reilly, C. A., III, & Wade, J. B. 1995. Accounting for the explanations of CEO compensation: Substance and symbolism. *Administrative Science Quarterly*, 40: 283-308.

Belleivieau, M. A., O'Reilly, C. A., III, & Wade, J. B. 1996. Social capital at the top: Effects of social similarity and status on CEO compensation. *Academy of Management Journal*, 39(6): 1568-1593.

Belous, R. S. 1989. *The Contingent Economy: The Growth of the Temporary, Part-Time and Subcontracted Workforce*. Washington, DC: National Planning Association.

Bendapudi, N., & Leone, R. P. 2002. Managing business-to-business customer relationships following key contact employee turnover in a vendor firm. *Journal of Marketing*, 66: 83-101.

Bentzin, B. 1999. Remarks to a University of Texas systems seminar for communications and government relations specialists. Reported by writer Mary Lenz in The University of Texas at Austin's *On Campus*, 9 November.

Berry, J. 2000. Employees cash in on KM-Knowledge management programs pay rewards to share ideas. *InternetWeek*, 22 May, 45-46.

Bettis, R. A., Bradley, S. P., & Hamel, G. 1992. Outsourcing and industrial decline. *Academy of Management Executive*, 6(1): 7-22.

Beyer, J. M., & Browning, L. D. 1999. Transforming an industry in crisis: Charisma, routinization, and supportive cultural leadership. *Leadership Quarterly*, 10: 483-520.

Bigley, G., & Roberts, K. H. 2001. The incident command system: High-reliability organization for complex and volatile task environments. *Academy of Management Journal*, 44(6): 1281-1300.

Blair, M. M., & Kochan, T. A. 2000. *The New Relationship: Human Capital in the American Corporation*. Washington, DC: Brookings Institution Press.

Bogner, W., & Barr, P. 2000. Making sense in hypercompetitive environments: A cognitive explanation for the persistence of high velocity competition. *Organization Science*, 11(2): 212-226.

Bolger, F., & Harvey, N. 1993. Context-sensitive heuristics in statistical reasoning. *Quarterly Journal of Experimental Psychology. A. Human Experimental Psychology*, 4: 779-811.

Boulding, K. E. 1978. *Ecodynamics: A New Theory of Societal Evolution*. Beverly Hills, CA: Sage.

Bowen, K. H., Clark, K. B., Holloway, C., Wheelwright, S. C., & Leonard-Barton, D. 1994. Regaining the lead in manufacturing: Three related articles. *Harvard Business Review*, 72(5): 108-143.

Bower, J. L., & Christensen, C. M. 1995. Disruptive technologies: Catching the wave. *Harvard Business Review*, 73(1): 48-49.

Bowman, E. H., Singh, H., Useem, M., & Bhadury, R. 1999. When does restructuring improve economic performance? *California Management Review*, 41(2): 33-54.

Bresnahan, T. F., Brynjolfsson, E., & Hitt, L. M. 2000. Technology, organization, and the demand for skilled labor. In M. M. Blair & T. A. Kochan (Eds.), *The New Relationship: Human Capital in the American Corporation*. Washington, DC: Brookings Institution Press.

Brockner, J., Grover, S., O'Malley, M. N., Reed, T. F., & Glynn, M. A. 1993. Threat of future layoffs, self-esteem, and survivors' reactions: Evidence from the laboratory and the field. *Strategic Management Journal*, 14(Summer): 153-166.

Brockner, J., Wiesenfeld, B. M., Reed, T., Grover, S., & Martin, C. 1993. Interactive effect of job content and context on the reactions of layoff survivors. *Journal of Personality and Social Psychology*, 64(2): 187-197.

Broschak, J. P. 1999. *Do the Actors Make the Play? Personnel Mobility and the Dissolution of Interorganizational Relationships*. Unpublished doctoral dissertation, University of Texas at Austin.

Broschak, J. P., & Davis-Blake, A. 2002a. Unintended consequences of using temporary workers: How temporary staffing affects attitudes and productivity of permanent and temporary employees. Working paper, University of Texas at Austin.

Broschak, J. P., & Davis-Blake, A. 2002b. When coworkers are contingent: The consequences of heterogeneity in employment arrangements. Working paper, University of Texas at Austin.

Brown, S. L., & Eisenhardt, K. M. 1995. Product development: Past research, present findings, and future directions. *Academy of Management Review,* 20(2): 343-378.

Brown, S. L., & Eisenhardt, K. M. 1997. The art of continuous change: Linking complexity theory and time-paced evolution in relentlessly shifting organizations. *Administrative Science Quarterly,* 42(1): 1-34.

Brown, S. L., & Eisenhardt, K. M. 1998. *Competing on the Edge: Strategy as Structured Chaos.* Cambridge, MA: Harvard Business School Press.

Browning, L. D., & Beyer, J. M. 1998. The structuring of shared voluntary standards in the U.S. semiconductor industry: Communicating to reach agreement. *Communication Monographs,* 65: 220-243.

Browning, L. D., Beyer, J. M., & Shetler, J. C. 1995. Building cooperation in a competitive industry: Sematech and the semiconductor industry. *Academy of Management Journal,* 38(1): 113-151.

Browning, L. D., & Shetler, J. C. 2000. *Sematech: Saving the U.S. Semiconductor Industry.* College Station: Texas A&M University Press.

Brusoni, S., Prencipe, A., & Pavitt, K. 2001. Knowledge specification, organizational coupling, and the boundaries of the firm: Why do firms know more than they make? *Administrative Science Quarterly,* 46: 597-621.

Bryce, James. 1901. *Studies in History and Jurisprudence.* New York: Oxford University Press.

Budget of the United States Government, 1977—Appendix; 1976. Washington, DC: U.S. Government Printing Office.

Budget of the United States Government, 1982—Appendix; 1981. Washington, DC: U.S. Government Printing Office.

Budget of the United States Government, 1987—Appendix; 1986. Washington, DC: U.S. Government Printing Office.

Budget of the United States Government, 1992—Appendix; 1991. Washington, DC: U.S. Government Printing Office.

Budget of the United States Government, 1997—Appendix; 1996. Washington, DC: U.S. Government Printing Office.

Bunderson, J. S., & Sutcliffe, K. M. 2002. Comparing alternative conceptualizations of functional diversity in management teams: Process and performance effects. *Academy of Management Journal,* 45: 875-893.

Burgelman, R. A. 1983. A process model of internal corporate venturing in the diversified major firm. *Administrative Science Quarterly,* 28(2): 223-244.

Burke, L., & Miller, M. 1999. Taking the mystery out of intuitive decision making. *Academy of Management Executive,* 13(4): 91-99.

Burke, P. 1991. *The Italian Renaissance: Culture and Society in Italy.* Princeton, NJ: Princeton University Press.

Burt, R. S., Gabbay, S. M., Holt, G., & Moran, P. 1994. Contingent organization as a network theory: The culture performance contingency function. *Acta Sociologica,* 37: 345-370.

BusinessWeek. 1984. Who's excellent now? 5 November: 76+.

BusinessWeek. 1989. From "bloody awful" to bloody awesome. 9 October: 97+.

BusinessWeek. 1992. Inside Hitachi. 28 September: 92+.

BusinessWeek. 2000. See the world, erase its borders. 28 August: 113+.

BusinessWeek. 2001. Sharing the wealth. 19 March: EB36.

BusinessWeek. 2001. Why the new economy is here to stay. 30 April: 26+.

Butler, P., Hall, T. W., Hanna, A. M., Mendonca, L., Auguste, B., Manyika, J., & Sahay, A. 1997. A revolution in interaction. *The McKinsey Quarterly,* 1: 4-23.

Byrne, J. A. 1999. 21 ideas for the 21st century. Management: The global corporation becomes the leaderless. *BusinessWeek,* 30 August: 88+.

California Management Review. Special issue on knowledge and the firm. Spring, 1998, 40(3).

Cameron, K. S. 1994. Strategies for successful organizational downsizing. *Human Resource Management,* 2(Summer): 189-211.

Cameron, K. S. 1998. Strategic organizational downsizing: An extreme case. In B. M. Staw & L. L. Cummings (Eds.), *Research in Organizational Behavior,* 20 (pp. 185-229). Greenwich, CT: JAI.

Cameron, K. S., Freeman, S. J., & Mishra, A. K. 1993. Downsizing and redesigning organizations. In G. P. Huber and W. H. Glick (Eds.), *Organizational Change and Redesign: Ideas and Insights for Improving Performance* (pp. 19-65). New York: Oxford University Press.

Campbell-Smith, D. 1986. *The British Airways Story: Struggle for Take-Off.* Columbus, OH: Coronet.

Canadian Business. 1997. In the service sector, they snoop to conquer. January.

Cangelosi, V. E., & Dill, W. R. 1965. Organizational learning: Observations toward a theory. *Administrative Science Quarterly,* 10: 175-203.

Cappelli, P. 1999. *The New Deal at Work.* Boston, MA: Harvard Business School Press.

Cappelli, P. 2000. Market-mediated employment: The historical context. In M. M. Blair & T. A. Kochan (Eds.), *The New Relationship: Human Capital in the American Corporation.* Washington, DC: Brookings Institution Press.

Cappelli, P. 2001. Making the most of on-line recruiting. *Harvard Business Review,* 79(3): 139-146.

Cappelli, P., & Neumark, D. 2001. Do "high performance" work practices improve establishment-level outcomes? *Industrial and Labor Relations Review,* 54(4): 737-775.

Carnoy, M., Castells, M., & Brenner, C. 1997. Labor markets and employment practices in the age of flexibility: A case study of Silicon Valley. *International Labor Review,* 136(1): 27-48.

Caron, J. R., Jarvenpaa, S. L., & Stoddard, D. B. 1994. Business reengineering at CIGNA Corporation: Lessons learned from the first five years. *MIS Quarterly,* 18(3): 233-250.

Carroll, G. R., & Hannan, M. T. 1995. *Organizations in Industry.* New York: Oxford University Press.

Carroll, J. S., Rudolph, J. W., & Hatakenaka, S. 2002. Learning from experience in high-hazard organizations. *Research in Organizational Behavior,* 24 (pp. 87-138).

Cascio, W. F. 1993. Downsizing: What do we know? What have we learned? *Academy of Management Executive,* 7(1): 95-104.

Cascio, W. F., Young, C. E., & Morris, J. R. 1997. Financial consequences of employment-change decisions in major U.S. corporations. *Academy of Management Journal,* 40(5): 1175-1189.

Casimiro, S. 1998. The spying game moves into the U.S. workplace. *Fortune,* 30 March: 152.

Cerf, C., & Navasky, V. 1998. *The Experts Speak.* New York: Villard.

Chandler, A. D, Jr 1962. *Strategy and Structure.* Cambridge: MIT Press.

Chapman, G. B., & Johnson, E. J. 1999. Anchoring, activation, and the construction of values. *Organizational Behavior and Human Decision Processes,* 79: 115-153.

Chattopadhyay, P., Glick, W. H., & Huber, G. P. 2001. Organizational actions in response to threats and opportunities. *Academy of Management Journal,* 44(5): 937-955.

Chattopadhyay, P., Glick, W. H., Miller, C. C., & Huber, G. P. 1999. Determinants of executive beliefs: Comparing functional conditioning and social influence. *Strategic Management Journal,* 20(8): 763-789.

Chesbrough, H. W., & Teece, D. J. 2002. Organizing for innovation: When is virtual virtuous? *Harvard Business Review,* 80(8): 127-134.

Child, J. 1972. Organization structure, environment, and performance: The role of strategic choice. *Sociology,* 6: 2-21.

Christensen, C. M. 1997. *The Innovator's Dilemma: When New Technologies Cause Great Firms to Fail.* Boston: Harvard Business School Press.

Cios, K. J., Pedrycz, W., & Swiniarski, R. 1998. *Data Mining Methods for Knowledge Discovery.* Boston: Kluwer.

Clark, K. B., & Wheelwright, S. C. 1992. Organizing and leading "heavyweight" development teams. *California Management Review,* 34(3): 9-28.

Clarke, T., & Clegg, S. 1998. *Changing Paradigms: The Transformation of Management Knowledge for the 21st Century.* London: Harper Collins Business.

Clegg, S. R., Hardy, C., & Nord, W. *Handbook of Organization Studies.* London, UK: Sage Publications.

Clifford, M. L. 1998. Showdown in Seoul: Can President Kim finally get the chaebol to change? *BusinessWeek,* 14 December: 56-57.

Coffey, W. 1983. *303 of the World's Worst Predictions.* New York: Tribeca.

Cohany, S. R. 1998. Workers in alternative employment arrangements: A second look. *Monthly Labor Review,* 121(11): 3- 21.

Cohen, W. M., & Levinthal, D. A. 1990. Absorptive capacity: A new perspective on learning and innovation. *Administrative Science Quarterly,* 35(1): 128-152.

Collins, J. C., & Porras, J. I. 1994. *Built to Last.* New York: HarperCollins.

Conlin, M. 2001. Where layoffs are a last resort. *BusinessWeek,* 8 October: 42+.

Constant, D., Sproull, L., & Kiesler, S. 1994. What's mine is ours, or is it? A study of attitudes about information sharing. *Information Systems Research,* 5: 400-421.

Constant, D., Sproull, L., & Kiesler, S. 1996. The kindness of strangers: The usefulness of electronic weak ties for technical advice. *Organization Science,* 7(2): 119-135.

Corke, A. 1986. *British Airways: Path to Profitability.* London: Pan Books Ltd.

Crainer, S., & Dearlove, D. 2002. The best way to best practices. *Across the Board: The Conference Board Magazine,* July: 25+.

Cramton, C. D. 2001. The mutual knowledge problem and its consequences for dispersed collaboration. *Organization Science,* 12: 346-371.

Creighton, S., & Hudson, L. 2002. *Participation Trends and Patterns in Adult Education: 1991 to 1999.* Washington, DC: U.S. Department of Education, National Center for Education Statistics.

Crock, S., & Moore, J. 1997. A crackdown on corporate spies. *BusinessWeek,* 14 July: 76+.

Crock, S., Smith, G., Weber, J., Melcher, R., & Himelstein, L. 1996. They snoop to conquer. *BusinessWeek,* 28 October: 172+.

Cross, R., & Baird, L. 2000. Technology is not enough: Improving performance by building organizational memory. *Sloan Management Review,* 41(3): 69-78.

Crossan, M. M., Lane, H. W., & White, R. E. 1999. An organizational learning framework: From intuition to institution. *Academy of Management Review,* 24(3): 522-537.

Daft, R. L., Bettenhausen, K. R., & Tyler, B. B. 1993. Implications of top managers' communication choices for strategic decisions. In G. P. Huber and W. H. Glick (Eds.), *Organizational Change and Redesign: Ideas and Insights for Improving Performance* (pp. 112-146). New York: Oxford University Press.

Daft, R. L., & Huber, G. P. 1987. How organizations learn: A communication framework. *Research in the Sociology of Organizations,* 5: 1-36.

Daft, R. L., & Lengel, R. H. 1984. Information richness: A new approach to managerial behavior and organization design. In B. M. Staw & L. L. Cummings (Eds.), *Research in Organizational Behavior,* 6 (pp. 191-233). Greenwich, CT: JAI.

Daft, R. L., & Lengel, R. H. 1988. The selection of communication media as an executive skill. *Academy of Management Executive,* 2(3): 225-232.

Daft, R. L., Lengel, R., & Trevino, L. 1987a. Media symbolism, media richness, and media choice in organizations: A symbolic interactionist perspective. *Communication Research,* 14: 553-574.

Daft, R. L., Lengel, R., & Trevino, L. 1987b. Message equivocality, media selection, and manager performance: Implication for information systems. *Management Information Systems Quarterly,* 11: 355-366.

Daft, R. L., Sormunen, J., & Parks, D. 1988. Chief executive scanning, environmental characteristics, and company performance: An empirical study. *Strategic Management Journal,* 9(2): 123-139.

Daft, R. L., & Weick, K. 1984. Toward a model of organizations as interpretation systems. *Academy of Management Review,* 9(2): 284-295.

Damanpour, F. 1991. Organizational innovation: A meta-analysis of effects of determinants and moderators. *Academy of Management Journal,* 34(3): 555-590.

Daniels, K., Johnson, G., & De Chernatony, L. 2002. Task and institutional influences on managers' mental models of competition. *Organization Studies,* 23(1): 31-62.

Darr, E. D., Argote, L., & Epple, D. 1995. The acquisition, transfer, and depreciation of knowledge in service organizations: Productivity in franchises. *Management Science,* 41(11): 1750-1762.

D'Aveni, R. A., & Gunther, R. 1994. *Hypercompetition: Managing the Dynamics of Strategic Maneuvering.* New York: Free Press.

Davenport, T. H. 1997. *Information Ecology: Mastering the Information and Knowledge Environment.* New York: Oxford University Press.

Davenport, T. H., & Prusak, L. 1998. *Working Knowledge: How Organizations Manage What They Know.* Boston: Harvard Business School Press.

Davidow, W. H., & Malone, M. S. 1992. *The Virtual Corporation.* New York: Harper Business.

Davis-Blake, A., Broschak, J. P., & George, E. 2003. Happy together? How using non-standard workers affects exit, voice, and loyalty among standard employees. *Academy of Management Journal.* 46(4): 475-485.

Davis-Blake, A., & Hui, P. P. 2003. Contracting talent for knowledge-based competition. In S. E. Jackson, M. A. Hitt, & A. DeNisi (Eds.), *Managing Knowledge for Sustained Competitive Advantage: Designing Strategies for Effective Human Resource Management.* San Francisco: Jossey-Bass.

Davis-Blake, A., & Uzzi, B. 1993. Determinants of employment externalization: A study of temporary workers and independent contractors. *Administrative Science Quarterly,* 38: 195-223.

Day, D., & Lord, R. 1992. Expertise and problem categorization: The role of expert processing in organizational sense-making. *Journal of Management Studies,* 29: 35-47.

Day, G. S., & Schoemaker, P. J. H. 2000. Avoiding the pitfalls of emerging technologies. *California Management Review,* 42(2): 8-33.

De Geus, A. 1997a. *The Living Company.* Boston: Harvard Business School Press.

De Geus, A. 1997b. The living company. *Harvard Business Review,* 75: 51-59.

De Solla Price, D. 1975. *Science Since Babylon* (enlarged ed.). New Haven, CT: Yale University Press.

Dean, J. W., & Sharfman, M. P. 1996. Does decision process matter? A study of strategic decision-making effectiveness. *Academy of Management Journal,* 39(2): 368-396.

Dearborn, D., & Simon, H. A. 1958. Selective perceptions: A note on the departmental identification of executives. *Sociometry,* 38: 140-144.

Deci, E. L., Koestner, R., & Ryan, R. M. 1999a. A meta-analytic review of experiments examining the effects of extrinsic rewards on intrinsic motivation. *Psychological Bulletin,* 125: 627-668.

Deci, E. L., Koestner, R., & Ryan, R. M. 1999b. The undermining effect is a reality after all—extrinsic rewards, task interest, and self-determination: Reply to Eisenberger, Pierce, and Cameron (1999) and Lepper, Henderlong, and Gingras (1999). *Psychological Bulletin,* 125: 692-700.

Deckop, J. R., Mangel, R., & Cirka, C. C. 1999. Getting more than you pay for: Organizational citizenship behavior and pay-for-performance plans. *Academy of Management Journal,* 42(4): 420-428.

Deeds, D. L. 2003. Alternative strategies for acquiring knowledge. In S. E. Jackson, M. A. Hitt, & A. S. DeNisi (Eds.), *Managing Knowledge for Sustained Competitive Advantage.* San Francisco: Jossey-Bass.

DeMatteo, J. S., Eby, L. T., & Sundstrom, E. 1998. Team-based rewards: Current empirical evidence and directions for future research. In B. M. Staw & L. L. Cummings (Eds.), *Research in Organizational Behavior,* 20 (pp. 141-183). Greenwich, CT: JAI.

Deng, Z., Lev, B, & Narin, F. 1999. Science and technology as predictors of stock performance. *Financial Analysts Journal,* May/June: 20-32.

DeSanctis, G., & Poole, M. S. 1997. Transitions in teamwork in new organizational forms. *Advances in Group Processes,* 14: 157-176.

Deutsch, C. H. 2002. Industry expertise has itself become a product. *New York Times,* May 13, p. C4.

Dill, W. R. 1958. Environment as an influence on managerial autonomy. *Administrative Science Quarterly,* 2: 409-443.

Dollinger, M. J. 1984. Environmental boundary spanning and information processing effects on organizational performance. *Academy of Management Journal,* 27(2): 351-368.

Donaldson, L. 2001. *The Contingency Theory of Organizations.* Thousand Oaks, CA: Sage.

Dougherty, D., & Bowman, E. H. 1995. The effects of organizational downsizing on product innovation. *California Management Review,* 37(4): 28-44.

Drago, R., & Garvey, G. T. 1998. Incentives for helping on the job: Theory and evidence. *Journal of Labor Economics,* 16: 1-25.

Drucker, P. 1995. *Managing in a Time of Great Change.* New York: Penguin.

Drucker, P. 2002. They're not employees, they're people. *Harvard Business Review,* 80(2): 70-77.

Druckman, D., Singer, J. E., & Van Cott, H. 1997. *Enhancing Organizational Performance.* Washington, DC: National Academy Press.

Dukerich, J., Waller, M., George, E., & Huber, G. 2000. Moral intensity and managerial problem solving. *Journal of Business Ethics,* 24: 29-38.

Dumaine, B. 1988. Corporate spies snoop to conquer. *Fortune,* 7 November: 68+.

The Dun and Bradstreet Corporation. 1996. *The Business Failure Record.* Murray Hill, NJ: Economic Analysis Department.

Duncan, R. 1973. Multiple decision-making structures in adapting to environmental uncertainty: The impact on organizational effectiveness. *Human Relations,* 26(3): 273-291.

Duncan, R., & Weiss, A. 1979. Organizational learning: Implications for organizational design. In B. Staw (Ed.), *Research in Organizational Behavior,* 1 (pp. 75-123). Greenwich, CT: JAI.

Dutton, J. E., Dukerich, J. M., & Harquail, C. V. 1994. Organizational images and member identification. *Administrative Science Quarterly,* 39(2): 239-263.

Dutton, J. E., & Jackson, S. E. 1987. Categorizing strategic issues: Links to organizational action. *Academy of Management Review,* 12(1): 76-90.

The Economist. 1997. The immaterial world. 28 June.

The Economist. 1997. Spying for pills, not projectiles. 12 July.

The Economist. 1999. The house that Jack built. 18 September.

The Economist. 2000. The rules of secession. 29 January.

The Economist. 2003. Coming of age: A survey of the IT industry. 10 May.

Edmondson, A. C. 1996. Learning from mistakes is easier said than done: Group and organizational influences on the detection and correction of human error. *Journal of Applied Behavioral Science,* 32(1): 5-28.

Edmondson, A., & Moingeon, B. 1996. When to learn how and when to learn why: Appropriate organizational learning processes as a source of competitive advantage. In B. Moingeon & A. Edmondson (Eds.), *Organizational Learning and Competitive Advantage* (pp. 16-37). Thousand Oaks, CA: Sage.

Einhorn, H. J., & Hogarth, R. M. 1978. Confidence in judgment: Persistence in the illusion of validity. *Psychology Review,* 85: 395-416.

Eisenberger, R., & Cameron, J. 1996. Detrimental effects of reward: Reality or myth. *American Psychologist,* 51: 1153-1166.

Eisenhardt, K. M. 1989. Making fast strategic decisions in high-velocity environments. *Academy of Management Journal,* 32(3): 543-576.

Eisenhardt, K. M. 1990. Speed and strategic choice: How managers accelerate decision making. *California Management Review,* 32(3): 39-54.

Eisenhardt, K. M. 1999. Strategy as strategic decision making. *Sloan Management Review,* Spring: 65-72.

Eisenhardt, K. M., & Tabrizi, B. N. 1995. Accelerating adaptive processes: Product innovation in the global computer industry. *Administrative Science Quarterly,* 40: 84-110.

Elsbach, K. D. 1999. An expanded model of organizational identification. In B. M. Staw & R. I. Sutton (Eds.), *Research in Organizational Behavior,* 21 (pp. 63-200). Greenwich, CT: JAI.

Evans, P. B., & Wurster, T. S. 1997. Strategy and the new economics of information. *Harvard Business Review,* 75(5): 70-82.

Ewing, J. 2001. Sharing the wealth. *Business Week,* 19 March: EB36.

Faraj, S., & Sproull, L. 2000. Coordinating expertise in software development teams. *Management Science,* 46: 1554-1568.

Feldman, M., & March, J. G. 1981. Information in organizations as signal and symbol. *Administrative Science Quarterly,* 26(2): 171-86.

Fialka, J. 1997. *War by Other Means: Economic Espionage in America.* New York: W. W. Norton.

Fine, C. H. 1998. *Clockspeed: Winning Industry Control in the Age of Temporary Advantage.* Reading, MA: Perseus.

Finkelstein, S., & Hambrick, D. C. 1990. Top management team tenure and organizational outcomes: The moderating role of managerial discretion. *Administrative Science Quarterly,* 35(3): 484-503.

Finkelstein, S., & Hambrick, D. C. 1996. *Strategic Leadership: Top Executives and Their Effects on Organizations.* St. Paul, MN: West.

Fiol, C. M. 1994. Consensus, diversity, and learning in organizations. *Organization Science,* 5(3): 403-420.

Fisher, S. R., & White, M. 2000. Downsizing in a learning organization: Are there hidden costs? *Academy of Management Review,* 25(1): 244-251.

Flatt, J. S. 1996. *Developing Innovative Strategies: How Top Management Teams Bring Creativity and Implementation Into the Firm.* Presented at the 16th Annual International Conference of the Strategic Management Society, Phoenix, AZ, November 1996.

Fogel, R. W. 1999. Catching up with the economy. *American Economic Review,* 89(1): 1-21.

Ford, R. C., & Randolph, W. A. 1992. Cross-functional structures: A review and integration of matrix organization and project management. *Journal of Management,* 18(2): 267-294.

Fort, R. D. 2001. *MLB Salaries.* Retrieved summer 2001 from http://users.pullman. com/rodfort/SportsBusiness/MLB/Salaries/MLBSalaries.htm

Friedman, T. L. 2000. *The Lexus and the Olive Tree.* New York: Anchor Books.

Fulk, J., & Collins-Jarvis, L. 2001. Wired meetings: Technological mediation of organizational gatherings. In F. M. Jablin and L. L. Putnam (Eds.), *The New Handbook of Organizational Communication: Advances in Theory, Research, and Methods.* Thousand Oaks, CA: Sage.

Galbraith, J. K. 1967. *The New Industrial State.* Boston: Houghton Mifflin.

Garg, V. K., Walters, B. A., & Priem, R. L. 2003. Chief executive scanning emphases, environmental dynamism, and manufacturing firm performance. *Strategic Management Journal,* 24(8): 725-744

Garvin, D. A. 1993. Building a learning organization. *Harvard Business Review,* 71(4): 78-91.

Garvin, D. A. 1998. The processes of organization and management. *Sloan Management Review,* 39(4): 33-50.

Garvin, D. A., & Roberto, M. A. 2001. What you don't know about making decisions. *Harvard Business Review,* 79(8): 108-116.

Gates, B. 1996. *The Road Ahead.* New York: Penguin.

Geary, J. F. 1992. Employment flexibility and human resource management: The case of three American electronics plants. *Work, Employment & Society,* 6: 251-270.

Geletkanycz, M. A., & Hambrick, D. C. 1997. The external ties of top executives: Implications for strategic choice and performance. *Administrative Science Quarterly,* 42(4): 654-681.

George, E. 2003. External solutions and internal problems: The effects of workers' attitudes. *Organization Science,* 14(4): 386-402.

Ghoshal, S., & Kim, S. K. 1986. Building effective intelligence systems for competitive advantage. *Sloan Management Review,* 28(1): 49-58.

Gilad, T., & Gilad, B. Business intelligence: The quiet revolution. *Sloan Management Review,* 27(4): 53-61.

Gilbert, D. T., Pinel, E. C., Wilson, T. D., Blumberg, S. J., & Wheatley, T. P. 1998. Immune neglect: A source of durability bias in affective forecasting. *Journal of Personality and Social Psychology,* 75: 617-638.

Goll, I., & Rasheed, A. M. A. 1997. Rational decision-making and firm performance: The moderating role of environment. *Strategic Management Journal,* 18(7): 583-591.

Goodstein, D. 1995. Peer review after the big crunch. *American Scientist,* 83: 401-402.

Gordon, G. G., & DiTomaso, N. 1992. Predicting corporate performance from organizational culture. *Journal of Management Studies,* 29: 783-799.

Grabowski, M., & Roberts, K. 1997. Risk mitigation in large-scale systems: Lessons from high reliability organizations. *California Management Review,* 39(4): 152-162.

Graham-Moore, B., & Ross, T. L. 1995. *Gainsharing and Employee Involvement.* Washington, DC: Bureau of National Affairs.

Granovetter, M. S. 1973. The strength of weak ties. *American Journal of Sociology,* 78(6): 1360-1380.

Granovetter, M. S. 1985. Economic action and social structure: The problem of embeddedness. *American Journal of Sociology,* 91: 481-510.

Granstrand, O., & Sjolander, S. 1990. The acquisition of technology and small firms by large firms. *Journal of Economic Behavior and Organization,* 13: 367-386.

Grant, R. M. 1996a. Toward a knowledge-based theory of the firm. *Strategic Management Journal,* 17(Winter): 109-122.

Grant, R. M. 1996b. Prospering in dynamically-competitive environments: Organizational capability as knowledge integration. *Organization Science,* 7(4): 375-387.

Greve, H. R., & Taylor, A. 2000. Innovations as catalysts for organizational change: Shifts in organizational cognition and search. *Administrative Science Quarterly,* 45(1): 54-80.

Griffith, T. L., & Neale, M. A. 2001. Information processing in traditional, hybrid, and virtual teams: From nascent knowledge to transactive memory. In B. M. Staw & R. I. Sutton (Eds.), *Research in Organizational Behavior,* 23 (pp. 1-42). Greenwich, CT: JAI.

Griffith, T. L., Sawyer, J. E., & Neale, M. A. 2003. Virtualness and knowledge in teams: Managing the love triangle of organizations, individuals, and information technology. *MIS Quarterly,* 27: 1-23.

Grove, A. S. 1996. *Only the Paranoid Survive: How to Exploit the Crisis Points That Challenge Every Company and Career.* New York: Currency/Doubleday.

Grove, A. S. 1998. Address to the Annual Academy of Management Convention. San Diego, CA, August 9.

Gupta, A. K., & Govindarajan, V. 2000a. Knowledge flows within multinational corporations. *Strategic Management Journal,* 21(4): 473-496.

Gupta, A. K., & Govindarajan, V. 2000b. Knowledge management's social dimension: Lessons from Nucor Steel. *Sloan Management Review,* 42(1): 71-80.

Hambrick, D. C., & D'Aveni, R. A. 1992. Top team deterioration as part of the downward spiral of large corporate bankruptcies. *Management Science,* 38: 1445-1466.

Hambrick, D. C., & Finklestein, S. 1987. Managerial discretion: A bridge between polar views of organizational outcomes. In L. L. Cummings & B. M. Staw (Eds.), *Research in Organizational Behavior,* 9 (pp. 369-406). Greenwich, CT: JAI.

Hamel, G., & Prahalad, C. K. 1994. *Competing for the Future: Breakthrough Strategies for Seizing Control of Your Industry and Creating the Markets of Tomorrow.* Boston: Harvard Business School Press.

Hannan, M. T., & Carroll, G. R. 1992. *Dynamics of Organizational Populations.* New York: Oxford University Press.

Hansen, M. T. 1999. The search-transfer problem: The role of weak ties in sharing knowledge across organization subunits. *Administrative Science Quarterly,* 44(1): 82-111.

Hansen, M. T., Nohria, N., & Tierney, T. 1999. What's your strategy for managing knowledge? *Harvard Business Review,* 77(2): 106-116.

Hargadon, A., & Sutton, R. I. 1997. Technology brokering and innovation in a product development firm. *Administrative Science Quarterly,* 42(4): 716-749.

Harrison, B., & Kelley, M. R. 1993. Outsourcing and the search for "flexibility." *Work, Employment & Society,* 7(2): 213-235.

Hartley, R. F. 1976. *Marketing Mistakes.* Columbus, OH: Grid.

Harvard Business Review. Special issue on the innovation enterprise. August 2002, 80(8).

Haunschild, P. R., & Miner, A. S. 1997. Modes of interorganizational imitation: The effects of outcome salience and uncertainty. *Administrative Science Quarterly,* 42(3): 472-500.

Heath, C., Larrick, R. P., & Klayman, J. 1998. Cognitive repairs: How organizational practices can compensate for individual shortcomings. In B. M. Staw and L. L. Cummings (Eds.), *Research in Organizational Behavior,* 20 (pp. 1-37). Greenwich, CT: JAI.

Hedberg, B. 1981. How organizations learn and unlearn. In P. C. Nystrom & W. H. Starbuck (Eds.), *Handbook of Organizational Design, Vol. 1.* New York: Oxford University Press.

Heilbroner, R. L. 1992. *The worldly philosophers: The lives, times, and ideas of the great economic thinkers.* New York: Simon & Shuster.

Heilbroner, R. L. 1995. *Visions of the Future: The Distant Past, Yesterday, Today, Tomorrow.* New York: Oxford University Press.

Henderson, R. M. 1996. Technological change and the management of architectural knowledge. In M. D. Cohen & L. S. Sproull (Eds.), *Organizational Learning.* Thousand Oaks: Sage.

Henderson, R., & Cockburn, I. 1996. Scale, scope, and spillovers: The determinants of research productivity in drug discovery. *Rand Journal of Economics,* 27(1): 32-59.

Henderson, R., & Mitchell, W. 1997. The interactions of organizational and competitive influences on strategy and performance. *Strategic Management Journal,* 18 (Summer): 5-14.

Hesselbein, F., Goldsmith, M., & Beckhard, R. (Eds.). 1997. *The Organization of the Future.* San Francisco: Jossey-Bass.

Hewitt Associates. 2000. *Salary Increases 1999-2000 (U.S.).* Lincolnshire, IL: Hewitt.

"The History of Technology." *Britannica Online. www.eb.com:180/cgi-bin/g?DocF= macro/5006/17/0.html* [Accessed 27 September 1997].

Hodgkinson, G. P. 2001. The psychology of strategic management: Diversity and cognition revisited. In L. Cooper & I. T. Robertson (Eds.), *International Review of Industrial and Organizational Psychology, Vol. 16.* Chichester, UK: Wiley.

Hoffer, E. 1973. *Reflections on the Human Condition.* New York: Harper & Row.

Houseman, S., & Erickcek, G. 2002. Temporary services and contracting out: Effects on low-skilled workers. *Employment Research,* 9(3): 1-3.

Huber, G. P. 1982. Organizational information systems: Determinants of their performance and behavior. *Management Science,* 28(2): 138-155.

Huber, G. P. 1984. The nature and design of post-industrial organizations. *Management Science,* 30(8): 928-951.

Huber, G. P. 1985. Strategies for inducing academic units to adopt innovations. In R. L. Kuhn (Ed.), *Frontiers in Creative and Innovative Management.* Cambridge, MA: Ballinger.

Huber, G. P. 1990. A theory of the effects of advanced information technologies on organizational design, intelligence, and decision making. *Academy of Management Review,* 15(1): 47-71.

Huber, G. P. 1991. Organizational learning: The contributing processes and the literatures. *Organization Science,* 2(1): 88-115.

Huber, G. P. 1996. Organizational learning: A guide for executives in technology-critical organizations. *International Journal of Technology Management,* 11(7/8): 821-832.

Huber, G. P. 1998. Synergies between organizational learning and creativity & innovation. *Creativity and Innovation Management,* 7(1): 3-8.

Huber, G. P. 1999. Facilitating project team learning and contributions to organizational knowledge. *Creativity and Innovation Management,* 8(2): 70-76.

Huber, G. P. 2000. The nature and improvement of organizational interpretations. In S. A. Carlsson, P. Brezillon, P. Humphreys, B. G. Lundberg, A. M. McCosh, & V. Rajkovic (Eds.), *Decision Support Through Knowledge Management.* Stockholm: Department of Computer and Systems Sciences, University of Stockholm and Royal Institute of Technology.

Huber, G. P. 2001a. Transfer of knowledge in knowledge management systems: Unexplored issues and suggested studies. *European Journal of Information Systems,* 10: 72-79.

Huber, G. P. 2001b. The knowledge explosion and the use of experts. Keynote address at the United Kingdom's Operational Research Society Annual Conference, Bath, September 2001.

Huber, G. P., & Crisp, C. B. 2002. Effect of information technologies on organizations. In *Encyclopedia of Information Systems.* San Diego, CA: Academic Press.

Huber, G. P., & Glick, W. H. 1993. *Organizational Change and Redesign: Ideas and Insights for Improving Organizational Performance.* New York: Oxford University Press.

Huber, G. P., & McDaniel, R. R. 1986. The decision-making paradigm of organizational design. *Management Science,* 32(5): 572-589.

Huber, G. P., Sutcliffe, K. M., Miller, C. C., & Glick, W. H. 1993. Understanding and predicting organizational change. In G. P. Huber and W. H. Glick (Eds.), *Organizational Change and Redesign* (pp. 215-265). New York: Oxford University Press.

Huber, G. P., Ullman, J. C., & Leifer, R. 1978. Optimum organization design: An analytic-adoptive approach. *Academy of Management Review,* 4(4): 556-578.

Huber, J. C. 2001. *Managing Innovation: Mining for Nuggets.* San Jose, CA: Authors Choice Press.

Huppes, T. 1987. *The Western Edge.* Dordrecht, The Netherlands: Kluwer.

Iansiti, M. 1995. Technology integration: Managing technological evolution in a complex environment. *Research Policy,* 24: 521-542.

Iaquinto, A. L., & Fredrickson, J. W. 1997. Top management team agreement about the strategic decision process: A test of some of its determinants and consequences. *Strategic Management Journal,* 18(1): 63-75.

Independent. 2001. MI5 offers to spy for British firms. 7 September.

Inkson, K., & Arthur, M. B. 2001. How to be a successful career capitalist. *Organizational Dynamics,* 30(1): 48-61.

Inmon, W. H. 1996. *Building the Data Warehouse.* New York: Wiley.

Internal Revenue Service. Summer 1995. *Statistics of Income Bulletin,* Publication 1136.

Irwin, D. A., & Klenow, P. J. 1994. Learning-by-doing spillovers in the semiconductor industry. *Journal of Political Economy,* 102(6): 1200-1227.

Jablin, F. M., & Putnam, L. L. (Eds.). 2001. *The New Handbook of Organizational Communication: Advances in Theory, Research, and Methods.* Thousand Oaks, CA: Sage.

Jackson, S. E., & Dutton, J. E. 1988. Discerning threats and opportunities. *Administrative Science Quarterly,* 33(3): 370-388.

Jacques, E. 1989. *Requisite Organization.* Falls Church, VA: Cason Hall.

Jacques, E. 1990. In praise of hierarchy. *Harvard Business Review,* 68(1): 127-133.

Janis, I. L. 1989. *Crucial Decisions.* New York: Free Press.

Jarvenpaa, S. L., & Staples, S. 2001. Exploring perceptions of organizational ownership of information and expertise. *Journal of Management Information Systems,* 18: 151-183.

Jones, T. Y. 2003. Top automakers turning to Dell for tips in efficient manufacturing. *Austin American-Statesman,* 14 March: pp. D1, D3.

Judge, W. Q., & Miller, A. 1991. Antecedents and outcomes of decision speed in different environmental contexts. *Academy of Management Journal,* 34(2): 449-463.

Kalakota, R., & Whinston, A. B. 1996. *Frontiers of Electronic Commerce.* Reading, MA: Addison-Wesley.

Kalakota, R., & Whinston, A. B. 1997. *Electronic Commerce: A Manager's Guide.* Reading, MA: Addison-Wesley.

Kalleberg, A. 2000. Nonstandard employment relations: Part-time, temporary and contract work. *Annual Review of Sociology,* 26: 341-365.

Kefalas, A., & Schoderbek, P. P. 1973. Scanning the business environment—Some empirical results. *Decision Sciences,* 4(1): 63-74.

Kelly, S. 1997. *Data Warehousing in Action.* New York: Wiley.

Kennedy Information Research Group. 2002. DataWatch Consulting by Numbers. *Consulting Magazine,* February: 52-53.

Kerr, S. 1975. On the folly of rewarding A, while hoping for B. *Academy of Management Journal,* 18(4): 769-783.

Kerr, S. 1995. On the folly of rewarding A, while hoping for B. *Academy of Management Executive,* 9(1): 7-16.

Kerr, S. 1997. *Ultimate Rewards: What Really Motivates People to Achieve.* Boston: Harvard Business School Press.

Kilduff, M., Angelmar, R., & Mehra, A. 2000. Top management-team diversity and firm performance: Examining the role of cognitions. *Organization Science,* 11(1): 21-34.

Kim, D. O. 1999. Determinants of the survival of gainsharing programs. *Industrial and Labor Relations Review,* 53(1): 21-42.

Klimoski, R., & Mohammed, S. 1994. Team mental model: Construct or metaphor? *Journal of Management,* 20(2): 403-437.

Knight, D., Pearce, C. L., Smith, K. G., Olian, J. D., Sims, H. P., Smith, K. A., & Flood, P. 1999. Top management team diversity, group process, and strategic consensus. *Strategic Management Journal,* 20(5): 445-465.

Kohn, A. 1993. Why incentive plans cannot work. *Harvard Business Review,* 71(5): 54-63.

Kolodner, J. 1993. *Case-Based Reasoning.* San Francisco: Morgan Kaufmann.

Kotabe, M., & Swan, K. S. 1995. The role of cooperative strategies in high technology new product development. *Strategic Management Journal,* 16(8): 621-636.

Kotter, J. P., & Haskett, J. L. 1992. *Corporate Culture and Performance.* New York: Free Press.

Koudsi, S. 2000. Actually, it's like brain surgery. *Fortune,* 20 March: 233+.

Kramer, R. M. 1991. Intergroup relations and organizational dilemmas: The role of categorization processes. In L. L. Cummings & B. M. Staw (Eds.), *Research in Organizational Behavior,* 13 (pp. 191-228). Greenwich, CT: JAI.

Krishnan, V., Eppinger, S. D., & Whitney, D. E. 1997. A model-based framework to overlap product development activities. *Management Science,* 43(4): 437-451.

Lane, P. J., & Lubatkin, M. 1998. Relative absorptive capacity and inter-organizational learning. *Strategic Management Journal,* 19(5): 461-477.

Laroche, H. 1995. From decision to action in organizations: Decision making as a social representation. *Organization Science,* 6(1): 62-75.

Larson, E. W., & Gobeli, D. H. 1987. Matrix management: Contradictions and insights. *California Management Review,* 29(4): 126-138.

Lawler, E. E., III. 2000. *Rewarding Excellence: Pay Strategies for the New Economy.* San Francisco: Jossey-Bass.

Lawler, E. E., III. 2003. Reward systems in knowledge-based organizations. In S. E. Jackson, M. A. Hitt, & A. S. Denisi (Eds.), *Managing Knowledge for Sustained Competitive Advantage.* San Francisco: Jossey-Bass.

Lawler, E. E., III, & Cohen, S. G. 1992. Designing pay systems for teams. *ACA Journal,* Autumn 1992: 6-19.

Lawton, T., Rennie, J., & Eisenschitz, T. 1988. Business information from industrial espionage—A state-of-the-art review. *Business Information Review,* 5(2): 3-13.

Leavitt, H. J. 2002. Technology and organizations: Where's the off button. *California Management Review,* 44(2): 126-140.

Lee, S. M., Yoo, S., & Lee, T. M. 1991. Korean chaebols: Corporate values and strategies. *Organizational Dynamics,* 19: 36-50.

Leifer, R., McDermott, C. M., O'Connor, G. C., Peters, L. S., Rice, M. P., & Veryzer, R.W. 2000. *Radical Innovation.* Boston: Harvard Business School Press.

Lepak, D. P., & Snell, S. A. 1999. The human resource architecture: Toward a theory of human capital allocation and development. *Academy of Management Review,* 24(1): 31-48.

Lesser, E., & Prusak, L. 2001. Preserving knowledge in an uncertain world. *Sloan Management Review,* 43(1): 101-103.

Levering, R., & Moskowitz, M. 2002. The best in the worst of times. *Fortune,* 4 February.

Levitt, B. L., and March, J. G. 1988. Organizational learning. *Annual Review of Sociology,* 14: 319-340.

Lewin, A. Y., & Kim, J. 2004. The nation-state and culture as influence on organizational change and innovation. In M. S. Poole and A. H. Van de Ven (Eds.), *Handbook of Organizational Change and Development*. New York: Oxford University Press, forthcoming.

Lewin, A. Y., Weigelt, C. B., & Emery, J. D. 2004. Adaptation and selection in strategy and change: Perspectives on strategic change in organization. In M. S. Poole and A. H. Van de Ven (Eds.), *Handbook of Organizational Change and Development*. New York: Oxford University Press.

Lewis, K. 1999. *The Impact of Interpersonal Relationships and Knowledge Exchange on Group Performance: A Field Study of Consulting Project Teams*. Unpublished doctoral dissertation, University of Maryland at College Park.

Lewis, K. 2003. Measuring transactive memory systems in the field: Scale development and validation. *Journal of Applied Psychology*, 88(4): 587-604.

Liang-Rulke, D., Moreland, R., & Argote, L. (1995). Group versus individual training and group performance; The mediating effects of transactive memory. *Personality and Social Psychology Bulletin*, 21: 384-393.

Loewenstein, G., & Schkade, D. A. 1999. Wouldn't it be nice? Predicting future feelings. In D. Kahneman, E. Diener, & N. Schwartz (Eds.), *Well Being: The Foundations of Hedonic Psychology*. New York: Russell Sage.

Lovett, S., Harrison, D., & Virick, M. 1997. Managing the boundary spanner—customer turnover connection. *Human Resource Management Review*, 7(4): 405-424.

Lynn, G. 1998. New product team learning: Developing and profiting from your knowledge capital. *California Management Review*, 40(4): 74-93.

Lynn, G., Morone, J., & Paulson, A. 1996. Marketing and discontinuous innovation: The probe and learn process. *California Management Review*, 38(3): 8-37.

Mael, F., & Ashforth, B. E. 1992. Alumni and their alma mater: A partial test of the reformulated model of organizational identification. *Journal of Organizational Behavior*, 13: 103-123.

March, J. G. 1995. The future, disposable organizations and the rigidities of imagination. *Organization*, 2(3/4): 427-440.

March, J. G., Sproull, L. S., & Tamuz, M. 1991. Learning from samples of one or fewer. *Organization Science*, 2(1): 1-13.

Martin, J. 1977. *Future Developments in Telecommunications*. Englewood Cliffs, NJ: Prentice Hall.

Martin, J. 1996. *Cybercorp: The New Business Revolution*. New York: AMACOM (American Management Association).

Matusik, S., & Hill, C. 1998. The utilization of contingent work, knowledge creation, and competitive advantage. *Academy of Management Review*, 23(4): 680-697.

McPhee, R. D., & Poole, M. S. 2001. Organizational structures and configurations. In F. M. Jablin and L. L. Putnam (Eds.), *The New Handbook of Organizational Communication: Advances in Theory, Research, and Methods*. Thousand Oaks, CA: Sage.

Meier, R. L. 1963. Communications overload: Proposals from the study of a university library. *Administrative Science Quarterly*, 7(1): 521-544.

Meier, R. L. 1973. Communications stress—Threats and remedies. *Organizational Dynamics*, 1(3): 69-80.

Meindl, J. R., Stubbart, C., & Porac, J. F. (Eds.). 1996. *Cognition Within and Between Organizations*. Thousand Oaks, CA: Sage.

Melcher, R. A. 1997. Dusting off the Britannica. *BusinessWeek*, 20 October: 143+.

Melone, N. P. 1994. Reasoning in the executive suite: The influence of role/experience-based expertise on decision processes of corporate executives. *Organization Science,* 5(3): 438-455.

Mendelson, H. 2000. Organizational architecture and success in the information technology industry. *Management Science,* 46(4): 513-529.

Mendelson, H., & Ravindran, R. P. 1999. Information age organizations, dynamics and performance. *Journal of Economic Behavior & Organization,* 38: 253-281.

Merman, J. 1985. The limits of tradition. *Forbes,* 20 May: 112+.

Meyer, A. D. 1982. Adapting to environmental jolts. *Administrative Science Quarterly,* 27(4): 515-537.

Meyer, C., & Ruggles, R. 2002. Search parties. *Harvard Business Review,* 80(8): 14-15.

Meyer, M. 2000. Does science push technology? Patents citing scientific literature. *Research Policy,* 29: 409-434.

Micklethwait, J., & Wooldridge, A. 2000. *A Future Perfect: The Challenge and Hidden Promise of Globalization.* New York: Crown.

Miles, R. E., & Snow, C. C. 1978. *Organizational Strategy, Structure, and Process.* New York: McGraw-Hill.

Miles, R. E., & Snow, C. C. 1996. Twenty-first-century careers. In M. B. Arthur & D. M. Rousseau (Eds.), *The Boundaryless Career.* New York: Oxford University Press.

Miller, D. 1991. Stale in the saddle: CEO tenure and the match between organization and environment. *Management Science,* 37(1): 34-52.

Miller, D., & Droge, C. 1986. Psychological and traditional determinants of structure. *Administrative Science Quarterly,* 31(4): 539-560.

Miller, D., Greenwood, R., & Hinings, B. 1997. Creative chaos versus munificent momentum: The schism between normative and academic views of organizational change. *Journal of Management Inquiry,* 6(1): 71-78.

Miller, D., & Shamsie, J. 2001. Learning across the life cycle: Experimentation and performance among the Hollywood studio heads. *Strategic Management Journal,* 22: 725-745.

Miller, J. G. 1978. *Living Systems.* New York: McGraw-Hill.

Miner, A. S., & Anderson, P. 1999. Industry and population-level learning: Organizational, interorganizational and collective learning processes. *Advances in Strategic Management,* 16(1): 1-30.

Mintzberg, H. 1975. The manager's job: Folklore and fact. *Harvard Business Review,* 53(4): 49-61.

Mintzberg, H. 1979. *The Structuring of Organizations: A Synthesis of the Research.* Englewood Cliffs, NJ: Prentice Hall.

Mintzberg, H. 1981. Organization design: Fashion or fit? *Harvard Business Review,* 59(1): 103-116.

Mintzberg, H. 1991a. The effective organization: Forces and forms. *Sloan Management Review,* 32(2): 54-68.

Mintzberg, H. 1991b. Learning 1, Planning 0: Reply to Igor Ansoff. *Strategic Management Journal,* 12(5): 463-466.

Mintzberg, H. 1993. *Structure in Fives: Designing Effective Organizations* (2nd ed.). Englewood Cliffs, NJ: Prentice Hall.

Mintzberg, H., Raisinghani, D., & Theoret, A. 1976. The structure of "unstructured decision process." *Administrative Science Quarterly,* 21(2): 246-275.

Mitchell, T. R., Holtom, B. C., Lee, T. W., Sablynski, C. J., & Erez, M. 2001. Why people stay: Using job embeddedness to predict voluntary turnover. *Academy of Management Journal*, 44(6): 1102-1122.

Moingeon, B., & Edmondson, A. 1996. *Organizational Learning and Competitive Advantage*. Thousand Oaks, CA: Sage.

Mokyr, J. 1990. *The Lever of Riches: Technological Creativity and Economic Progress*. New York: Oxford University Press.

Mokyr, J. 2002. *The Gift of Athena: Historical Origins of the Knowledge Economy*. Princeton, NJ: Princeton University Press.

Moore, J. F. 1997. *The Death of Competition: Leadership and Strategy in the Age of Business Ecosystems*. New York: Harper Business.

Moore, K., & Birkinshaw, J. 1998. Managing knowledge in global service firms: Centers of excellence. *Academy of Management Executive*, 12(1): 81-92.

Moreland, R. L., Argote, L., & Krishnan, R. 1996. Socially shared cognition at work: Transactive memory and group performance. In J. L. Nye and M. A. Brower (Eds.), *What's Social About Social Cognition?* (pp. 57-84). Thousand Oaks, CA: Sage.

Morris, M. W., & Moore, P. C. 2000. The lessons we (don't) learn: Counterfactual thinking and organizational accountability after a close call. *Administrative Science Quarterly*, 45(4): 737-765.

Moynihan, L. M, & Batt, R. 2000. Antecedents and consequences of transactive memory in shared services teams: Theory and scale development. Paper presented at the Academy of Management Meetings, Toronto, 2000.

Nahapiet, J., & Ghoshal, S. 1998. Social capital, intellectual capital, and the organizational advantage. *Academy of Management Review*, 23(2): 242-266.

Narin, F. 1991. *Globalization of Research, Scholarly Information, and Patents—Ten Year Trends. Plenary Session 2—Changing Information Worldwide*. Binghamton, NY: Haworth Press.

Narin, F., Hamilton, K. S., & Olivastro, D. 1997. The increasing linkage between U.S. technology and public science. *Research Policy*, 26(3): 317-330.

Narin, F., & Olivastro, D. 1998. Linkage between patents and papers: An interim EPO/US comparison. *Scientometrics*, 41: 51-59.

National Research Council. 1980. *Improving Aircraft Safety: FAA Certification of Commercial Passenger Aircraft*. Washington, DC: National Academy of Sciences.

National Science Board. 1996. *Science & Engineering Indicators—1996*. (NSB 96-21). Washington, DC: U.S. Government Printing Office.

National Science Board. 1998. *Science & Engineering Indicators—1998*. (NSB 98-1). Washington, DC: U.S. Government Printing Office.

National Science Board. 2000. *Science & Engineering Indicators—2000*. (NSB 00-1). Washington, DC: U.S. Government Printing Office.

National Science Foundation. 1993. *Human Resources for Science and Technology: The Asian Region*. (NSF 93-303). Washington, DC.

National Science Foundation. 1995. *Asia's New High-Tech Competitors*. (NSF 95-309). Arlington, VA.

National Science Foundation. 1996. *Human Resources for Science & Technology: The European Region*. (NSF 96-316, Special Report). Arlington, VA.

Nevins, J. L., & Whitney, D. E. 1989. *Concurrent Design of Products and Processes: A Strategy for the Next Generation in Manufacturing*. New York: McGraw-Hill.

Nisbett, R., & Ross, L. 1980. *Human Influence: Strategies and Shortcomings of Social Judgment.* Englewood Cliffs, NJ: Prentice Hall.

Nonaka, I. 1991. The knowledge-creating company. *Harvard Business Review,* 69(3): 79-91.

Nonaka, I. 1994. A dynamic theory of organizational knowledge creation. *Organization Science,* 5(1): 14-35.

Nutt, P. C. 2002. *Why Decisions Fail.* San Francisco: Berrett-Koehler.

Ocasio, W. 1995. The enactment of economic adversity: A reconciliation of theories of failure-induced change and threat-rigidity. In L. L. Cummings & B. M. Staw (Eds.), *Research in Organizational Behavior,* 17 (pp. 287-331). Greenwich, CT: JAI.

Ocasio, W. 1997. Towards an attention-based view of the firm. *Strategic Management Journal,* 18(3): 187-206.

O'Dell, C., & Grayson, C. J. 1998a. If only we knew what we know: Identification and transfer of internal best practices. *California Management Review,* 40(3): 154-174.

O'Dell, C., & Grayson, C. J. 1998b. *If Only We Knew What We Know: The Transfer of Internal Knowledge and Best Practices.* New York: Free Press.

Olson, G. M., & Olson, J. S. 2000. Distance matters. *Human-Computer Interaction,* 15: 139-178.

O'Mahony, S., & Barley, S. R. 1999. Do digital telecommunications affect work and organization? In L. L. Cummings & B. M. Staw (Eds.), *Research in Organizational Behavior,* 21 (pp. 125-161). Greenwich, CT: JAI.

Online courses the rage in corporate training. *USA Today,* April 30, 2002. Retrieved April 30, 2002, from www.usatoday.com/life/cyber/tech/2002/04/30/online-training.htm

O'Reilly, C. 1989. Corporations, culture, and commitment: Motivation and social control in organizations. *California Management Review,* 31(4): 9-25.

O'Reilly, C., & Chatman, J. A. 1996. Culture as social control: Corporations, cults and commitment. *Research in Organizational Behavior,* 18 (pp. 157-200).

Orlikowski, W. J. 1993. Learning from notes: Organizational issues in groupware implementation. *Information Society,* 9(3): 237-250.

Osterloh, M., & Frey, B. S. 2000. Motivation, knowledge transfer, and organizational forms. *Organization Science,* 11(5): 538-550.

Parker, G. G., & Anderson, E. G. 2002. From buyer to integrator: The transformation of the supply-chain manager in the vertically disintegrating firm. *Production and Operations Management,* 9(3): 239-261.

Parsons, T. 1977. *The Evolution of Societies.* Englewood Cliffs, NJ: Prentice Hall.

PC Magazine iBiz. 2002. A "eureka!" moment at Xerox. 26 March.

Pearce, J. L. 1993. Toward an organizational behavior of contract laborers: Their psychological involvement and effects on employee coworkers. *Academy of Management Journal,* 36: 1082-1096.

Pearson, C. M., & Clair, J. A. 1998. Reframing crisis management. *Academy of Management Review,* 23(1): 59-76.

Pelz, D. C., & Andrews, F. M. 1966. *Scientists in Organizations.* New York: Wiley.

Perrow, C. 1981. Normal accident at Three Mile Island. *Society,* 18: 17-26.

Perrow, C. 1983. The organizational context of human factors engineering. *Administrative Science Quarterly,* 28(4): 521-541.

Perrow, C. 1999. *Normal Accidents: Living With High-Risk Technologies*. Princeton, NJ: Princeton University Press.

Perry-Smith, J. E., & Blum, T. C. 2000. Work-family human resource bundles and perceived organizational performance. *Academy of Management Journal*, 43(6): 1107-1117.

Peters, T. 1987. Support fast failures. In *Thriving on Chaos*. New York: Harper & Row.

Peters, T. J., & Waterman, R. M., Jr. 1982. *In Search of Excellence*. New York: Warner Books.

Petersen, J. L. 1994. *The Road to 2015: Profiles of the Future*. Corte Madera, CA: Waite Group Press.

Pfeffer, J. 1994. *Competitive Advantage Through People*. Boston: Harvard Business School Press.

Pfeffer, J. 1998a. *The Human Equation: Building Profits by Putting People First*. Boston: Harvard Business School Press.

Pfeffer, J. 1998b. Six dangerous myths about pay. *Harvard Business Review*, 76(3): 109-119.

Pfeffer, J., & Salancik, G. R. 1978. *The External Control of Organizations: A Resource Dependence Perspective*. New York: Harper & Row.

Pierce, J., Kostova, T., & Dirks, K. 2001. Toward a theory of psychological ownership in organizations. *Academy of Management Review*, 26(2): 298-310.

Pletz, J. 2002. Dell turns productivity gains into market share. *Austin American-Statesman*, 26 August: p. D1.

Porter, M. E. 1985. *Competitive advantage: Creating and sustaining superior performance*. New York: The Free Press.

Prescott, J. E., & Smith, D. C. 1989. The largest survey of "leading-edge" competitor intelligence managers. *Planning Review*, May-June: 6-13.

Price, D. 1975. *Science Since Babylon*. New Haven, CT: Yale University Press.

Price, J. L. 1977. *The Study of Turnover*. Ames: Iowa State University Press.

Prokesch, S. E. 1997. Unleashing the power of learning: An interview with British Petroleum's John Browne. *Harvard Business Review*, 75(5): 147-168.

Prusak, L., & Cohen, D. 2001. How to invest in social capital. *Harvard Business Review*, 79(6): 86-93.

Puffer, S. M. 1999. Global executive: Intel's Andrew Grove on competitiveness. *Academy of Management Executive*, 13(1): 15-24.

Quarautelli, E. L. 1988. Disaster crisis management: A summary of research findings. *Journal of Management Studies*, 25(4): 373-385.

Quinn, J. B. 1992. *Intelligent Enterprise*. New York: Free Press.

Quinn, J. B., Anderson, P., & Finkelstein, S. 1996. Leveraging intellect. *Academy of Management Executive*, 10(3): 7-27.

Rappleye, W. C. 2000. Knowledge management: A force whose time has come. *Across the Board: The Conference Board Magazine*, January: 59-66.

Rau, D. 2000. The effect of transactive memory on the relationship between diversity of expertise and performance of top management teams. Paper presented at the Academy of Management Meetings, Toronto, 2000.

Reicheld, F. F. 1996. Learning from customer defections. *Harvard Business Review*, 74(2): 56-69.

Reinhardt, A. 1997. Intel: Can Andy Grove keep profits up in an era of cheap PCs? *BusinessWeek*, 22 December: 70+.

Rice, R. E. 1992. Task analyzability, use of new media, and effectiveness: A multi-site exploration of media richness. *Organization Science*, 3(4): 475-500.

Rice, R. E., & Gattiker, U. E. 2001. New media and organizational structuring. In F. M. Jablin and L. L. Putnam (Eds.), *The New Handbook of Organizational Communication: Advances in Theory, Research, and Methods.* Thousand Oaks, CA: Sage.

Ridderstrale, J. 1996. *Global Innovation: Managing International Innovation Projects at ABB and Electrolux.* Stockholm: Institute of International Business.

Riesbeck, C., & Schank, R. 1989. *Inside Case-Based Reasoning.* Hillsdale, NJ: Erlbaum.

Rifkin, J. 1996. *The End of Work: The Decline of the Global Labor Force and the Dawn of the Post-Market Era.* New York: G. P. Putnam's Sons.

Roberts, E. B., & Liu, W. K. 2001. Ally or acquire? How technology leaders decide? *Sloan Management Review,* 43: 26-34.

Rogers, E. M. 1995. *Diffusion of Innovations.* New York: Free Press.

Romanelli, E. 1991. The evolution of new organizational forms. *Annual Review of Sociology,* 17: 79-103.

Rosenberg, N. 1996. Uncertainty and technological change. In R. Landau, T. Taylor, & G. Wright, *The Mosaic of Economic Growth.* Stanford, CA: Stanford University Press.

Rosenkopf, L., & Nerkar, A. 2001. Beyond local search: Boundary-spanning, exploration, and impact in the optical disk industry. *Strategic Management Journal,* 22(4): 287-306.

Rowe, J. A., & Boulgarides, D. J. 1992. *Managerial Decision Making.* New York: Macmillan.

Ruefli, T. W. (Ed.). 1990. *Ordinal Time Series Analysis.* New York: Quorum Books.

Ruefli, T. W., & Jones, R. L. 1990. Excellent companies: An ordinal time series approach. In T. W. Ruefli (Ed.), *Ordinal Time Series Analysis* (pp. 81-97). New York: Quorum Books.

Ruggles, R. 1998. The state of the notion: Knowledge management in practice. *California Management Review,* 40(3): 80-89.

Rulke, D. L., Zaheer, S., & Anderson, M. H. 2000. Bringing the individual back in: Managers' transactive knowledge and organizational performance. Paper presented at the Academy of Management Meetings, Toronto, 2000.

Russo, J. E., & Schoemaker, P. J. H. 1989. *Decision Traps.* New York: Doubleday.

Rynes, S. L., & Gerhart, B. (Eds.). 2000. *Compensation in Organizations.* San Francisco: Jossey-Bass.

Sabatier, P. 1978. The acquisition and utilization of technical information by administrative agencies. *Administrative Science Quarterly,* 23(3): 396-417.

Sanchez, R. 1999. Modular architectures in the marketing process. *Journal of Marketing,* 63(Special Issue): 92-111.

Sarvary, M. 1999. Knowledge management and competition in the consulting industry. *California Management Review,* 41(2): 95-107.

Schein, E. H. 1992. *Organizational Culture and Leadership.* San Francisco: Jossey-Bass.

Schlender, B., Buffett, W., & Gates, B. 1998. The Bill & Warren Show. *Fortune,* 20 July: 48+.

Schlender, B., & Urresta, L. 1998. Peter Drucker takes the long view. *Fortune,* 28 September: 162+.

Schlesinger, J. R. 1970. Testimony of *Planning, Programming, Budgeting,* Inquiry of the Subcommittee on National Security and International Operations for the Senate Committee on Government Operations, 91 Congress 1 session, p. 482.

Schlosser, J. 2003. Looking for intelligence in ice cream. *Fortune,* 17 March: 114-120.

Schultz, H., & Yang, D. J. 1997. *Pour Your Heart Into It.* New York: Hyperion.

Schwenk, C. 1984. Cognitive simplification processes in strategic decision making. *Strategic Management Journal,* 5(2): 111-128.

Scott, W. R. 2001. *Institutions and Organizations* (2nd ed.). Thousand Oaks, CA: Sage.

Scott, W. R. 2003. *Organizations: Rational, Natural, and Open Systems* (5th ed.). Upper Saddle River, NJ: Prentice Hall.

Senge, P. 1990. *The Fifth Discipline: The Art and Practice of the Learning Organization.* New York: Doubleday.

Shaw, J. D., Gupta, N., & Delery, J. E. 2002. Pay dispersion and workforce performance: Moderating effects of incentives and interdependence. *Strategic Management Journal,* 23: 491-512.

Short, J., Williams, E., & Christie, B. 1976. *The Social Psychology of Telecommunications.* New York: Wiley.

Silver, B. L. 1998. *The Ascent of Science.* New York: Oxford University Press.

Silverman, G., & Spiro, L. N. 1999 Citigroup: So much for 50-50. *BusinessWeek,* 16 August: 80+.

Simon, H. A. 1973. Applying information technology to organization design. *Public Administrative Review,* 33(3): 268-278.

Simon, H. A. 1987. Making management decisions: The role of intuition and emotion. *Academy of Management Executive,* 1(1): 57-64.

Simon, H. A. 1991. Bounded rationality and organizational learning. *Organization Science,* 2(1): 125-134.

Simonin, B. L. 1999. Ambiguity and the process of knowledge transfer in strategic alliances. *Strategic Management Journal,* 20(7): 595-623.

Simons, T., Pelled, L. H., & Smith, K. A. 1999. Making use of difference: Diversity, debate, and decision comprehensiveness in top management teams. *Academy of Management Journal,* 42(6): 662-673.

Sitkin, S. B. 1992. Learning through failure: The strategy of small losses. In B. M. Staw & L. L. Cummings (Eds.), *Research in Organizational Behavior,* 14 (pp. 231-266). Greenwich, CT: JAI.

Skinner, B. F. 1948. "Superstition" in the pigeon. *Journal of Experimental Psychology,* 38(2): 168-172.

Smart, C., & Vertinsky, I. 1997. Designs for crisis decision units. *Administrative Science Quarterly,* 22(4): 640-655.

Smith, K., Grimm, C., Gannon, M., & Chen, M. J. 1991. Organizational information-processing, competitive responses and performance in the US domestic airline industry. *Academy of Management Journal,* 34(1): 60-85.

Smith, P. G., & Reinertsen, D. G. 1991. *Developing products in half the time.* New York: Van Nostrand Reinhold.

Smith, R. P. 1997. The historical roots of concurrent engineering fundamentals. *IEEE Transactions on Engineering Management,* 44: 67-78.

Smith, V. 1994. Institutionalizing flexibility in a service firm. *Work and Occupations,* 21: 284-307.

Sobel, R. 1999. *When Giants Stumble: Classic Business Blunders and How to Avoid Them.* New Jersey: Prentice Hall.

Sorenson, J. B. 2002. The strength of corporate culture and the reliability of firm performance. *Administrative Science Quarterly,* 47: 70-91.

Standing, C., & Benson, S. 2000. Knowledge management in a competitive environment. In S. A. Carlsson, P. Brezillon, P. Humphreys, B. G. Lundberg, A. M. Mccosh, & V. Rajkovic (Eds.), *Decision Support Through Knowledge Management.* Department of Computer and Systems Sciences, University of Stockholm and Royal Institute of Technology.

Starbuck, W. H. 1983. Organizations as action generators. *American Sociological Review,* 48: 91-102.

Starbuck, W. H. 1992. Learning by knowledge-intensive firms. *Journal of Management Studies,* 29(6): 713-740.

Starbuck, W. H. 1996. Unlearning ineffective or obsolete technologies. *International Journal of Technology Management,* 11: 725-737.

Starbuck, W. H., & Milliken, F. J. 1988. Executives' perceptual filters: What they notice and how they make sense. In D. Hambrick (Ed.), *The Executive Effect: Concepts and Methods for Studying Top Managers* (pp. 35-66). Greenwich, CT: JAI.

Staw, B. M., & Ross, J. 1987. Behavior in escalation situations: Antecedents, prototypes, and solutions. In L. L. Cummings & B. M. Staw (Eds.), *Research in Organizational Behavior,* 9 (pp. 39-78). Greenwich, CT: JAI.

Staw, B. M., Sandlelands, L. E., & Dutton, J. E. 1981. Threat-rigidity effects in organizational behavior: A multilevel analysis. *Administrative Science Quarterly,* 26(4): 501-524.

Steensma, H. K., & Corley, K. G. 2000. On the performance of technology-sourcing partnerships: The interaction between partner interdependence and technology attributes. *Academy of Management Journal,* 43(6): 1045-1067.

Stein, E. W., & Zwass, V. 1995. Actualizing organizational memory with information systems. *Information Systems Research,* 6(2): 85-117.

Steuer, J. 1992. Defining virtual reality: Dimensions determining telepresence. *Journal of Communication,* 42(4): 73-93.

Stewart, T. A. 1997. *Intellectual Capital.* New York: Doubleday/Currency.

Stewart, T. A. 2000. Water the grass, don't mow, and wait for lightening to strike. *Fortune,* 24 July: 376+.

Stuart, T. E. 2000. Interorganizational alliances and the performance of firms: A study of growth and innovation rates in a high-technology industry. *Strategic Management Journal,* 21(8): 791-811.

Sutcliffe, K. M. 2001. Organizational environments and organizational information processing. In F. Jablin and L. Putnam (Eds.), *The New Handbook of Organizational Communication: Advances in Theory, Research, and Methods.* Thousand Oaks, CA: Sage.

Sutcliffe, K. M., & Huber, G. P. 1998. Firm and industry as determinants of executive perceptions of the environment. *Strategic Management Journal,* 19(8): 793-807.

Sutcliffe, K. M., & McNamara, G. 2001. Controlling decision-making practice in organizations. *Organization Science,* 12(4): 484-501.

Sutton, H. 1988. *Competitive Intelligence (Research Report No. 913).* New York: The Conference Board.

Sutton, R. I., & Hargadon, A. 1996. Brainstorming groups in context: Effectiveness in a product design firm. *Administrative Science Quarterly,* 41(4): 685-718.

Szulanski, G. 1996. Exploring internal stickiness: Impediments to the transfer of best practices within the organization. *Strategic Management Journal,* 17(1): 27-44.

Tamuz, M. 1987. The impact of computer surveillance on air safety reporting. *Columbia Journal of World Business,* 22: 69-77.

Teece, D. J. 1998. Capturing value from knowledge assets: The new economy, markets for know-how, and intangible assets. *California Management Review,* 40(3): 55-79.

Tenopir, C., & King, D. 1998. Designing electronic journals with 30 years of lessons from print. *Journal of Electronic Publishing,* 4(2). *www.press.umich.edu/jep/04-02/king.html*

Terwiesch, C., & Loch, C. H. 1999. Measuring the effectiveness of overlapping development activities. *Management Science,* 45(4): 455-465.

Tetlock, P. E. 2000. Cognitive biases and organizational correctives: Do both disease and cure depend on the politics of the beholder? *Administrative Science Quarterly,* 45(2): 293-326.

Thietart, R. A., & Forgues, B. 1995. Chaos theory and organization. *Organization Science,* 6(1): 19-31.

Thomas, J. B., Clark, S. M., & Gioia, D. A. 1993. Strategic sensemaking and organizational performance: Linkages among scanning, interpretation, actions and outcomes. *Academy of Management Journal,* 36(2): 239-270.

Thomas, J. B., & McDaniel, R. R. 1990. Interpreting strategic issues: Effects of strategy and the information processing structure of top management teams. *Academy of Management Journal,* 33(2): 286-306.

Thomke, S. H. 1998. Simulation, learning and R & D performance: Evidence from automotive development. *Research Policy,* 27: 55-74.

Tripsas, M., & Gavetti, G. 2000. Capabilities, cognition, and inertia: Evidence from digital imaging. *Strategic Management Journal,* 21(10/11): 1147-1161.

Tsai, W. 2001. Knowledge transfer in intraorganizational networks: Effects of network position and absorptive capacity on business unit innovation. *Academy of Management Journal,* 44(5): 996-1004.

Tsui, A. S., Pearce, J. L., Porter, L. W., & Tripoli, A. M. 1997. Alternative approaches to the employee-organization relationship: Does investment in employees pay off? *Academy of Management Journal,* 40(5): 1089-1121.

Tushman, M. L., & Murmann, J. P. 1998. Dominant designs, technology cycles, and organizational outcomes. In B. M. Staw & L. L. Cummings (Eds.), *Research in Organizational Behavior,* 20 (pp. 231-266). Greenwich, CT: JAI.

Tushman, M. L., & O'Reilly, C. A., III. 1997. *Winning Through Innovation: A Practical Guide to Leading Organizational Change and Renewal.* Boston: Harvard Business School Press.

Tversky, A., & Kahneman, D. 1974. Judgment under uncertainty: Heuristics and biases. *Science,* 185: 1124-1131.

Tyson, K. 1998. Working one job for two companies: Employee leasing gains popularity. *Austin American-Statesman,* 23 December: p. D1.

Urwick, L. F. 1984. *The Golden Book of Management* (expanded ed.). New York: AMACOM (American Management Association).

U.S. Census Bureau. 1998. *Official Statistics.* December 2.

Utterback, J. M. 1971. The process of technological innovation within the firm. *Academy of Management Journal,* 14(1): 75-88.

Uzzi, B., & Barsness, Z. I. 1998. Contingent employment in British establishments: Organizational determinants of the use of fixed-term hires and part-time workers. *Social Forces,* 76(3): 967-1007.

Van de Ven, A. H., Angle, H. L., & Poole, M. S. 1989. *Research on the Management of Innovation.* New York: Harper & Row.

Van de Ven, A. H., Polley, D. E., Garud, R., & Vankataramen, S. 1999. *The Innovation Journey.* New York: Oxford University Press.

Van den Bosch, F. A. J., Volberda, H. W., & de Boer, M. 1999. Coevolution of firm absorptive capacity and knowledge environment: Organizational forms and combinative capabilities. *Organization Science,* 10(5): 551-568.

Van Doren, C. L. 1991. *A History of Knowledge: Past, Present, and Future.* Secaucus, NJ: Carol.

Venkatesh, V., & Johnson, P. 2002. Telecommuting technology implementations: A within- and between-subjects longitudinal field study. *Personnel Psychology,* 55: 661-687.

Vermeulen, F., & Barkema, H. 2001. Learning through acquisition. *Academy of Management Journal,* 44(3): 457-476.

Vickers, G. 1983. *Human Systems Are Different.* London: Harper & Row.

Vogl, A. J. 2001. The treadmill of the new economy. *Across the Board,* 37: 33-38.

Von Hippel, E. 1988. *The Sources of Innovation.* New York: Oxford University Press.

Von Hippel, E. 1994. "Sticky information" and the locus of problem solving: Implications for innovation. *Management Science,* 40: 429-439.

Vroom, V. H., & Yetton, P. W. 1973. *Leadership and Decision Making.* Pittsburgh, PA: University of Pittsburgh Press.

Wageman, R. 1995. Interdependence and group effectiveness. *Administrative Science Quarterly,* 40(1): 145-180.

Wall Street Journal. 1996. Call it dumbsizing: Why some companies regret cost-cutting. 14 May.

Wall Street Journal. 1997. Army devises a system to decide what does, and does not, work. 23 May.

Wall Street Journal. 1997. Secrets and lies: The dual career of a corporate spy. 23 October.

Wall Street Journal. 1998. Hand-held combat: How the competition got ahead of Intel in making cheap chips. 12 February.

Wall Street Journal. 1998. Internet commerce could pass $300 billion a year by 2002, the U.S. says. 16 April.

Wall Street Journal. 1999. What is the greatest technological innovation of the past 1000 years? 11 January.

Wall Street Journal. 2003. Midwest drought is threatening agriculture, rivers and tourism. 22 January.

Waller, M., Huber, G. P., & Glick, W. H. 1995. Functional background as a determinant of executives' selective perception. *Academy of Management Journal,* 38: 943-974.

Walsh, J. 1988. Selectivity and selective perception: An investigation of managers' belief structures and information processing. *Academy of Management Journal,* 31(4): 873-896.

Weick, K. E. 1983. Managerial thought in the context of action. In S. Srivastava (Ed.), *The Executive Mind* (pp. 221-242). San Francisco: Jossey-Bass.

Weick, K. E. 1985a. Cosmos vs. chaos: Sense and nonsense in electronic contexts. *Organizational Dynamics,* 14(2): 51-64.

Weick, K. E. 1985b. The significance of corporate culture. In P. J. Frost et al. (Eds.), *Organizational Cultures* (pp. 381-389). Beverly Hills, CA: Sage.

Weick, K. E. 1988. Enacted sensemaking in crisis situations. *Journal of Management Studies,* 25(4): 305-317.

Weick, K. E. 1995. *Sensemaking in Organizations.* Thousand Oaks, CA: Sage.

Weick, K. E., & Ashford, S. 2001. Learning in organizations. In F. M. Jablin and L. L. Putnam (Eds.), *The New Handbook of Organizational Communication: Advances in Theory, Research, and Methods.* Thousand Oaks, CA: Sage.

Weick, K. E., & Sutcliffe, K. M. 2001. *Managing the Unexpected*. San Francisco, CA: Jossey-Bass.

Wenger, E. 1998. *Communities of Practice*. New York: Oxford University Press.

Westphal, J. D., & Zajac, E. J. 1994. Substance and symbolism in CEO's long-term incentive plans. *Administrative Science Quarterly*, 39: 367-390.

Wheelwright, S. C., & Clark, K. B. 1992. *Revolutionizing Product Development: Quantum Leaps in Speed, Efficiency, and Quality*. New York: Free Press.

Whinston, A. B., Stahl, D. O., & Choi, S. Y. 1997. *The Economics of Electronic Commerce*. Indianapolis, IN: Macmillan Technical.

Wijnhoven, F. 1998. Designing organizational memories: Concept and method. *Journal of Organizational Computing and Electronic Commerce*, 8(1): 29-55.

Wilensky, H. L. 1967. *Organizational Intelligence*. New York: Basic Books.

Williams, K. Y., & O'Reilly, C. A., III. 1998. Demography and diversity in organizations: A review of 40 years of research. In B. M. Staw & L. L. Cummings (Eds.), *Research in Organizational Behavior*, 20 (pp. 77-140). Greenwich, CT: JAI.

Williamson, O. E. 1975. *Markets and Hierarchies: Analysis and Antitrust Implications*. New York: Free Press.

Williamson, O. E. 1981. The economies of organization: The transaction cost approach. *American Journal of Sociology*, 87: 548-577.

Winter, S., & Szulanski, G. 2001. Replication as strategy. *Organizational Science*, 12(6): 730-743.

Yang, C. 1997. Microsoft's lobbying blitz. *BusinessWeek*, 22 December: 34+.

Yimam-Seid, D., & Kobsa, A. 2003. Expert-finding systems for organizations: Problem and domain analysis and the DEMOIR approach. *Journal of Organizational Computing and Electronic Commerce*, 13: 1-24.

Yoo, Youngin. 2001. Developments of transactive memory systems and collective mind in virtual teams. *The International Journal of Organizational Analysis*, 9(2): 187-208.

Zack, M. H. 1999. Managing codified knowledge. *Sloan Management Review*, 40(4): 45-58.

Zahra, S., & George, G. 2002. Absorptive capacity: A review, reconceptualization, and extension. *Academy of Management Review*, 27(2): 185-203.

Zammuto, R. F., & Cameron, K. S. 1985. Environmental decline and organizational response. In L. L. Cummings & B. M. Staw (Eds.), *Research in Organizational Behavior*, 7 (pp. 223-262). Greenwich, CT: JAI.

Zeisset, P. T., & Wallace, M. E. 1998. How NAICS will affect data users, Bureau of the Census report. Retrieved March 1999 from www.census.gov/epcd/www/naicsusr.html [Revised 3/23/98].

Name Index

Adler, Paul, 230, 253n7
Aldrich, H., 10n5
Allen, T. J., 173n4
Amabile, Theresa, 229, 253n5, 253n6
Amason, A. C., 114n4
Ambrose, S. E., 24
Anderson, Edward, 207
Anderson, M. H., 76n15
Anderson, P., 138, 141n7, 211n8
Andrews, F. M., 173n4
Angelma, R., 76n16
Angle, H. L., 211n9
Argote, L., 176n22, 254n9
Argyris, C., 140n4
Arthur, M. B., 213n14
Ashby, W. R., 42n14
Ashford, S., 141n4
Ashforth, B. E., 175n18
Austin, J. R., 76n15
Avery, Sewell, 130

Baird, Lloyd, 141n11, 231
Baldwin, C. Y., 211n7
Barkema, H. G., 142n18
Barley, S., 114n9
Barnard, Chester, 92, 105, 108
Baron, James, 201, 223
Barr, P., 76n16
Barret, Craig, 173n1
Barsness, Z. I., 254n13
Batt, R., 76n15
Bell, Alexander Graham, 25
Bell, D., 41n2
Belleivieau, M. A., 255n21
Belous, R. S., 254n13

Bendapudi, N., 254n10
Benson, S., 150, 174n5, 174n7, 229
Bentzin, B., 127
Berry, J., 174n5
Bettis, R. A., 142n16
Beyer, J. M., 142n20, 145, 173n1
Bhadury, R., 253n3
Birkenshaw, J., 160, 174n13
Blumberg, S. J., 42n12
Bogner, W., 76n16
Boulding, Kenneth, 13n1
Bowen, K. H., 210n6
Bower, J. L., 74n4, 169
Bowman, E. H., 253n3, 253n5, 254n8
Bradley, S. P., 142n16
Brenner, C., 212n13
Bresnahan, T. F., 250
Brilliant, Ashley, 181
Brockner, J., 253n5, 253n6
Broschak, J. P., 212n13, 254n14, 255n15
Browne, John, 129
Browning, L. D., 142n20, 145, 173n1
Brusoni, S., 134
Brynjolfsson, E., 250
Bunderson, J. S., 75n13
Burke, L., 116n14
Burt, R. S., 255n16

Cameron, J., 175n15
Cameron, Kim S., 225, 252n2
Campbell-Smith, D., 255n17
Cangelosi, Vincent E., 120, 140n4
Cappelli, Peter, 199
Carnegie, Andrew, 148
Carnow, M., 212n13

289

Jones, R. L., 14n2
Jones, T. Y., 177
Jordan, Michael, 247, 249
Judge, W. Q., 114n5
Junkins, Jerry, 147, 227

Kahneman, D., 42n12
Kalleberg, Arne, 212n13, 235-236
Kefalas, A., 112n1
Kelley, M. R., 214n18, 254n13
Kelly, S., 115n10
Kelvin, Lord, 24
Kennedy, John F., 181-182
Kerr, Steve, 174n8, 175n15
Kiesler, S., 174n11, 174n12,
    175n14, 256n24
Kilduff, M., 76n16
Kim. J., 44n20
Kim, S. K., 51
King, D., 17, 41n4
Klayman, J., 113n3
Klein, Joe, 247
Klimoski, R., 74n5
Knight, D., 114n4
Kobsa, Al, 175n19
Kohn, A., 175n15
Kolodner, J., 116n15, 173n2
Kotabe, M., 142n15
Kotter, J. P., 255n16
Koudsi, S., 174n5
Kramer, R. M., 175n18
Kreps, David, 223
Krishnan, R., 254n9
Krishnan, V., 210n5, 210n6

Lane, P. J., 142n15
Larrick. R. P., 113n3
Larson, E. W., 209n4
Lawler, E. E., III, 175n17,
    255n22, 256n23
Lawton, T., 75n9
Leahy, Wililam D., 22
Leavitt, Harold. J., 132
Lee, S. M., 211n10
Lee, T. M., 211n10
Lee, T. W., 254n11
Leifer, R. L., 9n1, 114n8, 141n5, 211n9

Leinthal, D. A., 133
Lengel, R. H., 115-116n11
Leone, R. P., 254n10
Lesser, Eric, 253n4
Lev, B., 62
Levering, R., 235
Levinthal, D. A., 142n15
Lewin, A. Y., 10n7, 44n20
Lewis, K., 76n15, 254n9
Liang, D., 254n9
Lincoln, Abraham, 24
Lindberg, Charles, 179
Little, Arthur D., 146
Liu, W. K., 214n18
Loch, C. H., 210n6
Loewenstein, G., 42n12
Lord, R., 76n16
Lovett, S., 254n10
Lubatkin, M., 142n15
Lynn, G., 169

Mael, F., 175n18
Malone, M. S., 213n17
Mangel, R., 174n10
March, James G., 116n16, 128-129
Markels, A., 254n10
Martin, James, 25
Matusik, S., 212n12, 213n13
McDaniel, G. P., 114n7
McDaniel, R. R., 74n5, 114n7
McDermott, C. M., 114n8
McKinley, W., 22
McKnight, William, 152
McNamara, G., 114n6
Mehra, A., 76n16
Meindl, J. R., 75n12
Melone, N. P., 112-113n1
Mendelson, H., 74n6
Merwan, J., 140n2
Meyer, Alan, 67
Meyer, M., 42n10
Micklethwait, J., 153
Miles, R. E., 140n4, 213n14
Miller, A., 114n5
Miller, C. C., 75n12, 76n16, 113n1
Miller, Danny, 12, 63-64, 75n10
Miller, J. G., 9n4

Subject Index

Training, 136
Transportation technology, 16, 20, 24, 35, 198
Trends, in scientific knowledge, 16
Trust, employee, 243
Tulane University, 207
Turbulence, of change, 31-34
Turnover, 7, 232-233, 241, 243

U.S. Bureau of the Census, 28, 34
U.S. Department of Defense, 61, 144
U.S. Department of Education's National Center on The Educational Quality of the Workforce, 199
U.S. Department of Labor, 124, 126
U.S. Internal Revenue Service, 58-59
U.S. Patent Office, 22
U.S. Patent Statistics Report, 22
U.S. semiconductor research consortium (Sematech), 144
Uncertainty:
    income, 200
    strategic, 51
University of Alberta, 63
University of California—Berkeley, 2055
University of California—Irvine, 2388
University of Dublin, 238
University of North Carolina, 235
University of Stockholm, 118
University of Sussex, 134
University of Texas, 120
University of Texas at Austin, 207
Upjohn Institute for Employment Research, 236
User friendliness, 102-103

Value-added time, 183
Value-adding knowledge, 119
Variable income, 200
Variation, learning from, 125-126
Variety, environmental, 26-28

Velocity:
    of change, 31-34, 70
    of problem arrival, 109
Vendors. *See* Outsourcing
Vicarious learning, 131-137
    absorptive capacity and, 133-134
    by individuals, 136-137
    importing as expertise, 135-136
Videocassettes and digital disks, 27
Videoconferencing, 82, 102
Vigilance:
    in decision making, 89, 103, 109-111, 259
    in sensing, 51
Viruses, computer, 128-129

Wage inequality, 250
Wall Street Journal, 23, 47, 100
Webster's Encyclopedic Unabridged Dictionary of the English Language, 180
Western Union, 25
Westmark Systems, 61
Wharton School, University of Pennsylvania, 199
Where Layoffs Are a Last Resort (Conlin), 235
Workforce:
    knowledge, 58, 241
    mobile, 58
    specialized, 181
    temporary, 235-240, 243-244
World List of Scientific Periodicals, 17
Worldly Philosophers, The (Heilbronner), 181
Wright Aeronautical Corporation, 179

Xerox Corp., 159-160, 163, 167, 169

Zara Corp., 54

About the Author

George P. Huber teaches Organizational Change and Redesign in the Executive MBA program and Organizational Decision Making in the doctoral program at The University of Texas at Austin, where he holds the Charles and Elizabeth Prothro Regents Chair in Business Administration. His current research focuses on organizational change, organizational design, and organizational decision making. He has also conducted and published research in the areas of information technology and individual and group decision making. Dr. Huber is a Fellow of the Academy of Management and of the Decision Sciences Institute and is a charter member of the Academy of Management Journals Hall of Fame.

In 1993, his coedited book, *Organizational Change and Redesign: Ideas and Insights for Improving Performance,* was published by Oxford University Press, and in 1995 his coedited book, *Longitudinal Field Research Methods: Studying Processes of Organizational Change,* was published by Sage Publications.

Dr. Huber has held full-time positions with the Emerson Electric Manufacturing Company, the Procter and Gamble Manufacturing Company, the U.S. Department of Labor, and Execucom Systems Corporation, and has served as a consultant to many corporations and public agencies. Professor Huber has held full-time faculty appointments at the Universities of Wisconsin, California, and Texas.